D1030314

THE NATIONAL SYSTEM OF POLITICAL ECONOMY

THE

NATIONAL SYSTEM

OF

POLITICAL ECONOMY

BY

FRIEDRICH LIST

TRANSLATED FROM THE ORIGINAL GERMAN BY
SAMPSON S. LLOYD

AUGUSTUS M. KELLEY · PUBLISHERS

First edition 1885
(London: Longmans, Green and Co., 1885)

Reprinted 1991 with the addition of an introductory essay
by J. S. Nicholson from the edition of 1904 by
AUGUSTUS M. KELLEY, PUBLISHERS
Fairfield NJ 07004-0008

Library of Congress Cataloging-in-Publication Data

List, Friedrich, 1789-1846.
    [Nationale System der politischen Oekonomie. English]
    The national system of political economy / by Friedrich List :
translated from the original German by Sampson S. Lloyd ; with J. S.
Nicholson's introductory essay to the 1904 edition.
      p. cm. — (Reprints of economic classics)
    Translation of: Das nationale System der politischen Oekonomie.
    Reprint. Originally published: London : Longman's Green, 1885.
    Includes bibliographical references.
    ISBN 0-678-01454-X
    1. Economics. 2. Free trade. 3. Protectionism. I. Title. II.
Series.
HB165.L7413 1991
330.1—dc20
                                           90-35160

Manufactured in the United States of America

INTRODUCTORY ESSAY
[1904 Edition]
By J. S. Nicholson

INTRODUCTORY ESSAY.

As the demand for the re-publication of the work of Friedrich List is to be assigned mainly to the interest aroused by the fiscal controversy, the purpose of the Introduction which I have been requested to write, will be best served by indicating in the first place the bearing of the author's ideas and arguments on the present situation in this country. Those who expect to find an assortment of authoritative opinions which can be aggressively and conclusively quoted against upholders of the present system will surely be disappointed. The method of isolated extracts would probably be as favourable to the supporters as to the opponents of 'free trade.' List maintained, for example, that England would have gained by the abolition of the Corn Laws just after the restoration of the general peace (in 1815), but—these are the words—'Providence has taken care that trees should not grow quite up to the sky. Lord Castlereagh gave over the commercial policy of England into the hands of the landed aristocracy, and these killed the hen which had laid the golden eggs' (p. 297). Or, again, take this passage on retaliation : 'Thus it is Adam Smith who wants to introduce the principle of retaliation into commercial policy—a principle which would lead to the most absurd and most ruinous measures, especially if the retaliatory duties, as Smith demands, are to be repealed as soon as the foreign nation agrees to abolish its restrictions' (p. 254).

Nor if we abandon the dangerous and unfair method of isolated extracts, and look on List as the great critic and opponent of Adam Smith, can there be much doubt as to the general results of the comparison of the Scotsman with the German. List has made the mistake so common with popular writers, but inexcusable in the author of a systematic work, of attributing to Adam Smith the extravagant dogmas of his exponents. One would almost suppose that List had never read Adam Smith himself, but had taken for granted the *Smithianismus* bandied about in popular pamphlets. One passage from List may suffice to illustrate the unfairness of his rendering of Adam Smith. 'He [Adam Smith] entitles his work, "The Nature and Causes of the Wealth of Nations" (i.e. [on List's interpretation] of all nations of the whole human race). He speaks of the various systems of political economy in a separate part of his work solely for the purpose of demonstrating their non-efficiency, and of proving that "political" or *national* economy must be replaced by "cosmo-political or world-wide economy." Although here and there he speaks of wars, this only occurs incidentally. The idea of a perpetual state of peace forms the foundation of all his arguments' (p. 97). The real Adam Smith wrote that the first duty of the sovereign, that of protecting the society from the violence and the invasion of other independent societies, can be performed only by means of a military force. No nation, he declared, ever gave up voluntarily the dominion of any province how troublesome soever it might be to govern it. 'To propose that Great Britain should voluntarily give up all authority over her colonies, would be to propose such a measure as never was and never will be adopted by any nation.' 'The art of war is certainly the noblest of all arts.' And in a passage too long for quotation, Adam Smith maintained that even if the martial spirit of the people were of no use towards the defence of the society, yet to prevent that sort of mental mutilation, deformity, and wretchedness which cowardice necessarily involves in it from spreading themselves through the great body of the people, is a duty as incumbent on the Government as the prevention of leprosy or any other loathsome disease. The same Adam Smith approved of bounties on the export of sail-cloth and gun-powder so that the production at home might be encouraged and a larger supply be available for war in case of need.

Malthus, it may be observed incidentally, is another great writer whom List has utterly misrepresented through relying on popular dogma instead of going to the original source. The account given by List of the ' errors of Malthus ' (p. 103 *et seq.*) is curiously and perversely wrong.

When List is so weak on the history of economic theory, it is not to be expected that his history of economic facts and institutions should be above suspicion. On such important matters, for example, as the causes of the secession of the American colonies and the influence of the Navigation Acts, the opinions of List are not confirmed by the more recent work of Dr. Cunningham and Professor Ashley.[1]

And without insisting on details, for it must be expected that recent work in economic history should have upset many old opinions, List is open to the general charge of exaggeration. He is led away by preconceived ideas and induced to build up systems of policy on too little evidence. Notably as regards the industrial and commercial development of England he lays far too much stress on the benefits derived from legislation and governmental action. He is too ready to assume that if an idea is good in theory it must also be good in practice ; but, as every student of history knows, the wastage in ideas is as great as that in the ova of fishes— millions of ova for one good herring.

List shows on occasion that he was aware of this liability to over-emphasis. In his Preface he says authors of celebrity must be refuted in energetic terms, and this must be his

---

[1] *Cf.* 'England and America, 1660 to 1760,' in *Economic Surveys*, by Professor Ashley, and Dr. Cunningham's *Growth of English Industry and Commerce*, vol. ii. (edition 1903).

excuse if he appears to condemn in too strong language the opinions and works of authors and whole schools. And in the body of the work he occasionally reminds the reader that the prosperity of nations depends on a multitude of causes besides the commercial policy of governments. After insisting, as usual with a good deal of exaggeration, on the advantages England derived from trial by jury, and the early abolition of the use of the Latin language in her Law Courts and State departments, and comparing the happy history of England with the unhappy history of her neighbours on the Continent, List exclaims, ' But who can say how much of these happy results is attributable to the English national spirit and to the constitution; how much to England's geographical position and circumstances in the past; or again, how much to chance, to destiny, to fortune? ' (p. 42).

List's habit of 'contradicting energetically' is no doubt to be ascribed largely to the fact that he was engaged for the greater part of his life in political agitation. In this he resembled Cobden, who also excelled in exaggeration. The political agitator is like a person accustomed to shout to the deaf one idea at a time and as loud as possible, and even when a soft answer would be more suitable to the ears of the unafflicted he shouts still.

If, then, List is open to these charges, wherein lie his merits ? Why is List popularly regarded as the great critic of the free-traders ?

In the first place, it may be allowed that the defects just noticed are not constructive but superficial. The energetic language, which is absurdly wrong as applied to Adam Smith, is often just as applied to those who have tried to make his arguments popular by leaving out the difficulties and the qualifications. Indeed List himself constantly speaks of 'the school' alternatively with Adam Smith, and his mistake consists in not knowing or remembering that the extreme popular dogmas on free trade are not countenanced by Adam Smith. The principles on which List insists so strongly may for the most part be considered as the natural development of the modifications of what List calls *cosmopolitical* free trade, which are acknowledged throughout the 'Wealth of Nations.' It is clear from the passages already cited that Adam Smith took it for granted that the world consisted of nations, and that national interests were not always harmonious.

And if further proof were needed, it is furnished in his great chapter on colonial policy. He there distinguishes between the advantages which Europe in general has derived from the planting of new colonies and the particular advantages derived by particular nations. What any one nation ought to expect from her colonies is an increase of revenue or an increase of military power. It is true he showed that the various nations have sacrificed an absolute advantage to gain a less relative advantage by the monopoly of their respective colonial trades, but, on the other hand, he formulated the most thorough scheme of Imperial Federation to convert the 'project of an empire' into a reality. From the British standpoint Adam Smith is indeed more Nationalist than List himself; for whilst Adam Smith says the most visionary enthusiast would not propose the abandonment of the colonies, List (p. 216; see also p. 143) calmly assumes that Canada will secede as soon as she has reached the point of manufacturing power attained by the United States when they seceded, and that independent agricultural manufacturing commercial states will also arise in the countries of temperate climate in Australia in the course of time. But although Adam Smith himself always adopted the national standpoint, his followers of 'the school' have in general assumed that what is best for all the nations as a whole, must *ipso facto* be best for each individual nation, or that cosmopolitical and national interests always coincide. Against this extreme view List's central doctrine is directed, ' I would indicate, as the distinguishing characteristic of my system, NATIONALITY. On the nature of *nationality*, as the intermediate interest between those of *individualism* and of *entire humanity*, my whole structure is based' (Preface, p. xliii.). List's system is emphatically and explicitly the national system of political economy.

Next in importance to his doctrine of nationality must be placed his position on immaterial capital and productive powers. Adam Smith had included under the fixed capital of a nation the natural and acquired abilities of its inhabitants, but for a long time both in theory and practice the term 'capital' was narrowed down to purely material forms. If this change of definition had been made merely in deference to popular usage, in order to avoid confusion, no harm might have ensued ; but, unfortunately, with their exclusion from capital the immaterial productive forces and powers were dropped from the popular arguments altogether. Apparently the wealth of nations was supposed to depend principally on the accumulation of material capital, which was necessary to provide both the auxiliary aids to labour and its subsistence. List did good service in showing that mere accumulation is of minor importance compared with the organisation of the productive forces of society. ' The present state of the nations is the result of the accumulation of all discoveries, inventions, improvements, perfections, and exertions of all generations which have lived before us; they form the *mental capital of the present human race*, and every separate nation is productive only in the proportion in which it has known how to appropriate these attainments of former generations and to increase them by its own acquirements, in which the natural capabilities of its territory, its extent and geographical position, its population and political power, have been able to develop as completely and symmetrically as possible all sources of wealth within its boundaries, and to extend its moral, intellectual, commercial, and political influence over less advanced nations and especially over the affairs of the world' (p. 113).

Closely associated with these doctrines was the leading idea that from the national standpoint of productive power the cheapness of the moment might be far more than counterbalanced by the losses of the future measured by the loss of productive power. It follows that to buy at the time in the cheapest market and to sell in the dearest may not always be the wisest national policy.

The distinction between present and future advantage from the national standpoint is fundamental throughout the whole work. As soon as it is clearly apprehended the principle must be admitted, at least in theory, and the difficulty is to discover in practice the cases that may be brought under the rule. To Mill it seemed that there was only one case ' in which, on mere principles of political economy, protecting duties can be defensible,' that is, ' when they are imposed temporarily, especially in a young and rising nation, in hopes of naturalising a foreign industry, in itself perfectly suitable to the circumstances of the country.' This case so jejunely treated by Mill (though the bare admission has exposed him to the fierce attacks of extreme free-traders) is taken by List as one simple example capable of much more extended application by analogy. List maintains that in the early years of the nineteenth century England had obtained the manufacturing and commercial supremacy of the world to such a degree that all the other nations were in danger of becoming mere providers of food and raw materials in return for her manufactures. To List it seemed that the continental nations (just as much as the United States of America) must adopt protection until they were strong enough to compete with England (p. 294). But List goes much farther. He seeks for a wide inductive generalisation based on the experience of nations. In the chapter on the teachings of history the conclusion is reached that nations must modify their systems according to the measure of their own progress (p. 93). In the first stage they must adopt free trade with the more advanced nations as a means of raising themselves from a state of barbarism and of making advances in agriculture. In the second stage they must resort to commercial restrictions to promote the growth of manufactures, fisheries, navigation, and foreign trade. In the last stage, 'after reaching the highest degree of wealth and power,' they must gradually revert to the principle of free trade and of unrestricted competition in the home as well as in foreign markets, so that their agriculturists, manufacturers, and merchants may be preserved from indolence and stimulated to retain the supremacy which they have acquired. Writing in 1841, he concludes the survey: 'In the first stage, we see Spain, Portugal, and the Kingdom of Naples ; in the second, Germany and the United States of North America ; France apparently stands close upon the boundary line of the last stage ; but Great Britain alone at the present time has actually reached it' (p. 93).

This summary of historical tendencies is no doubt open to the usual charge of hasty and imperfect generalisation, but it shows very clearly the attitude of List towards protection. The main use of protection is to promote the growth of productive power in all the departments in which the nation has the requisite natural resources.

The attitude of List towards protection is made still clearer in the following passages, which fairly represent a large part of his main argument : '*The power of producing wealth* is therefore infinitely more important than *wealth itself;* it insures not only the possession and the increase of what has been gained, but also the replacement of what has been lost' (p. 108). 'The prosperity of a nation is not, as Say believes, greater in the proportion in which it has amassed more wealth (i.e. values of exchange), but in the proportion in which it has more *developed its powers of production*' (p. 117). On List's view there is no real opposition between free trade and protection, because neither is an end in itself, but simply a means to achieve a certain end, namely, the greatest development of productive power. Which policy may be better at any time depends on the stage of development of the nation in relation to the development of other nations. For the time being a protective duty involves a loss. But the present loss is justifiable if in the future there will be a greater gain. ' It is true that protective duties at first increase the price of manufactured goods; but it is just as true, and moreover acknowledged by the prevailing economical school, that in the course of time, by the nation being enabled to build up a completely developed manufacturing power of its own, those goods are produced more cheaply at home than the price at which they can be imported from foreign parts. If, therefore, a sacrifice of *value* is caused by protective duties, it is made good by the gain of a *power of production*, which not only secures to the nation an infinitely greater amount of material goods, but also industrial independence in case of war' (p. 117).

The reference to economical independence in the last phrase indicates that List did not consider that even as regards productive power the advantage was to be measured merely by the greater cheapness ultimately. As with Adam Smith, ' defence is of much more importance than opulence.' And with List the maxim is applied to all the industries that may be considered of vital importance to a nation. An interesting example is given in List's account of the methods of dumping (though the name is not used) practised by the English against the manufacturers of the Continent and America. ' Through their position as the manufacturing and commercial monopolists of the world, their manufactories from time to time fall into the state which they call "glut," and which arises from what they call "overtrading." At such periods everybody throws his stock of goods into the steamers. . . . The English manufacturers suffer for the moment, but they are saved, and they compensate themselves later on by better prices' (p. 119). This is, of course, a simpler form of dumping than the modern plan of continuous sale of goods at lower prices abroad than at home, but the principle involved is the same as regards the economic independence of the nation. List goes on to show that by this English method of dealing with gluts the whole manufacturing power, the system of credit, nay, the agriculture and generally the whole economical system of the nations who are placed in free competition with England, are shaken to their foundations.

List also insists on the importance, from the standpoint of national productive power, of the development of both manufactures and agriculture, as indeed of all industries, for which the nation is by nature adapted. When List wrote, dealing as he did mainly with the interests of other nations as against England, he was most concerned to show that without manufactures a nation must remain relatively unprogressive, even as regards its agriculture. 'A nation which possesses merely agriculture, and merely the most indispensable industries, is in want of the first and most necessary division of commercial operations among its inhabitants, and of the most important half of its productive powers, indeed it is in want of a useful division of commercial operations even in the separate branches of agriculture itself' (p. 124). 'The productive power of the cultivator and of the labourer in agriculture will always be greater or smaller according to the degree in which the exchange of agricultural produce for manufactures and other products of various kinds can proceed more or less readily. That in this respect the foreign trade of any nation which is but little advanced can prove in the highest degree beneficial, we have shown in another chapter by the example of England. But a nation which has already made considerable advances in civilisation, in possession of capital, and in population, will find the development of a manufacturing power of its own infinitely more beneficial to its agriculture than the most flourishing foreign trade can be without such manufactures' (p. 127). A number of reasons are assigned, but the final argument is 'especially because the reciprocal exchange between manufacturing power and agricultural power is so much greater, the closer the agriculturist and manufacturer are placed to one another, and the less they are liable to be interrupted in the exchange of their various products by accidents of all kinds.'

This is the argument which was developed in theory by Henry Sidgwick to show that ultimately the world at large might gain by the temporary protection of the constituent nations. And on the practical side it is this argument which is most popular in the British colonies. The colonies are protectionist because they wish to become complex industrial nations, and though it is the manufacturers who gain in the first place by protection, it is claimed that agriculture must also gain indirectly by the encouragement to various bye-products.

Even as regards manufactures the benefit of protection is limited by List to the educational or young industry stage of development. When nations have attained to their full powers protection is apt to check progress and lead to decadence. The case of Venice is given as typical (p. 8). Unrestricted freedom of trade was beneficial to the Republic in the first years of her existence, but a protective policy was also beneficial when she had attained to a certain stage of power and wealth, and protection first became injurious to her when she had attained the commercial supremacy of the world, because the exclusion of competition led to indolence. 'Therefore, not the introduction of a protective policy, but perseverance in maintaining it after the reasons for its introduction had passed away, was really injurious to Venice.' As regards protection to agriculture, curiously enough List confesses that he is in accord with the prevailing theory —that is, extreme free trade (p. 175). 'With regard to the interchange of raw products, the school is perfectly correct in supposing that the most extensive liberty of commerce is, under all circumstances, most advantageous to the individual as well as to the entire State. One can, indeed, augment this production by restrictions; but the advantage obtained thereby is merely apparent. We only thereby divert, as the school says, capital and labour into another and less useful channel.' The argument is given at length and is on familiar lines.

Nor is List's attitude towards free trade merely negative. It is not that protection should be abandoned when it becomes useless, and that free trade is the absence of useless restrictions, but positive virtue is ascribed to free trade as to other forms of freedom. List was an enthusiast for freedom. 'The real rise of the industry and the power of England dates only from the days of the actual foundation of England's national freedom, while the industry and power of Venice, of the Hanse Towns, of the Spanish and Portuguese, decayed concurrently with their loss of freedom' (p. 87). In this passage the reference is to freedom in the larger political sense, but in other places List extols the positive virtue of free trade once a nation has attained its full maturity. Protective duties ought never to be so high as to strangle healthy competition. 'It may in general be assumed that where any technical industry cannot be established by means of an original protection of forty to sixty per cent. and cannot continue to maintain itself under a continued protection of twenty to thirty per cent. the fundamental conditions of manufacturing power are lacking' (p. 251). Thus even in the educative stage the duties are to be moderate (relatively to the methods of production), and later on they are to be abandoned altogether. 'In order to allow freedom of trade to operate naturally, the less advanced nations must first be raised by artificial measures to that stage of cultivation to which the English nation has been artificially elevated' (p. 107). List was also a great enthusiast for the political union of kindred states, as exemplified in the case of Germany and Italy, but he thought that the political union must always precede the commercial union of the separate states (p. 102). Although the corner-stone of List's system is nationalism, his ultimate ideal is universal free trade. His difference with the *laissez-faire* school was that if under present conditions universal free trade were adopted, it would simply serve to subject the less advanced nations to the supremacy of the predominant manufacturing commercial and naval power (the England of his day); and in this way the development of the nations would be checked, and in the end the whole world would lose. The system of protection was the only means in his view of bringing other nations to the stage at which universal free trade would be possible and desirable.

This brief survey of the leading ideas of List's work confirms the suspicion, suggested by isolated extracts, that his arguments can only be brought to bear on the present controversy in this country by appealing to his fundamental ideas. List, like every other great writer, was influenced very much by the conditions under which he wrote and the atmosphere in which he moved. The predominance of England in industry and commerce was in fact considerable, and, according to the popular sentiment and jealousy of other nations, was altogether overbearing. The problem with List was to show the nations how they might upset this commercial overlordship and attain to an equality with England. The only method seemed to be that of temporary protection. To-day the fear has been expressed that England may succumb to other nations. It is plain that the case is altered. It would be absurd to argue that the manufactures of England must be protected until they have had time to grow up;

they are no longer young ; if they are weak, the weakness is that of age and not infancy.

Again, in List's day the conditions of agriculture and the means of transport were such that he himself argued in reference to England that with the abolition of the Corn Laws and other restraints on the import of raw produce, 'it is more than probable that thereby double and three times as much land could have been brought into cultivation as by unnatural restrictions' (p. 175). The idea at the time seemed reasonable that in the main every country must rely on its own food supplies, that agriculture was naturally protected, that the cultivator could resort to 'other things,' and that the growth of wealth through the increase of manufacturing power would increase the demand for these other things. And for nearly a generation after the repeal of the Corn Laws this view seemed justified. But again the conditions have changed; and it would be idle to quote the authority of List regarding raw products, that under all circumstances the most extensive liberty of commerce is most advantageous both to the individual and to the State.

Alike in agriculture and in manufactures the particular opinions of List are either irrelevant or adverse as regards the adoption by England of protection or retaliation, and even as regards federation he thought that political must precede commercial union. But the real value of List's work lies in the principles and fundamental ideas. These ideas are always to be reckoned with ; they suggest questions which the statesman must answer whatever the change in conditions. The questions which our statesmen have to answer, suggested by the ideas of List, are such as these : Will the productive powers of the nation suffice to maintain and increase its present prosperity ? Are the great national industries threatened with no signs of decay, and if there is decay where are substitutes to be looked for ? Is there any change in the character of our trade which indicates a lower standard of national life? Is there any danger from foreign monopolies? Will retaliation promote the industrial development of the nation?[1] Is the Empire capable of closer and more effective commercial and political union? And, lastly, there is the practical question, how far a change in tariffs is likely to prevent or remedy any of the evils of the present system?

The work of List will give no cut-and-dried answers to these questions, but it will suggest fruitful lines of inquiry in the search for the answers. Finally, it may be said, just as Adam Smith admitted exceptions to free trade, so List admitted exceptions to protection. And in both authors the exceptions in theory are so important that the divergence on balance is not nearly so great as the reader might suppose. List's work would have gained in power and in popularity if, instead of attacking Adam Smith for opinions which were only held by his extreme successors, he had emphasised his points of agreement with the original author.

J. Shield Nicholson.

[1] 'The principle of retaliation is reasonable and applicable only if it coincides with the principle of the *industrial development of the nation*, if it serves as it were as an assistance to this object' (p. 255).

TRANSLATOR'S PREFACE.

ABOUT five years ago, when the works of Friedrich List were republished and widely circulated in Germany, the Berlin correspondent of the 'Times' took occasion to comment on the powerful influence which those works were then exercising in that country in favour of the adoption of a protective commercial policy.

It was this testimony to the practical influence of List's economical theories which first attracted my attention to his writings, and a perusal of them induced me to undertake the translation of the following work, with a view to affording English readers an opportunity of judging for themselves as to the truth of his statements and the soundness of his arguments.

The work consists of four parts—the History, the Theory, the Systems, and the Politics of National Economy. It is important to bear in mind that all were written before 1844, and the fourth part in particular treats of political circumstances and of commercial policies which have now for the most part ceased to exist. The Corn Laws, the Navigation Laws, and the generally protectionist tariff of Great Britain were then still unrepealed; the manufacturing industry of Germany was still in its infancy, and the comparatively moderate tariff of the German States still permitted England to supply them with the greater part of the manufactured goods which they required.

At first sight, therefore, it would seem an anachronism to place before the reader of to-day a work having special relation to a state of things which existed forty years ago. The principles, however, enunciated by List are in their main features as applicable at one time as at another, and it will be found that they possess two especially powerful claims to consideration at the present moment.

In the first place, there is good reason for believing that they have directly inspired the commercial policy of two of the greatest nations of the world, Germany and the United States of America; and in the next, they supply a definite scientific basis for those protectionist doctrines which, although acted upon by our English-speaking colonies and held by not a few practical men as well as by some commercial economists in this country, have hitherto been only partially and inadequately formulated by English writers.

The fundamental idea of List's theory will be seen to be the free import of agricultural products and raw materials combined with an effective but not excessive protection (by means of customs duties) of native manufacturing industry against foreign competition. According to his views, the most efficient support of native production of agricultural products and raw materials is the maintenance within the nation of flourishing manufacturing industry thus protected. The system which he advocates differs, therefore, on the one hand from the unconditionally free import system of one-sided free trade adopted by England, and on the other from the system now apparently approved by Prince Bismarck, of imposing protective duties on the import of food and raw materials as well as on that of manufactured goods.

In fact, List draws a sharp line of demarcation between what he deems a truly 'political' economy and the 'cosmopolitical' economy of Adam Smith and his followers (English and foreign), and he vigorously defends a 'national' policy as opposed to the 'universal trade' policy which, although nearly forty years have elapsed since its adoption by England, has failed to commend itself in practice to any other civilised country.

In combating what he regarded as the mischievous fallacies of the cosmopolitical theory, List occasionally denounces with considerable asperity the commercial supremacy then exercised by England. But, so far from being an enemy of England, he was a sincere admirer of her political institutions and a warm advocate of an alliance between this country and Germany. 'England and Germany,' he wrote, 'have a common political interest in the Eastern Question, and by intriguing against the Customs Union of Germany and against her commercial and economical progress, England is sacrificing the highest political objects to the subordinate interests of trade, and will certainly have to rue hereafter her short-sighted shopkeeper policy.' He further addressed to the English and Prussian Governments a brief but forcible essay 'On the Value and Necessity of an Alliance between Great Britain and Germany.'

In translating the work, my aim has been to render the original as literally as possible. I have neither attempted to abridge my author's tautology nor to correct his style,

and where passages are emphasised by italics or capital
letters they are so in the original. Those, and they are
probably many in this country, who are prepared to accept
some or all of List's conclusions, will prefer to have his
theories and arguments stated in his own way, ungarbled
and unvarnished, while those who reject his doctrines may
perhaps still be interested in seeing the exact form in which
the intellectual founder of the German Zollverein gave his
opinions to the world.

CONTENTS.

———◦✧◦———

FIRST BOOK.

THE HISTORY.

SECOND BOOK.

THE THEORY.

THIRD BOOK.

THE SYSTEMS.

FOURTH BOOK.

THE POLITICS.

INTRODUCTORY ESSAY
[1904 Edition]
By J. S. Nicholson

MEMOIR.[1]

FRIEDRICH LIST was born August 6, 1789, at Reutlingen in Würtemberg, where his father, who, though not rich, was highly respected, carried on business as a currier and held several public appointments. At a very early age Friedrich manifested a strong dislike for his father's business, and determined to strike out a career for himself.

For a few years he found employment in the Town Clerks' offices at Blaubeeren, Ulm, and Tübingen; and after passing several Government examinations with distinction entered the Government Civil Service of Würtemberg, in which his promotion was so rapid that in 1816 he had risen to the post of Ministerial Under-Secretary. Von Wangenheim, who was Minister at the time, seems to have recognised his talents from the first, and cordially to have welcomed the assistance of so able a coadjutor in promoting his own projects of reform.

Among these was the establishment of a Chair of Political Economy in the University of Tübingen, an event which elicited from List an able and comprehensive pamphlet, in which he freely criticised the system of administration in Würtemberg, and pointed out that certain branches of knowledge in connection with the new Faculty, which it was of special importance to cultivate, had hitherto been almost entirely neglected. The pamphlet,

---

[1] Abridged from *Friedrich List, ein Vorläufer und ein Opfer für das Vaterland.* (Stuttgart, 1877.)

in fact, was rather a manifesto than an essay, and may be regarded as List's first open declaration of that war against officialism and red tape in which the rest of his life was to be spent.

Von Wangenheim showed his appreciation of the work by appointing the author Professor of Practical Administration (Staatspraxis) in the University, and encouraged him to persevere in his advocacy of reform in the State administration, of local representative government, and of freedom of the press.

Unhappily, so far from being of any advantage to List, the Minister's approval of his efforts was fatal to himself. The time was unpropitious for broaching schemes of reform which the nobility and bureaucracy were incapable of distinguishing from revolution—the King himself was alarmed, and the Minister had to resign.

This publication, however, was by no means List's only offence against the predominant official conservatism. At the close of the Napoleonic wars in 1815, German diplomatists appear with one consent to have shut their eyes to the industrial interests of the people. The Continental blockade as long as it lasted operated as a strongly protective system in favour of German home trade, particularly in the case of the minor States. But on the removal of the blockade, when the German ports were opened to foreign manufactures at low duties, the trade of the various German States with each other still remained restricted by a chain of internal custom-houses along every frontier. This state of things naturally excited just and general discontent, and an Association was formed for the abolition of these internal customs dues. Of this Association, List accepted the Presidency, a step which immediately brought down upon him the censure of the Government and deprivation of his office. His fellow-townsmen at Reutlingen testified their confidence in him by electing him their representative in the Würtemberg National Legislative Assembly, but so unpardonable was the crime which he had committed against those in authority that his election was cancelled by Ministerial veto.

Nothing daunted, however, List still devoted all his energies to agitating for the abolition of these internal tariffs and for the commercial union of all the German States, from which he foresaw that the political union of Germany must ultimately follow. He not only advocated these objects in the press in the shape of letters, articles, and pamphlets, but travelled, at a time when travelling. was both difficult and expensive, to Berlin, Munich, Vienna, and other German capitals, in order to make his views known to all the principal statesmen and leaders of commerce. His pilgrimage, however, produced but little practical result at the time; he found that the heads of the commercial houses, as usual, were timid, while Ministers, as usual, were jealous of any 'unauthorised' agitation for political objects.

A little later, in 1822, he was again elected as deputy from his native town to the Representative Assembly of Würtemberg. But a powerful petition, which he was chiefly instrumental in preparing, in favour of Commercial Union, and of other needful reforms, was resented so strongly by the King and his Ministers, that List was not only expelled from the Assembly, but condemned to ten months' imprisonment in a fortress, with hard labour, and to pay the costs of the proceedings against him.

To avoid the execution of this harsh sentence, he escaped to Strasburg; but after a brief stay, he was ordered by the authorities to quit that city, at the instance of the Würtemberg Government. From Strasburg he went to Baden, but only again to suffer the same indignity. From Baden he proceeded to Paris, where he was kindly welcomed by General Lafayette, who invited him to visit the United

States. Instead, however, of at once accepting the invitation, his intense love of his native country urged him to return to Würtemberg and appeal to the mercy of the King. His appeal was made to deaf ears. He was arrested and imprisoned in the State fortress of the Asberg, from which he was only released after several months' confinement, on condition of renouncing his nationality as a Würtemberger and quitting the country at once. Once more he proceeded to Strasburg, and once more his steps were dogged by the vindictive animosity of the King of Würtemberg, at whose request he was ordered by the French Government not to remain in French territory. He now determined to leave Europe altogether for a time, and took refuge in the United States, where he was again warmly welcomed by General Lafayette, whose introductions secured him the friendship of President Jackson, Henry Clay, James Madison, Edward Livingstone, and other influential American statesmen.

After an unsuccessful attempt to maintain himself by purchasing and cultivating a small piece of land, he started an American newspaper in the German language—the ' Adler.' The tariff disputes between Great Britain and the United States were at that time at their height, and List's friends urged him to write a series of popular articles on the subject in his journal. He accordingly published twelve letters addressed to J. Ingersoll, President of the Pennsylvanian ' Association for the Promotion of Manufacturing Industry.' In these he attacked the cosmopolitan system of free trade advocated by Adam Smith, and strongly urged the opposite policy, based on protection to native industry, pointing his moral by illustrations drawn from the existing economical condition of the United States.

The Association, which subsequently republished the letters under the title of ' Outlines of a New System of

Political Economy ' (Philadelphia, 1827), passed a series of resolutions affirming that List, by his arguments, had laid the foundation of a new and sound system of political economy, thereby rendering a signal service to the United States, and requesting him to undertake two literary works, one a scientific exposition of his theory, and the other a more popular treatise for use in the public schools, the Association binding itself to subscribe for fifty copies of each, and to recommend the Legislatures of all the other States to do the same.

The success of the ' Adler,' coupled with the fortunate discovery by himself of a new and important coalfield· in Pennsylvania, had now placed List in a position of comparative pecuniary ease ; but in spite of the ingratitude he had experienced at home from the King and the governing classes, his thoughts still turned to his native land. During 1828 and 1829 he warmly advocated, in a number of essays and articles, the formation of a national system of railways throughout Germany, and his desire to revisit Europe was heightened by his anxiety to promote his new scheme.

President Jackson accordingly, to whom List's views were familiar, sent him on a mission to Paris with a view to facilitating increased commercial intercourse between France and the United States, and subsequently in 1830 appointed him Consul for the United States at Hamburg. But the old spirit, which six years before had met his proposals of political reform with imprisonment and exile, was not yet dead. In the eyes of the servile official German press, List was still the ' hero of revolution,' and the American Minister, Van Buren, had to inform him with deep regret that the Senate of Hamburg refused to ratify his appointment. Forbidden to revisit his native Würtemberg, he again retired to Paris, where the American representative, Rives, introduced him to a number of influential friends. At this time Belgium had just gained her independence, and a more favourable prospect seemed opened for realising his plans both for a German national system of railways, and for increasing, through Belgium, the commercial inter ourse between Germany and the United States. After a brief visit to America, he returned to Europe as United States' Consul at Leipsic, in which capacity he was able to urge his railway schemes on the Goverment and people of Saxony, with such success that before ·long he had the satisfaction of witnessing the formation of powerful companies for the formation of several German lines. Whilst at Leipsic he also projected, and in great part wrote, two works which exercised considerable influence on public opinion in Germany—the 'Staats-Lexicon,' published in 1834, and the 'Railway Journal,' which appeared in 1835.

In the original survey of the railway from Halle to Cassel, the line had been projected so as to avoid the towns of Naumburg, Weimar, Gotha, Erfurt, and Eisenach. List exposed the impolicy of this arrangement both on strategical and commercial grounds, and by articles in the press and personal remonstrances at some of the smaller German courts succeeded in securing for these towns the benefit of railway communication. For his exertions on this occasion he received the personal thanks of the Duke of Gotha, an honorary doctor's degree from the University of Jena, and highly gratifying assurances on all hands that he had 'saved' the three Duchies of Weimar, Gotha, and Meiningen from a 'fatal danger.' These assurances were crowned by the munificent gift of one hundred louis d'or, which List received with the remark: 'So it appears that each of these " saved " principalities estimates the value of its salvation at exactly $33\frac{1}{3}$ louis.'

In 1837, on his way to Paris, he visited Belgium, where he was received with distinction, and renewed his acquaintance with Dr. Kolb, who had shared his imprisonment in the Asberg. Through Kolb's influence, List was persuaded to accept a permanent literary engagement in connection with the well-known 'Allgemeine Zeitung,' which at once began to devote greater space to questions affecting the material interests of Germany, especially in relation to tariffs and commercial law, and the commercial relations of Germany with Austria. List made ample use of this excellent opportunity of promulgating his opinions by a series of articles, some of which dealt more particularly with the commercial relations of Germany and Belgium with the United States. He also published his views in the columns of the Paris 'Constitutionnel' in 1839.

The agitation for the repeal of the Corn Laws in England, which aroused considerable interest throughout Europe, also gave him an opportunity for expounding his views in favour of a national protective policy and recommending its adoption by Germany.

In pointing out the prejudicial influence which he believed that restrictions on the importation of corn must necessarily exercise on the fully established manufacturing power of England, List argued that a national manufacturing power can only be successfully established and maintained by a free importation of raw materials combined with just protection to native industry against the importation of foreign manufactures.

Among many other results expected from the repeal of the English Corn Laws, it was anticipated that that measure would lead to the abolition of the protective duties imposed by Germany on foreign manufactures. But, according to List, it is only when a nation has reached such a stage of development that she can bear the strain of competition with foreign manufactures without injury in any respect, that she can safely dispense with protection to her own manufactures, and enter on a policy of general free trade. This, in fact, is the central idea of List's theory, which in

its economical aspect he opposed to the cosmopolitica
theory of Adam Smith and J. B. Say, and in its political
and national aspect to their theory of universal freedom
of trade.⌉ These views he maintained in many of his
essays, more particularly in those 'On Free Trade and
Protection,' and 'On the Nature and Value of a National
Manufacturing Industry.' It was not until List's articles
appeared that any public discussion of these questions
had taken place in Germany, and to him certainly belongs
the credit of having first awakened any general public
interest in them.

After leaving Leipsic, Augsburg became the permanent
residence of List and his family. Here it was that he
completed the first part of his 'National System of Political
Economy,' published in 1841. A second part was intended
to comprise 'The Policy of the Future,' and the third, 'The
Effect of Political Institutions on the Wealth and Power
of a Nation.' A commercial treaty had been concluded
between England and Prussia on behalf of the German
Zollverein, on March 2, 1841, just about the time when
List's work appeared. To this treaty List was bitterly
opposed, and his denunciation of it not only aroused the
wrath of the official newspapers, which reviled him as the
'German O'Connell,' but brought him again into collision
with 'the authorities.' In his despatch to Lord Aberdeen
of July 13, 1842, the English Ambassador, Lord Westmoreland, complains of List's proceedings, and describes him
as 'a very able writer in the pay of the German manufacturers.' As the English Anti-Corn-Law League had
paid their lecturers and agitators, and as the English
Government had paid Dr. Bowring to agitate in Germany,
France, and Switzerland, in favour of English commercial
interests, Lord Westmoreland's assumption that List was
also a paid agent was not unnatural, but it was wholly
without foundation. Whatever may have been the value

of List's services on this occasion, they were at least gratuitous.

As might have been expected, the 'National System' was vigorously attacked immediately on its publication; but such was the demand for it that three editions were called for within the space of a few months, and translations of it were published in French, Hungarian, and some other foreign languages. The principal objection raised against it was that the system it propounded was not one for the benefit of the whole world, but simply for the benefit of Germany. This List never sought to conceal. His avowed object was to free Germany from the overwhelming manufacturing supremacy of England, and on this subject some of his ablest opponents admitted that his was the best practical essay. But List never advocated a policy of prohibition. 'Any nation,' he declares, 'which decides to abandon a policy of absolute freedom of imports, must commence by imposing very moderate duties, and reach the protective system which she has decided to adopt by systematic degrees.' And again : 'Any tariff system which completely excludes foreign competition is injurious.' But 'the productions of foreign manufacturing industry must only be permitted to supply *a part* of the yearly national consumption,' and 'the maintenance of the foundation of the national industry at home must ever be the unvarying object of a nation's policy.'

In 1844 he published the fourth part of his principal work, 'The Politics' (of national economy). In this, after a graphic sketch of the negotiations and economical measures promoted by Canning, Huskisson, Labouchere, and Poulett Thompson, and censuring what he terms the 'crafty and spiteful commercial policy of England,' he advocates the establishment in Germany of thoroughly efficient transport facilities by river, canal, and railway, under united management—the creation of a German fleet

and the adoption of a universal German flag—the founding
of German colonies abroad—national supervision of emigration—the establishment of efficient German foreign consulates—of regular lines of German steamships—and the
negotiation of favourable commercial treaties with the
United States, Holland, and other countries.

The contemptuous bitterness with which this work was
criticised by the English press, led many of List's countrymen to conclude that he had 'hit the right nail on the
head,' and thus increased the influence of his writings.

In 1843 he had added to his other numerous literary
labours the editorship of the 'Zollvereinsblatt,' and continued to write in the 'Allgemeine Zeitung' and other
newspapers, on economical and commercial questions,
particularly on the development of the railway system in
Germany. He visited Hungary, where he was honourably
welcomed, Kossuth alluding to him in public as 'the man
who had best instructed the nations as to their true
national economical interests.' He received testimonials
from the Spinners' Association of Bohemia, the Congress of
Manufacturers of Leipsic, the Iron Manufacturers of the
Rhine, and various other public bodies. He enjoyed the
further satisfaction, amidst the bitter opposition which he
had to encounter, of witnessing the conclusion of the treaty
between the Zollverein and Belgium on September 1, 1844,
for which he had worked long and earnestly, both in the
press and by personal visits to Brussels, and by which, as
he observed, 'the Zollverein was enabled to carry on its
foreign trade with as much facility as if the ports of
Holland and North Germany were included in it.' Lastly,
at an audience with the King of Würtemberg, he received
a tardy acknowledgment of the injustice with which he had
formerly been treated in the words: 'My dear List, I bear
you no ill-will. What a pity it is that twenty-four years ago
we had not learnt to know each other as well as we do now!'

By this time his almost ceaseless labours had seriously undermined his health. He suffered from severe and frequent headache, and his bodily weakness increased, but he still continued his work. The repeal of the Corn Laws in England was imminent, and List dreaded lest the measure should enable England still further to encroach on German manufacturing industry. In spite of his failing health, he hastened to London in order that he might form a clear idea on the spot of the state of public opinion, and the probable effect of the impending change on the industrial interests of Germany. He was received with courtesy by many who had strongly opposed his policy, among others by Richard Cobden, who jokingly asked him, ' Have you actually come over here in order to get yourself converted ? ' His visit, however, only left List more strongly convinced than. ever of the earnest determination of England to secure for herself the manufacturing supremacy of the entire Continent, and the corresponding necessity for Germany to protect herself against it.

On his return from England his unfavourable symptoms both mental and bodily became more alarming, in spite of the affectionate care of his wife and family, to whom he was tenderly attached. A journey to the Tyrol was undertaken in the hope of restoring his shattered health, but it was already too late. After a few days' confinement to bed at Kufstein, on November 30, 1846, he left his lodging alone. He did not return. A desponding letter addressed to his friend Dr. Kolb was found in his room ; search was made, and his remains were found under some newly fallen snow under circumstances which left no doubt that in a moment of mental aberration he had died by his own hand. A monument in the cemetery at Kufstein marks his last resting place.

The news of his death was received with sincere and general regret throughout Germany and wherever he was known abroad. A subscription was set on foot to present to his bereaved family a substantial testimonial in recognition of his unselfish and devoted efforts to promote the unity, the power, and the welfare of Germany. King Louis of Bavaria was among the first to subscribe, as was also the Regent of Würtemberg, that native land whose rulers formerly so undervalued and ill-treated her able and patriotic son. Many of his most earnest political opponents joined in this endeavour to do honour to his memory, and even urged that ' it was the bounden duty of the German people to erect a statue to the noble patriot,' an appeal which has since been responded to by the erection of such a statue in his native town of Reutlingen.

The commercial policy suggested by List has been in great measure adopted by his native land. The internal tariffs have long since disappeared; under the Zollverein German manufactures and commerce have enormously increased; vigorous steps are being taken to found German colonies; an Imperial German flag floats over German shipping; a German empire has united the German people. And though to give effect to these great objects required the efforts of later and mightier men, a measure of the credit of them is surely due to the man who was long first and foremost in their advocacy, to which he sacrificed health, wealth, and ultimately his life.

List's talents were those of an original thinker, an able and laborious writer, and an earnest and untiring political agitator. For the latter career undoubtedly he was far more fitted by nature than for the service of the State. His was the thankless task of the political pioneer—the prophet who is not permitted to witness the full realisation of his own predictions, and whose message of a brighter future for his country is disbelieved and resented by those who should have been foremost to help him to hasten its advent.

SOME EXTRACTS

AUTHOR'S PREFACE TO THE FIRST EDITION.

———◆◇◆———

MORE than thirty-three years have elapsed since I first entertained doubts as to the truth of the prevailing theory of
political economy, and endeavoured to investigate (what
appeared to me) its errors and their fundamental causes.
My avocation (as Professor) gave me the motive to undertake that task—the opposition which it was my fate to meet
with forcibly impelled me to pursue it further.

My German contemporaries will remember to what a
low ebb the well-being of Germany had sunk in 1818. I
prepared myself by studying works on political economy.
I made myself as fully acquainted as others with what had
been thought and written on that subject. But I was
not satisfied with teaching young men that science in
its present form ; I desired also to teach them by what
economical policy the welfare, the culture, and the power
of Germany might be promoted. The popular theory
inculcated the principle of freedom of trade. That
principle appeared to me to be accordant with common
sense, and also to be proved by experience, when I considered the results of the abolition of the internal provincial
tariffs in France, and of the union of the three kingdoms
under one government in Great Britain. But the wonder-
fully favourable effects of Napoleon's Continental system,

and the destructive results of its abolition, were events too recent for me to overlook; they seemed to me to be directly contradictory of what I previously observed. And in endeavouring to ascertain on what that contradiction was founded, the idea struck me that *the theory was quite true, but only so in case all nations would reciprocally follow the principles of free trade, just as those provinces had done.* This led me to consider the nature of *nationality.* I perceived that the popular theory took no account of *nations,* but simply of the entire human race on the one hand, or of single individuals on the other. I saw clearly that free competition between two nations which are highly civilised can only be mutually beneficial in case both of them are in a nearly equal position of industrial development, and that any nation which owing to misfortunes is behind others in industry, commerce, and navigation, while she nevertheless possesses the mental and material means for developing those acquisitions, must first of all strengthen her own individual powers, in order to fit herself to enter into free competition with more advanced nations. In a word, I perceived the distinction between *cosmopolitical* and *political* economy. I felt that Germany must abolish her internal tariffs, and by the adoption of a common uniform commercial policy towards foreigners, strive to attain to the same degree of commercial and industrial development to which other nations have attained by means of their commercial policy.

In 1819 all Germany teemed with schemes and projects for new political institutions. Rulers and subjects, nobles and plebeians, officers of State and men of learning, were all occupied with them. Germany was like an estate which had been ravaged by war, whose former owners on resuming possession of it are about to arrange it afresh. Some wanted to restore everything exactly as it had been, down to every petty detail; others to have everything on a new plan and with entirely modern implements; while some, who paid regard both to common sense and to experience, desired to follow a middle course, which might accommodate the claims of the past with the necessities of the present. Everywhere were contradiction and conflict of opinion, everywhere leagues and associations for the promotion of patriotic objects. The constitution of the Diet itself was new, framed in a hurry, and regarded by the most enlightened and thoughtful diplomatists as merely an embryo from which a more perfect state of things might be hoped for in the future. One of its articles (the 19th) expressly left the door open for the establishment of a *national commercial system.* This article appeared to me to provide a basis on which the future industrial and commercial prosperity of the German Fatherland might rest, and hence the idea arose of establishing a league of German merchants and manufacturers for the abolition of our internal tariffs and the adoption of a common commercial policy for the whole of Germany. How this league took root, and led to united action between the noble-minded and enlightened rulers of Bavaria and Würtemberg, and later to the establishment of the German Zollverein, is well known.

As adviser of this German commercial league, I had a difficult position. All the scientifically educated Government employés, all the newspaper editors, all the writers on political economy, had been trained up in the cosmopolitical school, and regarded every kind of protective duty as a theoretical abomination. They were aided by the interests of England, and by those of the dealers in English goods in the ports and commercial cities of Germany. It is notorious what a powerful means of controlling public opinion abroad, is possessed by the English Ministry in their ' secret service money ; ' and they are not accustomed to be niggardly where it can be useful to their commercial interests. An innumerable army of correspondents and leader-writers, from Hamburg and Bremen, from Leipzig and Frankfort, appeared in the field to condemn the unreasonable desires of the German manufacturers for a niform protective duty, and to abuse their adviser in arsh and scornful terms; such as, that he was ignorant of the first principles of political economy as held by the most scientific authorities, or else had not brains enough to comprehend them. The work of these advocates of the interests of England was rendered all the easier by the fact that the popular theory and the opinions of German learned men were on their side.

The contest was clearly being fought with unequal weapons. On one side a theory thoroughly elaborated and uncontradicted, a compact school, a powerful party which had advocates in every legislature and learned society, but above all the great motive power—money. On the other side poverty and want, internal divisions, differences of opinion, and absolute lack of a theoretical basis.

In the course of the daily controversy which I had to conduct, I was led to perceive the distinction between the *theory of values* and the *theory of the powers of production*, and beneath the false line of argument which the popular school has raised out of the term *capital*. I learned to know the difference between *manufacturing power* and *agricultural power*. I hence discovered the basis of the fallacy of the arguments of the school, that it urges reasons which are only justly applicable to free trade in agricultural products, as grounds on which to justify free trade in manufactured goods. I began to learn to appreciate more thoroughly the principle of the division of labour, and to perceive how far it is applicable to the circumstances of *entire nations*. At a later period I travelled through Austria, North Germany, Hungary, Switzerland, France, and England, everywhere seeking instruction from observation of the actual condition of those countries as well as from written works. When afterwards I visited the United States, I cast all books aside—they would only have tended to mislead me. The best work on political economy which one can read in that modern land is actual life. There one may see wildernesses grow into rich and mighty States ; and progress which requires centuries in Europe, goes on there before one's eyes, viz. that from the condition of the mere hunter to the rearing of cattle—from that to agriculture, and from the latter to manufactures and commerce. There one may see how rents increase by degrees from nothing to important revenues. There the simple peasant knows practically far better than the most acute savans of the old world how agriculture and rents can be improved ; he endeavours to attract *manufacturers and artificers* to his vicinity. Nowhere so well as there can one learn the importance of means of transport, and their effect on the mental and material life of the people.

That book of actual life, I have earnestly and diligently studied, and compared with the results of my previous studies, experience, and reflections.

And the result has been (as I hope) the propounding of a system which, however defective it may as yet appear, is not founded on bottomless cosmopolitanism, but on the nature of things, on the lessons of history, and on the requirements of the nations. It offers the means of placing theory in accord with practice, and makes political economy comprehensible by every educated mind, by which previously, owing to its scholastic bombast, its contradictions, and its utterly false terminology, the sound sense of mankind had been bewildered.

I would indicate, as the distinguishing characteristic of my system, NATIONALITY. On the nature of *nationality*, as the intermediate interest between those of *individualism* and of *entire humanity*, my whole structure is based. I hesitated for some time whether I should not term mine the *natural* system of political economy, but was dissuaded from so doing by the remark of a friend, that under that title superficial readers might suppose my book to be a mere revival of the physiocratic system.

I have been accused by the popular school, of merely seeking to revive the (so-called) 'mercantile' system. But those who read my book will see that I have adopted in my theory merely the valuable parts of that much-decried system, whilst I have rejected what is false in it; that I have advocated those valuable parts on totally different grounds from those urged by the (so-called) mercantile school, namely on the grounds of history and of nature; also that I have refuted for the first time from those sources the arguments urged a thousand times by the cosmopolitical school, and have exposed for the first time the false train of reasoning which it bases on a bottomless cosmopolitanism, on the use of terms of double meaning, and on illogical arguments.

If I appear to condemn in too strong language the opinions and the works of individual authors or of entire schools, I have not done so from any personal arrogance. But as I hold that the views which I have controverted are injurious to the public welfare, it is necessary to contradict them energetically. And authors of celebrity do more harm by their errors than those of less repute, therefore they must be refuted in more energetic terms.

To candid and thoughtful critics I would remark (as respects tautology and recapitulation), that everyone who has studied political economy knows how in that science all individual items are interwoven in manifold ways, and that it is far better to repeat the same thing ten times over, than to leave one single point in obscurity. I have not followed the prevailing fashion of citing a multitude of quotations.   But I may say that I have read a hundred-fold more writings than those from which I have quoted.

In writing this preface I am humbly conscious that much fault may be found with my work; nay, that I myself might even now do much of it better. But my sole encouragement lies in the thought, that nevertheless much will be found in my book that is new and true, and also somewhat that may serve especially to benefit my German Fatherland.

FIRST BOOK

THE HISTORY

CHAPTER I.

At the revival of civilisation in Europe, no country was in so favourable a position as Italy in respect to commerce and industry. Barbarism had not been able entirely to eradicate the culture and civilisation of ancient Rome. A genial climate and a fertile soil, notwithstanding an unskilful system of cultivation, yielded abundant nourishment for a numerous population. The most necessary arts and industries remained as little destroyed as the municipal institutions of ancient Rome. Prosperous coast fisheries served everywhere as nurseries for seamen, and navigation along Italy's extensive sea-coasts abundantly compensated her lack of internal means of transport. Her proximity to Greece, Asia Minor, and Egypt, and her maritime intercourse with them, secured for Italy special advantages in the trade with the East which had previously, though not extensively, been carried on through Russia with the countries of the North. By means of this commercial intercourse Italy necessarily acquired those branches of knowledge and those arts and manufactures which Greece had preserved from the civilisation of ancient times.

From the period of the emancipation of the Italian cities by Otho the Great, they gave evidence of what history has testified alike in earlier and later times, namely, that freedom and industry are inseparable companions, even although not unfrequently the one has come into existence before the other. If commerce and industry are flourishing anywhere, one may be certain that there freedom is nigh at hand : if anywhere Freedom has unfolded her banner, it is as certain that sooner or later Industry will there establish herself; for nothing is more natural than that when man has acquired material or mental wealth he should strive to obtain guarantees for the transmission of his acquisitions to his successors, or that when he has acquired freedom, he should devote all his energies to improve his physical and intellectual condition.

For the first time since the downfall of the free states of antiquity was the spectacle again presented to the world by the cities of Italy of free and rich communities. Cities and territories reciprocally rose to a state of prosperity and received a powerful impulse in that direction from the Crusades. The transport of the Crusaders and their baggage and material of war not only benefited Italy's navigation, it afforded also inducements and opportunities for the conclusion of advantageous commercial relations with the East for the introduction of new industries, inventions, and plants, and for acquaintance with new enjoyments. On the other hand, the oppressions of feudal lordship were weakened and diminished in manifold ways, owing to the same cause, tending to the greater freedom of the cities and of the cultivation of the soil.

Next after Venice and Genoa, Florence became especially conspicuous for her manufactures and her monetary exchange business. Already, in the twelfth and thirteenth centuries, her silk and woollen manufactures were very flourishing; the guilds of those trades took part in the government, and under their influence the Republic was constituted. The woollen manufacture alone employed 200 manufactories, which produced annually 80,000 pieces of cloth, the raw material for which was imported from Spain. In addition to these, raw cloth to the amount of 300,000 gold gulden was imported annually from Spain, France, Belgium, and Germany, which, after being finished at Florence, was exported to the Levant. Florence conducted the banking business of the whole of Italy, and contained eighty banking establishments.[1] The annual revenue of her Government amounted to 300,000 gold

[1] De l'Ecluse, *Florence et ses Vicissitudes*, pp. 23, 26, 32, 103, 213.

gulden (fifteen million francs of our present money), considerably more than the revenue of the kingdoms of Naples and Aragon at that period, and more than that of Great Britain and Ireland under Queen Elizabeth.[1]

We thus see Italy in the twelfth and thirteenth centuries possessing all the elements of national economical prosperity, and in respect of both commerce and industry far in advance of all other nations. Her agriculture and her manufactures served as patterns and as motives for emulation to other countries. Her roads and canals were the best in Europe. The civilised world is indebted to her for banking institutions, the mariner's compass, improved naval architecture, the system of exchanges, and a host of the most useful commercial customs and commercial laws, as well as for a great part of its municipal and governmental institutions. Her commercial, marine, and naval power were by far the most important in the southern seas. She was in possession of the trade of the world; for, with the exception of the unimportant portion of it carried on over the northern seas, that trade was confined to the Mediterranean and the Black Sea. She supplied all nations with manufactures, with articles of luxury, and with tropical products, and was supplied by them with raw materials. One thing alone was wanting to Italy to enable her to become what England has become in our days, and because that one thing was wanting to her, every other element of prosperity passed away from her; she lacked *national union* and the power which springs from it. The cities and ruling powers of Italy did not act as members of one body, but made war on and ravaged one another like independent powers and states. While these wars raged externally, each commonwealth was successively overthrown by the internal conflicts between democracy, aristocracy, and autocracy. These conflicts, so destructive to national prosperity, were stimulated and increased by foreign powers and their invasions, and by the power of the priesthood at home and its pernicious influence, whereby

[1] Pechio, *Histoire de l'Economie Politique en Italie.*

the separate Italian communities were arrayed against one
another in two hostile factions.

How Italy thus destroyed herself may be best learned
from the history of her maritime states.   We first see
Amalfi great and powerful (from the eighth to the eleventh
century).[1] Her ships covered the seas, and all the coin
which passed current in Italy and the Levant was that of
Amalfi. She possessed the most practical code of maritime
laws, and those laws were in force in every port of the
Mediterranean. In the twelfth century her naval power
was destroyed by Pisa, Pisa in her turn fell under the
attacks of Genoa, and Genoa herself, after a conflict of a
hundred years, was compelled to succumb to Venice.

The fall of Venice herself appears to have indirectly
resulted from this narrow-minded policy. To a league of
Italian naval powers it could not have been a difficult task,
not merely to maintain and uphold the preponderance of
Italy in Greece, Asia Minor, the Archipelago, and Egypt,
but continually to extend and strengthen it; or to curb the
progress of the Turks on land and repress their piracies at
sea, while contesting with the Portuguese the passage round
the Cape of Good Hope.

As matters actually stood, however, Venice was not
merely left to her own resources, she found herself crippled
by the external attacks of her sister states and of the
neighbouring European powers.

It could not have proved a difficult task to a well-
organised league of Italian military powers to defend the
independence of Italy against the aggression of the great
monarchies. The attempt to form such a league was
actually made in 1526, but then not until the moment of
actual danger and only for temporary defence. The luke-
warmness and treachery of the leaders and members of
this league were the cause of the subsequent subjugation of

[1] Amalfi contained at the period of her prosperity 50,000 inhabitants.
Flavio Guio, the inventor of the mariner's compass, was a citizen of Amalfi.
It was at the sack of Amalfi by the Pisans (1135 or 1137) that that ancient
book was discovered which later on became so injurious to the reedom and
energies of Germany   the Pandects.

Milan and the fall of the Tuscan Republic. From that period must be dated the downfall of the industry and commerce of Italy.[1]

In her earlier as well as in her later history Venice aimed at being a nation for herself alone. So long as she had to deal only with petty Italian powers or with decrepid Greece, she had no difficulty in maintaining a supremacy in manufactures and commerce through the countries bordering on the Mediterranean and Black Seas. As soon, however, as united and vigorous nations appeared on the political stage, it became manifest at once that Venice was merely a city and her aristocracy only a municipal one. It is true that she had conquered several islands and even extensive provinces, but she ruled over them only as conquered territory, and hence (according to the testimony of all historians) each conquest increased her weakness instead of her power.

At the same period the spirit within the Republic by which she had grown great gradually died away. The power and prosperity of Venice—the work of a patriotic and heroic aristocracy which had sprung from an energetic and liberty-loving democracy—maintained itself and increased so long as the freedom of democratic energy lent it support, and that energy was guided by the patriotism, the wisdom, and the heroic spirit of the aristocracy. But in proportion as the aristocracy became a despotic oligarchy, destructive of the freedom and energies of the people, the roots of power and prosperity died away, notwithstanding that their branches and leading stem appeared still to flourish for some time longer.[2]

'A nation which has fallen into slavery,' says Montes-

[1] Hence Charles V. was the destroyer of commerce and industry in Italy, as he was also in the Netherlands and in Spain. He was the introducer of nobility by patent, and of the idea that it was disgraceful for the nobility to carry on commerce or manufactures—an idea which had the most destructive influence on the national industry. Before his time the contrary idea prevailed ; the Medici continued to be engaged in commerce long after they had become sovereign rulers.

[2] 'Quand les nobles, au lieu de verser leur sang pour la patrie, au lieu d'illustrer l'état par des victoires et de l'agrandir par des conquêtes, n'eurent plus qu'à jouir des honneurs et à se partager des impôts on dut se demander

quieu,[1] ' strives rather to retain what it possesses than to acquire more ; a free nation, on the contrary, strives rather to acquire than to retain.' To this very true observation he might have added—and because anyone strives only to retain without acquiring he must come to grief, for every nation which makes no forward progress sinks lower and lower, and must ultimately fall. Far from striving to extend their commerce and to make new discoveries, the Venetians never even conceived the idea of deriving benefit from the discoveries made by other nations. That they could be excluded from the trade with the East Indies by the discovery of the new commercial route thither, never occurred to them until they actually experienced it. What all the rest of the world perceived they would not believe ; and when they began to find out the injurious results of the altered state of things, they strove to maintain the old commercial route instead of seeking to participate in the benefits of the new one ; they endeavoured to maintain by petty intrigues what could only be won by making wise use of the altered circumstances by the spirit of enterprise and by hardihood. And when they at length had lost what they had possessed, and the wealth of the East and West Indies was poured into Cadiz and Lisbon instead of into their own ports, like simpletons or spendthrifts they turned their attention to alchemy.[2]

In the times when the Republic grew and flourished, to be inscribed in the Golden Book was regarded as a reward for distinguished exertions in commerce, in industry, or in the civil or military service of the State. On that condition this honour was open to foreigners; for example, to the most distinguished of the silk manufacturers who had immigrated from Florence.[3] But that book was closed

---

pourquoi il y avait huit ou neuf cents habitants de Venise qui se disaient propriétaires de toute la République.' (Daru, *Histoire de Venise*, vol. iv. ch. xviii.)

[1] *Esprit des Lois*, p. 192.

[2] A mere charlatan, Marco Brasadino, who professed to have the art of making gold, was welcomed by the Venetian aristocracy as a saviour. (Daru, *Histoire de Venise*, vol. iii. ch. xix.)

[3] Venice, as Holland and England subsequently did, made use of every

when men began to regard places of honour and State salaries as the family inheritance of the patrician class. At a later period, when men recognised the necessity of giving new life to the impoverished and enfeebled aristocracy, the book was reopened. But the chief title to inscription in it was no longer, as in former times, to have rendered services to the State, but the possession of wealth and noble birth. At length the honour of being inscribed in the Golden Book was so little esteemed, that it remained open for a century with scarcely any additional names.

If we inquire of History what were the causes of the downfall of this Republic and of its commerce, she replies that they principally consisted in the folly, neglect, and cowardice of a worn-out aristocracy, and in the apathy of a people who had sunk into slavery. The commerce and manufactures of Venice must have declined, even if the new route round the Cape of Good Hope had never been discovered.

The cause of it, as of the fall of all the other Italian republics, is to be found in the absence of national unity, in the domination of foreign powers, in priestly rule at home, and in the rise of other greater, more powerful, and more united nationalities in Europe.

If we carefully consider the commercial policy of Venice, we see at a glance that that of modern commercial and manufacturing nations is but a copy of that of Venice, only on an enlarged (i.e. a national) scale. By navigation laws and customs duties in each case native vessels and native manufactures were protected against those of foreigners, and the maxim thus early held good that it was sound policy to import raw materials from other states and to export to them manufactured goods.[1]

It has been recently asserted in defence of the principle

opportunity of attracting to herself manufacturing industry and capital from foreign states. Also a considerable number of silk manufacturers emigrated to Venice from Lucca, where already in the thirteenth century the manufacture of velvets and brocades was very flourishing, in consequence of the oppression of the Lucchese tyrant Castruccio Castracani. (Sandu, *Histoire de Venise*, vol. i. pp. 247–256.)

[1] Sismondi, *Histoire des Républiques Italiennes*, Pt. I. p. 285.

of absolute and unconditional free trade, that her protective
policy was the cause of the downfall of Venice. That assertion comprises a little truth with a great deal of error. If
we investigate the history of Venice with an unprejudiced
eye, we find that in her case, as in that of the great kingdoms at a later period, freedom of international trade as
well as restrictions on it have been beneficial or prejudicial to the power and prosperity of the State at different
epochs. Unrestricted freedom of trade was beneficial to
the Republic in the first years of her existence; for how
otherwise could she have raised herself from a mere fishing
village to a commercial power ? But a protective policy
was also beneficial to her when she had arrived at a certain
stage of power and wealth, for by means of it she attained
to manufacturing and commercial supremacy. Protection
first became injurious to her when her manufacturing and
commercial power had reached that supremacy, because by
it all competition with other nations became absolutely
excluded, and thus indolence was encouraged. Therefore,
not the introduction of a protective policy, but perseverance
in maintaining it after the reasons for its introduction had
passed away, was really injurious to Venice.

Hence the argument to which we have adverted has
this great fault, that it takes no account of the rise of great
nations under hereditary monarchy. Venice, although
mistress of some provinces and islands, yet being all the
time merely one Italian city, stood in competition, at the
period of her rise to a manufacturing and commercial
power, merely with other Italian cities ; and her prohibitory commercial policy could benefit her so long only as
whole nations with united power did not enter into competition with her. But as soon as that took place, she could
only have maintained her supremacy by placing herself at
the head of a united Italy and by embracing in her commercial system the whole Italian nation. No commercial
policy was ever clever enough to maintain continuously the
commercial supremacy of a single city over united nations.

From the example of Venice (so far as it may be
adduced against a protective commercial policy at the

present time) neither more nor less can be inferred than this—that a single city or a small state cannot establish and maintain such a policy successfully in competition with great states and kingdoms; also that any power which by means of a protective policy has attained a position of manufacturing and commercial supremacy, can (after she has attained it) revert with advantage to the policy of free trade.

In the argument before adverted to, as in every other when international freedom of trade is the subject of discussion, we meet with a misconception which has been the parent of much error, occasioned by the misuse of the term 'freedom.' Freedom of trade is spoken of in the same terms as religious freedom and municipal freedom. Hence the friends and advocates of freedom feel themselves especially bound to defend freedom in all its forms. And thus the term 'free trade' has become popular without drawing the necessary distinction between freedom of internal trade within the State and freedom of trade between separate nations, notwithstanding that these two in their nature and operation are as distinct as the heaven is from the earth. For while restrictions on the internal trade of a state are compatible in only very few cases with the liberty of individual citizens, in the case of international trade the highest degree of individual liberty may consist with a high degree of protective policy. Indeed, it is even possible that the greatest freedom of international trade may result in national servitude, as we hope hereafter to show from the case of Poland. In respect to this Montesquieu says truly, 'Commerce is never subjected to greater restrictions than in free nations, and never subjected to less ones than in those under despotic government.'[1]

[1] *Esprit des Lois*, livre xx. ch. xii.

CHAPTER II.

THE spirit of industry, commerce, and liberty having attained full influence in Italy, crossed the Alps, permeated Germany, and erected for itself a new throne on the shores of the northern seas, the Emperor Henry I., the father of the liberator of the Italian municipalities, promoted the founding of new cities and the enlargement of older ones which were already partly established on the sites of the ancient Roman colonies and partly in the Imperial domains.

Like the kings of France and England at a later period, he and his successors regarded the cities as the strongest counterpoise to the aristocracy, as the richest source of revenue to the State, as a new basis for national defence. By means of their commercial relations with the cities of Italy, their competition with Italian industry, and their free institutions, these cities soon attained to a high degree of prosperity and civilisation. Life in common fellow-citizenship created a spirit of progress in the arts and in manufacture, as well as zeal to achieve distinction by wealth and by enterprise; while, on the other hand, the acquisition of material wealth stimulated exertions to acquire culture and improvement in their political condition.

Strong through the power of youthful freedom and of flourishing industry, but exposed to the attacks of robbers by land and sea, the maritime towns of Northern Germany soon felt the necessity of a closer mutual union for protection and defence. With this object Hamburg and Lübeck formed a league in 1241, which before the close of that century embraced all the cities of any importance on the coasts of the Baltic and North Seas, or on the banks of the Oder, the Elbe, the Weser, and the Rhine (eighty-five in all). This confederation adopted the title of the 'Hansa,' which in the Low German dialect signifies a league.

Promptly comprehending what advantages the industry of individuals might derive from a union of their forces, the Hansa lost no time in developing and establishing a commercial policy which resulted in a degree of commercial prosperity previously unexampled. Perceiving that whatever power desires to create and maintain an extensive maritime commerce, must possess the means of defending it, they created a powerful navy; being further convinced that the naval power of any country is strong or weak in proportion to the extent of its mercantile marine and its sea fisheries, they enacted a law that Hanseatic goods should be conveyed only on board Hanseatic vessels, and established extensive sea fisheries. The English navigation laws were copied from those of the Hanseatic League, just as the latter were an imitation of those of Venice.[1]

England in that respect only followed the example of those who were her forerunners in acquiring supremacy at sea. Yet the proposal to enact a navigation Act in the time of the Long Parliament was then treated as a novel one. Adam Smith appears in his comment on this Act [2] not to have known, or to have refrained from stating, that already for centuries before that time and on various occasions the attempt had been made to introduce similar restrictions. A proposal to that effect made by Parliament in 1461 was rejected by Henry VI., and a similar one made by James I. rejected by Parliament; [3] indeed, long before these two proposals (viz. in 1381) such restrictions had been actually imposed by Richard II., though they soon proved inoperative and passed into oblivion. The nation was evidently not then ripe for such legislation. Navigation laws, like other

---

[1] Anderson, *Origin of Commerce*, Pt. I. p. 46.
[2] *Wealth of Nations*, Book IV. ch. ii.
[3] Hume, *History of England*, Part IV. ch. xxi.

measures for protecting native industry, are so rooted in the very nature of those nations who feel themselves fitted for future industrial and commercial greatness, that the United States of North America before they had fully won their independence had already at the instance of James Madison introduced restrictions on foreign shipping, and undoubtedly with not less great results (as will be seen in a future chapter) than England had derived from them a hundred and fifty years before.

The northern princes, impressed with the benefits which trade with the Hansards promised to yield to them—inasmuch as it gave them the means not only of disposing of the surplus products of their own territories, and of obtaining in exchange much better manufactured articles than were produced at home, but also of enriching their treasuries by means of import and export duties,[1] and of diverting to habits of industry their subjects who were addicted to idleness, turbulence, and riot—considered it as a piece of good fortune whenever the Hansards established factories on their territory, and endeavoured to induce them to do so by granting them privileges and favours of every kind. The kings of England were conspicuous above all other sovereigns in this respect.

The trade of England (says Hume) was formerly entirely in the hands of foreigners, but especially of the ' Easterlings '[2] whom Henry III. constituted a corpora-

---

[1] The revenues of the kings of England were derived at that time more from export duties than from import duties. Freedom of export and duties on imports (viz. of manufactures) betoken at once an advanced state of industry and an enlightened State administration. The governments and countries of the North stood at about the same stage of culture and statesmanship as the Sublime Porte does in our day. The Sultan has, notably, only recently concluded commercial treaties, by which he engages not to tax exports of raw materials and manufactures higher than fourteen per cent. but imports not higher than five per cent. And there accordingly that system of finance which professes to regard revenue as its chief object continues in full operation. Those statesmen and public writers who follow or advocate that system ought to betake themselves to Turkey ; there they might really stand at the head of the times.

[2] The Hansards were formerly termed ' Easterlings ' or Eastern merchants, in England, in contradistinction to those of the West, or the Belgians and Dutch. From this term is derived ' sterling ' or ' pound

tion, to whom he granted privileges, and whom he freed from restrictions and import duties to which other foreign merchants were liable. The English at that time were so inexperienced in commerce that from the time of Edward II. the Hansards, under the title of 'Merchants of the Steelyard,' monopolised the entire foreign trade of the kingdom. And as they conducted it exclusively in their own ships, the shipping interest of England was in a very pitiable condition.[1]

Some German merchants, viz. those of Cologne, after they had for a long time maintained commercial intercourse with England, at length established in London, in the year 1250, at the invitation of the King, the factory which became so celebrated under the name of 'The Steelyard'— an institution which at first was so influential in promoting culture and industry in England, but afterwards excited so much national jealousy, and which for 375 years, until its ultimate dissolution, was the cause of such warm and long-continued conflicts.

England formerly stood in similar relations with the Hanseatic League to those in which Poland afterwards stood with the Dutch, and Germany with the English; she supplied them with wool, tin, hides, butter, and other mineral and agricultural products, and received manufactured articles in exchange. The Hansards conveyed the raw products which they obtained from England and the northern states to their establishment at Bruges (founded in 1252), and exchanged them there for Belgian cloths and other manufactures, and for Oriental products and manufactures which came from Italy, which latter they carried back to all the countries bordering on the northern seas.

A third factory of theirs, at Novgorod in Russia (established in 1272), supplied them with furs, flax, hemp, and other raw products in exchange for manufactures. A fourth factory, at Bergen in Norway (also founded in

sterling,' an abbreviation of the word ' Easterling,' because formerly all the coin in circulation in England was that of the Hanseatic League.

[1] Hume, *History of England*, ch. xxxv.

1272), was occupied principally with fisheries and trade in train oil and fish products.[1]

The experience of all nations in all times teaches us that nations, so long as they remain in a state of barbarism, derive enormous benefit from free and unrestricted trade, by which they can dispose of the products of the chase and those of their pastures, forests, and agriculture—in short, raw products of every kind; obtaining in exchange better clothing materials, machines, and utensils, as well as the precious metals—the great medium of exchange—and hence that at first they regard free trade with approval. But experience also shows that those very nations, the farther advances that they make for themselves in culture and in industry, regard such a system of trade with a less favourable eye, and that at last they come to regard it as injurious and as a hindrance to their further progress. Such was the case with the trade between England and the Hansards. A century had scarcely elapsed from the foundation of the factory of the 'Steelyard' when Edward III. conceived the opinion that a nation might do something more useful and beneficial than to export raw wool and import woollen cloth. He therefore endeavoured to attract Flemish weavers into England by granting them all kinds of privileges; and as soon as a considerable number of them had got to work, he issued a prohibition against wearing any articles made of foreign cloth.[2]

The wise measures of this king were seconded in the most marvellous manner by the foolish policy pursued by the rulers of other countries—a coincidence which has not unfrequently to be noted in commercial history. If the earlier rulers of Flanders and Brabant did everything in their power to raise their native industry to a flourishing condition, the later ones did everything that was calculated to make the commercial and manufacturing classes discontented and to incite them to emigration.[3]

In the year 1413 the English woollen industry had

---

[1] M. I. Sartorius, *Geschichte der Hansa.*
[2] 11 Edward III. cap. 5.
[3] Rymer's *Fœdera*, p. 496. De Witte, *Interest of Holland*, p. 45.

already made such progress that Hume could write respecting that period, ' Great jealousy prevailed at this time against foreign merchants, and a number of restrictions were imposed on their trade, as, for instance, that they were required to lay out in the purchase of goods produced in England the whole value which they realised from articles which they imported into it.[1]

Under Edward IV. this jealousy of foreign traders rose to such a pitch that the importation of foreign cloth, and of many other articles, was absolutely prohibited.[2]

Notwithstanding that the king was afterwards compelled by the Hansards to remove this prohibition, and to reinstate them in their ancient privileges, the English woollen manufacture appears to have been greatly promoted by it, as is noted by Hume in treating of the reign of Henry VII., who came to the throne half a century later than Edward IV.

' The progress made in industry and the arts imposed limits, in a much more effective way than the rigour of laws could do, to the pernicious habit of the nobility of maintaining a great number of servants. Instead of vying with one another in the number and valour of their retainers, the nobility were animated by another kind of rivalry more in

[1] Hume, *History of England*, chap. xxv.

[2] 3 Edward IV. cap. iv. The preamble to this Act is so characteristic that we cannot refrain from quoting it verbatim.

' Whereas to the said Parliament, by the artificers men and women inhabitant and resident in the city of London and in other cities, towns, boroughs and villages within this realm and Wales, it has been piteously shewed and complained, how that all they in general and every of them be greatly impoverished and much injured and prejudiced of their worldly increase and living, by the great multitude of divers chaffers and wares pertaining to their mysteries and occupations, being fully wrought and ready made to sale, as well by the hand of strangers being the king's enemies as others, brought into this realm and Wales from beyond the sea, as well by merchant strangers as denizens or other persons, whereof the greatest part is deceitful and nothing worth in regard of any man's occupation or profits, by occasion whereof the said artificers cannot live by their mysteries and occupations, as they used to do in times past, but divers of them—as well householders as hirelings and other servants and apprentices—in great number be at this day unoccupied, and do hardly live, in great idleness, poverty, and ruin, whereby many inconveniences have grown before this time, and hereafter more are like to come (which God defend), if due remedy be not in their behalf provided.'

accordance with the spirit of civilisation, inasmuch as they now sought to excel one another in the beauty of their houses, the elegance of their equipages, and the costliness of their furniture. As the people could no longer loiter about in pernicious idleness, in the service of their chieftains and patrons, they became compelled, by learning some kind of handiwork, to make themselves useful to the community. Laws were again enacted to prevent the export of the precious metals, both coined and uncoined; but as these were well known to be inoperative, the obligation was again imposed on foreign merchants to lay out the whole proceeds of goods imported by them, in articles of English manufacture.' [1]

In the time of Henry VIII. the prices of all articles of food had considerably risen, owing to the great number of foreign manufacturers in London; a sure sign of the great benefit which the home agricultural industry derived from the development of home manufacturing industry.

The king, however, totally misjudging the causes and the operation of this phenomenon, gave ear to the unjust complaints of the English against the foreign manufacturers, whom the former perceived to have always excelled themselves in skill, industry, and frugality. An order of the Privy Council decreed the expulsion of 15,000 Belgian artificers, 'because they had made all provisions dearer, and had exposed the nation to the risk of a famine.' In order to strike at the root of this evil, laws were enacted to limit personal expenditure, to regulate the style of dress, the prices of provisions, and the rate of wages. This policy naturally was warmly approved by the Hansards, who acted towards this king in the same spirit of good-will which they had previously displayed towards all those former kings of England whose policy had favoured their interests, and which in our days the English display towards the kings of Portugal—they placed their ships of war at his disposition. During this king's whole reign the trade of the Hansards with England was very active. They possessed both ships and capital, and knew, not less cleverly than the English

Hume, chap. xxvi.

do in our days, how to acquire influence over peoples and governments who did not thoroughly understand their own interests. Only their arguments rested on quite a different basis from those of the trade monopolists of our day. The Hansards based their claim to supply all countries with manufactures on actual treaties and on immemorial possession of the trade, whilst the English in our day base a similar claim on a mere theory, which has for its author one of their own Custom-house officials. The latter demand in the name of a pretended science, what the former claimed in the name of actual treaties and of justice.

In the reign of Edward VI. the Privy Council sought for and found pretexts for abolishing the privileges of the 'Merchants of the Steelyard.' The Hansards made strong protests against this innovation. But the Privy Council persevered in its determination, and the step was soon followed by the most beneficial results to the nation. The English merchants possessed great advantages over the foreign ones, on account of their position as dwellers in the country, in the purchase of cloths, wool, and other articles, advantages which up to that time they had not so clearly perceived as to induce them to venture into competition with such a wealthy company. But from the time when all foreign merchants were subjected to the same commercial restrictions, the English were stimulated to enterprise, and the spirit of enterprise was diffused over the whole kingdom.[1]

After the Hansards had continued for some years to be entirely excluded from a market which they had for three centuries previously possessed as exclusively as England in our days possesses the markets of Germany and the United States, they were reinstated by Queen Mary in all their ancient privileges owing to representations made by the German Emperor.[2] But their joy was this time of short duration. Being earnestly desirous not merely of maintaining these privileges, but of increasing them, they made strong complaints at the beginning of the reign of Elizabeth

---

[1] Hume, chap. xxxv.; also Sir J. Hayward, *Life and Reign of Edward VI.*
[2] Hume, chap. xxxvii.; Heylyn.

of the treatment to which they had been subjected under Edward VI. and Mary. Elizabeth prudently replied that ' she had no power to alter anything, but she would willingly protect them still in the possession of those privileges and immunities which they then possessed.' This reply, however, did not satisfy them at all. Some time afterwards their trade was further suspended, to the great advantage of the English merchants, who now had an opportunity of showing of what they were capable ; they gained control over the entire export trade of their own country, and their efforts were crowned with complete success. They divided themselves into ' staplers and merchant adventurers,' the former carrying on business in some one place, the latter seeking their fortune in foreign cities and states with cloth and other English manufactures. This excited the jealousy of the Hansards so greatly, that they left no means untried to draw down on the English traders the ill opinion of other nations. At length, on August 1, 1597, they gained an imperial edict, by which all trade within the German Empire was forbidden to English merchants. The Queen replied (on January 13, 1598) by a proclamation, in consequence of which she sought reprisals by seizing sixty Hanseatic vessels which were engaged in contraband trade with Spain. In taking this step she had at first only intended, by restoring the vessels, to bring about a better understanding with the Hansards. But when she was informed that a general Hanseatic assembly was being held in the city of Lübeck in order to concert measures for harassing the export trade of England, she caused all these vessels with their cargoes to be confiscated, and then released two of them, which she sent to Lübeck with the message hat she felt the greatest contempt for the Hanseatic League and all their proceedings and measures.[1]

Thus Elizabeth acted towards these merchants, who had lent their ships to her father and to so many English kings to fight their battles ; who had been courted by all the potentates of Europe ; who had treated the kings of Denmark and Sweden as their vassals for centuries, and

---

[1] Campbell's *Lives of the Admirals*, vol. i. p. 386.

invited them into their territories and expelled them as they pleased ; who had colonised and civilised all the south-eastern coasts of the Baltic, and freed all seas from piracy ; who not very long before had, with sword in hand, compelled a king of England to recognise their privileges ; to whom on more than one occasion English kings had given their crowns in pledge for loans ; and who had once carried their cruelty and insolence towards England so far as to drown a hundred English fishermen because they had ventured to approach their fishing grounds. The Hansards, indeed, still possessed sufficient power to have avenged this conduct of the Queen of England ; but their ancient courage, their mighty spirit of enterprise, the power inspired by freedom and by co-operation, had passed from them. They dwindled gradually into powerlessness until at length, in 1630, their League was formally dissolved, after they had supplicated every court in Europe for import privileges, and had everywhere been repulsed with scorn.

Many external causes, besides the internal ones which we have to mention hereafter, contributed to their fall. Denmark and Sweden sought to avenge themselves for the position of dependence in which they had been so long held by the League, and placed all possible obstructions in the way of its commerce. The czars of Russia had conferred privileges on an English company. The order of Teutonic knights, who had for centuries been the allies as well as (originally) the children of the League, declined and was dissolved. The Dutch and the English drove them out of all markets, and supplanted them in every court. Finally, the discovery of the route to the East Indies by the Cape of Good Hope, operated most seriously to their disadvantage.

These leaguers, who during the period of their might and prosperity had scarcely deemed an alliance with the German Empire as worthy of consideration, now in their time of need betook themselves to the German Reichstag and represented to that body that the English exported annually 200,000 pieces of cloth, of which a great proportion went to Germany, and that the only means whereby he League could regain its ancient privileges in England, was to prohibit the import of English cloth into Germany. According to Anderson, a decree of the Reichstag to that effect was seriously contemplated, if not actually drawn up, but that author asserts that Gilpin, the English ambassador to the Reichstag, contrived to prevent its being .passed. A hundred and fifty years after the formal dissolution of the Hanseatic League, so completely had all memory of its former greatness disappeared in the Hanseatic cities that Justus Möser asserts (in some passage in his works) that when he visited those cities, and narrated to their merchants the power and greatness which their predecessors had enjoyed, they would scarcely believe him. Hamburg, formerly the terror of pirates in every sea, and renowned throughout Christendom for the services which she had rendered to civilisation in suppressing sea-robbers, had sunk so low that she had to purchase safety for her vessels by paying an annual tribute to the pirates of Algiers. Afterwards, when the dominion of the seas had passed into the hands of the Dutch another policy became prevalent in reference to piracy. When the Hanseatic League were supreme at sea, the pirate was considered as the enemy of the civilised world, and extirpated wherever that was possible. The Dutch, on the contrary, regarded the corsairs of Barbary as useful partisans, by whose means the marine commerce of other nations could be destroyed in times of peace, to the advantage of the Dutch. Anderson avails himself of the quotation of an observation of De Witt in favour of this policy to make the laconic comment, 'Fas est et ab hoste doceri,' a piece of advice which, in spite of its brevity, his countrymen comprehended and followed so well that the English, to the disgrace of Christianity, tolerated even until our days the abominable doings of the sea-robbers on the North African coasts, until the French performed the great service to civilisation of extirpating them.[1]

The commerce of these Hanseatic cities was not a *national* one; it was neither based on the equal preponderance and perfect development of internal powers of produc-

---

[1] Our author would appear to have forgotten, or else unfairly ignored, he exploits of the British fleet under Lord Exmouth.

tion, nor sustained by adequate political power. The bonds which held together the members of the League were too lax, the striving among them for predominant power and for separate interests (or, as the Swiss or the Americans would say, the cantonal spirit, the spirit of separate state right) was too predominant, and superseded Hanseatic patriotism, which alone could have caused the general common weal of the League to be considered before the private interests of individual cities. Hence arose jealousies, and not unfrequently treachery. Thus Cologne turned to her own private advantage the hostility of England towards the League, and Hamburg sought to utilise for her own advantage a quarrel which arose between Denmark and Lübeck.

The Hanseatic cities did not base their commerce on the production and consumption, the agriculture or the manufactures, of the land to which their merchants belonged. They had neglected to favour in any way the agricultural industry of their own fatherland, while that of foreign lands was greatly stimulated by their commerce. They found it more convenient to purchase manufactured goods in Belgium, than to establish manufactories in their own country. They encouraged and promoted the agriculture of Poland, the sheep-farming of England, the iron industry of Sweden, and the manufactures of Belgium. They acted for centuries on the maxim which the theoretical economists of our day commend to all nations for adoption—they ' bought only in the cheapest market.' But when the nations from whom they bought, and those to whom they sold, excluded them from their markets, neither their own native agriculture nor their own manufacturing industry was sufficiently developed to furnish employment for their surplus commercial capital. It consequently flowed over into Holland and England, and thus went to increase the industry, the wealth, and the power of their enemies ; a striking proof that mere private industry when left to follow its own course does not always promote the prosperity and the power of nations. In their exclusive efforts to gain material wealth, these cities had utterly neglected the promotion of their political interests. During the period of their power, they appeared no longer to belong at all to the German Empire. It flattered these selfish, proud citizens, within their circumscribed territories, to find themselves courted by emperors, kings, and princes, and to act the part of sovereigns of the seas. How easy would it have been for them during the period of their maritime supremacy, in combination with the cities of North Germany, to have founded a powerful Lower House as a counterpoise to the aristocracy of the empire, and by means of the imperial power to have thus brought about national unity—to have united under one nationality the whole sea-coast from Dunkirk to Riga—and by these means to have won and maintained for the German nation supremacy in manufactures, commerce, and maritime power. But in fact, when the sceptre of the seas fell from their grasp, they had not sufficient influence left to induce the German Reichstag to regard their commerce as a matter of national concern. On the contrary, the German aristocracy did all in their power thoroughly to oppress these humbled citizens. Their inland cities fell gradually under the absolute dominion of the various princes, and hence their maritime ones were deprived of their inland connections.

All these faults had been avoided by England. Her merchant shipping and her foreign commerce rested on the solid basis of her native agriculture and native industry; her internal trade developed itself in just proportion to her foreign trade, and individual freedom grew up without prejudice to national unity or to national power : in her case the interests of the Crown, the aristocracy, and the people became consolidated and united in the happiest manner.

If these historical facts are duly considered, can anyone possibly maintain that the English could ever have so widely extended their manufacturing power, acquired such an immeasurably great commerce, or attained such overwhelming naval power, save by means of the commercial policy which they adopted and pursued ? No ; the assertion that the English have attained to their present commercial eminence and power, not by means of their commercial policy, but in spite of it, appears to us to be one of the greatest falsehoods promulgated in the present century.

Had the English left everything to itself—' Laissé faire et laissé aller,' as the popular economical school recommends—the merchants of the Steelyard would be still carrying on their trade in London, the Belgians would be still manufacturing cloth for the English, England would have still continued to be the sheep-farm of the Hansards, just as Portugal became the vineyard of England, and has remained so till our days, owing to the stratagem of a cunning diplomatist. Indeed, it is more than probable that without her commercial policy England would never have attained to such a large measure of municipal and individual freedom as she now possesses, for such freedom is the daughter of industry and of wealth.

In view of such historical considerations, how has it happened that Adam Smith has never attempted to follow the history of the industrial and commercial rivalry between the Hanseatic League and England from its origin until its close ? Yet some passages in his work show clearly that he was not unacquainted with the causes of the fall of the League and its results. ' A merchant,' he says, ' is not necessarily the citizen of any particular country. It is in a great measure indifferent to him from what place he carries on his trade ; and a very trifling disgust will make him remove his capital, and together with it all the industry which it supports, from one country to another. No part of it can be said to belong to any particular country till it has been spread, as it were, over the face of that country, either in buildings or in the lasting improvement of lands. No vestige now remains of the great wealth said to have been possessed by the greater part of the Hanse Towns except in the obscure histories of the thirteenth and fourteenth centuries. It is even uncertain where some of them were situated, or to what towns in Europe the Latin names given to some of them belong.' [1]

How strange that Adam Smith, having such a clear insight into the secondary causes of the downfall of the

---

[1] Smith, *Wealth of Nations*, Book III. ch. iv.

Hanseatic League, did not feel himself compelled to examine into its primary causes! For this purpose it would not have been at all necessary to have ascertained the sites where the fallen cities had stood, or to which cities belonged the Latin names in the obscure chronicles. He need not even have consulted those chronicles at all. His own countrymen, Anderson, Macpherson, King, and Hume could have afforded him the necessary explanation.

How, therefore, and for what reason could such a profound inquirer permit himself to abstain from an investigation at once so interesting and so fruitful in results? We can see no other reason than this—that it would have led to conclusions which would have tended but little to support his principle of absolute free trade. He would infallibly have been confronted with the fact that after free commercial intercourse with the Hansards had raised English agriculture from a state of barbarism, the protective commercial policy adopted by the English nation at the expense of the Hansards, the Belgians, and the Dutch helped England to attain to manufacturing supremacy, and that from the latter, aided by her Navigation Acts, arose her commercial supremacy.

These facts, it would appear, Adam Smith was not willing to know or to acknowledge; for indeed they belong to the category of those inconvenient facts of which J. B. Say observes that they would have proved very adverse to his system.

CHAPTER III.

In respect to temperament and manners, to the origin and language of their inhabitants, no less than to their political connection and geographical position, Holland, Flanders, and Brabant constituted portions of the German Empire. The more frequent visits of Charlemagne and his residence in the vicinity of these countries must have exercised a much more powerful influence on their civilisation than on that of more distant German territories. Furthermore, Flanders and Brabant were specially favoured by nature as respects agriculture and manufactures, as Holland was as respects cattle-farming and commerce.

Nowhere in Germany was internal trade so powerfully aided by extensive and excellent sea and river navigation as in these maritime states. The beneficial effects of these means of water transport on the improvement of agriculture and on the growth of the towns must in these countries, even at an early period, have led to the removal of impediments which hindered their progress and to the construction of artificial canals. The prosperity of Flanders was especially promoted by the circumstance that her ruling Counts recognised the value of public security, of good roads, manufactures, and flourishing cities before all other German potentates, Favoured by the nature of their territory, they devoted themselves with zeal to the extirpation of the robber knights and of wild beasts. Active commercial intercourse between the cities and the country, the extension of cattle-farming, especially of sheep, and of the culture of flax and hemp, naturally followed; and wherever the raw material is abundantly produced, and security of property and of intercourse is maintained, labour and skill for working up that material will soon be found. Meanwhile the Counts of Flanders did not wait until chance should furnish them with woollen weavers, for history informs us that they imported such artificers from foreign countries.

Supported by the reciprocal trade of the Hanseatic League and of Holland, Flanders soon rose by her woollen manufactures to be the central point of the commerce of the North, just as Venice by her industry and her shipping had become the centre of the commerce of the South. The merchant shipping, and reciprocal trade of the Hanseatic League and the Dutch, together with the manufacturing trade of Flanders, constituted one great whole, a real national industry. A policy of commercial restriction could not in their case be deemed necessary, because as yet no competition had arisen against the manufacturing supremacy of Flanders. That under such circumstances manufacturing industry thrives best under free trade, the Counts of Flanders understood without having read Adam Smith. Quite in the spirit of the present popular theory, Count Robert III., when the King of England requested him to exclude the Scotch from the Flemish markets, replied, ' Flanders has always considered herself a free market for all nations, and it does not consist with her interests to depart from that principle.'

After Flanders had continued for centuries to be the chief manufacturing country, and Bruges the chief market, of Northern Europe, their manufactures and commerce passed over to the neighbouring province of Brabant, because the Counts of Flanders would not continue to grant them those concessions to which in the period of their great prosperity they had laid claim. Antwerp then became the principal seat of commerce, and Louvain the chief manufacturing city of Northern Europe. In consequence of this change of circumstances, the agriculture of Brabant soon rose to a high state of prosperity. The change in early times from payment of imposts in kind to their payment in money, and, above all, the limitation of the feudal system, also tended especially to its advantage.

In the meantime the Dutch, who appeared more and more upon the scene, with united power, as rivals to the Hanseatic League, laid the foundation of their future power at sea. Nature had conferred benefits on this small nation both by her frowns and smiles. Their perpetual contests with the inroads of the sea necessarily developed in them a spirit of enterprise, industry, and thrift, while the land which they had reclaimed and protected by such indescribable exertions must have seemed to them a property to which too much care could not be devoted. Restricted by Nature herself to the pursuits of navigation, of fisheries, and the production of meat, cheese, and butter, the Dutch were compelled to supply their requirements of grain, timber, fuel, and clothing materials by their marine-carrying trade, their exports of dairy produce, and their fisheries.

Those were the principal causes why the Hansards were at a later period gradually excluded by the Dutch from the trade with the north-eastern countries. The Dutch required to import far greater quantities of agricultural produce and of timber than did the Hansards, who were chiefly supplied with these articles by the territories immediately adjoining their cities. And, further, the vicinity to Holland of the Belgian manufacturing districts, and of the Rhine with its extensive, fertile, and vine-clad banks, and its stream navigable up to the mountains of Switzerland, constituted great advantages for the Dutch.

It may be considered as an axiom that the commerce and prosperity of countries on the sea coast is dependent on the greater or less magnitude of the river territories with which they have communication by water.[1] If we look at the map of Italy, we shall find in the great extent and fertility of the valley of the Po the natural reason why the commerce of Venice so greatly surpassed that of Genoa or of Pisa.

---

[1] The construction of good roads, and still more of railways, which has taken place in quite recent times, has materially modified this axiom.

The trade of Holland has its chief sources in the territories watered by the Rhine and its tributary streams, and in the same proportion as these territories were much richer and more fertile than those watered by the Elbe and the Weser must the commerce of Holland exceed that of the Hanse Towns. To the advantages above named was added another fortunate incident—the invention by Peter Böckels of the best mode of salting herrings. The best mode of catching and of 'böckelling' these fish (the latter term derived from the inventor) remained for a long period a secret known only to the Dutch, by which they knew how to prepare their herrings with a peculiar excellence surpassing those of all other persons engaged in sea fishery, and secured for themselves a preference in the markets as well as better prices.[1] Anderson alleges that after the lapse of centuries from the date of these inventions in Holland, the English and Scotch fishermen, notwithstanding their enjoyment of a considerable bounty on export, could not find purchasers for their herrings in foreign markets, even at much lower prices, in competition with the Dutch. If we bear in mind how great was the consumption of sea fish in all countries before the Reformation, we can well give credit to the fact that at a time when the Hanseatic shipping trade had already begun to decline, the Dutch found occasion for building 2,000 new vessels annually.

From the period when all the Belgian and Batavian provinces were united under the dominion of the House of Burgundy, these countries partly acquired the great benefit of national unity, a circumstance which must not be left out of sight in connection with Holland's success in maritime trade in competition with the cities of Northern Germany. Under the Emperor Charles V. the United Netherlands constituted a mass of power and capacity which would have insured to their Imperial ruler supremacy over the world, both by land and at sea, far more effectually

---

[1] It has been recently stated that the excellence of the Dutch herrings is attributable not only to the superior methods above named, but also to the casks in which they are 'böckelled' and exported being constructed of oak.

than all the gold mines on earth and all the papal favours and bulls could have done, had he only comprehended the nature of those powers and known how to direct and to make use of them.

Had Charles V. cast away from him the crown of Spain as a man casts away a burdensome stone which threatens to drag him down a precipice, how different would have been the destiny of the Dutch and the German peoples! As Ruler of the United Netherlands, as Emperor of Germany, and as Head of the Reformation, Charles possessed all the requisite means, both material and intellectual, for establishing the mightiest industrial and commercial empire, the greatest military and naval power which had ever existed—a maritime power which would have united under one flag all the shipping from Dunkirk as far as Riga.

The conception of but one idea, the exercise of but one man's will, were all that were needed to have raised Germany to the position of the wealthiest and mightiest empire in the world, to have extended her manufacturing and commercial supremacy over every quarter of the globe, and probably to have maintained it thus for many centuries.

Charles V. and his morose son followed the exactly opposite policy. Placing themselves at the head of the fanatical party, they made it their chief object to *hispanicise* the Netherlands. The result of that policy is matter of history. The northern Dutch provinces, strong by means of the element over which they were supreme, conquered their independence. In the southern provinces industry, the arts, and commerce, perished under the hand of the executioner, save only where they managed to escape that fate by emigrating to other countries. Amsterdam became the central point of the world's commerce instead of Antwerp. The cities of Holland, which already at an earlier period, in consequence of the disturbances in Brabant, had attracted a great number of Belgian woollen weavers, had now not room enough to afford refuge to all the Belgian fugitives, of whom a great number were consequently compelled to emigrate to England and to Saxony.

The struggle for liberty begot in Holland an heroic spirit at sea, to which nothing appeared too difficult or too adventurous, while on the contrary the spirit of fanaticism enfeebled the very nerves of Spain. Holland enriched herself principally by privateering against Spain, especially by the capture of the Spanish treasure fleets. By that means she carried on an enormous contraband trade with the Peninsula and with Belgium. After the union of Portugal with Spain, Holland became possessed of the most important Portuguese colonies in the East Indies, and acquired a part of Brazil. Up to the first half of the seventeenth century the Dutch surpassed the English in respect of manufactures and of colonial possessions, of commerce and of navigation, as greatly as in our times the English have surpassed the French in these respects. But with the English Revolution a mighty change developed itself. The spirit of freedom had become only a citizen spirit in Holland. As in all mere mercantile aristocracies, all went on well for a time ; so long as the preservation of life and limbs and of property, and mere material advantages, were the objects clearly in view, they showed themselves capable of great deeds. But statesmanship of a more profound character was beyond their ken. They did not perceive that the supremacy which they had won, could only be maintained if it were based on a great nationality and supported by a mighty national spirit. On the other hand, those states which had developed their nationality on a large scale by means of monarchy, but which were yet behindhand in respect of commerce and industry, became animated by a sentiment of shame that so small a country as Holland should act the part of master over them in manufactures and commerce, in fisheries, and naval power. In England this sentiment was accompanied by all the energy of the new-born Republic. The Navigation Laws were the challenge glove which the rising supremacy of England cast into the face of the reigning supremacy of Holland. And when the conflict came, it became evident that the English nationality was of far larger calibre than that of the Dutch. The result could not remain doubtful.

The example of England was followed by France. Colbert had estimated that the entire marine transport trade employed about 20,000 vessels, of which 16,000 were owned by the Dutch—a number altogether out of proportion for so small a nation. In consequence of the succession of the Bourbons to the Spanish throne, France was enabled to extend her trade over the Peninsula (to the great disadvantage of the Dutch), and equally so in the Levant. Simultaneously the protection by France of her native manufactures, navigation, and fisheries, made immense inroads on the industry and commerce of Holland.

England had gained from Holland the greater part of the trade of the latter with the northern European states, her contraband trade with Spain and the Spanish colonies, and the greater part of her trade with the East and West Indies, and of her fisheries. But the most serious blow was inflicted on her by the Methuen Treaty of 1703. From that the commerce of Holland with Portugal, the Portuguese colonies, and the East Indies, received a deadly wound.

When Holland thus commenced to lose so large a portion of her foreign trade, the same result took place which had previously been experienced by the Hanseatic cities and by Venice: the material and mental capital which could now find no employment in Holland, was diverted by emigration or in the shape of loans to those countries which had acquired the supremacy from Holland which she had previously possessed.

If Holland in union with Belgium, with the Rhenish districts, and with North Germany, had constituted one national territory, it would have been difficult for England and France to have weakened her naval power, her foreign commerce, and her internal industry by wars and by commercial policy, as they succeeded in doing. A nation such as that would have been, could have placed in competition with the commercial systems of other nations a commercial system of her own. And if owing to the development of the manufactures of those other nations her industry suffered some injury, her own internal resources, aided by founding colonies abroad, would have abundantly made good that loss. Holland suffered decline because she, a mere strip of sea coast, inhabited by a small population of German fishermen, sailors, merchants, and dairy farmers, endeavoured to constitute herself a national power, while she considered and acted towards the inland territory at her back (of which she properly formed a part) as a foreign land.

The example of Holland, like that of Belgium, of the Hanseatic cities, and of the Italian republics, teaches us that mere private industry does not suffice to maintain the commerce, industry, and wealth of entire states and nations, if the public circumstances under which it is carried on are unfavourable to it; and further, that the greater part of the productive powers of individuals are derived from the political constitution of the government and from the power of the nation. The agricultural industry of Belgium became flourishing again under Austrian rule. When united to France her manufacturing industry rose again to its ancient immense extent. Holland by herself was never in a position to establish and maintain an independent commercial system of her own in competition with great nations. But when by means of her union with Belgium after the general peace (in 1815) her internal resources, population, and national territory were increased to such an extent that she could rank herself among the great nationalities, and became possessed in herself of a great mass and variety of productive powers, we see the protective system established also in the Netherlands, and under its influence agriculture, manufactures, and commerce make a remarkable advance. This union has now been again dissolved (owing to causes which lie outside the scope and purpose of our present work), and thus the protective system in Holland has been deprived of the basis on which it rested, while in Belgium it is still maintained.

Holland is now maintained by her colonies and by her transport trade with Germany. But the next great naval war may easily deprive her of the former; and the more the German Zollverein attains to a clear perception of its interests, and to the exercise of its powers, the more clearly will it recognise the necessity of including Holland within the Zollverein.

CHAPTER IV.

THE ENGLISH.

In our account of the Hanseatic League we have shown how in England agriculture and sheep farming have been promoted by foreign trade ; how at a subsequent period, through the immigration of foreign artificers, fleeing from persecution in their native land, and also owing to the fostering measures adopted by the British Government, the English woollen manufacturing industry had gradually attained to a flourishing condition ; and how, as a direct consequence of that progress in manufacturing industry, as well as of the wise and energetic measures adopted by Queen Elizabeth, all the foreign trade which formerly had been monopolised by foreigners had been successfully diverted into the hands of the merchants at home.

Before we continue our exposition of the development of English national economy from the point where we left off in Chapter II., we venture here to make a few remarks as to the origin of British industry.

The source and origin of England's industrial and commercial greatness must be traced mainly to the breeding of sheep and to the woollen manufacture.

Before the first appearance of the Hansards on British soil the agriculture of England was unskilful and her sheep farming of little importance. There was a scarcity of winter fodder for the cattle, consequently a large proportion had to be slaughtered in autumn, and hence both stock and manure were alike deficient. Just as in all uncultivated territories—as formerly in Germany, and in the uncleared districts of America up to the present time— hog breeding furnished the principal supply of meat, and that for obvious reasons. The pigs needed little care—foraged for themselves, and found a plentiful supply of food on the waste lands and in the forests ; and by keeping only a moderate number of breeding sows through the winter, one was sure in the following spring of possessing considerable herds.

But with the growth of foreign trade hog breeding diminished, sheep farming assumed larger proportions, and agriculture and the breeding of horned cattle rapidly improved.

Hume, in his 'History of England,'[1] gives a very interesting account of the condition of English agriculture at the beginning of the fourteenth century :

'In the year 1327 Lord Spencer counted upon 68 estates in his possession, 28,000 sheep, 1,000 oxen, 1,200 cows, 560 horses, and 2,000 hogs : giving a proportion of 450 sheep, 35 head of cattle, 9 horses, and 32 hogs to each estate.'

From this statement we may perceive how greatly, even in those early days, the number of sheep in England exceeded that of all the other domestic animals put together. The great advantages derived by the English aristocracy from the business of sheep farming gave them an interest in industry and in improved methods of agriculture even at that early period, when noblemen in most Continental states knew no better mode of utilising the greater part of their possessions than by preserving large herds of deer, and when they knew no more honourable occupation than harassing the neighbouring cities and their trade by hostilities of various kinds.

And at this period, as has been the case in Hungary more recently, the flocks so greatly increased that many estates could boast of the possession of from 10,000 to 24,000 sheep. Under these circumstances it necessarily followed that, under the protection afforded by the measures introduced by Queen Elizabeth, the woollen manufacture, which had already progressed very considerably in the days

---

[1] Hume, vol. ii. p. 143.

of former English rulers, should rapidly reach a very high degree of prosperity.[1]

In the petition of the Hansards to the Imperial Diet, mentioned in Chapter II., which prayed for the enactment of retaliatory measures, England's export of cloth was estimated at 200,000 pieces; while in the days of James I. the total value of English cloths exported had already reached the prodigious amount of two million pounds sterling, while in the year 1354 the total money value of the wool exported had amounted only to 277,000*l*., and that of all other articles of export to no more than 16,400*l*. Down to the reign of the last-named monarch the great bulk of the cloth manufactured in England used to be exported to Belgium in the rough state and was there dyed and dressed; but owing to the measures of protection and encouragement introduced under James I. and Charles I. the art of dressing cloth in England attained so high a pitch of perfection that thenceforward the importation of the finer descriptions of cloth nearly ceased, while only dyed and finely dressed cloths were exported.

In order fully to appreciate the importance of these results of the English commercial policy, it must be here observed that, prior to the great development of the linen, cotton, silk, and iron manufactures in recent times, the manufacture of cloth constituted by far the largest proportion of the medium of exchange in the trade with all European nations, particularly with the northern kingdoms, as well as in the commercial intercourse with the Levant and the East and West Indies. To what a great extent this was the case we may infer from the undoubted fact that as far back as the days of James I. the export of woollen manufactures represented nine-tenths of all the English exports put together.[2]

This branch of manufacture enabled England to drive

---

[1] No doubt the decrees prohibiting the export of wool, not to mention the restrictions placed on the trade in wool in markets near the coast, were vexatious and unfair; yet at the same time they operated beneficially in the promotion of English industry, and in the suppression of that of the Flemings.

[2] Hume (in 1603). Macpherson, *Histoire du Commerce* (in 1651).

the Hanseatic League out of the markets of Russia, Sweden, Norway, and Denmark, and to acquire for herself the best part of the profits attaching to the trade with the Levant and the East and West Indies. It was this industry that stimulated that of coal mining, which again gave rise to an extensive coasting trade and the fisheries, both which, as constituting the basis of naval power, rendered possible the passing of the famous Navigation Laws which really laid the foundation of England's maritime supremacy. It was round the woollen industry of England that all other branches of manufacture grew up as round a common parent stem ; and it thus constitutes the foundation of England's greatness in industry, commerce, and naval power.

At the same time the other branches of English manufacture were in no way neglected.

Already under the reign of Elizabeth the importation of metal and leather goods, and of a great many other manufactured articles, had been prohibited, while the immigration of German miners and metal workers was encouraged. Formerly ships had been bought of the Hansards or were ordered to be built in the Baltic ports. But she contrived, by restrictions on the one hand and encouragements on the other, to promote shipbuilding at home.

The timber required for the purpose was brought to England from the Baltic ports, whereby again a great impetus was given to the British export trade to those regions.

The herring fishery had been learned from the Dutch, whale fishing from the dwellers on the shores of the Bay of Biscay ; and both these fisheries were now stimulated by means of bounties. James I. more particularly took a lively interest in the encouragement of shipbuilding and of fisheries. Though we may smile at his unceasing exhortations to his people to eat fish, yet we must do him the justice to say that he very clearly perceived on what the future greatness of England depended. The immigration into England, moreover, of the Protestant artificers who

had been driven from Belgium and France by Philip II.
and Louis XIV. gave to England an incalculable increase
of industrial skill and manufacturing capital. To these
men England owes her manufactures of fine woollen cloth,
her progress in the arts of making hats, linen, glass, paper,
silk, clocks and watches, as well as a part of her metal
manufacture; branches of industry which she knew how
speedily to increase by means of prohibition and high
duties.

The island kingdom borrowed from every country of the
Continent its skill in special branches of industry, and
planted them on English soil, under the protection of her
customs system. Venice had to yield (amongst other trades
in articles of luxury) the art of glass manufacture, while
Persia had to give up the art of carpet weaving and
dyeing.

Once possessed of any one branch of industry, England
bestowed upon it sedulous care and attention, for centuries
treating it as a young tree which requires support and care.
Whoever is not yet convinced that by means of diligence,
skill, and economy, every branch of industry must become
profitable in time—that in any nation already advanced in
agriculture and civilisation, by means of moderate protection, its infant manufactures, however defective and dear
their productions at first may be, can by practice, experience,
and internal competition readily attain ability to equal in
every respect the older productions of their foreign competitors; whoever is ignorant that the success of one
particular branch of industry depends on that of several
other branches, or to what a high degree a nation can
develop its productive powers, if she takes care that each
successive generation shall continue the work of industry
where former generations have left it; let him first study
the history of English industry before he ventures to frame
theoretical systems, or to give counsel to practical statesmen to whose hands is given the power of promoting the
weal or the woe of nations.

Under George I. English statesmen had long ago clearly
perceived the grounds on which the greatness of the nation

depends. At the opening of Parliament in 1721, the King is made to say by the Ministry, that 'it is evident that nothing so much contributes to promote the public well-being as the exportation of manufactured goods and the importation of foreign raw material.'[1]

This for centuries had been the ruling maxim of English commercial policy, as formerly it had been that of the commercial policy of the Venetian Republic. It is in force at this day (1841) just as it was in the days of Elizabeth. The fruits it has borne lie revealed to the eyes of the whole world. The theorists have since contended that England has attained to wealth and power not by means of, but in spite of, her commercial policy. As well might they argue that trees have grown to vigour and fruitfulness, not by means of, but *in spite of*, the props and fences with which they had been supported when they were first planted.

Nor does English history supply less conclusive evidence of the intimate connection subsisting between a nation's general political policy and political economy. Clearly the rise and growth of manufactures in England, with the increase of population resulting from it, tended to create an active demand for salt fish and for coals, which led to a great increase of the mercantile marine devoted to fisheries and the coasting trade. Both the fisheries and the coasting trade were previously in the hands of the Dutch. Stimulated by high customs duties and by bounties, the English now directed their own energies to the fishery trade, and by the Navigation Laws they secured chiefly to British sailors not only the transport of sea-borne coal, but the whole of the carrying trade by sea. The consequent increase in England's mercantile marine led to a proportionate augmentation of her naval power, which enabled the English to bid defiance to the Dutch fleet. Shortly after the passing of the Navigation Laws, a naval war broke out between

[1] See Ustaritz, *Théorie du Commerce*, ch. xxviii. Thus we see George I. did not want merely to export goods and import nothing but specie in return, which is stated as the fundamental principle of the so-called 'mercantile system,' and which in any case would be absurd. What he desired was to export manufactures and import raw material.

England and Holland, whereby the trade of the Dutch with countries beyond the English Channel suffered almost total suspension, while their shipping in the North Sea and the Baltic was almost annihilated by English privateers.' Hume estimates the number of Dutch vessels which thus fell into the hands of English cruisers at 1,600, while Davenant, in his 'Report on the Public Revenue,' assures us that in the course of the twenty-eight years next following the passing of the English Navigation Laws, the English shipping trade had increased to double its previous extent.[1]

Amongst the more important results of the Navigation Laws, the following deserve special mention, viz.:

1. The expansion of the English trade with all the northern kingdoms, with Germany and Belgium (export of manufactures and import of raw material), from which, according to Anderson's account, up to the year 1603 the English had been almost entirely shut out by the Dutch.

2. An immense extension of the contraband trade with Spain and Portugal, and their West Indian colonies.

3. A great increase of England's herring and whale fisheries, which the Dutch had previously almost entirely monopolised.

4. The conquest of the most important English colony in the West Indies—Jamaica—in 1655; and with that, the command of the West Indian sugar trade.

5. The conclusion of the Methuen Treaty (1703) with Portugal, of which we have fully treated in the chapters devoted to Spain and Portugal in this work. By the operation of this treaty the Dutch and the Germans were entirely excluded from the important trade with Portugal and her colonies: Portugal sank into complete political dependence upon England, while England acquired the means, through the gold and silver earned in her trade with Portugal, of extending enormously her own commercial intercourse with China and the East Indies, and thereby subsequently of laying the foundation for her great Indian empire, and dispossessing the Dutch from their most important trading stations.

[1] Hume, vol. v. p. 39.

The two results last enumerated stand in intimate connection one with the other. And the skill is especially noteworthy with which England contrived to make these two countries—Portugal and India—the instruments of her own future greatness. Spain and Portugal had in the main little to dispose of besides the precious metals, while the requirements of the East, with the exception of cloths, consisted chiefly of the precious metals. So far everything suited most admirably. But the East had principally only cotton and silk manufactures to offer in exchange, and that did not fit in with the principle of the English Ministry before referred to, namely, to export manufactured articles and import raw materials. How, then, did they act under the circumstances? Did they rest content with the profits accruing from the trade in cloths with Portugal and in cotton and silk manufactures with India? By no means. The English Ministers saw farther than that.

Had they sanctioned the free importation into England of Indian cotton and silk goods, the English cotton and silk manufactories must of necessity soon come to a stand. India had not only the advantage of cheaper labour and raw material, but also the experience, the skill, and the practice of centuries. The effect of these advantages could not fail to tell under a system of free competition.

But England was unwilling to found settlements in Asia in order to become subservient to Asia in manufacturing industry. She strove for commercial supremacy, and felt that of two countries maintaining free trade between one another, that one would be supreme which sold manufactured goods, while that one would be subservient which could only sell agricultural produce. In her North American colonies England had already acted on those principles in disallowing the manufacture in those colonies of even a single horseshoe nail, and, still more, that no horseshoe nails made there should be imported into England. How could it be expected of her that she would give up her own market for manufactures, the basis of her future greatness, to a people so numerous, so thrifty, so experienced and perfect in the old systems of manufacture as the Hindoos ?

Accordingly, England prohibited the import of the goods dealt in by her own factories, the Indian cotton and silk fabrics.[1] The prohibition was complete and peremptory. Not so much as a thread of them would England permit to be used. She would have none of these beautiful and cheap fabrics, but preferred to consume her own inferior and more costly stuffs. She was, however, quite willing to supply the Continental nations with the far finer fabrics of India at lower prices, and willingly yielded to them all the benefit of that cheapness; she herself would have none of it.

Was England a fool in so acting ? Most assuredly, according to the theories of Adam Smith and J. B. Say, the Theory of Values. For, according to them, England should have bought what she required where she could buy them cheapest and best : it was an act of folly to manufacture for herself goods at a greater cost than she could buy them at elsewhere, and at the same time give away that advantage to the Continent.

The case is quite the contrary, according to our theory, which we term the Theory of the Powers of Production, and which the English Ministry, without having examined the foundation on which it rests, yet practically adopted when enforcing their maxim of *importing produce* and *exporting fabrics*.

The English Ministers cared not for the acquisition of low-priced and perishable articles of manufacture, but for that of a more costly but enduring *manufacturing power*.

They have attained their object in a brilliant degree. At this day England produces seventy million pounds' worth of cotton and silk goods, and supplies all Europe, the entire world, India itself included, with British manufactures. Her home production exceeds by fifty or a hundred times the value of her former trade in Indian manufactured goods.

What would it have profited her had she been buying for a century the cheap goods of Indian manufacture ?

[1] Anderson for the year 1721.

And what have they gained who purchased those goods so cheaply of her? The English have gained power, incalculable power, while the others have gained the reverse of power.

That in the face of results like these, historically attested upon unimpeachable evidence, Adam Smith should have éxpressed so warped a judgment upon the Navigation Laws, can only be accounted for upon the same principle on which we shall in another chapter explain this celebrated author's fallacious conclusions respecting commercial restrictions. These facts stood in the way of his pet notion of unrestricted free trade. It was therefore necessary for him to obviate the objection that could be adduced against his principle from the effects of the Navigation Laws, by drawing a distinction between their political objects and their economical objects. He maintained that, although the Navigation Laws had been politically necessary and beneficial, yet that they were economically prejudicial and injurious. How little this distinction can be justified by the nature of things or by experience, we trust to make apparent in the course of this treatise.

J. B. Say, though he might have known better from the experience of North America, here too, as in every instance where the principles of free trade and protection clash, goes still farther than his predecessor. Say reckons up what the cost of a sailor to the French nation is, owing to the fishery bounties, in order to show how wasteful and unremunerative these bounties are.

The subject of restrictions upon navigation constitutes a formidable stumbling-block in the path of the advocates of unrestricted free trade, which they are only too glad to pass over in silence, especially if they are members of the mercantile community in seaport towns.

The truth of the matter is this. Restrictions on navigation are governed by the same law as restrictions upon any other kind of trade. Freedom of navigation and the carrying trade conducted by foreigners are serviceable and welcome to communities in the early stages of their civilisation, so long as their agriculture and manufactures still remain undeveloped. Owing to want of capital and of experienced seamen, they are willing to abandon navigation and foreign trade to other nations. Later on, however when they have developed their producing power to certain point and acquired skill in shipbuilding and navigation, then they will desire to extend their foreign trade, to carry it on in their own ships, and become a naval power themselves. Gradually their own mercantile marine grows to such a degree that they feel themselves in a position to exclude the foreigner and to conduct their trade to the most distant places by means of their own vessels. Then the time has come when, by means of restrictions on navigation, a nation can successfully exclude the more wealthy, more experienced, and more powerful foreigner from participation in the profits of that business. When the highest degree of progress in navigation and maritime power has been reached, a new era will set in, no doubt; and such was that stage of advancement which Dr. Priestley had in his mind when he wrote 'that the time may come when it may be as politic to repeal this Act as it was to make it.'[1]

Then it is that, by means of treaties of navigation based upon equality of rights, a nation can, on the one hand, secure undoubted advantages as against less civilised nations, who will thus be debarred from introducing restrictions on navigation in their own special behalf; while, on the other hand, it will thereby preserve its own seafaring population from sloth, and spur them on to keep pace with other countries in shipbuilding and in the art of navigation. While engaged in her struggle for supremacy, Venice was doubtless greatly indebted to her policy of restrictions on navigation; but as soon as she had acquired supremacy in trade, manufactures, and navigation, it was folly to retain them. For owing to them she was left behind in the race, both as respects shipbuilding, navigation, and seamanship of her sailors, with other maritime and commercial nations which were advancing in her footsteps. Thus England by her policy increased her

[1] Priestley, *Lectures on History and General Policy*, Pt. II. p. 289.

naval power, and by means of her naval power enlarged
the range of her manufacturing and commercial powers,
and again, by the latter, there accrued to her fresh accessions of maritime strength and of colonial possessions.
Adam Smith, when he maintains that the Navigation
Laws have not been beneficial to England in commercial
respects, admits that, in any case, these laws have increased her power. And power is more important than.
wealth. That is indeed the fact. Power is more important
than wealth. And why? Simply because national power
is a dynamic force by which new productive resources are
opened out, and because the forces of production are the
tree on which wealth grows, and because the tree which
bears the fruit is of greater value than the fruit itself.
Power is of more importance than wealth because a nation,
by means of power, is enabled not only to open up new
productive sources, but to maintain itself in possession of
former and of recently acquired wealth, and because the
reverse of power—namely, feebleness—leads to the relin-
quishment of all that we possess, not of acquired wealth
alone, but of our powers of production, of our civilisation,
of our freedom, nay, even of our national independence,
into the hands of those who surpass us in might, as
is abundantly attested by the history of the Italian republics, of the Hanseatic League, of the Belgians, the
Dutch, the Spaniards, and the Portuguese.

But how came it that, unmindful of this law of alternat-
ing action and reaction between political power, the forces
of production and wealth, Adam Smith could venture to
contend that the Methuen Treaty and the Act of Navigation
had not been beneficial to England from a commercial
point of view? We have shown how England by the policy
which she pursued acquired power, and by her political
power gained productive power, and by her productive power
gained wealth. Let us now see further how, as a result of
this policy, power has been added to power, and productive
forces to productive forces.

England has got into her possession the keys of every
sea, and placed a sentry over every nation: over the
Germans, Heligoland; over the French, Guernsey and

Jersey; over the inhabitants of North America, Nova Scotia and the Bermudas; over Central America, the island of Jamaica; over all countries bordering on the Mediterranean, Gibraltar, Malta, and the Ionian Islands. She possesses every important strategical position on both the routes to India with the exception of the Isthmus of Suez, which she is striving to acquire; she dominates the Mediterranean by means of Gibraltar, the Red Sea by Aden, and the Persian Gulf by Bushire and Karrack. She needs only the further acquisition of the Dardanelles, the Sound, and the Isthmuses of Suez and Panama, in order to be able to open and close at her pleasure every sea and every maritime highway. Her navy alone surpasses the combined maritime forces of all other countries, if not in number of vessels, at any rate in fighting strength.

Her manufacturing capacity excels in importance that of all other nations. And although her cloth manufactures have increased more than tenfold (to fourty-four and a half millions) since the days of James I., we find the yield of another branch of industry, which was established only in the course of the last century, namely the manufacture of cotton, amounting to a much larger sum, fifty-two and a half millions.[1]

Not content with that, England is now attempting to raise her linen manufacture, which has been long in a backward state as compared with that of other countries, to a similar position, possibly to a higher one than that of the two above-named branches of industry: it now amounts to fifteen and a half millions sterling. In the fourteenth century, England was still so poor in iron that she thought it necessary to prohibit the exportation of this indispensable metal; she now, in the nineteenth century, manufactures more iron and steel wares than all the other nations on earth (namely, thirty-one millions' worth), while she produces thirty-four millions in value of coal and other minerals.

[1] These and the following figures relating to English statistics are taken from a paper written by McQueen, the celebrated English statistician, and appearing in the July number of *Tait's Edinburgh Magazine* for the year 1839. Possibly they may be somewhat exaggerated for the moment. But even if so, it is more than probable hat the figures as stated will be reached within the present decade.

These two sums exceed by over sevenfold the value of the entire gold and silver production of all other nations, which amount to about two hundred and twenty million francs or nine millions sterling.

At this day she produces more silk goods than all the Italian republics produced in the Middle Ages together, namely, thirteen and a half million pounds. Industries which at the time of Henry VIII. and Elizabeth scarcely deserved classification, now yield enormous sums; as, for' instance, the glass, china, and stoneware manufactures, representing eleven millions; the copper and brass manufactures, four and a half millions; the manufactures of paper, books, colours, and furniture, fourteen millions.

England produces, moreover, sixteen millions' worth of leather goods, besides ten millions' worth of unenumerated articles. The manufacture of beer and spirituous liquors in England alone greatly exceeds in value the aggregate of national production in the days of James I., namely, forty-seven millions sterling.

The entire manufacturing production of the United Kingdom at the present time, is estimated to amount to two hundred and fifty-nine and a half millions sterling.

As a consequence, and *mainly* as a consequence, of this gigantic manufacturing production, the productive power of agriculture has been enabled to yield a total value exceeding twice that sum (five hundred and thirty-nine millions sterling).

It is true that for this increase in her power, and in her productive capacity, England is not indebted solely to her commercial restrictions, her Navigation Laws, or her commercial treaties, but in a large measure also to her conquests in science and in the arts.

But how comes it, that in these days one million of English operatives can perform the work of hundreds of millions? It comes from the great demand for manufactured goods which by her wise and energetic policy she has known how to create in foreign lands, and especially in her colonies; from the wise and powerful protection extended to her home industries; from the great rewards which by means of her patent laws she has offered to every new discovery; and from the extraordinary facilities for her inland transport afforded by public roads, canals, and railways.

England has shown the world how powerful is the effect of facilities of transport in increasing the powers of production, and thereby increasing the wealth, the population, and the political power of a nation. She has shown us what a free, industrious, and well-governed community can do in this respect within the brief space of half a century, even in the midst of foreign wars. That which the Italian republics had previously accomplished in these respects was mere child's play. It is estimated that as much as a hundred and eighteen millions sterling have been expended in England upon these mighty instruments of the nation's productive power.

England, however, only commenced and carried out these works when her manufacturing power began to grow strong. Since then, it has become evident to all observers that that nation only whose manufacturing power begins to develop itself upon an extensive scale is able to accomplish such works; that only in a nation which develops concurrently its internal manufacturing and agricultural resources will such costly engines of trade repay their cost; and that in such a nation only will they properly fulfil their purpose.

It must be admitted, too, that the enormous producing capacity and the great wealth of England are not the effect solely of national power and individual love of gain. The people's innate love of liberty and of justice, the energy, the religious and moral character of the people, have a share in it. The constitution of the country, its institutions, the wisdom and power of the Government and of the aristocracy, have a share in it. The geographical position, the fortunes of the country, nay, even good luck, have a share in it.

It is not easy to say whether the material forces exert a greater influence over the moral forces, or whether the moral outweigh the material in their operation; whether the social forces act upon the individual forces the more powerfully, or whether the latter upon the former. This

much is certain, however, namely, that between the two
there subsists an interchanging sequence of action and
reaction, with the result that the increase of one set of
forces promotes the increase of the other, and that the
enfeeblement of the one ever involves the enfeeblement of
the other.

Those who seek for the fundamental causes of England's
rise and progress in the blending of Anglo-Saxon with the
Norman blood, should first cast a glance at the condition
of the country before the reign of Edward III. Where
were then the diligence and the habits of thrift of the
nation? Those again who would look for them in the
constitutional liberties enjoyed by the people will do well
to consider how Henry VIII. and Elizabeth treated their
Parliaments. Wherein did England's constitutional freedom consist under the Tudors? At that period the cities
of Germany and Italy enjoyed a much greater amount of
individual freedom than the English did.

Only one jewel out of the treasure house of freedom
was preserved by the Anglo-Saxon-Norman race—before
other peoples of Germanic origin; and that was the germ
from which all the English ideas of freedom and justice
have sprung—the right of trial by jury.

While in Italy the Pandects were being unearthed, and
the exhumed remains (no doubt of departed greatness and
wisdom in their day) were spreading the pestilence of the
Codes amongst Continental nations, we find the English
Barons declaring they would not hear of any change in the
law of the land. What a store of intellectual force did
they not thereby secure for the generations to come! How
much did this intellectual force subsequently influence the
forces of material production!

How greatly did the early banishment of the Latin
language from social and literary circles, from the State
departments, and the courts of law in England influence,
the development of the nation, its legislation, law admi
nistration, literature, and industry! What has been the
effect upon Germany of the long retention of the Latin in
conjunction with foreign Codes, and what has been its

effect in Hungary to the present day? What an effect have the invention of gunpowder, the art of printing, the Reformation, the discovery of the new routes to India and of America, had on the growth of English liberties, of English civilisation, and of English industry? Compare with this their effect upon Germany and France. In Germany—discord in the Empire, in the provinces, even within the walls of cities; miserable controversies, barbarism in literature, in the administration of the State and of the law; civil war, persecutions, expatriation, foreign invasion, depopulation, desolation; the ruin of cities, the decay of industry, agriculture, and trade, of freedom and civic institutions; supremacy of the great nobles; decay of the imperial power, and of nationality; severance of the fairest provinces from the Empire. In France—subjugation of the cities and of the nobles in the interest of despotism; alliance with the priesthood against intellectual freedom, but at the same time national unity and power; conquest with its gain and its curse, but, as against that, downfall of freedom and of industry. In England—the rise of cities, progress in agriculture, commerce, and manufactures; subjection of the aristocracy to the law of the land, and hence a preponderating participation by the nobility in the work of legislation, in the administration of the State and of the law, as also in the advantages of industry; development of resources at home, and of political power abroad; internal peace; influence over all less advanced communities; limitation of the powers of the Crown, but gain by the Crown in royal revenues, in splendour and stability. Altogether, a higher degree of well-being, civilisation, and freedom at home, and preponderating might abroad.

But who can say how much of these happy results is attributable to the English national spirit and to the constitution; how much to England's geographical position and circumstances in the past; or again, how much to chance, to destiny, to fortune?

Let Charles V. and Henry VIII. change places, and, in consequence of a villanous divorce trial, it is conceivable

(the reader will understand why we say ' conceivable ') that
Germany and the Netherlands might have become what
England and Spain have become. Place in the position of
Elizabeth, a weak woman allying herself to a Philip II.,
and how would it have fared with the power, the civilisation,
and the liberties of Great Britain ?

If the force of national character will alone account for
everything in this mighty revolution, must not then the
greatest share of its beneficial results have accrued to the
nation from which it sprang, namely, to Germany ? Instead
of that, it is just the German nation which reaped nothing
save trouble and weakness from this movement in the
direction of progress.

In no European kingdom is the institution of an aristocracy more judiciously designed than in England for
securing to the nobility, in their relation to the Crown and
the commonalty, individual independence, dignity, and stability; to give them a Parliamentary training and position ;
to direct their energies to patriotic and national aims; to
induce them to attract to their own body the *élite* of the
commonalty, to include in their ranks every commoner
who earns distinction, whether by mental gifts, exceptional
wealth, or great achievements ; and, on the other hand, to
cast back again amongst the commons the surplus progeny
of aristocratic descent, thus leading to the amalgamation of
the nobility and the commonalty in future generations.
By this process the nobility is ever receiving from the
Commons fresh accessions of civic and patriotic energy, of
science, learning, intellectual and material resources, while
it is ever restoring to the people a portion of the culture
and of the spirit of independence peculiarly its own, leaving
its own children to trust to their own resources, and supplying the commonalty with incentives to renewed exertion.
In the case of the English lord, however large may be the
number of his descendants, only one can hold the title at a
time.   The other members of the family are commoners,
who gain a livelihood either in one of the learned professions,
or in the Civil Service, in commerce, industry, or agriculture.
The story goes that some time ago one of the first dukes

in England conceived the idea of inviting all the blood relations of his house to a banquet, but he was fain to abandon
the design because their name was legion, notwithstanding
that the family pedigree had not reached farther back than
for a few centuries. It would require a whole volume to
show the effect of this institution upon the spirit of enterprise, the colonisation, the might and the liberties, and
especially upon the forces of production of this nation.[1]

The geographical position of England, too, has exercised
an immense influence upon the independent development of
the nation. England in its relation to the continent of
Europe has ever been a world by itself; and was always
exempt from the effects of the rivalries, the prejudices, the
selfishness, the passions, and the disasters of her Continental
neighbours. To this isolated condition she is mainly indebted for the independent and unalloyed growth of her
political constitution, for the undisturbed consummation of
the Reformation, and for the secularisation of ecclesiastical
property which has proved so beneficial to her industries.
To the same cause she is also indebted for that continuous
peace, which, with the exception of the period of the civil
war, she has enjoyed for a series of centuries, and which
enabled her to dispense with standing armies, while
facilitating the early introduction of a consistent customs
system.

By reason of her insular position, England not only
enjoyed immunity from territorial wars, but she also derived immense advantages for her manufacturing supremacy
from the Continental wars. Land wars and devastations
of territory inflict manifold injury upon the manufactures
at the seat of hostilities; directly, by interfering with the
farmer's work and destroying the crops, which deprives
the tiller of the soil of the means wherewithal to purchase
manufactured goods, and to produce raw material and food
for the manufacturer; indirectly, by often destroying the
manufactories, or at any rate ruining them, because hos-

---

[1] Before his lamented death, the gifted author of this remark, in his
Letters on England, read the nobles of his native country a lesson in this
respect which they would do well to lay to heart.

tilities interfere with the importation of raw material an
with the exportation of goods, and because it becomes a
difficult matter to procure capital and labour just at the
very time when the masters have to bear extraordinary
imposts and heavy taxation; and lastly, the injurious
effects continue to operate even after the cessation of the
war, because both capital and individual effort are ever
attracted towards agricultural work and diverted from
manufactures, precisely in that proportion in which the
war may have injured the farmers and their crops, and
thereby opened up a more directly profitable field for the
employment of capital and of labour than the manufacturing industries would then afford. While in Germany
this condition of things recurred twice in every hundred
years, and caused German manufactures to retrograde,
those of England made uninterrupted progress. English
manufacturers, as opposed to their Continental competitors,
enjoyed a double and treble advantage whenever England,
by fitting out fleets and armies, by subsidies, or by both
these means combined, proceeded to take an active part in
foreign wars.

We cannot agree with the defenders of unproductive
expenditure, namely of that incurred by wars and the maintenance of large armies, nor with those who insist upon
the positively beneficial character of a public debt; but
neither do we believe that the dominant school are in the
right when they contend that all consumption which is not
directly reproductive—for instance, that of war—is absolutely injurious without qualification. The equipment of
armies, wars, and the debts contracted for these purposes,
may, as the example of England teaches, under certain
circumstances, very greatly conduce to the increase of the
productive powers of a nation. Strictly speaking, material
wealth may have been consumed unproductively, but this
consumption may, nevertheless, stimulate manufacturers
to extraordinary exertions, and lead to new discoveries and
improvements, especially to an increase of productive
powers. This productive power then becomes a permanent
acquisition; it will increase more and more, while the

expense of the war is incurred only once for all.[1] And thus it may come to pass, under favouring conditions such as have occurred in England, that a nation has gained immeasurably more than it has lost from that very kind of expenditure which theorists hold to be unproductive. That such was really the case with England, may be shown by figures. For in the course of the war, that country had acquired in the cotton manufacture alone a power of production which yields annually a much larger return in value than the amount which the nation has to find to defray the interest upon the increased national debt, not to mention the vast development of all other branches of industry, and the additions to her colonial wealth.

Most conspicuous was the advantage accruing to the English manufacturing interest during the Continental wars, when England maintained army corps on the Continent or paid subsidies. The whole expenditure on these was sent, in the shape of English manufactures, to the seat of war, where these imports then materially contributed to crush the already sorely suffering foreign manufacturers, and permanently to acquire the market of the foreign country for English manufacturing industry. It operated precisely like an export bounty instituted for the benefit of British and for the injury of foreign manufacturers.[2]

In this way, the industry of the Continental nations has ever suffered more from the English as allies, than from the English as enemies. In support of this statement we

[1] England's national debt would not be so great an evil as it now appears to us, if England's aristocracy would concede that this burden should be borne by the class who were benefited by the cost of wars, namely, by the rich. McQueen estimates the capitalised value of property in the three kingdoms at 4,000 million pounds sterling, and Martin estimates the capital invested in the colonies at about 2,600 millions sterling. Hence we see that one ninth part of Englishmen's private property would suffice to cover the entire national debt. Nothing could be more just than such an appropriation, or at least than the payment of the interest on the national debt out of the proceeds of an income tax. The English aristocracy, however, deem it more convenient to provide for this charge by the imposition of taxes upon articles of consumption, by which the existence of the working classes is embittered beyond the point of endurance.

[2] See Appendix A.

need refer only to the Seven Years' War, and to the wars against the French Republic and Empire.

Great, however, as have been the advantages heretofore mentioned, they have been greatly surpassed in their effect by those which England derived from immigrations attracted by her political, religious, and geographical conditions.

As far back as the twelfth century political circumstances induced Flemish woollen weavers to emigrate to Wales. Not many centuries later exiled Italians came over to London to carry on business as money changers and bankers. That from Flanders and Brabant entire bodies of manufacturers thronged to England at various periods, we have shown in Chapter II. From Spain and Portugal came persecuted Jews; from the Hanse Towns, and from Venice in her decline, merchants who brought with them their ships, their knowledge of business, their capital, and their spirit of enterprise. Still more important were the immigrations of capital and of manufacturers in consequence of the Reformation and the religious persecutions in Spain, Portugal, France, Belgium, Germany, and Italy; as also of merchants and manufacturers from Holland in consequence of the stagnation of trade and industry in that country occasioned by the Act of Navigation and the Methuen Treaty. Every political movement, every war upon the Continent, brought England vast accessions of fresh capital and talents, so long as she possessed the privileges of freedom, the right of asylum, internal tranquillity and peace, the protection of the law, and general well-being. So more recently did the French Revolution and the wars of the Empire; and so did the political commotions, the revolutionary and reactionary movements and the wars in Spain, in Mexico, and in South America. By means of her Patent Laws, England long monopolised the inventive genius of every nation. It is no more than fair that England, now that she has attained the culminating point of her industrial growth and progress, should restore again to the nations of Continental Europe a portion of those productive forces which she originally derived from them.

CHAPTER V.

THE SPANIARDS AND PORTUGUESE.

WHILST the English were busied for centuries in raising the structure of their national prosperity upon the most solid foundations, the Spaniards and the Portuguese made a fortune rapidly by means of their discoveries and attained to great wealth in a very short space of time. But it was only the wealth of a spendthrift who had won the first prize in a lottery, whereas the wealth of the English may be likened to the fortune accumulated by the diligent and saving head of a family. The former may for a time appear more to be envied than the latter on account of his lavish expenditure and luxury; but wealth in his case is only a means for prodigality and momentary enjoyment, whereas the latter will regard wealth chiefly as a means of laying a foundation for the moral and material well-being of his latest posterity.

The Spaniards possessed flocks of well-bred sheep at so early a period that Henry I. of England was moved to prohibit the importation of Spanish wool in 1172, and that as far back as the tenth and eleventh centuries Italian woollen manufacturers used to import the greater portion of their wool supplies from Spain. Two hundred years before that time the dwellers on the shores of the Bay of Biscay had already distinguished themselves in the manufacture of iron, in navigation, and in fisheries. They were the first to carry on the whale fishery, and even in the year 1619 they still so far excelled the English in that business that they were asked to send fishermen to England to instruct the English in this particular branch of the fishing rade.[1]

[1] Anderson, vol. i. p. 127, vol. ii. p. 350.

Already in the tenth century, under Abdulrahman III.
(912 to 950), the Moors had established in the fertile plains
around Valencia extensive plantations of cotton, sugar, and
rice, and carried on silk cultivation.   Cordova, Seville, and
Granada contained at the time of the Moors important
cotton and silk manufactories.[1]   Valencia, Segovia, Toledo,
and several other cities in Castile were celebrated for their
woollen manufactures.   Seville alone at an early period of
history contained as many as 16,000 looms, while the
woollen manufactories of Segovia in the year 1552 were
employing 13,000 operatives.   Other branches of industry,
notably the manufacture of arms and of paper, had become
developed on a similar scale.   In Colbert's day the French
were still in the habit of procuring supplies of cloth from
Spain.[2]   The Spanish seaport towns were the seat of an
extensive trade and of important fisheries, and up to the
time of Philip II. Spain possessed a most powerful navy.
In a word, Spain possessed all the elements of greatness
and prosperity, when bigotry, in alliance with despotism,
set to work to stifle the high spirit of the nation.   The first
commencement of this work of darkness was the expulsion
of the Jews, and its crowning act the expulsion of the Moors,
whereby two millions of the most industrious and well-to-do
inhabitants were driven out of Spain with their capital.

While the Inquisition was thus occupied in driving
native industry into exile, it at the same time effectually
prevented foreign manufacturers from settling down in the
country.   The discovery of America and of the route round
the Cape only increased the wealth of both kingdoms after
a specious and ephemeral fashion—indeed, by these events
a death-blow was first given to their national industry and
to their power.   For then, instead of exchanging the
produce of the East and West Indies against home manufactures, as the Dutch and the English subsequently did,
the Spaniards and Portuguese purchased manufactured
goods from foreign nations with the gold and the silver which

---

[1] M. G. Simon, *Recueil d'Observations sur l'Angleterre. Mémoires et
Considérations sur le Commerce et les Finances d'Espagne.* Ustaritz,
Théorie et Pratique du Commerce.

[2] Chaptal, *De l'Industrie Française*, vol. ii. p. 245.

they had wrung from their colonies.[1] They transformed
their useful and industrious citizens into slave-dealers and
colonial tyrants : thus they promoted the industry, the
trade, and the maritime power of the Dutch and English,
in whom they raised up rivals who soon grew strong
enough to destroy their fleets and rob them of the sources
of their wealth. In vain the kings of Spain enacted laws
against the exportation of specie and the importation of
manufactured goods. The spirit of enterprise, industry,
and commerce can only strike root in the soil of religious
and political liberty ; gold and silver will only abide where
industry knows how to attract and employ them.

Portugal, however, under the auspices of an enlightened
and powerful minister, did make an attempt to develop her
manufacturing industry, the first results of which strike
us with astonishment. That country, like Spain, had
possessed from time immemorial fine flocks of sheep.
Strabo tells us that a fine breed of sheep had been introduced into Portugal from Asia, the cost of which amounted
to one talent per head. When the Count of Ereceira became minister in 1681, he conceived the design of establishing cloth manufactories, and of thus working up the
native raw material in order to supply the mother country
and the colonies with home-manufactured goods. With
that view cloth workers were invited from England, and so
speedily did the native cloth manufactories flourish in
consequence of the protection secured to them, that three
years later (in 1684) it became practicable to prohibit the
importation of foreign cloths. From that period Portugal
supplied herself and her colonies with native goods manufactured of home-grown raw material, and prospered ex-
ceedingly in so doing for a period of nineteen years, as
attested by the evidence of English writers themselves.[2]

---

[1] The chief export trade of the Portuguese from Central and Southern
America consisted of the precious metals. From 1748 to 1753, the exports
amounted to 18 millions of piastres. See Humboldt's *Essai Politique sur
le Royaume de la Nouvelle Espagne*, vol. ii. p. 652. The goods trade with
those regions, as well as with the West Indies, first assumed important
proportions, by the introduction of the sugar, coffee, and cotton planting.

[2] *British Merchant*, vol. iii. p. 69.

It is true that even in those days the English gave proof of that ability which at subsequent times they have managed to bring to perfection. In order to evade the tariff restrictions of Portugal, they manufactured woollen fabrics, which slightly differed from cloth though serving the same purpose, and imported these into Portugal under the designation of woollen serges and woollen druggets. This trick of trade was, however, soon detected and rendered innocuous by a decree prohibiting the importation of such goods.[1] The success of these measures is all the more remarkable because the country, not a very great while before, had been drained of a large amount of capital, which had found its way abroad owing to the expulsion of the Jews, and was suffering especially from all the evils of bigotry, of bad government, and of a feudal aristocracy, which ground down popular liberties and agriculture.[2]

In the year 1703, after the death of Count Ereceira, however, the famous British ambassador Paul Methuen succeeded in persuading the Portuguese Government that Portugal would be immensely benefited if England were to permit the importation of Portuguese wines at a duty one-third less than the duty levied upon wines of other countries, in consideration of Portugal admitting English cloths at the same rate of import duty (viz. twenty-three per cent.) which had been charged upon such goods prior to the year 1684. It seems as though on the part of the King the hope of an increase in his customs revenue, and on the part of the nobility the hope of an increased income from rents, supplied the chief motives for the conclusion of that commercial treaty in which the Queen of England (Anne) styles the King of Portugal ' her oldest friend and ally '— on much the same principle as the Roman Senate was formerly wont to apply such designations to those rulers who had the misfortune to be brought into closer relations with that assembly.

Directly after the conclusion of this treaty, Portugal was deluged with English manufactures, and the first

---

[1] *British Merchant,* vol. iii. p. 71.
[2] *Ibid.* p. 76.

result of this inundation was the sudden and complete ruin of the Portuguese manufactories—a result which had its perfect counterparts in the subsequent so-called Eden treaty with France and in the abrogation of the Continental system in Germany.

According to Anderson's testimony, the English, even in those days, had become such adepts in the art of understating the value of their goods in their custom-house bills of entry, that in effect they paid no more than half the duty chargeable on them by the tariff.[1]

'After the repeal of the prohibition,' says 'The British Merchant,' 'we managed to carry away so much of their silver currency that there remained *but very little for their necessary occasions*; thereupon we attacked their gold.'[2] This trade the English continued down to very recent times. They exported all the precious metals which the Portuguese had obtained from their colonies, and sent a large portion of them to the East Indies and to China, where, as we saw in Chapter IV., they exchanged them for goods which they disposed of on the continent of Europe against raw materials. The yearly exports of England to Portugal exceeded the imports from that country by the amount of one million sterling. This favourable balance of trade lowered the rate of exchange to the extent of fifteen per cent. to the disadvantage of Portugal. 'The balance of trade is more favourable to us in our dealings with Portugal than it is with any other country,' says the author of 'The British Merchant' in his dedication to Sir Paul Methuen, the son of the famous minister, 'and our imports of specie from that country have risen to the sum of one and a half millions sterling, whereas formerly they amounted only to 300,000*l.*'[3]

All the merchants and political economists, as well as all the statesmen of England, have ever since eulogised this treaty as the masterpiece of English commercial policy. Anderson himself, who had a clear insight enough

---

[1] Anderson, vol. iii. p. 67.
[2] *British Merchant*, vol. iii. p. 267.
[3] *Ibid.* vol. iii. pp. 15, 20, 33, 38, 110, 253, 254.

into all matters affecting English commercial policy, and who in his way always treats of them with great candour, calls it ' an extremely fair and advantageous treaty ; ' nor could he forbear the *naïve* exclamation, ' May it endure for ever and ever ! ' [1]

For Adam Smith alone it was reserved to set up a theory directly opposed to this unanimous verdict, and to maintain that the Methuen Tréaty had in no respect proved a special boon to British commerce. Now, if anything will suffice to show the blind reverence with which public opinion has accepted the (partly very paradoxical) views of this celebrated man, surely it is the fact that the particular opinion above mentioned has hitherto been left unrefuted.

In the sixth chapter of his fourth book, Adam Smith says, that inasmuch as under the Methuen Treaty the wines of Portugal were admitted upon paying only two-thirds of the duty which was paid on those of other nations, a decided advantage was conceded to the Portuguese; whereas the English, being bound to pay quite as high a duty in Portugal on their exports of cloth as any other nation, had, therefore, no special privilege granted to them by the Portuguese. But had not the Portuguese been previously importing a large proportion of the foreign goods which they required from France, Holland, Germany, and Belgium ? Did not the English thenceforth exclusively command the Portuguese market for a manufactured product, the raw material for which they possessed in their own country ? Had they not discovered a method of reducing the Portuguese customs duty by one-half ? Did not the course of exchange give the English consumer of Portuguese wines a profit of fifteen per cent. ? Did not the consumption of French and German wines in England almost entirely cease? Did not the Portuguese gold and silver supply the English with the means of bringing vast quantities of goods from India and of deluging the continent of Europe with them ? Were not the Portuguese cloth manufactories totally ruined, to the advantage of the English ? Did not all the Portuguese colonies, especially

Anderson for the year 1703.

the rich one of Brazil, by this means become practically English colonies ? Certainly this treaty conferred a privilege upon Portugal, but only in name; whereas it conferred a privilege upon the English in its actual operation and effects. A like tendency underlies all subsequent treaties of commerce negotiated by the English. By profession they were always cosmopolites and philanthropists, while in their aims and endeavours they were always monopolists.

According to Adam Smith's second argument, the English gained no particular advantages from this treaty, because they were to a great extent obliged to send away to other countries the money which they received from the Portuguese for their cloth, and with it to purchase goods there; whereas it would have been far more profitable for them to make a direct exchange of their cloths against such commodities as they might need, and thus by one exchange accomplish that which by means of the trade with Portugal they could only effect by two exchanges. Really, but for the very high opinion which we entertain of the character and the acumen of this celebrated savant, we should in the face of this argument be driven to despair either of his candour or of his clearness of perception. To avoid doing either, nothing is left for us but to bewail the weakness of human nature, to which Adam Smith has paid a rich tribute in the shape of these paradoxical, almost laughable, arguments among other instances ; being evidently dazzled by the splendour of the task, so noble in itself, of pleading a justification for absolute freedom of trade.

In the argument just named there is no more sound sense or logic than in the proposition that a baker, because he sells bread to his customers for money, and with that money buys flour from the miller, does an unprofitable trade, because if he had exchanged his bread directly for flour, he would have effected his purpose by a single act of exchange instead of by two such acts. It needs surely no great amount of sagacity to answer such an allegation by hinting that the miller might possibly not want so much bread as the baker could supply him with, that the miller might perhaps understand and undertake baking himself, and that, therefore, the baker's business could not go on at all without these two acts of exchange. Such in effect were the commercial conditions of Portugal and England at the date of the treaty. Portugal received gold and silver from South America in exchange for manufactured goods which she then exported to those regions ; but too indolent or too shiftless to manufacture these goods herself, she bought them of the English in exchange for the precious metals. The latter employed the precious metals, in so far as they did not require them for the circulation at home, in exportation to India or China, and bought goods there which they sold again on the European continent, whence they brought home agricultural produce, raw material, or precious metals once again.

We now ask, in the name of common sense, who would have purchased of the English all those cloths which they exported to Portugal, if the Portuguese had chosen either to make them at home or procure them from other countries ? The English could not in that case have sold them to Portugal, and to other nations they were already selling as much as those nations would take. Consequently the English would have manufactured so much less cloth than they had been disposing of to the Portuguese ; they would have exported so much less specie to India than they had obtained from Portugal. They would have brought to Europe and sold on the Continent just that much less of East Indian merchandise, and consequently would have taken home with them that much less of raw material.

Quite as untenable is Adam Smith's third argument that, if Portuguese money had not flowed in upon them, the English might have supplied their requirements of this article in other ways. Portugal, he conceived, must in any case have exported her superfluous store of precious metals, and these would have reached England through some other channel. We here assume that the Portuguese had manufactured their cloths for themselves, had themselves exported their superfluous stock of precious metals to India and China, and had purchased the return cargoes in other countries ; and we take leave to ask the question whether under these circumstances the English would have seen much of Portuguese money? It would have been just the same if Portugal had concluded a Methuen Treaty with Holland or France. In both these cases, no doubt, some little of the money would have gone over to England, but only so much as she could have acquired by the sale of her raw wool. In short, but for the Methuen Treaty, the manufactures, the trade, and the shipping of the English could never have reached such a degree of expansion as they have attained to.

But whatever be the estimate formed of the effects of the Methuen Treaty as respects England, this much at least appears to be made out, that, in respect to Portugal, they have in no way been such as to tempt other nations to deliver over their home markets for manufactured goods to English competition, for the sake of facilitating the exportation of agricultural produce. Agriculture and trade, commerce and navigation, instead of improving from the intercourse with England, went on sinking lower and lower in Portugal. In vain did Pombal strive to raise them, English competition frustrated all his efforts. At the same time it must not be forgotten that in a country like Portugal, where the whole social conditions are opposed to progress in agriculture, industry, and commerce, commercial policy can effect but very little. Nevertheless, the little which Pombal did effect proves how much can be done for the benefit of industry by a government which is anxious to promote its interests, if only the internal hindrances which the social condition of a country presents can first be removed.

The same experience was made in Spain in the reigns of Philip V. and his two immediate successors. Inadequate as was the protection extended to home industries under the Bourbons, and great as was the lack of energy in fully enforcing the customs laws, yet the remarkable animation which pervaded every branch of industry and every district of the country as the result of transplanting the commercial policy of Colbert from France to Spain was unmistakable.[1] The statements of Ustaritz and Ulloa [2] in regard to these results under the then prevailing circumstances are astonishing. For at that time were found everywhere only the most wretched mule-tracks, nowhere any well-kept inns, nowhere any bridges, canals, or river navigation, every province was closed against the rest of Spain by an internal customs cordon, at every city gate a royal toll was demanded, highway robbery and mendicancy were pursued as regular professions, the contraband trade was in the most flourishing condition, and the most grinding system of taxation existed; these and such as these the above-named writers adduce as the causes of the decay of industry and agriculture. The causes of these evils—fanaticism, the greed and the vices of the clergy, the privileges of the nobles, the despotism of the Government, the want of enlightenment and freedom amongst the people—Ustaritz and Ulloa dared not denounce.

A worthy counterpart to the Methuen Treaty with Portugal is the Assiento Treaty of 1713 with Spain, under which power was granted to the English to introduce each year a certain number of African negroes into Spanish America, and to visit the harbour of Portobello with one ship once a year, whereby an opportunity was afforded them of smuggling immense quantities of goods into these countries.

We thus find that in all treaties of commerce concluded by the English, there is a tendency to extend the sale of their manufactures throughout all the countries with whom they negotiate, by offering them apparent advantages in respect of agricultural produce and raw materials. Everywhere their efforts are directed to ruining the native manufacturing power of those countries by means of

[1] Macpherson, *Annals of Commerce* for the years 1771 and 1774. The obstacles thrown in the way of the importation of foreign goods greatly promoted the development of Spanish manufactures. Before that time Spain had been obtaining nineteen-twentieths of her supplies of manufactured goods from England.—Brougham, *Inquiry into the Colonial Policy of the European Powers*, Part I. p. 421.

[2] Ustaritz, *Théorie du Commerce.* Ulloa, *Rétablissement des Manufactures à'Espagne.*

cheaper goods and long credits. If they cannot obtain low tariffs, then they devote their exertions to defrauding the custom-houses, and to organising a wholesale system of contraband trade. The former device, as we have seen, succeeded in Portugal, the latter in Spain. The collection of import dues upon the *ad valorem* principle has stood them in good stead in this matter, for which reason of late they have taken so much pains to represent the principle of paying duty by weight—as introduced by Prussia—as being injudicious.

CHAPTER VI.

THE FRENCH.

FRANCE, too, inherited many a remnant of Roman civilisation. On the irruption of the German Franks, who loved nothing but the chase, and changed many districts again into forests and waste which had been long under cultivation, almost everything was lost again. To the monasteries, however, which subsequently became such a great hindrance to civilisation, France, like all other European countries, is indebted for most of her progress in agriculture during the Middle Ages. The inmates of religious houses kept up no feuds like the nobles, nor harassed their vassals with calls to military service, while their lands and cattle were less exposed to rapine and extermination. The clergy loved good living, were averse to quarrels, and sought to gain reputation and respect by supporting the necessitous. Hence the old adage ' It is good to dwell under the crosier.' The Crusades, the institution of civic communities and of guilds by Louis IX. (Saint Louis), and the proximity of Italy and Flanders, had considerable effect at an early period in developing industry in France. Already in the fourteenth century, Normandy and Brittany supplied woollen and linen cloths for home consumption and for export to England. At this period also the export trade in wines and salt, chiefly through the agency of Hanseatic middlemen, had become important.

By the influence of Francis I. the silk manufacture was introduced into the South of France. Henry IV. favoured this industry, as well as the manufacture of glass, linen, and woollens ; Richelieu and Mazarin favoured the silk manufactories, the velvet and woollen manufactures of Rouen and Sedan, as well as the fisheries and navigation.

On no country did the discovery of America produce more favourable effects than upon France. From Western France quantities of corn were sent to Spain. Many peasants migrated every year from the Pyrenean districts to the north-east of Spain in search of work. Great quantities of wine and salt were exported to the Spanish Netherlands, while the silks, the velvets, as also especially the articles of luxury of French manufacture, were sold in considerable quantities in the Netherlands, England, Spain, and Portugal. Owing to this cause a great deal of Spanish gold and silver got into circulation in France at an early period.

But the palmy days of French industry first commenced with Colbert.

At the time of Mazarin's death, neither manufacturing industry, commerce, navigation, nor the fisheries had attained to importance, while the financial condition of the country was at its worst.

Colbert had the courage to grapple single-handed with an undertaking which England could only bring to a successful issue by the persevering efforts of three centuries, and at the cost of two revolutions. From all countries he obtained the most skilful workmen, bought up trade secrets, and procured better machinery and tools. By a general and efficient tariff he secured the home markets for native industry. By abolishing, or by limiting as much as possible, the provincial customs collections, by the construction of highways and canals, he promoted internal traffic. These measures benefited agriculture even more than manufacturing industry, because the number of consumers was thereby doubled and trebled, and the producers were brought into easy and cheap communication with the consumers. He further promoted the interests of agriculture by lowering the amounts of direct imposts levied upon landed property, by mitigating the severity of the stringent measures previously adopted in collecting the revenue, by equalising the incidence of taxation, and lastly by introducing measures for the reduction of the rate of nterest. He prohibited the exportation ot corn only in times of scarcity and high prices. To the extension of the foreign trade and the promotion of fisheries he devoted special attention. He re-established the trade with the Levant, enlarged that with the colonies, and opened up a trade with the North. Into all branches of the administration he introduced the most stringent economy and perfect order. At his death France possessed 50,000 looms engaged in the manufacture of woollens; she produced annually silk manufactures to the value of 50 millions of francs. The State revenues had increased by 28 millions of francs. The kingdom was in possession of flourishing fisheries, of an extensive mercantile marine, and a powerful navy.[1]

A century later, the economists have sharply censured Colbert, and maintained that this statesman had been anxious to promote the interests of manufactures at the expense of agriculture: a reproach which proves nothing more than that these authorities were themselves incapable of appreciating the nature of manufacturing industry.[2]

If, however, Colbert was in error in opposing periodical obstacles to the exportation of raw materials, yet by fostering the growth and progress of native industries he so greatly increased the demand for agricultural produce that he gave the agricultural interest tenfold compensation for any injury which he caused to it by the above-named obstacles. If, contrary to the dictates of enlightened statesmanship, he prescribed new processes of manufacture, and compelled

[1] 'Eloge de Jean Baptiste Colbert, par Necker' (1773) (*Œuvres Completes*, vol. xv.)

[2] See Quesnay's paper entitled, 'Physiocratie, ou du Gouvernement le plus avantageux au Genre Humain (1768),' Note 5, 'sur la maxime viii.,' wherein Quesnay contradicts and condemns Colbert in two brief pages, whereas Necker devoted a hundred pages to the exposition of Colbert's system and of what he accomplished. It is hard to say whether we are to wonder most at the ignorance of Quesnay on matters of industry, history, and finance, or at the presumption with which he passes judgment upon such a man as Colbert without adducing grounds for it. Add to that, that this ignorant dreamer was not even candid enough to mention the expulsion of the Huguenots; nay, that he was not ashamed to allege, contrary to all truth, that Colbert had restricted the trade in corn between province an province by vexatious police ordinances.

the manufacturers by penal enactments to adopt them, it should be borne in mind that these processes were the best and the most profitable known in his day, and that he had to deal with a people which, sunk into the utmost apathy by reason of a long despotic rule, resisted every innovation even though it was an improvement.

The reproach, however, that France had lost a large portion of her native industry through Colbert's protective system, could be levelled against Colbert only by that school which utterly ignored the revocation of the Edict of Nantes with its disastrous consequences. In consequence of these deplorable measures, in the course of three years after Colbert's death half a million of the most industrious, skilful, and thriving inhabitants of France were banished; who, consequently, to the double injury of France which they had enriched, transplanted their industry and their capital to Switzerland, to every Protestant country in Germany, especially to Prussia, as also to Holland and England. Thus the intrigues of a bigoted courtesan ruined in three years the able and gifted work of a whole generation, and cast France back again into its previous state of apathy; while England, under the ægis of her Constitution, and invigorated by a Revolution which called forth all the energies of the nation, was prosecuting with increasing ardour and without intermission the work commenced by Elizabeth and her predecessors.

The melancholy condition to which the industry and the finances of France had been reduced by a long course of misgovernment, and the spectacle of the great prosperity of England, aroused the emulation of French statesmen shortly before the French revolution. Infatuated with the hollow theory of the economists, they looked for a remedy, in opposition to Colbert's policy, in the establishment of free trade. It was thought that the prosperity of the country could be restored at one blow if a better market were provided for French wines and brandies in England, at the cost of permitting the importation of English manufactures upon easy terms (a twelve per cent. duty). England, delighted at the proposal, willingly granted to the

French a second edition of the Methuen Treaty, in the shape of the so-called Eden Treaty of 1786 ; a copy which was soon followed by results not less ruinous than those produced by the Portuguese original.

The English, accustomed to the strong wines of the Peninsula, did not increase their consumption to the extent which had been expected, whilst the French perceived with horror that all they had to offer the English were simply fashions and fancy articles, the total value of which was insignificant : whereas the English manufacturers, in all articles of prime necessity, the total amount of which was enormous, could greatly surpass the French manufacturers in cheapness of prices, as well as in quality of their goods, and in granting of credit. When, after a brief competition, the French manufacturers were brought to the brink of ruin, while French wine-growers had gained but little, then the French Government sought to arrest the progress of this ruin by terminating the treaty, but only acquired the conviction that it is much easier to ruin flourishing manufactories in a few years than to revive ruined manufactories in a whole generation. English competition had engendered a taste for English goods in France, the consequence of which was an extensive and long-continued contraband trade which it was difficult to suppress. Meanwhile it was not so difficult for the English, after the termination of the treaty, to accustom their palates again to the wines of the Peninsula.

Notwithstanding that the commotions of the revolution and the incessant wars of Napoleon could not have been favourable to the prosperity of French industry, notwithstanding that the French lost during this period most of their maritime trade and all their colonies, yet French manufactories, solely from their exclusive possession of their home markets, and from the abrogation of feudal restrictions, attained during the Empire to a higher degree of prosperity than they had ever enjoyed under the preceding *ancien régime*. The same effects were noticeable in Germany and in all countries over which the Continental blockade extended.

Napoleon said in his trenchant style, that under the existing circumstances of the world any State which adopted the principle of free trade must come to the ground. In these words he uttered more political wisdom in reference to the commercial policy of France than all contemporary political economists in all their writings. We cannot but wonder at the sagacity with which this great genius, without any previous study of the systems of political economy, comprehended the nature and importance of manufacturing power. Well was it for him and for France that he had not studied these systems. 'Formerly,' said Napoleon, 'there was but one description of property, the possession of land; but a new property has now risen up, namely, industry.' Napoleon saw, and in this way clearly enunciated, what contemporary economists did not see, or did not clearly enunciate, namely, that a nation which combines in itself the power of manufactures with that of agriculture is an immeasurably more perfect and more wealthy nation than a purely agricultural one. What Napoleon did to found and promote the industrial education of France, to improve the country's credit, to introduce and set going new inventions and improved processes, and to perfect the means of internal communication in France, it is not necessary to dwell upon in detail, for these things are still too well remembered. But what, perhaps, does call for special notice in this connection, is the biassed and unfair judgment passed upon this enlightened and powerful ruler by contemporary theorists.

With the fall of Napoleon, English competition, which had been till then restricted to a contraband trade, recovered its footing on the continents of Europe and America. Now for the first time the English were heard to condemn protection and to eulogise Adam Smith's doctrine of free trade, a doctrine which heretofore those practical islanders considered as suited only to an ideal state of Utopian perfection. But an impartial, critical observer might easily discern the entire absence of mere sentimental motives of philanthropy in this conversion, for only when increased facilities for the exportation of English goods to the continents of Europe and America were in question were cosmopolitan arguments resorted to ; but so soon as the question turned upon the free importation of corn, or whether foreign goods might be allowed to compete at all with British manufactures in the English market, in that case quite different principles were appealed to.[1] Unhappily, it was said, the long continuance in England of a policy contrary to natural principles had created an artificial state of things, which could not be interfered with suddenly without incurring the risk of dangerous and mischievous consequences. It was not to be attempted without the greatest caution and prudence. It was England's misfortune, not her fault. All the more gratifying ought it to be for the nations of the European and American continents, that their happy lot and condition left them quite free to partake without delay of the blessings of free trade.

In France, although her ancient dynasty reascended the throne under the protection of the banner of England, or at any rate by the influence of English gold, the above

---

[1] A highly accomplished American orator, Mr. Baldwin, Chief Justice of the United States, when referring to the Canning-Huskisson system of free trade, shrewdly remarked, that, like most English productions, it had been manufactured not so much for home consumption as for exportation.

Shall we laugh most or weep when we call to mind the rapture of enthusiasm with which the Liberals in France and Germany, more particularly the cosmopolitan theorists of the philanthropic school, and notably Mons. J. B. Say, hailed the announcement of the Canning-Huskisson system ? So great was their jubilation, that one might have thought the millennium had come. But let us see what Mr. Canning's own biographer says about this minister's views on the subject of free trade.

' Mr. Canning was perfectly convinced of the truth of the abstract principle, that commerce is sure to flourish most when wholly unfettered; but since such had not been the opinion either of our ancestors or of surrounding nations, and since in consequence restraints had been imposed upon all commercial transactions, a state of things had grown up to which the unguarded application of the abstract principle, however true it was in theory, might have been somewhat mischievous in practice.' (The Political Life of Mr. Canning, by Stapleton, p. 3.)

In the year 1828, these same tactics of the English had again assumed a prominence so marked that Mr. Hume, the Liberal Member of Parliament, felt no hesitation in stigmatising them in the House as the strangling of Continental industries.

arguments did not obtain currency for very long. England's free trade wrought such havoc amongst the manufacturing industries which had prospered and grown strong under the Continental blockade system, that a prohibitive *régime* was speedily resorted to, under the protecting ægis of which, according to Dupin's testimony,[1] the producing power o French manufactories was doubled between the years 1815 and 1827.

[1] *Forces productives de la France.*

CHAPTER VII.

THE GERMANS.

In the chapter on the Hanseatic League we saw how, next in order to Italy, Germany had flourished, through extensive commerce, long before the other European states. We have now to continue the industrial history of that nation, after first taking a rapid survey of its earliest industrial circumstances and their development.

In ancient Germania, the greater part of the land was devoted to pasturage and parks for game. The insignificant and primitive agriculture was abandoned to serfs and to women. The sole occupation of the freemen was warfare and the chase ; and that is the origin of all the German nobility.

The German nobles firmly adhered to this system throughout the Middle Ages, oppressing agriculturists and opposing manufacturing industry, while quite blind to the benefits which must have accrued to them, as the lords of the soil, from the prosperity of both.

Indeed, so deeply rooted has the passion for their hereditary favourite occupation ever continued with the German nobles, that even in our days, long after they have been enriched by the ploughshare and the shuttle, they still dream in legislative assemblies about the preservation of game and the game laws, as though the wolf and the sheep, the bear and the bee, could dwell in peace side by side ; as though landed property could be devoted at one and the same time to gardening, timber growing, and scientific farming, and to the preservation of wild boars, deer, and hares.

German husbandry long remained in a barbarous condition, notwithstanding that the influence of towns and monasteries on the districts in their immediate vicinity could not be ignored.

Towns sprang up in the ancient Roman colonies, at the seats of the temporal and ecclesiastical princes and lords, near monasteries, and, where favoured by the Emperor, to a certain extent within their domains and inclosures, also on sites where the fisheries, combined with facilities for land and water transport, offered inducements to them. They flourished in most cases only by supplying the local requirements, and by the foreign transport trade. An extensive system of native industry capable of supplying an export trade could only have grown up by means of extensive sheep farming and extensive cultivation of flax. But flax cultivation implies a high standard of agriculture, while extensive sheep farming needs protection against wolves and robbers. Such protection could not be maintained amid the perpetual feuds of the nobles and princes between themselves and against the towns. Cattle pastures served always as the principal field for robbery; while the total extermination of beasts of prey was out of the question with those vast tracts of forest which the nobility so carefully preserved for their indulgence in the chase. The scanty number of cattle, the insecurity of life and property, the entire lack of capital and of freedom on the part of the cultivators of the soil, or of any interest in agriculture on the part of those who owned it, necessarily tended to keep agriculture, and with it the prosperity of the towns, in a very low state.

If these circumstances are duly considered, it is easy to understand the reason why Flanders and Brabant under totally opposite conditions attained at so early a period to a high degree of liberty and prosperity.

Notwithstanding these impediments, the German cities on the Baltic and the German Ocean flourished, owing to the fisheries, to navigation, and the foreign trade at sea; in Southern Germany and at the foot of the Alps, owing to the influence of Italy, Greece, and the transport trade by

land ; on the Rhine, the Elbe, and the Danube, by means
of viticulture and the wine trade, owing to the exceptional
fertility of the soil and the facilities of water communication, which in the Middle Ages was of still greater importance than even in our days, because of the wretched condition of the roads and the general state of insecurity.

This diversity of origin will explain the diversity charac-
terising the several confederations of German cities, such
as the Hanseatic, the Rhenish, the Swabian, the Dutch, and
the Helvetic.

Though they continued powerful for a time owing to the
spirit of youthful freedom which pervaded them, yet these
leagues lacked the internal guarantee of stability, the
principle of unity, the cement.   Separated from each
other by the estates of the nobility, by the serfdom of the
population of the country, their union was doomed sooner
or later to break down, owing to the gradual increase and
enrichment of the agricultural population, among whom,
through the power of the princes, the principle of unity was
maintained.   The cities, inasmuch as they tended to promote the prosperity of agriculture, by so doing necessarily
were working at their own effacement, unless they contrived
to incorporate the agricultural classes or the nobility as
members of their unions.   For the accomplishment of that
object, however, they lacked the requisite higher political
instincts and knowledge.   Their political vision seldom extended beyond their own city walls.

Two only of these confederations, Switzerland and the
Seven United Provinces, actually carried out this incorporation, and that not as the result of reflection, but because
they were compelled to it, and favoured by circumstances,
and for that reason those confederations still exist.   The
Swiss Confederation is nothing but a conglomerate of
German imperial cities, established and cemented together
by the free populations occupying the intervening tracts of
country.

The remaining leagues of German cities were ruined
owing to their contempt for the rural population, and from
their absurd burgher arrogance, which delighted in keeping

that population in subjection, rather than in raising them to their own level.

These cities could only have attained unity by means of an hereditary royal authority. But this authority in Germany lay in the hands of the princes, who, in order to avert restraints upon their own arbitrary rule, and to keep both the cities and the minor nobles in subjection, were interested in resisting the establishment of an hereditary empire.

Hence the persevering adherence to the idea of the Imperial Roman Empire amongst German kings. Only at the head of armies were the emperors rulers; only when they went to war were they able to bring together princes and cities under their banner. Hence their protection of civic liberty in Germany, and their hostility to it and persecution of it in Italy.

The expeditions to Rome not only weakened more and more the kingly power in Germany, they weakened those very dynasties through which, within the Empire, in the heart of the nation, a consolidated power might have grown up. But with the extinction of the house of Hohenstaufen the nucleus of consolidated power was broken up into a thousand fragments.

The sense of the impossibility of consolidating the heart of the nation impelled the House of Hapsburg, originally so weak and poor, to utilise the nation's vigour in founding a consolidated hereditary monarchy on the south-eastern frontier of the German Empire, by subjugating alien races, a policy which in the north-east was imitated by the Margraves of Brandenburg. Thus in the south-east and north-east there arose hereditary sovereignties founded upon the dominion over alien races, while in the two western corners of the land two republics grew into existence which continually separated themselves more and more from the parent nation; and within, in the nation's heart, disintegration, impotence, and dissolution continually progressed. The misfortunes of the German nation were completed by the inventions of gunpowder and of the art of printing, the revival of the Roman law, the Reformation, and lastly the discovery of America and of the new route to India.

The intellectual, social, and economic revolution which we have described produced divisions and disruption between the constituent members of the Empire, disunion between the princes, disunion between the cities, disunion even between the various guilds of individual cities, and between neighbours of every rank. The energies of the nation were now diverted from the pursuit of industry, agriculture, trade, and navigation ; from the acquisition of colonies, the amelioration of internal institutions, in fact from every kind of substantial improvement, the people contended about dogmas and the heritage of the Church.

At the same time came the decline of the Hanseatic League and of Venice, and with it the decline of Germany's wholesale trade, and of the power and liberties of the German cities both in the north and in the south.

Then came the Thirty Years' War with its devastations of all territories and cities. Holland and Switzerland seceded, while the fairest provinces of the Empire were conquered by France. Whereas formerly single cities, such as Strasburg, Nürnberg, Augsburg, had surpassed in power entire electorates, they now sank into utter impotence in consequence of the introduction of standing armies.

If before this revolution the cities and the royal power had been more consolidated—if a king exclusively belonging to the German nation had obtained a complete mastery of the Reformation, and had carried it out in the interests of the unity, power, and freedom of the nation—how very differently would the agriculture, industry, and trade of the Germans have been developed. By the side of considerations such as these, how pitiable and unpractical seems that theory of political economy which would have us refer the material welfare of nations solely to the production of individuals, wholly losing sight of the fact that the producing power of all individuals is to a great extent determined by the social and political circumstances of the nation. The introduction of the Roman law weakened no nation so much as the German. The unspeakable confusion which it brought into the legal status and relations of private individuals, was not the worst of its bad effects.

More mischievous was it by far, in that it created a caste of learned men and jurists differing from the people in spirit and language, which treated the people as a class unlearned in the law, as minors, which denied the authority of all sound human understanding, which everywhere set up secrecy in the room of publicity, which, living in the most abject dependence and living upon arbitrary power, everywhere advocated it and defended its interests, everywhere gnawed at the roots of liberty." Thus we see even to the beginning of the eighteenth century in Germany, barbarism in literature and language, barbarism in legislation, State administration, and administration of justice; barbarism in agriculture, decline of industry and of all trade upon a large scale, want of unity and of force in national cohesion; powerlessness and weakness on all hands in dealing with foreign nations.

One thing only the Germans had preserved; that was their aboriginal character, their love of industry, order, thrift, and moderation, their perseverance and endurance in research and in business, their honest striving after improvement, and a considerable natural measure of morality, prudence, and circumspection.

This character both the rulers and the ruled had in common. After the almost total decay of nationality and the restoration of tranquillity, people began in some individual isolated circles to introduce order, improvement, and progress. Nowhere was witnessed more zeal in cherishing education, manners, religion, art and science; nowhere was absolute power exercised with greater moderation or with more advantage to general enlightenment, order, and morality, to the reform of abuses and the advancement of the common welfare.

The foundation for the revival of German nationality was undoubtedly laid by the Governments themselves, by their conscientious devotion of the proceeds of the secularised Church lands to the uses of education and instruction, of art and science, of morality and objects of public utility. By these measures light made its way into the State administration and the administration of justice, into education and literature, into agriculture, industry, and commerce, and above all amongst the masses. Thus Germany developed herself in a totally different way from all other nations. Elsewhere high mental culture rather grew out of the evolution of the material powers of production, whilst in Germany the growth of material powers of production was the outcome chiefly of an antecedent intellectual development. Hence at the present day the whole culture of the Germans is theoretical. Hence also those many unpractical and odd traits in the German character which other nations notice in us.

For the moment the Germans are in the position of an individual who, having been formerly deprived of the use of his limbs, first learned theoretically the arts of standing and walking, of eating and drinking, of laughing and weeping, and then only proceeded to put them in practice. Hence comes the German predilection for philosophic systems and cosmopolitan dreams. The intellect, which was not allowed to stir in the affairs of this world, strove to exercise itself in the realms of speculation. Hence, too, we find that nowhere has the doctrine of Adam Smith and of his disciples obtained a larger following than in Germany; nowhere else have people more thoroughly believed in the cosmopolitan magnanimity of Messrs. Canning and Huskisson.

For the first progress in manufactures Germany is indebted to the revocation of the Edict of Nantes and to the numerous refugees who by that insane measure were driven to emigrate to almost every part of Germany, and established everywhere manufactures of wool, silk, jewellery, hats, glass, china, gloves, and industries of every kind.

The first Government measures for the promotion of manufactures in Germany were introduced by Austria and Prussia; in Austria under Charles VI. and Maria Theresa, but even more under Joseph II. Austria had formerly suffered enormously from the banishment of the Protestants, her most industrious citizens; nor can it be exactly affirmed that she distinguished herself in the immediate sequel by promoting enlightenment and mental culture.

Afterwards, in consequence of a protective tariff, improved sheep farming, better roads, and other encouragements, industry made considerable strides even under Maria Theresa.

More energetically still was this work pushed forward under Joseph II. and with immensely greater success. At first, indeed, the results could not be called important, because the Emperor, according to his wont, was too precipitate in these as in all his other schemes of reform, and Austria, in relation to other states, still occupied too backward a position. Here as elsewhere it became evident that one might get 'too much of a good thing' at once, and that protective duties, in order to work beneficially and not as a disturbing element upon an existing state of things, must not be made too high at the commencement. But the longer that system continued, the more clearly was its wisdom demonstrated. To that tariff Austria is indebted for her present prosperous industries and the flourishing condition of her agriculture.

The industry of Prussia had suffered more than that of any other country from the devastations of the Thirty Years' War. Her most important industry, the manufacture of cloth in the Margravate of Brandenburg, was almost entirely annihilated. The majority of cloth workers had migrated to Saxony, while English imports at the time held every competition in check. To the advantage of Prussia now came the revocation of the Edict of Nantes and the persecution of the Protestants in the Palatinate and in Salzburg. The great Elector saw at a glance what Elizabeth before him had so clearly understood. In consequence of the measures devised by him a great number of the fugitives directed their steps to Prussia, fertilised the agricultural industry of the land, established a large number of manufactures, and cultivated science and art. All his successors followed in his footsteps, none with more zeal than the great King—greater by his policy in times of peace than by his successes in war. Space is wanting to treat at length of the countless measures whereby Frederick II. attracted to his dominions large numbers of foreign agriculturists, brought tracts of waste land into cultivation, and established the cultivation of meadows, of cattle fodder, vegetables, potatoes, and tobacco, improved sheep farming, cattle breeding, horse breeding, the use of mineral manures, &c., by which means he created capital and credit for the benefit of the agricultural classes.   Still more than by these direct measures he promoted indirectly the interests of agriculture by means of those branches of manufacture which, in consequence of the customs tariff and the improved means of transport which he established, as well as the establishment of a bank, made greater advances in Prussia than in any other German state, notwithstanding that that country's geographical position, and its division into several provinces separated from one another, were much less favourable for the success of such measures, and that the disadvantages of a customs cordon, namely the damaging effects of a contraband trade, must be felt more acutely there than in great states whose territories are compact and well protected by boundaries of seas, rivers, and chains of mountains.

At the same time we are nowise anxious, under cover of this eulogy, to defend the faults of the system, such as, for example, the restrictions laid upon the exportation of raw material.   Still, that in despite of these faults the national industry was considerably advanced by it, no enlightened and impartial historian would venture to dispute.

To every unprejudiced mind, unclouded by false theories, it must be clear that Prussia gained her title to rank amongst the European powers not so much by her conquests as by her wise policy in promoting the interests of agriculture, industry, and trade, and by her progress in literature and science ; and all this was the work of one great genius alone.

And yet the Crown was not yet supported by the energy of free institutions, but simply by an administrative system, well ordered and conscientious, but unquestionably trammelled by the dead mechanical routine of a hierarchical bureaucracy.

Meanwhile all the rest of Germany had for centuries been under the influence of free trade—that is to say, th whole world was free to export manufactured products into Germany, while no one consented to admit German manufactured goods into other countries. This rule had its exceptions, but only a few. It cannot, however, be asserted that the predictions and the promises of the school about the great benefits of free trade have been verified by the experience of this country, for everywhere the movement was rather retrograde than progressive. Cities like Augsburg, Nürnberg, Mayence, Cologne, &c. numbered no more than a third or a fourth part of their former population, and wars were often wished for merely for the sake of getting rid of a valueless surplus of produce.

The wars came in the train of the French Revolution, and with them English subsidies together with increased English competition. Hence a new downward tendency in manufactures coupled with an increase in agricultural prosperity, which, however, was only apparent and transitory.

Next followed Napoleon's Continental blockade, an event which marked an era in the history of both German and French industry, notwithstanding that Mons. J. B. Say, Adam Smith's most famous pupil, denounced it as a calamity. Whatever theorists, and notably the English, may urge against it, this much is clearly made out—and all who are conversant with German industry must attest it, for there is abundant evidence of the fact in all statistical writings of that day—that, as a result of this blockade, German manufactures of all and every kind for the first time began to make an important advance;[1] that then only did the improved breeding of sheep (which had been commenced some time before) become general and successful; that then only was activity displayed in improving the means of transport. It is true, on the other hand, that Germany lost the greater part of her former export trade, especially in linens. Yet the gain was considerably greater than the loss, particularly for the Prussian and Austrian

---

[1] The system must necessarily have affected France in a different manner than Germany, because Germany was mostly shut out from the French markets, while the German markets were all open to the French manufacturer.

manufacturing establishments, which had previously gained a start over all other manufactories in the German states.

But with the return of peace the English manufacturers again entered into a fearful competition with the German; for during the reciprocal blockade, in consequence of new inventions and a great and almost exclusive export trade to foreign lands, the manufactories of the island had far outstripped that of Germany; and for this reason, as well as because of their large acquired capital, the former were first in a position to sell at much lower prices, to offer much superior articles, and to give much longer credit than the latter, which had still to battle with the difficulties of a first beginning. Consequently general ruin followed and loud wailings amongst the latter, especially in the lower Rhenish provinces, in those regions which, having formerly belonged to France, were now excluded from the French market. Besides, the Prussian customs tariff had undergone many changes in the direction of absolute free trade, and no longer afforded any sufficient protection against English competition. At the same time the Prussian bureaucracy long strove against the country's cry for help. They had become too strongly imbued with Adam Smith's theory at the universities to discern the want of the times with sufficient promptness. There even still existed political economists in Prussia who harboured the bold design of reviving the long-exploded 'physiocratic' system. Meanwhile the nature of things here too proved a mightier force than the power of theories. The cry of distress raised by the manufacturers, hailing as it did from districts still yearning after their former state of connection with France, whose sympathies it was necessary to conciliate, could not be safely disregarded too long. More and more the opinion spread at the time that the English Government were favouring in an unprecedented manner a scheme for glutting the markets on the Continent with manufactured goods in order to stifle the Continental manufactures in the cradle. This idea has been ridiculed, but it was natural enough that it should prevail, first, because this glutting really took place in such a manner as though it had been deliberately planned, and, secondly, because a celebrated Member of Parliament, Mr. Henry Brougham (afterwards Lord Brougham), had openly said, in 1815, ' that it was well worth while to incur a loss on the exportation of English manufactures in order to stifle in the cradle the foreign manufactures.' [1] This idea of this lord, since so renowned as a philanthropist, cosmopolist, and Liberal, was repeated ten years later almost in the same words by Mr. Hume, a Member of Parliament not less distinguished for liberalism, when he expressed a wish that ' Continental manufactures might be nipped in the bud.'

At length the prayer of the Prussian manufacturers found a hearing—late enough, indeed, as must be admitted when one considers how painful it is to be wrestling with death year after year—but at last their cry was heard to real good purpose. The Prussian customs tariff of 1818 answered, for the time in which it was established, all the requirements of Prussian industry, without in any way overdoing the principle of protection or unduly interfering with the country's beneficial intercourse with foreign countries. Its scale of duties was much lower than those of the English and French customs systems, and necessarily so ; for in this case there was no question of a gradual transition from a prohibitive to a protective system, but of a change from free trade (so called) to a protective system. Another great advantage of this tariff, considered as a whole, was that the duties were mostly levied according to the weight of goods and not according to their value. By this means not only were smuggling and too low valuations obviated, but also the great object was gained, that articles of general consumption, which every country can most easily manufacture for itself, and the manufacture of which, because of their great total money value, is the most important of any for the country, were burdened with the highest import duty, while the protective duty fell lower and lower in proportion to the fineness and costliness of the goods, also as the difficulty of making such articles at

[1] *Report of the Committee of Commerce and Manufactures to the House of Representatives of the Congress of the United States*, Feb. 13, 1816.

home increased, and also as both the inducements and the facilities for smuggling increased.

But this mode of charging the duty upon the weight would of course, for very obvious reasons, affect the trade with the neighbouring German states much more injuriously than the trade with foreign nations. The second-rate and smaller German states had now to bear, in addition to their exclusion from the Austrian, French, and English markets, almost total exclusion from that of Prussia, which hit them all the harder, since many of them were either totally or in great part hemmed in by Prussian provinces.

Just in proportion as these measures pacified the Prussian manufacturers, was the loudness of the outcry against them on the part of the manufacturers of the other German states. Add to that, that Austria had shortly before imposed restrictions on the importation of German goods into Italy, notably of the linens of Upper Swabia. Restricted on all sides in their export trade to small strips of territory, and further being separated from one another by smaller internal lines of customs duties, the manufacturers of these countries were well-nigh in despair.

It was this state of urgent necessity which led to the formation of that private union of five to six thousand German manufacturers and merchants, which was founded in the year 1819 at the spring fair held in Frankfort-on-the-Main, with the object of abolishing all the separate tariffs of the various German states, and on the other hand of establishing a common trade and custom-house system for the whole of Germany.

This union was formally organised. Its articles of association were submitted to the Diet, and to all the rulers and governments of the German states for approval. In every German town a local correspondent was appointed ; each German state had its provincial correspondent. All the members and correspondents bound themselves to promote the objects of the union to the best of their ability. The city of Nürnberg was selected as the head-quarters of the union, and authorised to appoint a central commit ee, which should direct the business of the union, under the advice of an assessor, for which office the author of this book was selected. In a weekly journal of the union, bearing the title of 'Organ des deutschen Handels- und Fabrikantenstandes,'[1] the transactions and measures of the central committee were made known, and ideas, proposals, treatises, and statistical papers relating to the objects of the union were published. Each year at the spring fair in Frankfort a general meeting of the union was held, at which the central committee gave an account of its stewardship.

After this union had presented a petition to the German Diet showing the need and expediency of the measures proposed by their organisation, the central committee at Nürnberg commenced operations. Deputations were sent to every German Court, and finally one to the congress of plenipotentiaries held at Vienna in 1820. At this congress so much at least was gained, that several of the second-class and smaller German states agreed to hold a separate congress on the subject at Darmstadt. The effect of the deliberations of this last-named congress was, first, to bring about a union between Würtemberg and Bavaria ; secondly, a union of some of the German states and Prussia ; then a union between the middle German states ; lastly, and chiefly in consequence of the exertions of Freiherr von Cotta, to fuse the above-named three unions into a general customs confederation, so that at this present time, with the exception of Austria, the two Mecklenburgs, Hanover, and the Hanse Towns, the whole of Germany is associated in a single customs union, which has abolished the separate customs lines amongst its members, and has established a uniform tariff in common against the foreigner, the revenue derived from which is distributed *pro rata* amongst the several states according to their populations.

The tariff of this union is substantially the same as that established by Prussia in 1818; that is to say, it is a moderate protectionist tariff.

In consequence of this unification of customs, the industry, trade, and agriculture of the German states forming the union have already made enormous strides.

[1] *Organ of the German Commercial and Manufacturing Interests.*

CHAPTER VIII.

THE RUSSIANS.

RUSSIA owes her first progress in civilisation and industry to her intercourse with Greece, to the trade of the Hanseatic Towns with Novgorod and (after the destruction of that town by Ivan Wassiljewitsch) to the trade which arose with the English and Dutch, in consequence of the discovery of the water communication with the coasts of the White Sea.

But the great increase of her industry, and especially of her civilisation, dates from the reign of Peter the Great. The history of Russia during the last hundred and forty years offers a most striking proof of the great influence of national unity and political circumstances on the economic welfare of a nation.

To the imperial power which established and maintained this union of innumerable barbaric hordes, Russia owes the foundations of her manufactures, her vast progress in agriculture and population, the facilities offered to her interior traffic by the construction of canals and roads, a very large foreign trade, and her standing as a commercial power.

Russia's independent system of trade dates, however, only from the year 1821.

Under Catherine II. trade and manufactures had certainly made some progress, on account of the privileges she offered to foreign artisans and manufacturers; but the culture of the nation was still too imperfect to allow of its getting beyond the first stages in the manufacture of iron, glass, linen, &c., and especially in those branches of industry in which the country was specially favoured by its agricultural and mineral wealth.

Besides this, further progress in manufactures would

not, at that time, have been conducive to the economic interests of the nation. If foreign countries had taken in payment the provisions, raw material, and rude manufactures which Russia was able to furnish—if, further, no wars and exterior events had intervened, Russia by means of intercourse with nations more advanced than herself would have been much more prosperous, and her culture in general would in consequence of this intercourse have made greater progress than under the manufacturing system. But wars and the Continental blockade, and the commercial regulations of foreign nations, compelled her to seek prosperity in other ways than by the export of raw materials and the import of manufactures. In consequence of these, the previous commercial relations of Russia by sea were disturbed. Her overland trade with the western continent could not make up for these losses; and she found it necessary, therefore, to work up her raw materials herself. After the establishment of the general peace, a desire arose to return to the old system. The Government, and even the Emperor, were inclined to favour free trade. In Russia, the writings of Herr Storch enjoyed as high a reputation as those of Mons. Say in Germany. People were not alarmed by the first shocks which the home manufactories, which had arisen during the Continental blockade, suffered owing to English competition. The theorists maintained that if these shocks could only be endured once for all, the blessings of free trade would follow. And indeed the circumstances of the commercial world at the time were uncommonly favourable to this transition. The failure of crops in Western Europe caused a great export of agricultural produce, by which Russia for a long time gained ample means to balance her large importation of manufactured goods.

But when this extraordinary demand for Russian agricultural produce had ceased, when, on the other hand, England had imposed restrictions on the import of corn for the benefit of her aristocracy, and on that of foreign timber for the benefit of Canada, the ruin of Russia's home manufactories and the excessive import of foreign manufactures made itself doubly felt. Although people had formerly, with Herr Storch, considered the balance of trade as a chimera, to believe in the existence of which was, for a reasonable and enlightened man, no less outrageous and ridiculous than the belief in witchcraft in the seventeenth century had been, it was now seen with alarm that there must be something of the nature of a balance of trade as between independent nations. The most enlightened and discerning statesman of Russia, Count Nesselrode, did not hesitate to confess to this belief. He declared in an official circular of 1821 : ' Russia finds herself compelled by circumstances to take up an independent system of trade ; the products of the empire have found no foreign market, the home manufactures are ruined or on the point of being so, all the ready money of the country flows towards foreign lands, and the most substantial trading firms are nearly ruined.'

The beneficial effects of the Russian protective system contributed no less than the injurious consequences of the re-establishment of free trade had done to bring into discredit the principles and assertions of the theorists. Foreign capital, talent, and labour flowed into the country from all civilised lands, especially from England and Germany, in order to share in the advantages offered by the home manufactories.

The nobility imitated the policy of the Empire at large. As they could obtain no foreign market for their produce, they attempted to solve the problem inversely by bringing the market into proximity with the produce—they established manufactories on their estates. In consequence of the demand for fine wool produced by the newly created woollen manufactories, the breed of sheep was rapidly improved. Foreign trade increased, instead of declining, particularly that with China, Persia, and other neighbouring countries of Asia. The commercial crises entirely ceased, and one need only read the latest reports of the Russian Minister of Commerce, to be convinced that Russia owes a large measure of prosperity to this system, and that she is increasing her national wealth and power by enormous strides.

It is foolish for Germans to try to make little of this progress and to complain of the injury which it has caused to the north-eastern provinces of Germany. Each nation, like each individual, has its own interests nearest at heart. Russia is not called upon to care for the welfare of Germany; Germany must care for Germany, and Russia for Russia. It would be much better, instead of complaining, instead of hoping and waiting and expecting the Messiah of a future free trade, to throw the cosmopolitan system into the fire and take a lesson from the example of Russia.

That England should look with jealousy on this commercial policy of Russia is very natural. By its means Russia has emancipated herself from England, and has qualified herself to enter into competition with her in Asia. Even if England manufactures more cheaply, this advantage will in the trade with Central Asia be outweighed by the proximity of the Russian Empire and by its political influence. Although Russia may still be, in comparison with Europe, but a slightly civilised country, yet, as compared with Asia, she is a civilised one.

Meantime, it cannot be denied that the want of civilisation and political institutions will greatly hinder Russia in her further industrial and commercial progress, especially if the Imperial Government does not succeed in harmonising her political conditions with the requirements of industry, by the introduction of efficient municipal and provincial constitutions, by the gradual limitation and final abolition of serfdom, by the formation of an educated middle class and a free peasant class, and by the completion of means of internal transport and of communication with Central Asia. These are the conquests to which Russia is called in the present century, and on them depends her further progress in agriculture and industry, in trade, navigation and naval power. But in order to render reforms of this kind possible and practicable, the Russian aristocracy must first learn to feel that their own material interests will be most promoted by them.

CHAPTER IX.

THE NORTH AMERICANS.

AFTER our historical examination of the commercial policy of the European nations, with the exception of those from which there is nothing of importance to be learnt, we will cast a glance beyond the Atlantic Ocean at a people of colonists which has been raising itself almost before our eyes from the condition of entire dependence on the mother country, and of separation into a number of colonial provinces having no kind of political union between themselves, to that of a united, well-organised, free, powerful, industrious, rich, and independent nation, which will perhaps in the time of our grandchildren exalt itself to the rank of the first naval and commercial power in the world. The history of the trade and industry of North America is more instructive for our subject than any other can be, because here the course of development proceeds rapidly, the periods of free trade and protection follow closely on each other, their consequences stand out clearly and sharply defined, and the whole machinery of national industry and State administration moves exposed before the eyes of the spectator.

The North American colonies were kept, in respect of trade and industry, in such complete thraldom by the mother country, that no sort of manufacture was permitted to them beyond domestic manufacture and the ordinary handicrafts. So late as the year 1750 a hat manufactory in the State of Massachusetts created so great sensation and jealousy in Parliament, that it declared all kinds of manufactories to be 'common nuisances,' not excepting iron works, notwithstanding that the country possessed in the greatest abundance all the requisite materials for the manufacture of iron. Even more recently, namely in 1770, the great Chatham, made uneasy by the first manufacturing attempts of the New Englanders, declared that the colonies should not be permitted to manufacture so much as a horseshoe nail.

To Adam Smith belongs the merit of having first pointed out the injustice of this policy.

The monopoly of all manufacturing industry by the mother country was one of the chief causes of the American Revolution; the tea duty merely afforded an opportunity for its outbreak.

Freed from restrictions, in possession of all material and intellectual resources for manufacturing work, and separated from that nation from which they had previously been supplied with manufactured goods, and to which they had been selling their produce, and thus thrown with all their wants upon their own resources, manufactures of every kind in the North American free states received a mighty stimulus during the war of revolution, which in its turn had the effect of benefiting agriculture to such an extent that, notwithstanding the burdens and the devastation consequent upon the then recent war, the value of land and the rate of wages in these states everywhere rose immensely. But as, after the peace of Paris, the faulty constitution of the free states made the introduction of a united commercial system impossible, and consequently English manufactured goods again obtained free admission, competition with which the newly established American manufactories had not strength enough to bear, the prosperity which had arisen during the war vanished much more quickly than it had grown up. An orator in Congress said afterwards of this crisis: 'We did buy, according to the advice of modern theorists, where we could buy cheapest, and our markets were flooded with foreign goods; English goods sold cheaper in our seaport towns than in Liverpool or London. Our manufacturers were being ruined; our merchants, even those who thought to enrich themselves by importation, became bankrupt; and all these causes together were so detrimental to agriculture, that landed property became very generally worthless, and consequently bankruptcy became general even among our landowners.'

This condition of things was by no means temporary; it lasted from the peace of Paris until the establishment of the federal constitution, and contributed more than any other circumstance to bring about a more intimate union between the free states and to impel them to give to Congress full powers for the maintenance of a united commercial policy. Congress was inundated with petitions from all the states—New York and South Carolina not excepted —in favour of protective measures for internal industry; and Washington, on the day of his inauguration, wore a suit of home-manufactured cloth, 'in order,' said a contemporary New York journal, 'in the simple and impressive manner so peculiar to this great man, to give to all his successors in office and to all future legislators a memorable lesson upon the way in which the welfare of this country is to be promoted.' Although the first American tariff (1789) levied only light duties on the importation of the most important manufactured articles, it yet worked so beneficially from the very first years of its introduction that Washington in his 'Message' in 1791 was able to congratulate the nation on the flourishing condition of its manufactures, agriculture, and trade.

The inadequacy of this protection was, however, soon apparent; for the effect of the slight import duties was easily overcome by English manufacturers, who had the advantage of improved methods of production. Congress did certainly raise the duty on the most important manufactured articles to fifteen per cent., but this was not till the year 1804, when it was compelled, owing to deficient customs receipts, to raise more revenue, and long after the inland manufacturers had exhausted every argument in favour of having more protection, while the interests opposed to them were equally strenuous upon the advantages of free trade and the injurious effects of high import duties.

In striking contrast with the slight progress which had,

on the whole, been made by the manufacturers of the country, stood the improved condition of its navigation, which since the year 1789, upon the motion of James Madison, had received effectual protection. From a tonnage of 200,000 in 1789 their mercantile marine had increased in 1801 to more than 1,000,000 tons. Under the protection of the tariff of 1804, the manufacturing interest of the United States could just barely maintain itself against the English manufactories, which were continually being improved, and had attained a colossal magnitude, and it would doubtless have had to succumb entirely to English competition, had it not been for the help of the embargo and declaration of war of 1812. In consequence of these events, just as at the time of the War of Independence, the American manufactories received such an extraordinary impetus that they not only sufficed for the home demand, but soon began to export as well. According to a report of the Committee on Trade and Manufactures to Congress in 1815, 100,000 hands were employed in the woollen and cotton manufactures alone, whose yearly production amounted to the value of more than sixty million dollars. As in the days of the War of Independence, and as a necessary consequence of the increase in manufacturing power, there occurred a rapid rise in all prices, not only of produce and in wages, but also of landed property, and hence universal prosperity amongst landowners, labourers, and all engaged in internal trade.

After the peace of Ghent, Congress, warned by the experience of 1786, decreed that for the first year the previous duties should be doubled, and during this period the country continued to prosper. Coerced, however, by powerful private interests which were opposed to those of the manufacturers, and persuaded by the arguments of theorists, it resolved in the year 1816 to make a considerable reduction in the import duties, whereupon the same effects of external competition reappeared which had been experienced from 1786 to 1789, viz. ruin of manufactories, unsaleability of produce, fall in the value of property, and general calamity among landowners. After the country had for a second time enjoyed in war time the blessings of peace, it suffered, for a second time, greater evils through peace than the most devastating war could have brought upon it. It was only in the year 1824, after the effects of the English corn laws had been made manifest to the full extent of their unwise tendency, thus compelling the agricultural interest of the central, northern, and western states to make common cause with the manufacturing interest, that a somewhat higher tariff was passed in Congress, which, however, as Mr. Huskisson immediately brought forward counteracting measures with the view of paralysing the effects of this tariff on English competition, soon proved insufficient, and had to be supplemented by the tariff of 1828, carried through Congress after a violent struggle.

Recently published official statistics [1] of Massachusetts give a tolerable idea of the start taken by the manufactures of the United States, especially in the central and northern states of the Union, in consequence of the protective system, and in spite of the subsequent modification of the tariff of 1828. In the year 1837, there were in this State (Massachusetts) 282 cotton mills and 565,031 spindles in operation, employing 4,997 male and 14,757 female hands; 37,275,917· pounds' of cotton were worked up, and 126,000,000 yards of textile fabrics manufactured, of the value of 13,056,659 dollars, produced by a capital of 14,369,719 dollars.

In the woollen manufacture there were 192 mills, 501 machines, and 3,612 male and 3,485 female operatives employed, who worked up 10,858,988 pounds of wool, and produced 11,313,426 yards of cloth, of the value of 10,399,807 dollars on a working capital of 5,770,750 dollars.

16,689,877 pairs of shoes and boots were manufactured (large quantities of shoes being exported to the western states), to the value of 14,642,520 dollars.

---

[1] *Statistical Table of Massachusetts for the Year ending April* 1, 1837, by J. P. Bigelow, Secretary of the Commonwealth (Boston, 1838). No American state but Massachusetts possesses similar statistical abstracts. We owe those here referred to, to Governor Everett, distinguished alike as a scholar, an author, and a statesman.

The other branches of manufacture stood in relative proportion to the above.

The combined value of the manufactures of the State (deducting shipbuilding) amounted to over 86 million dollars, with a working capital of about 60 million dollars.

The number of operatives (men) was 117,352; and the total number of inhabitants of the State (in 1837) was 701,331.

Misery, brutality, and crime are unknown among the manufacturing population here. On the contrary, among the numerous male and female factory workers the strictest morality, cleanliness, and neatness in dress, exist; libraries are established to furnish them with useful and instructive books; the work is not exhausting, the food nourishing and good. Most of the women save a dowry for themselves.[1]

This last is evidently the effect of the cheap prices of the common necessaries of life, light taxation, and an equitable customs tariff. Let England repeal the restrictions on the import of agricultural produce, decrease the existing taxes on consumption by one-half or two-thirds, cover the loss by an income tax, and her factory workers will be put into the same position.

No nation has been so misconstrued and so misjudged as respects its future destiny and its national economy as the United States of North America, by theorists as well as by practical men. Adam Smith and J. B. Say had laid it down that the United States were, ' like Poland,' destined for agriculture. This comparison was not very flattering for the union of some dozen of new, aspiring, youthful republics, and the prospect thus held out to them for the future not very encouraging. The above-mentioned theorists had demonstrated that Nature herself had singled out the people of the United States exclusively for agriculture, so long as the richest arable land was to be had in their country for a mere trifle. Great was the commendation which had been bestowed upon them for so willingly

---

[1] The American papers of July 1839 report that in the manufacturing town of Lowell alone there are over a hundred workwomen who have each over a thousand dollars deposited to their credit in the savings bank.

acquiescing in Nature's ordinances, and thus supplying theorists with a beautiful example of the splendid working of the principle of free trade. The school, however, soon had to experience the mortification of losing this cogent proof of the correctness and applicability of their theories in practice, and had to endure the spectacle of the United States seeking their nation's welfare in a direction exactly opposed to that of absolute freedom of trade.

As this youthful nation had previously been the very apple of the eye of the schoolmen, so she now became the object of the heaviest condemnation on the part of the theorists of every nation in Europe. It was said to be a proof of the slight progress of the New World in political knowledge, that while the European nations were striving with the most honest zeal to render universal free trade possible, while England and France especially were actually engaged in endeavouring to make important advances towards this great philanthropic object, the United States of North America were seeking to promote their national prosperity by a return to that long-exploded mercantile system which had been clearly refuted by theory. A country like the United States, in which such measureless tracts of fruitful land still remained uncultivated and where wages ruled so high, could not utilise its material wealth and increase of population to better purpose than in agriculture ; and when this should have reached complete development, then manufactures would arise in the natural course of events without artificial forcing. But by an artificial development of manufactures the United States would injure not only the countries which had long before enjoyed civilisation, but themselves most of all.

With the Americans, however, sound common sense, and the instinct of what was necessary for the nation, were more potent than a belief in theoretical propositions. The arguments of the theorists were thoroughly investigated, and strong doubts entertained of the infallibility of a doctrine which its own disciples were not willing to put in practice.

To the argument concerning the still uncultivated tracts

of fruitful land, it was answered that tracts of such land in the populous, well-cultivated states of the Union which were ripe for manufacturing industry, were as rare as in Great Britain ; that the surplus population of those states would have to migrate at great expense to the west, in order to bring tracts of land of that description into cultivation, thus not only annually causing the eastern states large losses in material and intellectual resources, but also, inasmuch as such emigration would transform customers into competitors, the value of landed property and agricultural produce would thereby be lessened. It could not be to the advantage of the Union that all waste land belonging to it should be cultivated up to the Pacific Ocean before either the population, the civilisation, or the military power of the old states had been fully developed. On the contrary, the cultivation of distant virgin lands could confer no benefit on the eastern states unless they themselves devoted their attention to manufacturing, and could exchange their manufactures against the produce of the west. People went still farther : Was not England, it was asked, in much the same position ? Had not England also under her dominion vast tracts of fertile land still uncultivated in Canada, in Australia, and in other quarters of the world ? Was it not almost as easy for England to transplant her surplus population to those countries as for the North Americans to transplant theirs from the shores of the Atlantic to the banks of the Missouri ? If so, what occasion had England not only continuously to protect her home manufactures, but to strive to extend them more and more ?

The argument of the school, that with a high rate of wages in agriculture, manufactures could not succeed by the natural course of things, but only by being forced like hothouse plants, was found to be partially well-founded ; that is to say, it was applicable only to those manufactured goods which, being small in bulk and weight as compared to their value, are produced principally by hand labour, but was not applicable to goods the price of which is less influenced by the rate of wages, and as to which the disadvantage of higher wages can be neutralised by the use of machinery, by water power as yet unused, by cheap raw materials and food, by abundance of cheap fuel and building materials, by light taxation and increased efficiency of labour.

Besides, the Americans had long ago learnt from experience that agriculture cannot rise to a high state of prosperity unless the exchange of agricultural produce for manufactures is guaranteed for all future time ; but that, when the agriculturist lives in America and the manufacturer in England, that exchange is not unfrequently interrupted by wars, commercial crises, or foreign tariffs, and that consequently, if the national well-being is to rest on a secure foundation, 'the manufacturer,' to use Jefferson's words, ' must come and settle down in close proximity to the agriculturist.'

At length the Americans came to realise the truth that it behoves a great nation not exclusively to set its heart upon the enjoyment of proximate material advantages ; that civilisation and power—more important and desirable possessions than mere material wealth, as Adam Smith himself allows—can only be secured and retained by the creation of a manufacturing power of its own ; that a country which feels qualified to take and to maintain its place amongst the powerful and civilised nations of the earth must not shrink from any sacrifice in order to secure such possessions for itself; and that at that time the Atlantic states were clearly the region marked out for such possessions.

It was on the shores of the Atlantic that European settlers and European civilisation first set a firm foot. Here, at the first, were populous, wealthy, and civilised states created ; here was the cradle and seat of their sea fisheries, coasting trade, and naval power ; here their independence was won and their union founded. Through these states on the coast the foreign trade of the Union is carried on ; through them it is connected with the civilised world ; through them it acquires the surplus population, material, capital, and mental powers of Europe ; upon the civilisation, power, and wealth of these sea-board states depend the future civilisation, power, wealth, and independence of the whole nation and its future influence over less civilised communities. Suppose that the population of these Atlantic states decreased instead of growing larger, that their fisheries, coasting trade, shipping engaged in foreign trade and foreign trade itself, and, above all, their general prosperity, were to fall off or remain stationary instead of progressing, then we should see the resources of civilisation of the whole nation, the guarantees for its independence and external power, diminish too in the same degree. It is even conceivable that, were the whole territory of the United States laid under cultivation from sea to sea, covered with agricultural states, and densely populated in the interior, the nation itself might nevertheless be left in a low grade as respects civilisation, independence, foreign power, and foreign trade. There are certainly many nationalities who are in such a position and whose shipping and naval power are *nil*, though possessing a numerous inland population !

If a power existed that cherished the project of keeping down the rise of the American people and bringing them under subjection to itself industrially, commercially, or politically, it could only succeed in its aim by trying to depopulate the Atlantic states of the Union and driving all increase of population, capital, and intellectual power into the interior. By that means it would not only check the further growth of the nation's naval power, but might also indulge the hope of getting possession in time of the principal defensive strategical positions on the Atlantic coast and at the mouths of the rivers. The means to this end would not be difficult to imagine ; it would only be necessary to hinder the development of manufacturing power in the Atlantic states and to insure the acceptance of the principle of absolute freedom of foreign trade in America.

If the Atlantic states do not become manufacturers, they will not only be unable to keep up their present degree of civilisation, but they must sink, and sink in every respect. Without manufactures how are the towns along the Atlantic

coast to prosper ?   Not by the forwarding of inland produce
to Europe and of English manufactured goods to the interior, for a very few thousand people would be sufficient
to transact this business.   How are the fisheries to prosper ?
The majority of the population who have moved inland
prefer fresh meat and fresh-water fish to salted ; they
require no train oil, or at least but a small quantity.   How
is the coasting trade along the Atlantic sea-board to thrive ?
As the largest portion of the coast states are peopled by
cultivators of land who produce for themselves all the
provisions, building materials, fuel, &c. which they require,
there is nothing along the coast to sustain a transport
trade.   How are foreign trade and shipping to distant
places to increase ?   The country has nothing to offer but
what less cultivated nations possess in superabundance,
and those manufacturing nations to which it sends its
produce encourage their own shipping.   How can a naval
power arise when fisheries, the coasting trade, ocean navigation, and foreign trade decay ?   How are the Atlantic
states to protect themselves against foreign attacks without
a naval power ?   How is agriculture even to thrive in these
states, when by means of canals, railways, &c. the produce
of the much more fertile and cheaper tracts of land in the
west which require no manure, can be carried to the east
much more cheaply than it could be there produced upon
soil exhausted long ago ?   How under such circumstances
can civilisation thrive and population increase in the
eastern states, when it is clear that under free trade with
England all increase of population and of agricultural
capital must flow to the west ?   The present state of
Virginia gives but a faint idea of the condition into which
the Atlantic states would be thrown by the absence of
manufactures in the east; for Virginia, like all the southern
states on the Atlantic coast, at present takes a profitable
share in providing the Atlantic states with agricultural
produce.

All these things bear quite a different complexion, owing
to the existence of a flourishing manufacturing power in
the Atlantic states.   Now population, capital, technical

skill and intellectual power, flow into them from all European countries; now the demand for the manufactured products of the Atlantic states increases simultaneously with their consumption of the raw materials supplied by the west. Now the population of these states, their wealth, and the number and extent of their towns increase in equal proportion with the cultivation of the western virgin lands; now, on account of the larger population, and the consequently increased demand for meat, butter, cheese, milk, garden produce, oleaginous seeds, fruit, &c., their own agriculture is increasing; now the sea fisheries are flourishing in consequence of the larger demand for salted fish and train oil; now quantities of provisions, building materials, coal, &c. are being conveyed along the coast to furnish the wants of the manufacturing population; now the manufacturing population produce a large quantity of commodities for export to all the nations of the earth, from whence result profitable return freights; now the nation's naval power increases by means of the coasting trade, the fisheries, and navigation to distant lands, and with it the guarantee of national independence and influence over other nations, particularly over those of South America; now science and art, civilisation and literature, are improving in the eastern states, whence they are being diffused amongst the western states.

These were the circumstances which induced the United States to lay restrictions upon the importation of foreign manufactured goods, and to protect their native manufactures. With what amount of success this has been done, we have shown in the preceding pages. That without such a policy a manufacturing power could never have been maintained successfully in the Atlantic states, we may learn from their own experience and from the industrial history of other nations.

The frequently recurring commercial crises in America have been very often attributed to these restrictions on importation of foreign goods, but without reasonable grounds. The earlier as well as the later experience of North America shows, on the contrary, that such crises have never been more frequent and destructive than when commercial intercourse with England was least subject to restrictions. Commercial crises amongst agricultural nations, who procure their supplies of manufactured goods from foreign markets, arise from the disproportion between imports and exports. Manufacturing nations richer in capital than agricultural states, and ever anxious to increase the quantity of their exports, deliver their goods on credit and encourage consumption. In fact, they make advances upon the coming harvest. But if the harvest turn out so poor that its value falls greatly below that of the goods previously consumed ; or if the harvest prove so rich that the supply of produce meets with no adequate demand and falls in price; while at the same time the markets still continue to be overstocked with foreign goods —then a commercial crisis will occur by reason of the disproportion existing between the means of payment and the quantity of goods previously consumed, as also by reason of the disproportion between supply and demand in the markets for produce and manufactured goods.   The operations of foreign and native banks may increase and promote such a crisis, but they cannot create it. In a future chapter we shall endeavour more closely to elucidate this subject.

CHAPTER X.

THE TEACHINGS OF HISTORY.

EVERYWHERE and at all times has the well-being of the nation been in equal proportion to the intelligence, morality, and industry of its citizens; according to these, wealth has accrued or been diminished; but industry and thrift, invention and enterprise, on the part of individuals, have never as yet accomplished aught of importance where they were not sustained by municipal liberty, by suitable public institutions and laws, by the State administration and foreign policy, but above all by the unity and power, of the nation.

History everywhere shows us a powerful process of reciprocal action between the social and the individual powers and conditions. In the Italian and the Hanseatic cities, in Holland and England, in France and America, we find the powers of production, and consequently the wealth of individuals, growing in proportion to the liberties enjoyed, to the degree of perfection of political and social institutions, while these, on the other hand, derive material and stimulus for their further improvement from the increase of the material wealth and of the productive power of individuals. The real rise of the industry and power of England dates only from the days of the actual foundation of England's national freedom, while the industry and power of Venice, of the Hanse Towns, of the Spanish and Portuguese, decayed concurrently with their loss of freedom. However industrious, thrifty, inventive, and intelligent, individual citizens might be, they could not make up for the lack of free institutions. History also teaches that individuals derive the greater part of their productive powers from the social institutions and conditions under which they are placed.

The influence of liberty, intelligence, and enlightenment over the power, and therefore over the productive capacity and wealth of a nation, is exemplified in no respect so clearly as in navigation. Of all industrial pursuits, navigation most demands energy, personal courage, enterprise, and endurance; qualifications that can only flourish in an atmosphere of freedom. In no other calling do ignorance, superstition, and prejudice, indolence, cowardice, effeminacy, and weakness produce such disastrous consequences; nowhere else is a sense of self-reliance so indispensable. Hence history cannot point to a single example of an enslaved people taking a prominent part in navigation. The Hindoos, the Chinese, and the Japanese have ever strictly confined their efforts to canal and river navigation and the coasting trade. In ancient Egypt maritime navigation was held in abhorrence, probably because priests and rulers dreaded lest by means of it the spirit of freedom and independence should be encouraged. The freest and most enlightened states of ancient Greece were also the most powerful at sea; their naval power ceased with their freedom, and however much history may narrate of the victories of the kings of Macedonia on land, she is silent as to their victories at sea.

When were the Romans powerful at sea, and when is nothing more heard of their fleets? When did Italy lay down the law in the Mediterranean, and since when has her very coasting trade fallen into the hands of foreigners? Upon the Spanish navy the Inquisition had passed sentence of death long ere the English and the Dutch fleets had executed the decree. With the coming into power of the mercantile oligarchies in the Hanse Towns, power and the spirit of enterprise took leave of the Hanseatic League.

Of the Spanish Netherlands only the maritime provinces achieved their freedom, whereas those held in subjection by the Inquisition had even to submit to the closing of their rivers. The English fleet, victorious over the Dutch in the Channel, now took possession of the dominion of the seas, which the spirit of freedom had assigned to England long before; and yet Holland, down to our own days, has retained a large proportion of her mercantile marine, whereas that of the Spaniards and the Portuguese is almost annihilated. In vain were the efforts of a great individual minister now and then under the despotic kings of France to create a fleet, for it invariably went again to ruin.

But how is it that at the present day we witness the growing strength of French navigation and naval power ? Hardly had the independence of the United States of North America come to life, when we find the Americans contending with renown against the giant fleets of the mother country. But what is the position of the Central and South American nations ? So long as their flags wave not over every sea, but little dependence can be placed upon the effectiveness of their republican forms of government. Contrast these with Texas, a territory that has scarcely attained to political life, and yet already claims its. share in the realm of Neptune.

But navigation is merely one part of the industrial power of a nation—a part which can flourish and attain to importance only in conjunction with all the other complementary parts. Everywhere and at all times we see navigation, inland and foreign trade, and even agriculture itself, flourish only where manufactures have reached a high state of prosperity. But if freedom be an indispensable condition for the prosperity of navigation, how much more must it be so for the prosperity of the manufacturing power, for the growth of the entire producing power of a nation ? History contains no record of a rich, commercial, and industrial community that was not at the same time in the enjoyment of freedom.

Manufactures everywhere first brought into operation improved means of transport, improved river navigation, improved highways, steam navigation and railways, which constitute the fundamental elements of improved systems of agriculture and of civilisation.

History teaches that arts and trades migrated from city to city, from one country to another. Persecuted and oppressed at home, they took refuge in cities and in countries where freedom, protection, and support were

assured to them. In this way they migrated from Greece
and Asia to Italy; from Italy to Germany, Flanders, and
Brabant; and from thence to Holland and England.
Everywhere it was want of sense and despotism that drove
them away, and the spirit of freedom that attracted them.
But for the folly of the Continental governments, England
would have had difficulty in attaining supremacy in industry. But does it appear more consistent with wisdom
for us in Germany to wait patiently until other nations are
impolitic enough to drive out their industries and thus
compel them to seek a refuge with us, or that we should,
without waiting for such contingencies, invite them by
proffered advantages to settle down amongst us?

It is true that experience teaches that the wind bears
the seed from one region to another, and that thus waste
moorlands have been transformed into dense forests; but
would it on that account be wise policy for the forester to
wait until the wind in the course of ages effects this trans-
formation?

Is it unwise on his part if by sowing and planting he
seeks to attain the same object within a few decades?
History tells us that whole nations have successfully accomplished that which we see the forester do. Single free
cities, or small republics and confederations of such cities
and states, limited in territorial possessions, of small population and insignificant military power, but fortified by the
energy of youthful freedom and favoured by geographical
position as well as by fortunate circumstances and opportunities, flourished by means of manufactures and commerce
long before the great monarchies; and by free commercial
intercourse with the latter, by which they exported to them
manufactured goods and imported raw produce in exchange,
raised themselves to a high degree of wealth and power.
Thus did Venice, the Hanse Towns, the Belgians and the
Dutch.

Nor was this system of free trade less profitable at first
to the great monarchies themselves, with whom these
smaller communities had commercial intercourse. For,
having regard to the wealth of their natural resources and

to their undeveloped social condition, the free importation
of foreign manufactured goods and the exportation of
native produce presented the surest and most effectual
means of developing their own powers of production, of
instilling habits of industry into their subjects who were
addicted to idleness and turbulence, of inducing their landowners and nobles to feel an interest in industry, of arousing
the dormant spirit of enterprise amongst their merchants,
and especially of raising their own civilisation, industry,
and power.

These effects were learned generally by Great Britain
from the trade and manufacturing industry of the Italians,
the Hansards, the Belgians, and the Dutch. But having
attained to a certain grade of development by means of
free trade, the great monarchies perceived that the highest
degree of civilisation, power, and wealth can only be attained
by a combination of manufactures and commerce with
agriculture. They perceived that their newly established
native manufactures could never hope to succeed in free
competition with the old and long-established manufactures
of foreigners ; that their native fisheries and native mercantile marine, the foundations of their naval power, could
never make successful progress without special privileges ;
and that the spirit of enterprise of their native merchants
would always be kept down by the overwhelming reserves
of capital, the greater experience and sagacity of the
foreigners. Hence they sought, by a system of restrictions,
privileges, and encouragements, to transplant on to their
native soil the wealth, the talents, and the spirit of enterprise of the foreigners. This policy was pursued with
greater or lesser, with speedier or more tardy success, just
in proportion as the measures adopted were more or less
judiciously adapted to the object in view, and applied and
pursued with more or less energy and perseverance.

England, above all other nations, has adopted this
policy. Often interrupted in its execution from the want
of intelligence and self-restraint on the part of her rulers,
or owing to internal commotions and foreign wars, it first
assumed the character of a settled and practically efficient

policy under Edward VI., Elizabeth, and the revolutionary period. For how could the measures of Edward III. work satisfactorily when it was not till under Henry VI. that the law permitted the carriage of corn from one English county to another, or the shipment of it to foreign parts ; when still under Henry VII. and Henry VIII. all interest on money, even discount on bills, was held to be usury, and when it was still thought at the time that trade might be encouraged by fixing by law at a low figure the price of woollen goods and the rate of wages, and that the production of corn could be increased by prohibiting sheep farming on a large scale ?

And how much sooner would England's woollen manufactures and maritime trade have reached a high standard of prosperity had not Henry VIII. regarded a rise in the prices of corn as an evil; had he, instead of driving foreign workmen by wholesale from the kingdom, sought like his predecessors to augment their number by encouraging their immigration ; and had not Henry VII. refused his sanction to the Act of Navigation as proposed by Parliament ?

In France we see native manufactures, free internal intercourse, foreign trade, fisheries, navigation, and naval power—in a word, all the attributes of a great, mighty, and rich nation (which it had cost England the persevering efforts of centuries to acquire)—called into existence by a great genius within the space of a few years, as it were by a magician's wand ; and afterwards all of them yet more speedily annihilated by the iron hand of fanaticism and despotism.

We see the principle of free trade contending in vain under unfavourable conditions against restriction powerfully enforced; the Hanseatic League is ruined, while Holland sinks under the blows of England and France.

That a restrictive commercial policy can be operative for good only so far as it is supported by the progressive civilisation and free institutions of a nation, we learn from the decay of Venice, Spain, and Portugal, from the relapse of France in consequence of the revocation of the Edict of Nantes, and from the history of England, in which country liberty kept pace at all times with the advance of industry, trade, and national wealth.

That, on the contrary, a highly advanced state of civilisation, with or without free institutions, unless supported by a suitable system of commercial policy, will prove but a poor guarantee for a nation's economic progress, may be learnt on the one hand from the history of the North American free states, and on the other from the experience of Germany.

Modern Germany, lacking a system of vigorous and united commercial policy, exposed in her home markets to competition with a foreign manufacturing power in every way superior to her own, while excluded at the same time from foreign markets by arbitrary and often capricious restrictions, and very far indeed from making that progress in industry to which her degree of culture entitles her, cannot even maintain her previously acquired position, and is made a convenience of (like a colony) by that very nation which centuries ago was worked upon in like manner by the merchants of Germany, until at last the German states have resolved to secure their home markets for their own industry, by the adoption of a united vigorous system of commercial policy.

The North American free states, who, more than any other nation before them, are in a position to benefit by freedom of trade, and influenced even from the very cradle of their independence by the doctrines of the cosmopolitan school, are striving more than any other nation to act on that principle. But owing to wars with Great Britain, we find this nation twice compelled to manufacture at home the goods which it previously purchased under free trade from other countries, and twice, after the conclusion of peace, brought to the brink of ruin by free competition with foreigners, and thereby admonished of the fact that under the present conditions of the world every great nation must seek the guarantees of its continued prosperity and independence, before all other things, in the independent and uniform development of its own powers and resources.

Thus history shows that restrictions are not so much the inventions of mere speculative minds, as the natural consequences of the diversity of interests, and of the strivings of nations after independence or overpowering ascendency, and thus of national emulation and wars, and therefore that they cannot be dispensed with until this conflict of national interests shall cease, in other words until all nations can be united under one and the same system of law. Thus the question as to whether, and how, the various nations can be brought into one united federation, and how the decisions of law can be invoked in the place of military force to determine the differences which arise between independent nations, has to be solved concurrently with the question how universal free trade can be established in the place of separate national commercial systems.

The attempts which have been made by single nations to introduce freedom of trade in face of a nation which is predominant in industry, wealth, and power, no less than distinguished for an exclusive tariff system—as Portugal did in 1703, France in 1786, North America in 1786 and 1816, Russia from 1815 till 1821, and as Germany has done for centuries—go to show us that in this way the prosperity of individual nations is sacrificed, without benefit to mankind in general, solely for the enrichment of the predominant manufacturing and commercial nation. Switzerland (as we hope to show in the sequel) constitutes an exception, which proves just as much as it proves little for or against one or the other system.

Colbert appears to us not to have been the inventor of that system which the Italians have named after him; for, as we have seen, it was fully elaborated by the English long before his time. Colbert only put in practice what France, if she wished to fulfil her destinies, was bound to carry out sooner or later. If Colbert is to be blamed at all, it can only be charged against him that he attempted to put into force under a despotic government a system which could subsist only after a fundamental reform of the political conditions.

But against this reproach to Colbert's memory it may very well be argued that, had his system been continued by wise princes and sagacious ministers, it would in all probability have removed by means of reforms all those hindrances which stood in the way of progress in manufactures, agriculture, and trade, as well as of national freedom ; and France would then have undergone no revolution, but rather, impelled along the path of development by the reciprocating influences of industry and freedom, she might for the last century and a half have been successfully competing with England in manufactures, in the promotion of her internal trade, in foreign commerce, and in colonisation, as well as in her fisheries, her navigation, and her naval power.

Finally, history teaches us how nations which have been endowed by Nature with all resources which are requisite for the attainment of the highest grade of wealth and power, may and must—without on that account forfeiting the end in view—modify their systems according to the measure of their own progress : in the first stage, adopting free trade with more advanced nations as a means of raising themselves from a state of barbarism, and of making advances in agriculture ; in the second stage, promoting the growth of manufactures, fisheries, navigation, and foreign trade by means of commercial restrictions ; and in the last stage, after reaching the highest degree of wealth and power, by gradually reverting to the principle of free trade and of unrestricted competition in the home as well as in foreign markets, that so their agriculturists, manufacturers, and merchants may be preserved from indolence, and stimulated to retain the supremacy which they have acquired. In the first stage, we see Spain, Portugal, and the Kingdom of Naples ; in the second, Germany and the United States of North America ; France apparently stands close upon the boundary line of the last stage ; but Great Britain alone at the present time has actually reached it.

SECOND BOOK

THE THEORY

CHAPTER XI.

BEFORE Quesnay and the French economists there existed only a *practice* of political economy which was exercised by the State officials, administrators, and authors who wrote about matters of administration, occupied themselves exclusively with the agriculture, manufactures, commerce, and navigation of those countries to which they belonged, without analysing the causes of wealth, or taking at all into consideration the interests of the whole human race.

Quesnay (from whom the idea of universal free trade originated) was the first who extended his investigations to the whole human race, without taking into consideration the idea of the nation. He calls his work 'Physiocratie, ou du Gouvernement le plus avantageux au Genre Humain,' his demands being that we must imagine that *the merchants of all nations formed one commercial republic.* Quesnay undoubtedly speaks of *cosmopolitical* economy, i.e. of that science which teaches how the entire human race may attain prosperity; in opposition to political economy, or that science which limits its teaching to the inquiry how a *given nation* can obtain (under the existing conditions of the world) prosperity, civilisation, and power, by means of agriculture, industry, and commerce.

Adam Smith [1] treats his doctrine in a similarly extended sense, by making it his task to indicate the cosmopolitical idea of the absolute freedom of the commerce of the whole

---

[1] It is alleged that Adam Smith intended to have *dedicated* his great work to Quesnay.—TR. (See *Life of Smith*, published by T. and J. Allman. 1825.)

world in spite of the gross mistakes made by the physiocrates against the very nature of things and against logic. Adam Smith concerned himself as little as Quesnay did with true political economy, i.e. that policy which each separate nation had to obey in order to make progress in its economical conditions. He entitles his work, ' The Nature and Causes of the Wealth of Nations' (i.e. of all nations of the whole human race). He speaks of the various systems of political economy in a separate part of his work solely for the purpose of demonstrating their non-efficiency, and of proving that 'political' or *national* economy must be replaced by ' cosmo-political or world-wide economy.' Although here and there he speaks of wars, this only occurs incidentally. The idea of a perpetual state of peace forms the foundation of all his arguments. Moreover, according to the explicit remarks of his biographer, Dugald Stewart, his investigations from the commencement are based upon the principle that ' most of the State regulations for the promotion of public prosperity are unnecessary, and a nation in order to be transformed from the lowest state of barbarism into a state of the highest possible prosperity needs nothing but bearable taxa-tion, fair administration of justice, and *peace*.' Adam Smith naturally understood under the word ' peace ' the ' perpetual universal peace ' of the Abbé St. Pierre.

J. B. Say openly demands that we should imagine the existence of a *universal republic* in order to comprehend the idea of general free trade. This writer, whose efforts were mainly restricted to the formation of a system out of the materials which Adam Smith had brought to light, says explicitly in the sixth volume (p. 288) of his ' Economie politique pratique : ' ' We may take into our consideration the economical interests of the family with the father at its head ; the principles and observations referring thereto will constitute *private economy*. Those principles, however, which have reference to the interests of whole nations, whether in themselves or in relation to other nations, form *public economy* (l'économie publique). *Political economy*, lastly, relates to the interests of all nations, to *human society in general*.'

It must be remarked here, that in the first place Say recognises the existence of a national economy or political economy, under the name ' économie publique,' but that he nowhere treats of the latter in his works ; secondly, that he attributes the name *political* economy to a doctrine which is evidently of *cosmopolitical* nature ; and that in this doctrine he invariably merely speaks of an economy which has for its sole object the interests of the whole human society, without regard to the separate interests of distinct nations.

This substitution of terms might be passed over if Say, after having explained what he calls political economy (which, however, is nothing else but cosmopolitical or worldwide economy, or economy of the whole human race), had acquainted us with the principles of the doctrine which he calls ' économie publique,' which however is, properly speaking, nothing else but the economy of given nations, or true political economy.

In defining and developing this doctrine he could scarcely forbear to proceed from the idea and the nature of the nation, and to show what material modifications the ' economy of the whole human race ' must undergo by the fact that at present that race is still separated into distinct nationalities each held together by common powers and interests, and distinct from other societies of the same kind which in the exercise of their natural liberty are opposed to one another. However, by giving his cosmopolitical economy the name *political*, he dispenses with this explanation, effects by means of a transposition of terms also a transposition of meaning, and thereby masks a series of the gravest theoretical errors.

All later writers have participated in this error. Sismondi also calls political economy explicitly, ' La science qui se charge du bonheur de l'espèce humaine.' Adam Smith and his followers teach us from this mainly nothing more than what Quesnay and his followers had taught us already, for the article of the ' Revue Méthodique ' treating of the physiocratic school states, in almost the same words : ' *The well-being of the individual is dependent altogether on the well-being of the whole human race.*'

The first of the North American advocates of free trade, as understood by Adam Smith—Thomas Cooper, President of Columbia College—denies even the existence of nationality; he calls the nation ' a grammatical invention,' created only to save periphrases, a nonentity, which has no actual existence save in the heads of politicians.   Cooper is moreover perfectly consistent with respect to this, in fact much more consistent than his predecessors and instructors, for it is evident that as soon as the existence of nations with their distinct nature and interests is recognised, it becomes necessary to modify the economy of human society in accordance with these special interests, and that if Cooper intended to represent these modifications as errors, it was very wise on his part from the beginning to disown the very existence of nations.

For our own part, we are far from rejecting the theory of *cosmopolitical* economy, as it has been perfected by the prevailing school ; we are, however, of opinion that political economy, or as Say calls it ' économie publique,' should also be developed scientifically, and that it is always better to call things by their proper names than to give them significations which stand opposed to the true import of words.

If we wish to remain true to the laws of logic and of the nature of things, we must set the economy of individuals against the economy of societies, and discriminate in respect to the latter between true political or national economy (which, emanating from the idea and nature of the nation, teaches how a given *nation* in the present state of the world and its own special national relations can maintain and improve its economical conditions) and cosmopolitical economy, which originates in the assumption that all nations of the earth form but one society living in a perpetual state of peace.

If, as the prevailing school requires, we assume a universal union or confederation of all nations as the guarantee for an everlasting peace, the principle of international free trade seems to be perfectly justified.   The less every individual is restrained in pursuing his own individual prosperity, the greater the number and wealth of those with whom he has free intercourse, the greater the area over which his individual activity can exercise itself, the easier it will be for him to utilise for the increase of his prosperity the properties given him by nature, the knowledge and talents which he has acquired, and the forces of nature placed at his disposal. As with separate individuals, so is it also the case with individual communities, provinces, and countries. A simpleton only could maintain that a union for free commercial intercourse between themselves is not as advantageous to the different states included in the United States of North America, to the various departments of France, and to the various German allied states, as would be their separation by internal provincial customs tariffs.

In the union of the three kingdoms of Great Britain and Ireland the world witnesses a great and irrefragable example of the immeasurable efficacy of free trade between united nations. Let us only suppose all other nations of the earth to be united in a similar manner, and the most vivid imagination will not be able to picture to itself the sum of prosperity and good fortune which the whole human race would thereby acquire.

Unquestionably the idea of a universal confederation and a perpetual peace is commended both by common sense and religion.[1] If single combat between individuals is at present considered to be contrary to reason, how much more must combat between two nations be similarly condemned? The proofs which social economy can produce from the history of the civilisation of mankind of the reasonableness of bringing about the union of all mankind under the law of right, are perhaps those which are the clearest to sound human understanding.

---

[1] The Christian religion inculcates perpetual peace. But until the promise, ' There shall be *one fold and one shepherd*,' has been fulfilled, the principle of the Quakers, however true it be in itself, can scarcely be acted upon. There is no better proof for the Divine origin of the Christian religion than that its doctrines and promises are in perfect agreement with the demands of both the material and spiritual well-being of the human race.

History teaches that wherever individuals are engaged in wars, the prosperity of mankind is at its lowest stage, and that it increases in the same proportion in which the concord of mankind increases. In the primitive state of the human race, first unions of families took place, then towns, then confederations of towns, then union of whole countries, finally unions of several states under one and the same government. If the nature of things has been powerful enough to extend this union (which commenced with the family) over hundreds of millions, we ought to consider that nature to be powerful enough to accomplish the union of all nations. If the human mind were capable of comprehending the advantages of this great union, so ought we to venture to deem it capable of understanding the still greater benefits which would result from a union of the whole human race. Many instances indicate this tendency in the spirit of the present times. We need only hint at the progress made in sciences, arts, and discoveries, in industry and social order. [It may be already foreseen with certainty, that after a lapse of a few decades the civilised nations of the earth will, by the perfection of the means of conveyance, be united as respects both material and mental interchange in as close a manner as (or even closer than) that in which a century ago the various counties of England were connected.] Continental governments possess already at the present moment in the telegraph the means of communicating with one another, almost as if they were at one and the same place. Powerful forces previously unknown have already raised industry to a degree of perfection hitherto never anticipated, and others still more powerful have already announced their appearance. But the more that industry advances, and proportionately extends over the countries of the earth, the smaller will be the possibility of wars. Two nations equally well developed in industry could mutually inflict on one another more injury in one week than they would be able to make good in a whole generation. But hence it follows that the same new forces which have hitherto served particularly for production will not withhold their services from destruction, and will principally favour the side of defence, and especially the European Continental nations, while they threaten the insular State with the loss of those advantages which have been gained by her insular position for her defence. In the congresses of the great European powers Europe possesses already the embryo of a future congress of nations. The endeavours to settle differences by protocol are clearly already prevailing over those which obtain justice by force of arms. A clearer insight into the nature of wealth and industry has led the wiser heads of all civilised nations to the conviction that both the civilisation of barbarous and semi-barbarous nations, and of those whose culture is retrograding, as well as the formation of colonies, offer to civilised nations a field for the development of their productive powers which promises them much richer and safer fruits than mutual hostilities by wars or restrictions on trade. The farther we advance in this perception, and the more the uncivilised countries come into contact with the civilised ones by the progress made in the means of transport, so much more will the civilised countries comprehend that the civilisation of barbarous nations, of those distracted by internal anarchy, or which are oppressed by bad government, is a task which offers to all equal advantages—a duty incumbent on them all alike, but one which can only be accomplished by unity.

That the civilisation of all nations, the culture of the whole globe, forms a task imposed on the whole human race, is evident from those unalterable laws of nature by which civilised nations are driven on with irresistible power to extend or transfer their powers of production to less cultivated countries. We see everywhere, under the influence of civilisation, population, powers of mind, material capital attaining to such dimensions that they must necessarily flow over into other less civilised countries. If the cultivable area of the country no longer suffices to sustain the population and to employ the agricultural population, the redundant portion of the latter seeks territories suitable for cultivation in distant lands ; if the talents and technical abilities of a nation have become so numerous as to find no longer sufficient rewards within it, they emigrate to places where they are more in demand; if in consequence of the accumulation of material capital, the rates of interest fall so considerably that the smaller capitalist can no longer live on them, he tries to invest his money more satisfactorily in less wealthy countries.]

A true principle, therefore, underlies the system of the popular school, but a principle which must be recognised and applied by science if its design to enlighten practice is to be fulfilled, an idea which practice cannot ignore without getting astray; only the school has omitted to take into consideration the nature of nationalities and their special interests and conditions, and to bring these into accord with the idea of universal union and an everlasting peace.

The popular school has assumed as being actually in existence a state of things which has yet to come into existence. It assumes the existence of a universal union and a state of perpetual peace, and deduces therefrom the great benefits of free trade. In this manner it confounds effects with causes. Among the provinces and states which are already politically united, there exists a state of perpetual peace; from this political union originates their commercial union, and it is in consequence of the perpetual peace thus maintained that the commercial union has become so beneficial to them. All examples which history can show are those in which the political union has led the way, and the commercial union has followed.[1] Not a single instance can be adduced in which the latter has taken the lead, and the former has grown up from it. That, however, under the existing conditions of the world, the result of general free trade would not be a universal republic, but, on the contrary, a universal subjection of the less advanced nations to the supremacy of the predominant manufacturing, commercial, and naval power, is a conclusion for which the reasons are very strong and, according to our views, irrefragable. A universal

[1] This statement was probably accurate up to the period when List wrote, but a notable exception to it may now be adduced. The commercial union of the various German states under the Zollverein preceded by many years their political union under the Empire, and powerfully promoted it.—Tr.

republic (in the sense of Henry IV. and of the Abbé St. Pierre), i.e. a union of the nations of the earth whereby they recognise the same conditions of right among themselves and renounce self-redress, can only be realised if a large number of nationalities attain to as nearly the same degree as possible of industry and civilisation, political cultivation, and power. Only with the gradual formation of this union can free trade be developed, only as a result of this union can it confer on all nations the same great advantages which are now experienced by those provinces and states which are politically united. [The system of protection, inasmuch as it forms the only means of placing those nations which are far behind in civilisation on equal terms with the one predominating nation (which, however, never received at the hands of Nature a perpetual right to a monopoly of manufacture, but which merely gained an advance over others in point of time), the system of protection regarded from this point of view appears to be the most efficient means of furthering the final union of nations, and hence also of promoting true freedom of trade.] And national economy appears from this point of view to be that science which, correctly appreciating the existing interests and the individual circumstances of nations, teaches how *every separate nation* can be raised to that stage of industrial development in which union with other nations equally well developed, and consequently freedom of trade, can become possible and useful to it.

The popular school, however, has mixed up both doctrines with one another ; it has fallen into the grave error of judging of the conditions of nations according to purely cosmopolitical principles, and of ignoring from merely political reasons the cosmopolitical tendency of the productive powers.

Only by ignoring the cosmopolitical tendency of the productive powers could Malthus be led into the error of desiring to restrict the increase of population, or Chalmers and Torrens maintain more recently the strange idea that augmentation of capital and unrestricted production are evils the restriction of which the welfare of the community imperatively demands, or Sismondi declare that manufactures are things injurious to the community. Their theory in this case resembles Saturn, who devours his own children—the same theory which allows that from the increase of population, of capital and machinery, division of labour takes place, and explains from this the welfare of society, finally considers these forces as monsters which threaten the prosperity of nations, because it merely regards the present conditions of individual nations, and does not take into consideration the conditions of the whole globe and the future progress of mankind.

It is not true that population increases in a larger proportion than production of the means of subsistence; it is at least foolish to assume such disproportion, or to attempt to prove it by artificial calculations or sophistical arguments, so long as on the globe a mass of natural forces still lies inert by means of which ten times or perhaps a hundred times more people than are now living can be sustained. It is mere narrow-mindedness to consider the present extent of the productive forces as the test of how many persons could be supported on a given area of land. The savage, the hunter, and the fisherman, according to his own calculation, would not find room enough for one million persons, the shepherd not for ten millions, the raw agriculturist not for one hundred millions on the whole globe; and yet two hundred millions are living at present in Europe alone. The culture of the potato and of food-yielding plants, and the more recent improvements made in agriculture generally, have increased tenfold the productive powers of the human race for the creation of the means of subsistence. In the Middle Ages the yield of wheat of an acre of land in England was fourfold, to-day it is ten to twenty fold, and in addition to that five times more land is cultivated. In many European countries (the soil of which possesses the same natural fertility as that of England) the yield at present does not exceed fourfold. Who will venture to set further limits to the discoveries, inventions, and improvements of the human race? Agricultural chemistry is still in its infancy; who can tell that to-morrow, by means of a new invention or discovery, the produce of the soil may not be increased five or ten fold ? We already possess, in the artesian well, the means of converting unfertile wastes into rich corn fields ; and what unknown forces may not yet be hidden in the interior of the earth ? Let us merely suppose that through a new discovery we were enabled to produce heat everywhere very cheaply, and without the aid of the fuels at present known : what spaces of land could thus be utilised for cultivation, and in what an incalculable degree would the yield of a given area of land be increased ? If Malthus' doctrine appears to us in its tendency narrow-minded, it is also in the methods by which it could act an unnatural one, which destroys morality and power, and is simply horrible. It seeks to destroy a desire which nature uses as the most active means for inciting men to exert body and mind, and to awaken and support their nobler feelings—a desire to which humanity for the greater part owes its progress. It would elevate the most heartless egotism to the position of a law ; it requires us to close our hearts against the starving man, because if we hand him food and drink, another might starve in his place in thirty years' time. It substitutes cold calculation for sympathy. This doctrine tends to convert the hearts of men into stones. But what could be finally expected of a nation whose citizens should carry stones instead of hearts in their bosoms ? What else than the total destruction of all morality, and with it of all productive forces, and therefore of all the wealth, civilisation, and power of the nation ?

If in a nation the population increases more than the production of the means of subsistence, if capital accumulates at length to such an extent as no longer to find investment, if machinery throws a number of operatives out of work and manufactured goods accumulate to a large excess, this merely proves, that nature will not allow industry, civilisation, wealth, and power to fall exclusively to the lot of a single nation, or that a large portion of the globe suitable for cultivation should be merely inhabited by wild animals, and that the largest portion of the human race should remain sunk in savagery, ignorance, and poverty.

We have shown into what errors the school has fallen by judging the productive forces of the human race from a political point of view ; we have now also to point out the mistakes which it has committed by regarding the separate interests of nations from a cosmopolitcal point of view.

If a confederation of all nations existed in reality, as is the case with the separate states constituting the Union of North America, the excess of population, talents, skilled abilities, and material capital would flow over from England to the Continental states, in a similar manner to that in which it travels from the eastern states of the American Union to the western, provided that in the Continental states the same security for persons and property, the same constitution and general laws prevailed, and that the English Government was made subject to the united will of the universal confederation. Under these suppositions there would be no better way of raising all these countries to the same stage of wealth and cultivation as England than free trade. This is the argument of the school. But how would it tally with the actual operation of free trade under the existing conditions of the world ?

[The Britons as an independent and separate nation would henceforth take their national interest as the sole guide of their policy. The Englishman, from predilection for his language, for his laws, regulations, and habits, would wherever it was possible devote his powers and his capital to develop his own native industry, for which the system of free trade, by extending the market for English manufactures over all countries, would offer him sufficient opportunity; he would not readily take a fancy to establish manufactures in France or Germany. All excess of capital in England would be at once devoted to trading with foreign parts of the world. If the Englishman took it into his head to emigrate, or to invest his capital elsewhere than in England, he would as he now does prefer those more distant countries where he would find already existing his language, his laws, and regulations, rather than the benighted countries of the Continent. All England would thus be developed into one immense manufacturing city. Asia, Africa, and Australia

Marginal handwritten notes: Englishmen naturally look to the interests of England, including English manufacturers. This would extend to English colonies, to the detriment of Continental Europe, which would be little more than England's plantations, assuming free trade.

would be civilised by England, and covered with new states modelled after the English fashion. In time a world of English states would be formed, under the presidency of the mother state, in which the European Continental nations would be lost as unimportant, unproductive races. By this arrangement it would fall to the lot of France, together with Spain and Portugal, to supply this English world with the choicest wines, and to drink the bad ones herself: at most France might retain the manufacture of a little millinery. Germany would scarcely have more to supply this English world with than children's toys, wooden clocks, and philological writings, and sometimes also an auxiliary corps, who might sacrifice themselves to pine away in the deserts of Asia or Africa, for the sake of extending the manufacturing and commercial supremacy, the literature and language of England. It would not require many centuries before people in this English world would think and speak of the Germans and French in the same tone as we speak at present of the Asiatic nations.

True political science, however, regards such a result of universal free trade as a very unnatural one ; it will argue that had universal free trade been introduced at the time of the Hanseatic League, the German nationality instead of the English would have secured an advance in commerce and manufacture over all other countries.

It would be most unjust, even on cosmopolitical grounds, now to resign to the English all the wealth and power of the earth, merely because by them the political system of commerce was first established and the cosmopolitical principle for the most part ignored. In order to allow freedom of trade to operate naturally, the less advanced nations must first be raised by artificial measures to that stage of cultivation to which the English nation has been artificially elevated. In order that, through that cosmopolitical tendency of the powers of production to which we have alluded, the more distant parts of the world may not be benefited and enriched before the neighbouring European countries, those nations which feel themselves to be capable, owing to their moral, intellectual, social, and political circumstances, of developing

The lesson to be learned

a manufacturing power of their own must adopt the system of protection as the most effectual means for this purpose. The effects of this system for the purpose in view are of two kinds; in the first place, by gradually excluding foreign manufactured articles from our markets, a surplus would be occasioned in foreign nations, of workmen, talents, and capital, which must seek employment abroad; and secondly, by the premium which our system of protection would offer to the immigration into our country of workmen, talents, and capital, that excess of productive power would be induced to find employment with us, instead of emigrating to distant parts of the world and to colonies. Political science refers to history, and inquires whether England has not in former times drawn from Germany, Italy, Holland, France, Spain, and Portugal by these means a mass of productive power. She asks: Why does the cosmopolitical school, when it pretends to weigh in the balance the advantages and the disadvantages of the system of protection, utterly ignore this great and remarkable instance of the results of that system?

[handwritten margin note: I.e., don't listen to British political economists]

CHAPTER XII.

THE THEORY OF THE POWERS OF PRODUCTION AND THE THEORY OF VALUES.

ADAM SMITH's celebrated work is entitled, ' The Nature and Causes of the Wealth of Nations.' The founder of the prevailing economical school has therein indicated the double point of view from which the economy of nations, like that of private separate individuals, should be regarded.

The causes of wealth are something totally different from *wealth itself.* [A person may possess wealth, i.e. exchangeable value ; if, however, he does not possess the power of producing objects of more value than he consumes, he will become poorer. A person may be poor ; if he, however, possesses the power of producing a larger amount of valuable articles than he consumes, he becomes rich.]

The power of producing wealth is therefore infinitely more important than *wealth itself*; it insures not only the possession and the increase of what has been gained, but also the replacement of what has been lost. This is still more the case with entire nations (who cannot live out of mere rentals) than with private individuals. Germany has been devastated in every century by pestilence, by famine, or by civil or foreign wars ; she has, nevertheless, always retained a great portion of her powers of production, and has thus quickly reattained some degree of prosperity ; while rich and mighty but despot- and priest-ridden Spain, notwithstanding her comparative enjoyment of internal peace,[1] has sunk deeper into poverty and misery. The

[1] This is true respecting Spain up to the period of her invasion by Napoleon, but not subsequently. Our author's conclusions are, however, scarcely invalidated by that exception.—TR.

same sun still shines on the Spaniards, they still possess the same area of territory, their mines are still as rich, they are still the same people as before the discovery of America, and before the introduction of the Inquisition; but that nation has gradually lost her powers of production, and has therefore become poor and miserable.   The War of Independence of the United States of America cost that nation hundreds of millions, but her powers of production were immeasurably strengthened by gaining independence, and it was for this reason that in the course of a few years after the peace she obtained immeasurably greater riches than she had ever possessed before.   If we compare the state of France in the year 1809 with that of the year 1839, what a difference in favour of the latter!   Nevertheless, France has in the interim lost her sovereignty over a large portion of the European continent; she has suffered two devastating invasions, and had to pay milliards of money in war contributions and indemnities.

It was impossible that so clear an intellect as Adam Smith possessed could altogether ignore the difference between wealth and its causes and the overwhelming influence of these causes on the condition of nations.   In the introduction to his work, he says in clear words in effect: 'Labour forms the fund from which every nation derives its wealth, and the increase of wealth depends first on the *productive power* of labour, namely on the degree of skill, dexterity, and judgment with which the labour of the nation is generally applied, and secondly on the proportion between the number of those employed productively and the number of those who are not so employed.'   From this we see how clearly Smith in general perceived that the condition of nations is principally dependent on the sum of their *productive powers*.

It does not, however, appear to be the plan of nature that complete sciences should spring already perfected from the brain of individual thinkers.   It is evident that Smith was too exclusively possessed by the cosmopolitical idea of the physiocrats, 'universal freedom of trade,' and by his own great discovery, 'the division of labour,' to follow up the idea of the importance to a nation of its *powers of pro-duction*. However much science may be indebted to him in respect of the remaining parts of his work, the idea 'division of labour' seemed to him his most brilliant thought. It was calculated to secure for his book a name, and for himself posthumous fame.

He had too much worldly wisdom not to perceive that whoever wishes to sell a precious jewel does not bring the treasure to market most profitably by burying it in a sack of wheat, however useful the grains of wheat may be, but better by exposing it at the forefront. He had too much experience not to know that a *débutant* (and he was this as regards political economy at the time of the publication of his work) who in the first act creates a *furore* is easily excused if in the following ones he only occasionally raises himself above mediocrity; he had every motive for making the introduction to his book, the doctrine of division of labour. Smith has not been mistaken in his calculations; his first chapter has made the fortune of his book, and founded his authority as an economist.

However, we on our part believe ourselves able to prove that just this zeal to put the important discovery '*division of labour*' in an advantageous light, has hindered Adam Smith from following up the idea '*productive power*' (which has been expressed by him in the introduction, and also frequently afterwards, although merely incidentally) and from exhibiting his doctrines in a much more perfect form. By the great value which he attached to his idea '*division of labour*' he has evidently been misled into representing labour itself as the 'fund' of all the wealth of nations, although he himself clearly perceives and also states that the productiveness of labour principally depends on the degree of skill and judgment with which the labour is performed. We ask, can it be deemed scientific reasoning if we assign as the cause of a phenomenon that which in itself is the result of a number of deeper lying causes? It cannot be doubted that all wealth is obtained by means of mental and bodily exertions (labour), but yet from that circumstance no reason is indicated from which useful conclusions may be drawn; for history teaches that whole nations have, in spite of the exertions and of the thrift of their citizens, fallen into poverty and misery. Whoever desires to know and investigate how one nation from a state of poverty and barbarism has attained to one of wealth and prosperity, and how another has fallen from a condition of wealth and well-being into one of poverty and misery, has always, after receiving the information that labour is the cause of wealth and idleness the cause of poverty (a remark which King Solomon made long before Adam Smith), to put the further question, what are the causes of labour, and what the causes of idleness?

It would be more correct to describe the limbs of men (the head, hands, and feet) as the causes of wealth (we should thus at least approach far nearer to the truth), and the question then presents itself, what is it that induces these heads, arms, and hands to produce, and calls into activity these exertions? What else can it be than the spirit which animates the individuals, the social order which renders their energy fruitful, and the powers of nature which they are in a position to make use of? The more a man perceives that he must provide for the future, the more his intelligence and feelings incite him to secure the future of his nearest connections, and to promote their well-being; the more he has been from his youth accustomed to fore-thought and activity, the more his nobler feelings have been developed, and body and mind cultivated, the finer examples that he has witnessed from his youth, the more opportunities he has had for utilising his mental and bodily powers for the improvement of his condition, also the less he has been restrained in his legitimate activity, the more successful his past endeavours have been, and the more their fruits have been secured to him, the more he has been able to obtain public recognition and esteem by orderly conduct and ac-tivity, and the less his mind suffers from prejudices, super-stition, false notions, and ignorance, so much the more will he exert his mind and limbs for the object of production, so much the more will he be able to accomplish, and so much the better will he make use of the fruits of his labour.

However, most depends in all these respects on the conditions of the society in which the individual has been brought up, and turns upon this, whether science and arts flourish, and public institutions and laws tend to promote religious character, morality and intelligence, security for person and for property, freedom and justice ; whether in the nation all the factors of material prosperity, agriculture, manufactures, and trade, have been equally and harmoniously cultivated ; whether the power of the nation is strong enough to secure to its individual citizens progress in wealth and education from generation to generation, and to enable them not merely to utilise the natural powers of their own country to their fullest extent, but also, by foreign trade and the possession of colonies, to render the natural powers of foreign countries serviceable to their own.

Adam Smith has on the whole recognised the nature of these powers so little, that he does not even assign a productive character to the mental labours of those who maintain laws and order, and cultivate and promote instruction, religion, science, and art. His investigations are limited to that human activity which creates material values. With regard to this, he certainly recognises that its productiveness depends on the ' skill and judgment ' with which it is exercised ; but in his investigations as to the causes of this skill and judgment, he does not go farther than the division of labour, and that he illustrates solely by exchange, augmentation of material capital, and extension of markets. His doctrine at once sinks deeper and deeper into materialism, particularism, and individualism. If he had followed up the idea ' *productive power*,' without allowing his mind to be dominated by the idea of ' value,' ' exchangeable value,' he would have been led to perceive that an independent *theory of the 'productive power* ' must be considered by the side of a ' *theory of values* ' in order to explain the economical phenomena. But he thus fell into the mistake of explaining mental forces from material circumstances and conditions, and thereby laid the foundation for all the absurdities and contradictions from which his school (as we propose to prove) suffers up to the present day, and to which alone it must be attributed that the doctrines of political economy are those which are the least accessible to the most intelligent minds. That Smith's school teaches nothing else than the theory of values, is not only seen from the fact that it bases its doctrine everywhere on the conception of 'value of exchange,' but also from the definition which it gives of its doctrine. It is (says J. B. Say) that science which teaches how riches, or exchangeable values, are produced, distributed, and consumed. This is undoubtedly not the science which teaches how the *productive powers* are awakened and developed, and how they become repressed and destroyed. M'Culloch calls it explicitly ' *the science of values*,' and recent English writers ' *the science of exchange*.'

Examples from private economy will best illustrate the difference between the theory of productive powers and the theory of values.

Let us suppose the case of two fathers of families, both being landed proprietors, each of whom saves yearly 1,000 thalers and has five sons. The one puts out his savings at interest, and keeps his sons at common hard work, while the other employs his savings in educating two of his sons as skilful and intelligent landowners, and in enabling the other three to learn a trade after their respective tastes; the former acts according to the theory of values, the latter according to the theory of productive powers. The first at his death may prove much richer than the second in mere exchangeable value, but it is quite otherwise as respects productive powers. The estate of the latter is divided into two parts, and every part will by the aid of improved management yield as much total produce as the whole did before; while the remaining three sons have by their talents obtained abundant means of maintenance. The landed property of the former will be divided into five parts, and every part will be worked in as bad a manner as the whole was heretofore. In the latter family a mass of different mental forces and talents is awakened and cultivated, which will increase from generation to generation, every succeeding generation possessing more power of obtaining material wealth than the preceding one, while in the former family stupidity and poverty must increase with the diminution of the shares in the landed property. So the slaveholder increases by slave-breeding the sum of his values of exchange, but he ruins the productive forces of future generations. All expenditure in the instruction of youth, the promotion of justice, defence of nations, &c. is a consumption of present values for the behoof of the productive powers. The greatest portion of the consumption of a nation is used for the education of the future generation, for promotion and nourishment of the future national productive powers.

The Christian religion, monogamy, abolition of slavery and of vassalage, hereditability of the throne, invention of printing, of the press, of the postal system, of money, weights and measures, of the calendar, of watches, of police, the introduction of the principle of freehold property, of means of transport, are rich sources of productive power. To be convinced of this, we need only compare the condition of the European states with that of the Asiatic ones. In order duly to estimate the influence which liberty of thought and conscience has on the productive forces of nations, we need only read the history of England and then that of Spain. The publicity of the administration of justice, trial by jury, parliamentary legislation, public control of State administration, self-administration of the commonalties and municipalities, liberty of the press, liberty of association for useful purposes, impart to the citizens of constitutional states, as also to their public functionaries, a degree of energy and power which can hardly be produced by other means. We can scarcely conceive of any law or any public legal decision which would not exercise a greater or smaller in-fluence on the increase or decrease of the productive power of the nation.[1]

If we consider merely bodily labour as the cause of wealth, how can we then explain why modern nations are incomparably richer, more populous, more powerful, and

[1] Say states in his *Economie Politique Pratique*, vol. iii. p. 242, 'Les lois ne peuvent pas créer des richesses.' Certainly they cannot do this, but they create productive power, which is more important than riches, i.e. than possession of values of exchange.

prosperous than the nations of ancient times ? The ancient nations employed (in proportion to the whole population) infinitely more hands, the work was much harder, each individual possessed much more land, and yet the masses were much worse fed and clothed than is the case in modern nations. In order to explain these phenomena, we must refer to the progress which has been made in the course of the last thousand years in sciences and arts, domestic and public regulations, cultivation of the mind and capabilities of production. The present state of the nations is the result of the accumulation of all discoveries, inventions, improvements, perfections, and exertions of all generations which have lived before us ; they form the *mental capital of the present human race*, and every separate nation is productive only in the proportion in which it has known how to appropriate these attainments of former generations and to increase them by its own acquirements, in which the natural capabilities of its territory, its extent and geographical position, its population and political power, have been able to develop as completely and symmetrically as possible all sources of wealth within its boundaries, and to extend its moral, intellectual, commercial, and political influence over less advanced nations and especially over the affairs of the world.

The popular school of economists would have us believe that politics and political power cannot be taken into consideration in political economy. So far as it makes only values and exchange the subjects of its investigations, this may be correct ; we can define the ideas of value and capital, profit, wages, and rent ; we can resolve them into their elements, and speculate on what may influence their rising or falling &c. without thereby taking into account the political circumstances of the nation. Clearly, however, these matters appertain as much to private economy as to the economy of whole nations. We have merely to consider the history of Venice, of the Hanseatic League, of Portugal, Holland, and England, in order to perceive what reciprocal influence material wealth and political power exercise on each other.

The school also always falls into the strangest inconsistencies whenever this reciprocal influence forces itself on their consideration. Let us here only call to mind the remarkable dictum of Adam Smith on the English Navigation Laws.[1]

The popular school, inasmuch as it does not duly consider the nature of the powers of production, and does not take into account the conditions of nations in their aggregate, disregards especially the importance of developing in an equal ratio agriculture, manufactures and commerce, political power and internal wealth, and disregards especially the value of a manufacturing power belonging specially to the nation and fully developed in all its branches. It commits the error of placing manufacturing power in the same category with agricultural power, and of speaking of labour, natural power, capital &c. in general terms without considering the differences which exist between them. It does not perceive that between a State devoted merely to agriculture and a State possessing both agriculture and manufactures, a much greater difference exists than between a pastoral State and an agricultural one. In a condition of merely agricultural industry, caprice and slavery, superstition and ignorance, want of means of culture, of trade, and of transport, poverty and political weakness exist. In the merely agricultural State only the least portion of the mental and bodily powers existing in the nation is awakened and developed, and only the least part of the powers and resources placed by nature at its disposal can be made use of, while little or no capital can be accumulated.

Let us compare Poland with England : both nations at one time were in the same stage of culture ; and now what a difference. Manufactories and manufactures are the mothers and children of municipal liberty, of intelligence, of the arts and sciences, of internal and external commerce, of navigation and improvements in transport, of civilisation and political power. They are the chief means of liberating agriculture from its chains, and of elevating it to a commercial character and to a degree of art and science, by

[1] *Wealth of Nations*, Book IV. chap. ii.

which the rents, farming profits, and wages are increased, and greater value is given to landed property. The popular school has attributed this civilising power to foreign trade, but in that it has confounded the mere exchanger with the originator. Foreign manufactures furnish the goods for the foreign trade, which the latter conveys to us, and which occasion consumption of products and raw materials which we give in exchange for the goods in lieu of money payments.

If, however, trade in the manufactures of far distant lands exercises admittedly so beneficial an influence on our agricultural industry, how much more beneficial must the influence be of those manufactures which are bound up with us locally, commercially, and politically, which not only take from us a small portion, but the largest portion of their requirements of food and of raw materials, which are not made dearer to us by great costs of transport, our trade in which cannot be interrupted by the chance of foreign manufacturing nations learning to supply their own wants themselves, or by wars and prohibitory import duties ?

We now see into what extraordinary mistakes and contradictions the popular school has fallen in making material wealth or value of exchange the sole object of its investigations, and by regarding mere bodily labour as the sole productive power.

The man who breeds pigs is, according to this school, a productive member of the community, but he who educates men is a mere non-productive. The maker of bagpipes or jews-harps for sale is a productive, while the great composers and virtuosos are non-productive simply because that which they play cannot be brought into the market. The physician who saves the lives of his patients does not belong to the productive class, but on the contrary the chemist's boy does so, although the values of exchange (viz. the pills) which he produces may exist only for a few minutes before they pass into a valueless condition. A Newton, a Watt, or a Kepler is not so productive as a donkey, a horse, or a draught-ox (a class of labourers who have been recently introduced by M'Culloch into the series of the productive members of human society).

We must not believe that J. B. Say has remedied this defect in the doctrine of Adam Smith by his fiction of '*immaterial goods*' or products; he has thus merely somewhat varnished over the folly of its results, but not raised it out of its intrinsic absurdity. The mental (immaterial) producers are merely productive, according to his views, because they are remunerated with values of exchange, and because their attainments have been obtained by sacrificing values of exchange, and *not because they produce productive powers.*[1] They merely seem to him an accumulated capital. M'Culloch goes still further; he says that man is as much a product of labour as the machine which he produces, and it appears to him that in all economical investigations he must be regarded from this point of view. He thinks that Smith comprehended the correctness of this principle, only he did not deduce the correct conclusion from it. Among other things he draws the conclusion that eating and drinking are productive occupations. Thomas Cooper values a clever American lawyer at 3,000 dollars, which is about three times as much as the value of a strong slave.

The errors and contradictions of the prevailing school to which we have drawn attention, can be easily corrected from the standpoint of *the theory of the productive powers.* Certainly those who fatten pigs or prepare pills are productive, but the instructors of youths and of adults, virtuosos, musicians, physicians, judges, and administrators, are productive in a much higher degree. The former *produce values of exchange*, and the latter *productive powers*, some by enabling the future generation to become producers, others by furthering the morality and religious character of the present generation, a third by ennobling and raising the powers of the human mind, a fourth by preserving the productive powers of his patients, a fifth by rendering human rights and justice secure, a sixth by constituting and pro-

[1] From the great number of passages wherein J. B. Say explains this view, we merely quote the newest—from the sixth volume of *Economie Politique Pratique*, p. 307: 'Le talent d'un avocat, d'un médecin, qui a été acquis au prix de quelque sacrifice et qui produit un revenu, est une valeur capitale, non transmissible à la vérité, mais qui réside néanmoins dans un corps visible, celui de la personne qui le possède.'

tecting public security, a seventh by his art and by the enjoyment which it occasions fitting men the better to produce values of exchange. In the doctrine of mere values, these *producers of the productive powers* can of course only be taken into consideration so far as their services are rewarded by values of exchange; and this manner of regarding their services may in some instances have its practical use, as e.g. in the doctrine of public taxes, inasmuch as these have to be satisfied by values of exchange. But whenever our consideration is given to the nation (as a whole and in its international relations) it is utterly insufficient, and leads to a series of narrow-minded and false views.

The prosperity of a nation is not, as Say believes, greater in the proportion in which it has amassed more wealth (i.e. values of exchange), but in the proportion in which it has more *developed its powers of production*. Although laws and public institutions do not produce immediate values, they nevertheless produce productive powers, and Say is mistaken if he maintains that nations have been enabled to become wealthy under all forms of government, and that by means of laws no wealth can be created. The foreign trade of a nation must not be estimated in the way in which individual merchants judge it, solely and only according to the theory of values (i.e. by regarding merely the gain at any particular moment of some material advantage); the nation is bound to keep steadily in view all these conditions on which its present and future existence, prosperity, and power depend.

The nation must sacrifice and give up a measure of material property in order to gain culture, skill, and powers of united production; it must sacrifice some present advantages in order to insure to itself future ones. If, therefore, a manufacturing power developed in all its branches forms a fundamental condition of all higher advances in civilisation, material prosperity, and political power in every nation (a fact which, we think, we have proved from history); if it be true (as we believe we can prove) that in the present conditions of the world a new unprotected manufacturing power cannot possibly be raised up under free competition with a power which has long since grown in strength and is protected on its own territory ; how can anyone possibly undertake to prove by arguments only based on the mere theory of values, that a nation ought to buy its goods like individual merchants, at places where they are to be had the cheapest—that we act foolishly if we manufacture anything at all which can be got cheaper from abroad—that we ought to place the industry of the nation at the mercy of the self-interest of individuals—that protective duties constitute monopolies, which are granted to the individual home manufacturers at the expense of the nation ? It is true that protective duties at first increase the price of manufactured goods; but it is just as true, and moreover acknowledged by the prevailing economical school, that in the course of time, by the nation being enabled to build up a completely developed manufacturing power of its own, those goods are produced more cheaply at home than the price at which they can be imported from foreign parts.   If, therefore, a sacrifice of *value* is caused by protective duties, it is made good by the gain of a *power of production*, which not only secures to the nation an infinitely greater amount of material goods, but also industrial independence in case of war.   Through industrial independence and the internal prosperity derived from it the nation obtains the means for successfully carrying on foreign trade and for extending its mercantile marine ; it increases its civilisation, perfects its institutions internally, and strengthens its external power. A nation capable of developing a manufacturing power, if it makes use of the system of protection, thus acts quite in the same spirit as that landed proprietor did who by the sacrifice of some material wealth allowed some of his children to learn a productive trade.

Into what mistakes the prevailing economical school has fallen by judging conditions according to the mere theory of values which ought properly to be judged according to the theory of powers of production, may be seen very clearly by the judgment which J. B. Say passes upon the bounties which foreign countries sometimes offer in order to facilitate exportation; he maintains that ' *these are presents made to our nation.'* Now if we suppose that France considers a protective duty of twenty-five per cent. sufficient for her not yet perfectly developed manufactures, while England were to grant a bounty on exportation of thirty per cent., what would be the consequence of the 'present' which in this manner the English would make to the French ? The French consumers would obtain for a few years the manufactured articles which they needed much cheaper than hitherto, but the French manufactories would be ruined, and millions of men be reduced to beggary or obliged to emigrate, or to devote themselves to agriculture for employment. Under the most favourable circumstances, the present consumers and customers of the French agriculturists would be converted into competitors with the latter, agricultural production would be increased, and the consumption lowered. The necessary consequence would be diminution in value of the products, decline in the value of property, national poverty and national weakness in France. The English 'present' in mere value would be dearly paid for in loss of power; it would seem like the present which the Sultan is wont to make to his pashas by sending them valuable *silken cords.*

Since the time when the Trojans were 'presented' by the Greeks with a wooden horse, the acceptance of 'presents' from other nations has become for the nation which receives them a very questionable transaction. The English have given the Continent presents of immense value in the form of subsidies, but the Continental nations have paid for them dearly by the loss of power. These subsidies acted like a bounty on exportation in favour of the English, and were detrimental to the German manufactories.[1] If England bound herself to-day to supply the Germans gratuitously for years with all they required in manufactured articles, we could not recommend them to accept such an offer. If the English are enabled through new inventions to produce linen forty per cent. cheaper than the Germans can by using the old process, and if in the use of their new process they merely obtain a start of a few years over the Germans, in such a case, were it not for protective duties, one of the

[1] See Appendix A.

most important and oldest branches of Germany's industry will be ruined. It will be as if a limb of the body of the German nation had been lost. And who would be consoled for the loss of an arm by knowing that he had nevertheless bought his shirts forty per cent. cheaper?

If the English very often find occasion to offer presents to foreign nations, very different are the forms in which this is done; it is not unfrequently done against their will; always does it behove foreign nations well to consider whether or not the present should be accepted. Through their position as the manufacturing and commercial monopolists of the world, their manufactories from time to time fall into the state which they call 'glut,' and which arises from what they call 'overtrading.' At such periods everybody throws his stock of goods into the steamers. After the lapse of eight days the goods are offered for sale in Hamburg, Berlin, or Frankfort, and after three weeks in New York, at fifty per cent. under their real value. The English manufacturers suffer for the moment, but they are saved, and they compensate themselves later on by better prices. The German and American manufacturers receive the blows which were deserved by the English—they are ruined. The English nation merely sees the fire and hears the report of the explosion; the fragments fall down in other countries, and if their inhabitants complain of bloody heads, the intermediate merchants and dealers say, 'The crisis has done it all!' If we consider how often by such crises the whole manufacturing power, the system of credit, nay the agriculture, and generally the whole economical system of the nations who are placed in free competition with England, are shaken to their foundations, and that these nations have afterwards notwithstanding richly to recompense the English manufacturers by higher prices, ought we not then to become very sceptical as to the propriety of the commercial conditions of nations being regulated according to the mere theory of values and according to cosmopolitical principles? The prevailing economical school has never deemed it expedient to elucidate the causes and effects of such commercial crises.

The great statesmen of all modern nations, almost without exception, have comprehended the great influence of manufactures and manufactories on the wealth, civilisation, and power of nations, and the necessity of protecting them. Edward III. comprehended this like Elizabeth; Frederick the Great like Joseph II.; Washington like Napoleon. Without entering into the depths of the theory, their foreseeing minds comprehended the nature of industry in its entirety, and appreciated it correctly. It was reserved for the school of physiocrats to regard this nature from another point of view in consequence of a sophistical line of reasoning. Their castle in the air has disappeared; the more modern economical school itself has destroyed it; but even the latter has also not disentangled itself from the original errors, but has merely advanced somewhat farther from them. Since it did not recognise the difference between productive power and mere values of exchange, and did not investigate the former independently of the latter, but subordinated it to the theory of values of exchange, it was impossible for that school to arrive at the perception how greatly the nature of the agricultural productive power differs from the nature of the manufacturing productive power. It does not discern that through the development of a manufacturing industry in an agricultural nation a mass of mental and bodily powers, of natural powers and natural resources, and of instrumental powers too (which latter the prevailing school terms 'capital'), is brought to bear, and brought into use, which had not previously been active, and would never have come into activity but for the formation and development of an internal manufacturing power; it imagines that by the establishment of manufacturing industry these forces must be taken away from agriculture, and transferred to manufacture, whereas the latter to a great extent is a perfectly new and additional power, which, very far indeed from increasing at the expense of the agricultural interest, is often the means of helping that interest to attain a higher degree of prosperity and development.

CHAPTER XIII.

THE NATIONAL DIVISION OF COMMERCIAL OPERATIONS AND THE CONFEDERATION OF THE NATIONAL PRODUCTIVE FORCES.

THE school is indebted to its renowned founder for the discovery of that natural law which it calls ' *division of labour*,' but neither Adam Smith nor any of his successors have thoroughly investigated its essential nature and character, or followed it out to its most important consequences.

The expression ' *division of labour* ' is an indefinite one, and must necessarily produce a false or indefinite idea.

It is ' *division of labour* ' if one savage on one and the same day goes hunting or fishing, cuts down wood, repairs his wigwam, and prepares arrows, nets, and clothes ; but it is also ' *division of labour* ' if (as Adam Smith mentions as an example) ten different persons share in the different occupations connected with the manufacture of a pin : the former is an objective, and the latter a subjective division of labour ; the former hinders, the latter furthers production. The essential difference between both is, that in the former instance one person divides his work so as to produce *various* objects, while in the latter *several* persons share in the production of a single object.

Both operations, on the other hand, may be called with equal correctness *a union of labour* ; the savage unites various tasks in his person, while in the case of the pin manufacture various persons are united in one work of production in common.

The essential character of the natural law from which the popular school explains such important phenomena in social economy, is evidently not merely *a division of labour*, but *a division of different commercial operations between several individuals*, and at the same time *a confederation or union of various energies, intelligences, and powers on behalf of a common production*. The cause of the productiveness of these operations is not merely that *division*, but essentially this *union*. Adam Smith well perceives this himself when he states, ' The necessaries of life of the lowest members of society are a product of *joint* labour and of the co-operation of a number of individuals.' [1]   What a pity that he did not follow out this idea (which he so clearly expresses) of *united labour*.

If we continue to consider the example of the pin manufacture adduced by Adam Smith in illustration of the advantages of division of labour, and seek for the causes of the phenomenon that ten persons united in that manufacture can produce an infinitely larger number of pins than if every one carried on the entire pin manufacture separately, we find that the division of commercial operations without *combination of the productive powers towards one common object* could but little further this production.

In order to create such a result, the different individuals must co-operate bodily as well as mentally, and work together.   The one who makes the heads of the pins must be certain of the co-operation of the one who makes the points if he does not want to run the risk of producing pin heads in vain.   The labour operations of all must be in the proper proportion to one another, the workmen must live as near to one another as possible, and their co-operation must be insured.   Let us suppose e.g. that every one of these ten workmen lives in a different country ; how often might their co-operation be interrupted by wars, interruptions of transport, commercial crises, &c. ; how greatly would the cost of the product be increased, and consequently the advantage of the division of operation diminished ; and would not the separation or secession of a single person from the union, throw all the others out of work ?

The popular school, because it has regarded the division of operation alone as the essence of this natural law, has committed the error of applying it merely to the separate

[1] *Wealth of Nations*, Book I. chap. i.

manufactory or farm; it has not perceived that the same law extends its action especially over the *whole manufacturing* and *agricultural power*, over *the whole economy of the nation.*

As the pin manufactory only prospers by the confederation of the productive force of the individuals, so does every kind of manufacture prosper only by the confederation of its productive forces with those of all other kinds of manufacture. For the success of a machine manufactory, for instance, it is necessary that the mines and metal works should furnish it with the necessary materials, and that all the hundred different sorts of manufactories which require machines, should buy their products from it. Without machine manufactories, a nation would in time of war be exposed to the danger of losing the greater portion of its manufacturing power.

In like manner the entire manufacturing industry of a State in connection with its agricultural interest, and the latter in connection with the former, will prosper the more the nearer they are placed to one another, and the less they are interrupted in their mutual exchanges with one another. The advantages of their confederation under one and the same political Power in times of war, of national differences, of commercial crises, failure of crops, &c., are not less perceptible than are the advantages of the union of the persons belonging to a pin manufactory under one and the same roof.

Smith affirms that the division of labour is less applicable to agriculture than to manufactures.[1] Smith had in view only the separate manufactory and the separate farm. He has, however, neglected to extend his principle over whole districts and provinces. Nowhere has the division of commercial operations and the confederation of the productive powers greater influence than where every district and every province is in a position to devote itself exclusively, or at least chiefly, to those branches of agricultural production for which they are mostly fitted by nature. In one district corn and hops chiefly thrive, in another vines and fruit, in a third timber production and cattle rearing &c. If every district is devoted to all these branches of produc-

---

[1] *Wealth of Nations*, Book I. chap. i.

tion, it is clear that its labour and its land cannot be nearly so productive as if every separate district were devoted mainly to those branches of production for which it is specially adapted by nature, and as if it exchanged the surplus of its own special products for the surplus produce of those provinces which in the production of other necessaries of life and raw materials possess a natural advantage equally peculiar to themselves. This division of commercial operations, this confederation of the productive forces occupied in agriculture, can only take place in a country which has attained the greatest development of all branches of manufacturing industry ; for in such a country only can a great demand for the greatest variety of products exist, or the demand for the surplus of agricultural productions be so certain and considerable that the producer can feel certain of disposing of any quantity of his surplus produce during this or at least during next year at suitable prices ; in such a country only can considerable capital be devoted to speculation in the produce of the country and holding stocks of it, or great improvements in transport, such as canals and railway systems, lines of steamers, improved roads, be carried out profitably ; and only by means of thoroughly good means of transport can every district or province convey the surplus of its peculiar products to all other provinces, even to the most distant ones, and procure in return supplies of the peculiar products of the latter. Where everybody supplies himself with what he requires, there is but little opportunity for exchange, and therefore no need for costly facilities of transport.

We may notice how the augmentation of the powers of production in consequence of the separation of occupations and the co-operation of the powers of individuals begins in the separate manufactory and extends to the united nation. The manufactory prospers so much the more in proportion as the commercial operations are divided, the more closely the workmen are united, and the more the co-operation of each person is insured for the whole. The productive powers of every separate manufactory are also increased in proportion as the whole manufacturing power of the country is developed in all its branches, and the more intimately it is united with all other branches of industry. The agricultural power of production is so much greater the more intimately a manufacturing power developed in all its branches is united locally, commercially, and politically with agriculture. In proportion as the manufacturing power is thus developed will the division of the commercial operations and the co-operation of the productive powers in agriculture also develop themselves and be raised to the highest stage of perfection. That nation will therefore possess most productive power, and will consequently be the richest, which has cultivated manufacturing industry in all branches within its territory to the highest perfection, and whose territory and agricultural production is large enough to supply its manufacturing population with the largest part of the necessaries of life and raw materials which they require.

Let us now consider the opposite side of this argument. A nation which possesses merely agriculture, and merely the most indispensable industries, is in want of the first and most necessary division of commercial operations among its inhabitants, and of the most important half of its productive powers, indeed it is in want of a useful division of commercial operations even in the separate branches of agriculture itself. A nation thus imperfect will not only be merely half as productive as a perfect nation, but with an equal or even with a much larger territory, with an equal or a much larger population, it will perhaps scarcely obtain a fifth, probably scarcely a tenth, part of that material wealth which a perfect nation is able to procure ; and this for the same reason owing to which in a very complicated manufactory ten persons produce not merely ten times more, but perhaps thirty times more, than one person, or a man with one arm cannot merely work half as little, but infinitely less, than a man with two arms. This loss in productive power will be so much greater, the more that the manufacturing operations can be furthered by machinery, and the less that machinery can be applied in agriculture. A part of the productive power which the agricultural nation thus loses, will fall to the lot of that nation which exchanges its manufactured goods for agricultural products. This will, however, be a positive loss only in case the agricultural nation has already reached that stage of civilisation and political development which is necessary for the establishment of a manufacturing power. If it has not yet attained that stage, and still remains in a barbarous or half-, civilised state, if its agricultural power of production has not yet developed itself even from the most primitive condition, if by the importation of foreign fabrics and the exportation of raw products its prosperity nevertheless increases considerably from year to year, and its mental and social powers continue to be awakened and increased, if such commerce as it can thus carry on is not interrupted by foreign prohibition of importation of raw products, or by wars, or if the territory of the agricultural nation is situated in a tropical climate, the gain on both sides will then be equal and in conformity with the laws of nature, because under the influence of such an exchange of the native products for foreign fabrics, a nation so situated will attain to civilisation and development of its productive powers more quickly and safely than when it has to develop them entirely out of its resources. If, however, the agricultural nation has already reached the culminating point of its agricultural development, as far as that can be attained by the influence of foreign commerce, or if the manufacturing nation refuses to take the products of the agricultural nation in exchange for its manufactured goods, and if nevertheless, owing to the successful competition of the manufacturing nation in the markets of the agricultural nation, no manufactures can spring up in the latter, in such a case the agricultural productive power of the agricultural nation is exposed to the danger of being crippled.

By a *crippled state of agriculture* we mean that state of things in which, from want of a powerful and steadily developing manufacturing industry, the entire increase of population tends to throw itself on agriculture for employment, consumes all the surplus agricultural production of the country, and as soon as it has considerably increased either has to emigrate or share with the agriculturists already in existence the land immediately at hand, till the landed property of every family has become so small that it produces only the most elementary and necessary portion of that family's requirements of food and raw materials, but no considerable surplus which it might exchange with the manufacturers for the manufactured products which it requires. Under a normal development of the productive powers of the State, the greater part of the increase of population of an agricultural nation (as soon as it has attained a certain degree of culture) should transfer itself to manufacturing industry, and the excess of the agricultural products should partly serve for supplying the manufacturing population with provisions and raw materials, and partly for procuring for the agriculturists the manufactured goods, machines, and utensils which they require for their consumption, and for the increase of their own production.

If this state of things sets in at the proper time, agricultural and industrial productive power will increase reciprocally, and indeed *ad infinitum*. The demand for agricultural products on the part of the industrial population will be so great, that no greater number of labourers will be diverted to agriculture, nor any greater division of the existing land be made, than is necessary to obtain the greatest possible surplus produce from it. In proportion to this surplus produce the population occupied in agriculture will be enabled to consume the products of the workmen employed in manufacturing. A continuous increase of the agricultural surplus produce will occasion a continuous increase of the demand for manufacturing workmen. The excess of the agricultural population will therefore continually find work in the manufactories, and the manufacturing population will at length not only equal the agricultural population in numbers, but will far exceed it. This latter is the condition of England; that which we formerly described is that of part of France and Germany. England was principally brought to this natural division of industrial pursuits between the two great branches of industry, by means of her flocks of sheep and woollen manufactures, which existed there on a large scale much sooner than in other countries. In other countries agriculture was crippled mainly by the influence of feudalism and arbitrary power. The possession of land gave influence and power, merely because by it a certain number of retainers could be maintained which the feudal proprietor could make use of in his feuds. The more vassals he possessed, so many more warriors he could muster. It was besides impossible, owing to the rudeness of those times, for the landed proprietor to consume his income in any other manner than by keeping a large number of servants, and he could not pay these better and attach them to his own person more surely than by giving them a bit of land to cultivate under the condition of rendering him personal service and of paying a smaller tax in produce. Thus the foundation for excessive division of the soil was laid in an artificial manner; and if in the present day the Government seeks by artificial means to alter that system, in so doing it is merely restoring the original state of things.

In order to restrain the continued depreciation of the agricultural power of a nation, and gradually to apply a remedy to that evil in so far as it is the result of previous institutions, no better means exists (apart from the promotion of emigration) than to establish an internal manufacturing power, by which the increase of population may be gradually drawn over to the latter, and a greater demand created for agricultural produce, by which consequently the cultivation of larger estates may be rendered more profitable, and the cultivator induced and encouraged to gain from his land the greatest possible amount of surplus produce.

The productive power of the cultivator and of the labourer in agriculture will always be greater or smaller according to the degree in which the exchange of agricultural produce for manufactures and other products of various kinds can proceed more or less readily. That in this respect the foreign trade of any nation which is but little advanced can prove in the highest degree beneficial, we have shown in another chapter by the example of England. But a nation which has already made considerable advances in civilisation, in possession of capital, and in population, will find the development of a manufacturing power of its own infinitely more beneficial to its agriculture than the most flourishing foreign trade can be without such manufactures, because it thereby secures itself against all fluctuations to which it may be exposed by war, by foreign restrictions on trade, and by commercial crises, because it thereby saves the greatest part of the costs of transport and commercial charges incurred in exporting its own products and in importing manufactured articles, because it derives the greatest advantages from the improvements in transport which are called into existence by its own manufacturing industry, while from the same cause a mass of personal and natural powers hitherto unemployed will be developed, and *especially because the reciprocal exchange between manufacturing power and agricultural power is so much greater, the closer the agriculturist and manufacturer are placed to one another, and the less they are liable to be interrupted in the exchange of their various products by accidents of all kinds.*

In my letters to Mr. Charles J. Ingersoll, President of the Society for Promoting Arts and Industries in Philadelphia, of the year 1828 (entitled, ' Outlines of a New System of Political Economy '), I tried to explain the advantages of a union of the manufacturing power with agriculture in one and the same country, and under one and the same political power, in the following manner. Supposing you did not understand the art of grinding corn, which has certainly been a great art in its time ; supposing further that the art of baking bread had remained unknown to you, as (according to Anderson) the real art of salting herrings was still unknown to the English in the seventeenth century ; supposing, therefore, that you had to send your corn to England to be ground into flour and baked into bread, how large a quantity of your corn would not the English retain as pay for the grinding and baking ; how much of it would the carters, seamen, and merchants consume, who would have to be employed in exporting the corn and importing the bread ; and how much would come back into the hands of those who cultivated the corn ? There is no doubt that by such a process the foreign trade would receive a considerable impetus, but it is very doubtful whether this intercourse would be specially advantageous to the welfare and independence of the nation. Consider only in case of a war breaking out between your country (the United States) and Great Britain, what would be the situation of those who produced corn for the English mills and bakehouses, and on the other hand the situation of those who had become accustomed to the taste of the English bread. Just as, however, the economical prosperity of the corn-cultivating interest requires that the corn millers should live in its vicinity, so also does the prosperity of the farmer especially require that the manufacturer should live close to him, so also does the prosperity of a flat and open country require that a prosperous and industrial town should exist in its centre, and so does the prosperity of the whole agriculture of a country require that its own manufacturing power should be developed in the highest possible degree.

Let us compare the condition of agriculture in the vicinity of a populous town with its condition when carried on in distant provinces. In the latter case the farmer can only cultivate for sale those products which can bear a long transport, and which cannot be supplied at cheaper prices and in better quality from districts lying nearer to those who purchase them. A larger portion of his profits will be absorbed by the costs of transport. He will find it difficult to procure capital which he may employ usefully on his farm. From want of better examples and means of education he will not readily be led to avail himself of new processes, of better implements, and of new methods of cultivation. The labourer himself, from want of good example, of stimulus to exertion, and to emulation in the exercise of his productive powers, will only develop those powers inefficiently, and will indulge himself in loitering about and in idleness.

On the other hand, in the proximity of the town, the farmer is in a position to use every patch of land for those crops which best suit the character of the soil. He will produce the greatest variety of things to the best advantage.

Garden produce, poultry, eggs, milk, butter, fruit, and especially articles which the farmer residing at a distance considers insignificant and secondary things, will bring to the farmer near the town considerable profit. While the distant farmer has to depend mainly on the mere breeding of cattle, the other will make much better profits from fattening them, and will thereby be led to perfect his cultivation of root crops and fodder. He can utilise with much profit a number of things which are of little or no use to the distant farmer ; e.g. stone, sand, water power, &c. The most numerous and best machines and implements, as well as all means for his instruction, are close at hand. It will be easy for him to accumulate the capital necessary for the improvement of his farm. Landed proprietors and workmen, by the means of recreation which the town affords, the emulation which it excites among them, and the facility of making profits, will be incited to exert all their mental and bodily powers for the improvement of their condition. And precisely the same difference exists between a nation which unites agriculture and manufactures on its own territory, and a nation which can only exchange its own agricultural products for foreign manufactured goods.

The whole social state of a nation will be chiefly *determined by the principle of the variety and division of occupations and the co-operation of its productive powers.* What the pin is in the pin manufactory, that the national well-being is to the large society which we term ' the nation.' *The most important division of occupations in the nation is that between the mental and material ones.* Both are mutually dependent on one another. The more the mental producers succeed in promoting morality, religion, enlightenment, increase of knowledge, extension of liberty and of perfection of political institutions—security of persons and property within the State, and the independence and power of the nation externally—so much greater will be the production of material wealth. On the other hand, the more goods that the material producers produce, the more will *mental production be capable of being promoted.*

The most important division of occupations, and the most

*important co-operation of productive powers in material pro-
duction, is that of agriculture and manufacture.* Both depend
mutually upon one another, as we have shown.

As in the pin manufactory, so also in the nation does
the productiveness of every individual—of every separate
branch of production—and finally of the whole nation depend
on the exertions of all individuals standing in proper relation to one another. We call this relation the *balance* or
the *harmony of the productive powers.* It is possible for
a nation to possess too many philosophers, philologers, and
literati, and too few skilled artisans, merchants, and seamen.
This is the consequence of highly advanced and learned
culture which is not supported by a highly advanced manufacturing power and by an extensive internal and external
trade ; it is as if in a pin manufactory far more pin heads
were manufactured than pin points. The surplus pin
heads in such a nation are : a mass of useless books, sub-
tle theoretical systems, and learned controversies, through
which the mind of the nation is more obscured than cultivated, and is withdrawn from useful occupations ; consequently its productive powers are retarded in their progress
almost as much as if it possessed too many priests and too
few instructors of youth, too many soldiers and too few
politicians, too many administrators and too few judges
and defenders of justice and right.

*A nation which only carries on agriculture, is an individual
who in his material production lacks one arm.* Commerce is
merely the medium of exchange between the agricultural
and the manufacturing power, and between their separate
branches. A nation which exchanges agricultural products
for foreign manufactured goods is an individual with *one*
arm, which is supported by a foreign arm. This support
may be useful to it, but not so useful as if it possessed two
arms itself, and this because its activity is dependent on the
caprice of the foreigner. In possession of a manufacturing
power of its own, it can produce as much provisions and
raw materials as the home manufacturers can consume ;
but if dependent upon foreign manufacturers, it can merely
produce as much surplus as foreign nations do not care to

produce for themselves, and which they are obliged to buy from another country.

As between the different districts of one and the same country, so does the division of labour and the co-operation of the productive powers operate between the various nations of the earth.   The former is conducted by internal or national, the latter by international commerce.   The international co-operation of productive powers is, however, a very imperfect one, inasmuch as it may be frequently interrupted by wars, political regulations, commercial crises, &c.   Although it is the most important in one sense, inasmuch as by it the various nations of the earth are connected with one another, it is nevertheless the least important with regard to the prosperity of any separate nation which is already far advanced in civilisation.   This is admitted by writers of the popular school, who declare that the home market of a nation is without comparison more important than its foreign market.   It follows from this, that it is the interest of every great nation to make the *national* confederation of its productive powers the main object of its exertions, and to consider their *international* confederation as second in importance to it.

Both *international* and *national division of labour* are chiefly determined by climate and by Nature herself.   We cannot produce in every country tea as in China, spices as in Java, cotton as in Louisiana, or corn, wool, fruit, and manufactured goods as in the countries of the temperate zone.   It would be folly for a nation to attempt to supply itself by means of national division of labour (i.e. by home production) with articles for the production of which it is not favoured by nature, and which it can procure better and cheaper by means of international division of labour (i.e. through foreign commerce).   And just as much does it betoken a want of national intelligence or national industry if a nation does not employ all the natural powers which it possesses in order to satisfy its own internal wants, and then by means of the surplus of its own productions to purchase those necessary articles which nature has forbidden it to produce on its own territory.

The countries of the world most favoured by nature, with regard to both national and international division of labour, are evidently those whose soil brings forth the most common necessaries of life of the best quality and in the largest quantity, and whose climate is most conducive to bodily and mental exertion, and these are *the countries of the temperate zone*; for in these countries the manufacturing power especially prospers, by means of which the nation not merely attains to the highest degree of mental and social development and of political power, but is also enabled to make the countries of tropical climates and of inferior civilisation tributary in a certain measure to itself. The countries of the temperate zone therefore are above all others called upon to bring their own national division of labour to the highest perfection, and to use the international division of labour for their enrichment.

CHAPTER XIV.

PRIVATE ECONOMY AND NATIONAL ECONOMY.

WE have proved historically that the unity of the nation forms the fundamental condition of lasting national prosperity ; and we have shown that only where the interest of individuals has been subordinated to those of the nation, and where successive generations have striven for one and the same object, the nations have been brought to harmonious development of their productive powers, and how little private industry can prosper without the united efforts both of the individuals who are living at the time, and of successive generations directed to one common object. We have further tried to prove in the last chapter how the law of union of powers exhibits its beneficial operation in the individual manufactory, and how it acts with equal power on the industry of whole nations. In the present chapter we have now to demonstrate how the popular school has concealed its misunderstanding of the national interests and of the effects of national union of powers, by confounding the principles of private economy with those of national economy.

'What is prudence in the conduct of every private family,' says Adam Smith,[1] 'can scarce be folly in that of a great kingdom.' Every individual in pursuing his own interests necessarily promotes thereby also the interests of the community. It is evident that every individual, inasmuch as he knows his own local circumstances best and pays most attention to his occupation, is far better able to judge than the statesman or legislator how his capital can most profitably be invested. He who would venture to give

---

[1] *Wealth of Nations*, Book IV. chap. ii.

advice to the people how to invest their capital would not
merely take upon himself a useless task, but would also
assume to himself an authority which belongs solely to the
producer, and which can be entrusted to those persons
least of all who consider themselves equal to so difficult a
task.   Adam Smith concludes from this : ['Restrictions on
trade imposed on the behalf of the internal industry of a
country, are mere folly ; every nation, like every individual,
ought to buy articles where they can be procured the
cheapest ; in order to attain to the highest degree of
national prosperity, we have simply to follow the maxim of
letting things alone (laisser faire et laisser aller).'] Smith
and Say compare a nation which seeks to promote its
industry by protective duties, to a tailor who wants to
make his own boots, and to a bootmaker who would
impose a toll on those who enter his door, in order to
promote his prosperity.   As in all errors of the popular
school, so also in this one does Thomas Cooper go to
extremes in his book[1] which is <u>directed against</u> the
<u>American system of protection</u>.   'Political economy,' he
alleges, ' is almost synonymous with the private economy
of all individuals ; *politics* are no essential ingredient of
political economy ; it is folly to suppose that the community
is something quite different from the individuals of whom
it is composed.   [Every individual knows best how to invest
his labour and his capital.   The wealth of the community
is nothing else than the aggregate of the wealth of all its
individual members ; and if every individual can provide
best for himself, that nation must be the richest in which
every individual is most left to himself.']   The adherents of
the American system of protection had opposed themselves
to this argument, which had formerly been adduced by
importing merchants in favour of free trade ; the American
navigation laws had greatly increased the carrying trade,
the foreign commerce, and fisheries of the United States ;
and for the mere protection of their mercantile marine
millions had been annually expended on their fleet ; according to his theory those laws and this expense also

[1] *Lectures on Political Economy*, by Thomas Cooper, pp. 1, 15, 19, 117.

would be as reprehensible as protective duties. 'In any case,' exclaims Mr. Cooper, 'no commerce by sea is worth a naval war; the merchants may be left to protect themselves.'

Thus the popular school, which had begun by ignoring the principles of nationality and national interests, finally comes to the point of altogether denying their existence, and of leaving individuals to defend them as they may solely by their own individual powers.

How? Is the wisdom of private economy, also wisdom in national economy? Is it in the nature of individuals to take into consideration the wants of future centuries, as those concern the nature of the nation and the State? Let us consider only the first beginning of an American town; every individual left to himself would care merely for his own wants, or at the most for those of his nearest successors, whereas all individuals united in one community provide for the convenience and the wants of the most distant generations; they subject the present generation for this object to privations and sacrifices which no reasonable person could expect from individuals. Can the individual further take into consideration in promoting his private economy, the defence of the country, public security, and the thousand other objects which can only be attained by the aid of the whole community? Does not the State require individuals to limit their private liberty according to what these objects require? Does it not even require that they should sacrifice for these some part of their earnings, of their mental and bodily labour, nay, even their own life? We must first root out, as Cooper does, the very ideas of 'State' and 'nation' before this opinion can be entertained.

No; that may be wisdom in national economy which would be folly in private economy, and *vice versâ*; and owing to the very simple reason, that a tailor is no nation and a nation no tailor, that one family is something very different from a community of millions of families, that one house is something very different from a large national territory. Nor does the individual merely by understanding his own interests best, and by striving to further them, if left to his own devices, always further the interests of the community. We ask those who occupy the benches of justice, whether they do not frequently have to send individuals to the tread-mill on account of their excess of inventive power, and of their all too great industry. Robbers, thieves, smugglers, and cheats know their own local and personal circumstances and conditions extremely well, and pay the most active attention to their business; but it by no means follows therefrom, that society is in the best condition where such individuals are least restrained in the exercise of their private industry.

In a thousand cases the power of the State is compelled to impose restrictions on private industry.[1] It prevents the shipowner from taking on board slaves on the west coast of Africa, and taking them over to America. It imposes regulations as to the building of steamers and the rules of navigation at sea, in order that passengers and sailors may not be sacrificed to the avarice and caprice of the captains. In England certain rules have recently been enacted with regard to shipbuilding, because an infernal union between assurance companies and shipowners has been brought to light, whereby yearly thousands of human lives and millions in value were sacrificed to the avarice of a few persons. In North America millers are bound under a penalty to pack into each cask not less than 198 lbs. of good flour, and for all market goods market inspectors are appointed, although in no other country is individual liberty more highly prized. Everywhere does the State consider it to be its duty to guard the public against danger and loss, as in the sale of necessaries of life, so also in the sale of medicines, &c.

But the cases which we have mentioned (the school will reply) concern unlawful damages to property and to the person, not the honourable exchange of useful objects, not the harmless and useful industry of private individuals; to impose restrictions on these latter the State has no right whatever. Of course not, so long as they remain harmless

[1] See Appendix B.

and useful; that which, however, is harmless and useful in
itself, in general commerce with the world, can become
dangerous and injurious in national internal commerce,
and *vice versâ*. In time of peace, and considered from a
cosmopolitan point of view, privateering is an injurious
profession; in time of war, Governments favour it. The
deliberate killing of a human being is a crime in time of
peace, in war it becomes a duty. Trading in gunpowder,
lead, and arms in time of peace is allowed; but whoever
provides the enemy with them in time of war, is punished
as a traitor.

For similar reasons the State is not merely justified in
imposing, but bound to impose, certain regulations and
restrictions on commerce (which is in itself harmless) for
the best interests of the nation. By prohibitions and protective duties it does not give directions to individuals how
to employ their productive powers and capital (as the
popular school sophistically alleges); it does not tell the
one, 'You must invest your money in the building of a
ship, or in the erection of a manufactory;' or the other,
'You must be a naval captain or a civil engineer;' it leaves
it to the judgment of every individual how and where to invest his capital, or to what vocation he will devote himself.
It merely says, 'It is to the advantage of our nation that
we manufacture these or the other goods ourselves; but as
by free competition with foreign countries we can never obtain possession of this advantage, we have imposed restrictions on that competition, so far as in our opinion is necessary, to give those among us who invest their capital in
these new branches of industry, and those who devote their
bodily and mental powers to them, the requisite guarantees
that they shall not lose their capital and shall not miss their
vocation in life; and further to stimulate foreigners to come
over to our side with their productive powers. In this
manner, it does not in the least degree restrain private industry; on the contrary, it secures to the personal, natural,
and moneyed powers of the nation a greater and wider field
of activity. It does not thereby do something which its
individual citizens could understand better and do better

than it ; on the contrary, it does something which the individuals, even if they understood it, would not be able to do for themselves.

The allegation of the school, that the system of protection occasions unjust and anti-economical encroachments by the power of the State against the employment of the capital and industry of private individuals, appears in the least favourable light if we consider that it is the *foreign* commercial regulations which allow such encroachments on *our* private industry to take place, and that only by the aid of the system of protection are we enabled to counteract those injurious operations of the foreign commercial policy. If the English shut out our corn from their markets, what else are they doing than compelling our agriculturists to grow so much less corn than they would have sent out to England under systems of free importation ? If they put such heavy duties on our wool, our wines, or our timber, that our export trade to England wholly or in great measure ceases, what else is thereby effected than that the power of the English nation restricts proportionately our branches of production ? In these cases a direction is evidently given by *foreign legislation* to *our* capital and *our* personal productive powers, which but for the regulations made by it they would scarcely have followed. It follows from this, that were we to disown giving, by means of *our* own legislation, a direction to our own national industry in accordance with our own national interests, we could not prevent foreign nations from regulating our national industry after a fashion which corresponds with their own real or presumed advantage, and which in any case operates disadvantageously to the development of our own productive powers. But can it possibly be wiser on our part, and more to the advantage of those who nationally belong to us, for us to allow our private industry to be regulated by a foreign national Legislature, in accordance with foreign national interests, rather than regulate it by means of our own Legislature and in accordance with our own interests ? Does the German or American agriculturist feel himself less restricted if he has to study every year the English

Acts of Parliament, in order to ascertain whether that body deems it advantageous to encourage or to impose restrictions on his production of corn or wool, than if his own Legislature imposes certain restrictions on him in respect of foreign manufactured goods, but at the same time insures him a market for all his products, of which he can never again be deprived by foreign legislation ?

If the school maintains that protective duties secure to the home manufacturers a monopoly to the disadvantage of the home consumers, in so doing it makes use of a weak argument. For as every individual in the nation is free to share in the profits of the home market which is thus secured to native industry, this is in no respect a private monopoly, but a privilege, secured to all those who belong to our nation, as against those who nationally belong to foreign nations, and which is the more righteous and just inasmuch as those who nationally belong to foreign nations possess themselves the very same monopoly, and those who belong to us are merely thereby put on the same footing with them. It is neither a privilege to the exclusive advantage of the producers, nor to the exclusive disadvantage of the consumers ; for if the producers at first obtain higher prices, they run great risks, and have to contend against those considerable losses and sacrifices which are always connected with all beginnings in manufacturing industry. But the consumers have ample security that these extraordinary profits shall not reach unreasonable limits, or become perpetual, by means of the competition at home which follows later on, and which, as a rule, always lowers prices further than the level at which they had steadily ranged under the free competition of the foreigner. If the agriculturists, who are the most important consumers to the manufacturers, must also pay higher prices, this disadvantage will be amply repaid to them by increased demands for agricultural products, and by increased prices obtained for the latter.

It is a further sophism, arrived at by confounding the theory of mere values with that of the powers of production, when the popular school infers from the doctrine,

' *that the wealth of the nation is merely the aggregate of the wealth of all individuals in it, and that the private interest of every individual is better able than all State regulations to incite to production and accumulation of wealth,*' the conclusion that the national industry would prosper best if only every individual were left undisturbed in the occupation of accumulating wealth. That doctrine can be conceded without the conclusion resulting from it at which the school desires thus to arrive; for the point in question is not (as we have shown in a previous chapter) that of immediately increasing by commercial restrictions the amount of *the values of exchange* in the nation, but of increasing *the amount of its productive powers.* But that the aggregate of the productive powers of the nation is not synonymous with the aggregate of the productive powers of all individuals, each considered separately—that the total amount of these powers depends chiefly on social and political conditions, but especially on the degree in which the nation has rendered effectual the division of labour and the confederation of the powers of production within itself—we believe we have sufficiently demonstrated in the preceding chapters.

This system everywhere takes into its consideration only individuals who are in free unrestrained intercourse among themselves, and who are contented if we leave everyone to pursue his own private interests according to his own private natural inclination. This is evidently not a system of national economy, but a system of the private economy of the human race, as that would constitute itself were there no interference on the part of any Government, were there no wars, no hostile foreign tariff restrictions. Nowhere do the advocates of that system care to point out by what means those nations which are now prosperous have raised themselves to that stage of power and prosperity which we see them maintain, and from what causes others have lost that degree of prosperity and power which they formerly maintained. We can only learn from it how in private industry, natural ability, labour and capital, are combined in order to bring into exchange valuable products, and in what manner these latter are distributed among the human race and consumed by it. But what means are to be adopted in order to bring the natural powers belonging to any individual nation into activity and value, to raise a poor and weak nation to prosper ty and power, cannot be gathered from it, because the school totally ignoring politics, ignores the special conditions of the nation, and concerns itself merely about the prosperity of the whole human race. Wherever international commerce is in question, the native individual is throughout simply pitted against the foreign individual; examples from the private dealings of separate merchants are throughout the only ones adduced—goods are spoken of in general terms (without considering whether the question is one of raw products or of manufactured articles) —in order to prove that it is equally for the benefit of the nation whether its exports and imports consist of money, of raw materials, or of manufactured goods, and whether or not they balance one another. If we, for example, terrified at the commercial crises which prevail in the United States of North America like native epidemics, consult this theory as to the means of averting or diminishing them, it leaves us utterly without comfort or instruction; nay, it is indeed impossible for us to investigate these phenomena scientifically, because, under the penalty of being taken for muddleheads and ignoramuses, we must not even utter the term '*balance of trade*,' while this term is, notwithstanding, made use of in all legislative assemblies, in all bureaux of administration, on every exchange. For the sake of the welfare of humanity, the belief is inculcated on us that exports always balance themselves spontaneously by imports; notwithstanding that we read in public accounts how the Bank of England comes to the assistance of the nature of things; notwithstanding that corn laws exist, which make it somewhat difficult for the agriculturist of those countries which deal with England to pay with his own produce for the manufactured goods which he consumes.

The school recognises no distinction between nations which have attained a higher degree of economical development, and those which occupy a lower stage. Everywhere

it seeks to exclude the action of the power of the State ;
everywhere, according to it, will the individual be so much
better able to produce, the less the power of the State concerns itself for him.   In fact, according to this doctrine
savage nations ought to be the most productive and wealthy
of the earth, for nowhere is the individual left more to
himself than in the savage state, nowhere is the action of
the power of the State less perceptible.

Statistics and history, however, teach, on the contrary,
that the necessity for the intervention of legislative power
and administration is everywhere more apparent, the further the economy of the nation is developed.   As individual
liberty is in general a good thing so long only as it does
not run counter to the interests of society, so is it reasonable to hold that private industry can only lay claim to
unrestricted action so long as the latter consists with the
well-being of the nation.   But whenever the enterprise and
activity of individuals does not suffice for this purpose, or
in any case where these might become injurious to the
nation, there does private industry rightly require support
from the whole power of the nation, there ought it for the
sake of its own interests to submit to legal restrictions.

If the school represents the free competition of all producers as the most effectual means for promoting the prosperity of the human race, it is quite right from the point of
view which it assumes.   On the hypothesis of a universal
union, every restriction on the honest exchange of goods
between various countries seems unreasonable and injurious.
But so long as other nations subordinate the interests
of the human race as a whole to their national interests,
it is folly to speak of free competition among the individuals
of various nations.   The arguments of the school in favour
of free competition are thus only applicable to the exchange
between those who belong to one and the same nation.
Every great nation, therefore, must endeavour to form an
aggregate within itself, which will enter into commercial
intercourse with other similar aggregates so far only as
that intercourse is suitable to the interests of its own special
community.   These interests of the community are, how-

ever, infinitely different from the private interests of all the separate individuals of the nation, if each individual is to be regarded as existing for himself alone and not in the character of a member of the national community, if we regard (as Smith and Say do) individuals as mere producers and consumers, not citizens of states or members of nations; for as such, mere individuals do not concern themselves for the prosperity of future generations—they deem it foolish (as Mr. Cooper really demonstrates to us) to make certain and present sacrifices in order to endeavour to obtain a benefit which is as yet uncertain and lying in the vast field of the future (if even it possess any value at all); they care but little for the continuance of the nation —they would expose the ships of their merchants to become the prey of every bold pirate—they trouble themselves but little about the power, the honour, or the glory of the nation, at the most they can persuade themselves to make some material sacrifices for the education of their children, and to give them the opportunity of learning a trade, provided always that after the lapse of a few years the learners are placed in a position to earn their own bread.

Indeed, according to the prevailing theory, so analogous is national economy to private economy that J. B. Say, where (exceptionally) he allows that internal industry may be protected by the State, makes it a condition of so doing, that every probability must exist that after the lapse of a *few years* it will attain independence, just as a shoemaker's apprentice is allowed only a few years' time in order to perfect himself so far in his trade as to do without parental assistance.

CHAPTER XV.

NATIONALITY AND THE ECONOMY OF THE NATION.

THE system of the school suffers, as we have already shown in the preceding chapters, from three main defects : firstly, from boundless *cosmopolitanism*, which neither recognises the principle of nationality, nor takes into consideration the satisfaction of its interests ; secondly, from a dead *materialism*, which everywhere regards chiefly the mere exchangeable value of things without taking into consideration the mental and political, the present and the future interests, and the productive powers of the nation ; thirdly, from *a disorganising particularism* and *individualism*, which, ignoring the nature and character of social labour and the operation of the union of powers in their higher consequences, considers private industry only as it would develop itself under a state of free interchange with society (i.e. with the whole human race) were that race not divided into separate national societies.

Between each individual and entire humanity, however, stands THE NATION, with its special language and literature, with its peculiar origin and history, with its special manners and customs, laws and institutions, with the claims of all these for existence, independence, perfection, and continuance for the future, and with its separate territory ; a society which, united by a thousand ties of mind and of interests, combines itself into one independent whole, which recognises the law of right for and within itself, and in its united character is still opposed to other societies of a similar kind in their national liberty, and consequently can only under the existing conditions of the world maintain self-existence and independence by its own power and resources. As the individual chiefly obtains by means of the nation and in the nation mental culture, power of production, security, and prosperity, so is the civilisation of the human race only conceivable and possible by means of the civilisation and development of the individual nations.

Meanwhile, however, an infinite difference exists in the condition and circumstances of the various nations : we observe among them giants and dwarfs, well-formed bodies and cripples, civilised, half-civilised, and barbarous nations ; but in all of them, as in the individual human being, exists the impulse of self-preservation, the striving for improvement which is implanted by nature. It is the task of politics to civilise the barbarous nationalities, to make the small and weak ones great and strong, but, above all, to secure to them existence and continuance. It is the task of national economy to accomplish *the economical development of the nation*, and to prepare it for admission into the universal society of the future.

A nation in its normal state possesses one common language and literature, a territory endowed with manifold natural resources, extensive, and with convenient frontiers and a numerous population. Agriculture, manufactures, commerce, and navigation must be all developed in it proportionately ; arts and sciences, educational establishments, and universal cultivation must stand in it on an equal footing with material production. Its constitution, laws, and institutions must afford to those who belong to it a high degree of security and liberty, and must promote religion, morality, and prosperity ; in a word, must have the well-being of its citizens as their object. It must possess sufficient power on land and at sea to defend its independence and to protect its foreign commerce. It will possess the power of beneficially affecting the civilisation of less advanced nations, and by means of its own surplus population and of their mental and material capital to found colonies and beget new nations.

A large population, and an extensive territory endowed with manifold national resources, are essential requirements of the normal nationality; they are the fundamental conditions of mental cultivation as well as of material development and political power. A nation restricted in the number of its population and in territory, especially if it has a separate language, can only possess a crippled literature, crippled institutions for promoting art and science. A small State can never bring to complete perfection within its territory the various branches of production In it all protection becomes mere private monopoly. Only through alliances with more powerful nations, by partly sacrificing the advantages of nationality, and by excessive energy, can it maintain with difficulty its independence.

A nation which possesses no coasts, mercantile marine, or naval power, or has not under its dominion and control the mouths of its rivers, is in its foreign commerce dependent on other countries; it can neither establish colonies of its own nor form new nations; all surplus population, mental and material means, which flows from such a nation to uncultivated countries, is lost to its own literature, civilisation and industry, and goes to the benefit of other nationalities.

A nation not bounded by seas and chains of mountains lies open to the attacks of foreign nations, and can only by great sacrifices, and in any case only very imperfectly, establish and maintain a separate tariff system of its own.

Territorial deficiencies of the nation can be remedied either by means of hereditary succession, as in the case of England and Scotland; or by purchase, as in the case of Florida and Louisiana; or by conquests, as in the case of Great Britain and Ireland.

In modern times a fourth means has been adopted, which leads to this object in a manner much more in accordance with justice and with the prosperity of nations than conquest, and which is not so dependent on accidents as hereditary succession, namely, the union of the interests of various States by means of free conventions.

By its Zollverein, the German nation first obtained one

of the most important attributes of its nationality. But this measure cannot be considered complete so long as it does not extend over the whole coast, from the mouth of the Rhine to the frontier of Poland, including *Holland* and *Denmark*. A natural consequence of this union must be the admission of both these countries into the German Bund, and consequently into the German nationality, whereby the latter will at once obtain what it is now in need of, namely, fisheries and naval power, maritime commerce and colonies. Besides, both these nations belong, as respects their descent and whole character, to the German nationality. The burden of debt with which they are oppressed is merely a consequence of their unnatural endeavours to maintain themselves as independent nationalities, and it is in the nature of things that this evil should rise to a point when it will become intolerable to those two nations themselves, and when incorporation with a larger nationality must seem desirable and necessary to them.

Belgium can only remedy by means of confederation with a neighbouring larger nation her needs which are inseparable from her restricted territory and population. *The United States* and *Canada*, the more their population increases, and the more the protective system of the United States is developed, so much the more will they feel themselves drawn towards one another, and the less will it be possible for England to prevent a union between them.

As respects their economy, nations have to pass through the following stages of development: original barbarism, pastoral condition, agricultural condition, agricultural-manufacturing condition, and agricultural-manufacturing-commercial condition.

The industrial history of nations, and of none more clearly than that of England, proves that the transition from the savage state to the pastoral one, from the pastoral to the agricultural, and from agriculture to the first beginnings in manufacture and navigation, is effected most speedily and advantageously by means of free commerce with further advanced towns and countries, but that a perfectly developed manufacturing industry, an important mercantile marine, and foreign trade on a really large scale, can only be attained by means of the interposition of the power of the State.

The less any nation's agriculture has been perfected, and the more its foreign trade is in want of opportunities of exchanging the excess of native agricultural products and raw materials for foreign manufactured goods, the deeper that the nation is still sunk in barbarism and fitted only for an absolute monarchical form of government and legislation, the more will free trade (i.e. the exportation of agricultural products and the importation of manufactured goods) promote its prosperity and civilisation.

On the other hand, the more that the agriculture of a nation, its industries, and its social, political, and municipal conditions, are thoroughly developed, the less advantage will it be able to derive for the improvement of its social conditions, from the exchange of native agricultural products and raw materials for foreign manufactured goods, and the greater disadvantages will it experience from the successful competition of a foreign manufacturing power superior to its own.

Solely in nations of the latter kind, namely those which possess all the necessary mental and material conditions and means for establishing a manufacturing power of their own, and of thereby attaining the highest degree of civilisation, and development of material prosperity and political power, but which are retarded in their progress by the competition of a foreign manufacturing Power which is already farther advanced than their own—only in such nations are commercial restrictions justifiable for the purpose of establishing and protecting their own manufacturing power; and even in them it is justifiable only until that manufacturing power is strong enough no longer to have any reason to fear foreign competition, and thenceforth only so far as may be necessary for protecting the inland manufacturing power in its very roots.

The system of protection would not merely be contrary

to the principles of cosmopolitical economy, but also to the rightly understood advantage of the nation itself, were it to exclude foreign competition at once and altogether, and thus isolate from other nations the nation which is thus protected. If the manufacturing Power to be protected be still in the first period of its development, the protective duties must be very moderate, they must only rise gradually with the increase of the mental and material capital, of the technical abilities and spirit of enterprise of the nation. Neither is it at all necessary that all branches of industry should be protected in the same degree. Only the most important branches require special protection, for the working of which much outlay of capital in building and management, much machinery, and therefore much technical knowledge, skill, and experience, and many workmen are required, and whose products belong to the category of the first necessaries of life, and consequently are of the greatest importance as regards their total value as well as regards national independence (as, for example, cotton, woollen and linen manufactories, &c.). If these main branches are suitably protected and developed, all other less important branches of manufacture will rise up around them under a less degree of protection. It will be to the advantage of nations in which wages are high, and whose population is not yet great in proportion to the extent of their territory, e.g. in the United States of North America, to give less protection to manufactures in which machinery does not play an important part, than to those in which machinery does the greater part of the work, providing that those nations which supply them with similar goods allow in return free importation to their agricultural products.

The popular school betrays an utter misconception of the nature of national economical conditions if it believes that such nations can promote and further their civilisation, their prosperity, and especially their social progress, equally well by the exchange of agricultural products for manufactured goods, as by establishing a manufacturing power of their own. A mere agricultural nation can never develop to any considerable extent its home and foreign commerce, its inland means of transport, and its foreign navigation, increase its population in due proportion to their well-being, or make notable progress in its moral, intellectual, social, and political development : it will never acquire important political power, or be placed in a position to influence the cultivation and progress of less advanced nations and to form colonies of its own. A mere agricultural State is an infinitely less perfect institution than an agricultural-manufacturing State. The former is always more or less economically and politically dependent on those foreign nations which take from it agricultural products in exchange for manufactured goods. It cannot determine for itself how much it will produce ; it must wait and see how much others will buy from it. These latter, on the contrary (the agricultural-manufacturing States), produce for themselves large quantities of raw materials and provisions, and supply merely the deficiency by importation from the purely agricultural nations. The purely agricultural nations are thus in the first place dependent for their power of effecting sales on the chances of a more or less plentiful harvest in the agricultural-manufacturing nations ; in the next place they have to compete in these sales with other purely agricultural nations, whereby their power of sale, in itself very uncertain, thus becomes still more uncertain. Lastly, they are exposed to the danger of being totally ruined in their trading with foreign manufacturing nations by wars, or new foreign tariff regulations whereby they suffer the double disadvantage of finding no buyers for their surplus agricultural products, and of failing to obtain supplies of the manufactured goods which they require. An agricultural nation is, as we have already stated, an individual with *one* arm, who makes use of a foreign arm, but who cannot make sure of the use of it in all cases ; an agricultural-manufacturing nation is an individual who has *two* arms *of his own* always at his disposal.

It is a fundamental error of the school when it represents the system of protection as a mere device of speculative politicians which is contrary to nature. History is there to prove that protective regulations originated either in the natural efforts of nations to attain to prosperity, independence, and power, or in consequence of wars and of the hostile commercial legislation of predominating manufacturing nations.

The idea of independence and power originates in the very idea of ' the nation.' The school never takes this into consideration, because it does not make the economy of the separate nation, but the economy of society generally, i.e. of the whole human race, the object of its investigations. If we imagine, for instance, that all nations were united by means of a universal confederation, their individual independence and power would cease to be an object of regard. The security for the independence of every nation would in such a case rest on the legal provisions of the universal society, just as e.g. the security of the independence of the states of Rhode Island and Delaware lies in the union of all the free states constituting the American Union. Since the first foundation of that Union it has never yet occurred to any of these smaller states to care for the enlargement of its own political power, or to consider its independence less secured than is that of the largest states of the Union.

In proportion, however, as the principle of a universal confederation of nations is reasonable, in just the same degree would a given nation act contrary to reason if, in anticipation of the great advantages to be expected from such a union, and from a state of universal and perpetual peace, it were to regulate the principles of its national policy as though this universal confederation of nations existed already. We ask, would not every sane person consider a government to be insane which, in consideration of the benefits and the reasonableness of a state of universal and perpetual peace, proposed to disband its armies, destroy its fleet, and demolish its fortresses? But such a government would be doing nothing different in principle from what the popular school requires from governments when, because of the advantages which would be derivable from general free trade, it urges that they should abandon the advantages derivable from protection.

War has a ruinous effect on the reciprocal commercial relations between nation and nation. The agriculturist living in one country is by it forcibly separated from the manufacturer living in another country. While, however, the manufacturer (especially if he belongs to a nation powerful at sea, and carrying on extensive commerce) readily finds compensation from the agriculturists of his own country, or from those of other accessible agricultural countries, the inhabitant of the purely agricultural country suffers doubly through this interruption of intercourse.

The market for his agricultural products will fail him entirely, and he will consequently lose the means of paying for those manufactured goods which have become necessaries to him owing to previously existing trade ; his power both of production and consumption will be diminished.

If, however, one agricultural nation whose production and consumption are thus diminished by war has already made considerable advances in population, civilisation, and agriculture, manufactures and factories will spring up in it in consequence of the interruption of international commerce by war. War acts on it like a prohibitive tariff system. It thereby becomes acquainted with the great advantages of a manufacturing power of its own, it becomes convinced by practical experience that it has gained more than it has lost by the commercial interruptions which war has occasioned. The conviction gains ground in it, that it is called to pass from the condition of a mere agricultural State to the condition of an agricultural-manufacturing State, and in consequence of this transition, to attain to the highest degree of prosperity, civilisation, and power. But if after such a nation has already made considerable progress in the manufacturing career which was opened to it by war, peace is again established, and should both nations then contemplate the resumption of their previously existing commercial intercourse, they will both find that during the war new interests have been formed, which would be destroyed by re-establishing the former commercial interchange.[1] The former agricultural

---

[1] Vide *Wealth of Nations*, Book IV. chap. ii. (TR.)

nation will feel, that in order to resume the sale of its agricultural products to the foreigner, it would have to sacrifice its own manufacturing industry which has in the meanwhile been created; the manufacturing nation will feel that a portion of its home agricultural production, which has been formed during the war, would again be destroyed by free importation. Both, therefore, try to protect these interests by means of imposing duties on imports. This is the history of commercial politics during the last fifty years.

It is war that has called into existence the more recent systems of protection; and we do not hesitate to assert, that it would have been to the interest of the manufacturing nations of the second and third rank to retain a protective policy and further develop it, even if England after the conclusion of peace had not committed the monstrous mistake of imposing restrictions on the importation of necessaries of life and of raw materials, and consequently of allowing the motives which had led to the system of protection in the time of the war, to continue during peace. As an uncivilised nation, having a barbarous system of agriculture, can make progress only by commerce with civilised manufacturing nations, so after it has attained to a certain degree of culture, in no other way can it reach the highest grade of prosperity, civilisation, and power, than by possessing a manufacturing industry of its own. A war which leads to the change of the purely agricultural State into an agricultural-manufacturing State is therefore a blessing to a nation, just as the War of Independence of the United States of North America, in spite of the enormous sacrifices which it required, has become a blessing to all future generations. But a peace which throws back into a purely agricultural condition a nation which is fitted to develop a manufacturing power of its own, becomes a curse to it, and is incomparably more injurious to it than a war.

It is fortunate for the manufacturing Powers of the second and third rank, that England after the restoration of the general peace has herself imposed a limit to her main tendency (of monopolising the manufacturing market of the whole earth), by imposing restrictions on the importation of foreign means of subsistence and raw materials. Certainly the English agriculturists, who had enjoyed a monopoly of supplying the English market with products during the war, would of course have painfully felt the foreign competition, but that only at first ; at a later period (as we will show more particularly elsewhere), these losses would have been made up to them tenfold by the fact that England had obtained a monopoly of manufacturing for the whole world. But it would have been still more injudicious if the manufacturing nations of the second and third rank, after their own manufacturing power had just been called into existence, in consequence of wars lasting for twenty-five years, and after (in consequence of twenty-five years' exclusion of their agricultural products from the English market) that power has been strengthened so far that possibly it only required another ten or fifteen years of strict protection in order to sustain successfully free competition with English manufactures—if (we say) these nations, after having endured the sacrifices of half a century, were to give up the immense advantages of possessing a manufacturing power of their own, and were to descend once more from the high state of culture, prosperity, and independence, which is peculiar to agricultural-manufacturing countries, to the low position of dependent agricultural nations, merely because it now pleases the English nation to perceive its error and the closely impending advances of the Continental nations which enter into competition with it.

Supposing also that the manufacturing interest of England should obtain sufficient influence to force the House of Lords, which chiefly consists of large landed proprietors, and the House of Commons, composed mostly of country squires, to make concessions in respect of the importation of agricultural products, who would guarantee that after a lapse of a few years a new Tory ministry would not under different circumstances again pass a new Corn Law ? Who can guarantee that a new naval war or a new Continental system may not separate the agriculturists of the

Continent from the manufacturers of the island kingdom, and compel the Continental nations to recommence their manufacturing career, and to spend their best energies in overcoming its primary difficulties, merely in order at a later period to sacrifice everything again at the conclusion of peace ?

In this manner the school would condemn the Continental nations for ever to be rolling the stone of Sisyphus, for ever to erect manufactories in time of war in order to allow them to fall to ruin in time of peace.

To results so absurd as these the school could never have arrived had it not (in spite of the name which it gives to the science which it professes) completely excluded politics from that science, had it not completely ignored the very existence of nationality, and left entirely out of consideration the effects of war on the commercial intercourse between separate nations.

How utterly different is the relation of the agriculturist to the manufacturer if both live in one and the same country, and are consequently really connected with one another by perpetual peace. Under those circumstances, every extension or improvement of an already existing manufactory increases the demand for agricultural products. This demand is no uncertain one; it is not dependent on foreign commercial regulations or foreign commercial fluctuations, on foreign political commotions or wars, on foreign inventions and improvements, or on foreign harvests; the native agriculturist has not to share it with other nations, it is certain to him every year. However the crops of other nations may turn out, whatever misunderstandings may spring up in the political world, he can depend on the sale of his own produce, and on obtaining the manufactured goods which he needs at suitable and regular prices. On the other hand, every improvement of the native agriculture, every new method of culture, acts as a stimulant on the native manufacture, because every augmentation of native agricultural production must result in a proportionate augmentation of native manufacturing production. Thus, by means of

this reciprocal action, progress is insured for all time to
both these main sources of the nation's strength and
support.

Political power not merely secures to the nation the
increase of its prosperity by foreign commerce and by
colonies abroad, it also secures to it the possession of
internal prosperity, and secures to it its own existence,
which is far more important to it than mere material
wealth. England has obtained political power by means
of her navigation laws; and by means of political power
she has been placed in a position to extend her manufacturing power over other nations. Poland, however, was
struck out of the list of nations because she did not possess
a vigorous middle class, which could only have been called
into existence by the establishment of an internal manufacturing power.

The school cannot deny that the internal market of a
nation is ten times more important to it than its external
one, even where the latter is in the most flourishing condition; but it has omitted to draw from this the conclusion,
which is very obvious, that it is ten times more important
to cultivate and secure the home market, than to seek for
wealth abroad, and that only in those nations which have
developed their internal industry to a high degree can foreign
commerce attain importance.

The school has formed its estimate of the nature and
character of the market only from a cosmopolitical, but
not from a political point of view. Most of the maritime
countries of the European continent are situated in the
natural market district of the manufacturers of London,
Liverpool, or Manchester; only very few of the inland
manufacturers of other nations can, under free trade,
maintain in their own seaports the same prices as the
English manufacturers. The possession of larger capital,
a larger home market of their own, which enables them
to manufacture on a larger scale and consequently
more cheaply, greater progress in manufacture itself, and
finally cheaper sea transport, give at the present time to
the English manufacturers advantages over the manu-

facturers of other countries, which can only be gradually diverted to the native industry of the latter by means of long and continuous protection of their home market, and through perfection of their inland means of transport. The market of the inhabitants of its coasts is, however, of great importance to every nation, both with reference to the home market, and to foreign commerce ; and a nation the market of whose coasts belongs more to the foreigner than to itself, is a divided nation not merely in economical respects, but also in political ones. Indeed, there can be no more injurious position for a nation, whether in its economical or political aspect, than if its seaports sympathise more with the foreigner than with itself.

Science must not deny the nature of special national circumstances, nor ignore and misrepresent it, in order to promote cosmopolitical objects. Those objects can only be attained by paying regard to nature, and by trying to lead the separate nations in accordance with it to a higher aim. We may see what small success has hitherto attended the doctrines of the school in practice. This is not so much the fault of practical statesmen, by whom the character of the national circumstances has been comprehended tolerably correctly, as the fault of the theories themselves, the practice of which (inasmuch as they are opposed to all experience) must necessarily err. Have those theories prevented nations (like those of South America) from introducing the protectionist system, which is contrary to the requirements of their national circumstances ? Or have they prevented the extension of protectionism to the production of provisions and raw materials, which, however, needs no protection, and in which the restriction of commercial intercourse must be disadvantageous under all circumstances to both nations—to that which imposes, as well as to that which suffers from such restrictions ?[1] Has this theory prevented the finer manufactured goods, which are essentially articles of luxury, from being comprehended among objects requiring protection, while it is nevertheless clear that these can be exposed to competition without the

[1] See Appendix C.

least danger to the prosperity of the nation? No; the theory has till now not effected any thorough reform, and further will never effect any, so long as it stands opposed to the very nature of things. But it can and must effect great reforms as soon as it consents to base itself on that nature.

It will first of all establish a benefit extending to all nations, to the prosperity and progress of the whole human race, if it shows that the prevention of free trade in natural products and raw materials causes to the nation itself which prevents it the greatest disadvantage, and that the system of protection can be justified solely and only for the purpose of the *industrial development* of the nation. It may then, by thus basing the system of protection as regards manufactures on correct principles, induce nations which at present adopt a rigidly prohibitive system, as e.g. the French, to give up the prohibitive system by degrees. The manufacturers will not oppose such a change as soon as they become convinced that the theorists, very far from planning the ruin of existing manufactures, consider their preservation and their further development as the basis of every sensible commercial policy.

If the theory will teach the Germans, that they can further their manufacturing power advantageously only by protective duties previously fixed, and on a gradually increasing scale at first, but afterwards gradually diminishing, and that under all circumstances partial but carefully limited foreign competition is really beneficial to their own manufacturing progress, it will render far better service in the end to the cause of free trade than if it simply helps to strangle German industry.

The theory must not expect from the United States of North America that they are to sacrifice to free competition from the foreigner, those manufactures in which they are protected by cheap raw materials and provisions, and by machine power. It will, however, meet no contradiction if it maintains that the United States, as long as wages are disproportionately higher there than in the older civilised States, can best promote the development of their productive powers, their civilisation and political power, by allowing the free import as much as possible of those manufactured articles in the cost of which wages are a principal element, provided that other countries admit their agricultural products and raw materials.

The theory of free trade will then find admission into Spain, Portugal, Naples, Turkey, Egypt, and all barbarous and half-civilised or hot countries. In such countries as these the foolish idea will not be held any longer, of wanting to establish (in their present state of culture) a manufacturing power of their own by means of the system of protection.

England will then give up the idea that she is designed to monopolise the manufacturing power of the whole world. She will no longer require that France, Germany, and North America should sacrifice their own manufactures in consideration of the concession by England of permitting the import, duty free, of agricultural products and raw materials. She will recognise the legitimacy of protective systems in those nations, although she will herself more and more favour free trade; the theory having taught her that a nation which has already attained manufacturing supremacy, can only protect its own manufacturers and merchants against retrogression and indolence, by the free importation of means of subsistence and raw materials, and by the competition of foreign manufactured goods.

England will then follow a practice totally opposed to her present commercial policy, instead of lecturing, as hitherto, other nations to adopt free trade, whilst herself maintaining the strictest prohibitory system; she will herself permit competition without regard to the foreign systems of protection. She will defer her hopes of the general adoption of free trade, until other nations have no longer to fear that the ruin of their manufactories would result from free competition.

Meanwhile, and until that period has arrived, England will be able to compensate herself for the losses which she suffers from foreign systems of protection, in respect of

her export trade in manufactures of every-day use, by a
greater export of goods of finer quality, and by opening,
establishing, and cultivating new markets for her manufactures.

She will endeavour to bring about peace in Spain, in
the East, and in the states of Central and South America,
and will use her influence in all the barbarous and half-
civilised countries of Central and South America, of Asia
and Africa, in order that powerful and civilised governments may be formed in them, that security of persons
and of property may be introduced into them, for the
construction in them of roads and canals, the promotion
of education and civilisation, morality and industry, and
for rooting out fanaticism, superstition, and idleness. If
concurrently with these endeavours she abolishes her restrictions on the importation of provisions and raw
materials, she will increase her exports of manufactures
immensely, and much more successfully than by continually speculating on the ruin of the Continental manufactories.

If, however, these operations of civilisation on the part
of England are to be successful as respects barbarous and
half-civilised nations, she must not act in an exclusive
manner, she must not endeavour by special commercial
privileges, such as, for instance, she has managed to procure in Brazil, to monopolise these markets, and to shut
out other nations from them. Such a policy as the latter
will always excite the just jealousy of other nations, and
give them a motive for opposing the exertions of England.
It is evident that this selfish policy is the cause why the
influence of the civilised powers on the civilisation of such
countries as we have specified has been hitherto so unimportant. England ought therefore to introduce into the
law of nations the maxim : that in all such countries the
commerce of all manufacturing nations should have equal
rights. England would thereby not merely secure the aid
of all civilised powers in her own work of civilisation, but
also no disadvantage would result to her own commerce if
similar experiments of civilisation were undertaken by other

manufacturing nations. On account of their superiority in all branches of manufacture and commerce, the English would everywhere always obtain the greatest share of the exports to such markets.

The striving and ceaseless intrigues of the English against the manufactures of other nations might still be justified, if a world-manufacturing monopoly were indispensable for the prosperity of England, if it could not be proved by evidence that the nations which aspire, after the example of England, to attain to a large manufacturing power can very well attain their object without the humiliation of England; that England need not become poorer than she is because others become richer; and that nature offers sufficient means for the creation in Germany, France, and North America (without detriment to the prosperity of England), of a manufacturing power equal to that of the English.

With regard to this, it must further be remarked, that every nation which gains entire possession of its own home market for manufactures, gains in the course of time, by its home production and consumption of manufactured goods, infinitely more than the nation which has hitherto provided the former with manufactured goods loses by being excluded; because a nation which manufactures for itself, and which is perfectly developed in its economical conditions, becomes more than proportionately richer and more populous, consequently is enabled to consume infinitely more fabrics, than it could import while depending on a foreign manufacturing nation for its supply.

As respects the exportation of manufactured goods, however, the *countries of the temperate zone* (being specially fitted by nature for manufacturing) have a special field for their efforts in supplying the consumption of the countries of the torrid zone, which latter provide the former with colonial produce in exchange for their manufactured goods. The consumption of manufactured goods by the countries of the torrid zone, however, is partly determined by their ability to produce a surplus of the articles peculiar to their climate, and partly according to the proportion in which the countries of the temperate zone augment their demand for the products of the torrid zone.

If it can now be proved, that in the course of time the countries of the torrid zone can produce sugar, rice, cotton, coffee, &c. to an extent five or ten times greater than hitherto, and that the countries of the temperate zone can consume five or ten times more of these articles than hitherto, it will be simultaneously proved that the countries of the temperate zone can increase their exportation of manufactured goods to the countries of the torrid zone by from five to ten times their present total quantity.

The capability of the Continental nations to increase their consumption of colonial produce thus considerably, is indicated by the increase of consumption in England for the last fifty years; in reference to which it must further be borne in mind, that that increase would probably have become very much greater still were it not for the excessive taxes on consumption.

Of the possibility of augmenting the productions of the torrid zone, Holland in Sumatra and Java, and England in the East Indies, have given us during the last five years irrefragable proofs. England has quadrupled her importation of sugar from the East Indies from 1835 to 1839; her importation of coffee has increased even in a still larger proportion, while the importation of East India cotton is also greatly increasing. In one word, the latest English papers (February 1840) announced with great rejoicing that the capability of the East Indies for the production of these articles is unlimited, and that the time is not far distant when England will make herself independent of the importation of these articles from America and the West Indies. Holland on her part is already embarrassed for means of sale of her colonial products, and seeks actively for new markets. Let us further remember that North America continues to augment her cotton production —that in Texas a State has risen up which without doubt will become possessed of the whole of Mexico, and will make out of that fertile country a territory such as the Southern States of the North American Union now are. We may well imagine that order and law, industry and intelligence, will extend themselves gradually over the South American States from Panama to Cape Horn, then over the whole of Africa and Asia, and augment everywhere production and a surplus of products ; and we may then comprehend without difficulty that here there is room enough for more than *one* nation for the sale of manufactured goods.

By calculating the area of the land which has up to this time been actually used for the production of colonial produce, and comparing it with the entire area which is fitted by nature for such production, we shall find that at present scarcely the fiftieth part of the land fitted for this production is actually used.

How, then, could England be able to monopolise the manufacturing markets of all countries which yield colonial produce, if she is able to supply her own entire requirements of such produce by means of importation from the East Indies alone ? How can England indulge the hope of selling manufactured goods to countries whose colonial products she cannot take in exchange ? Or how can a great demand for colonial produce spring up in the continent of Europe, if the Continent is not enabled by its manufacturing production to pay for, and thus to consume, these goods ?

It is therefore evident, that keeping down the manufacturing industry of the Continent, though it certainly hinders the progress of the Continental nations, does not in the least further the prosperity of England.

It is further clear, that at present, as well as for some long time to come, the countries of the torrid zone will offer to all nations which are fitted for manufacturing production abundant materials for exchange.

Lastly, it is evident that a world-manufacturing monopoly such as is at present established by the free competition of English manufactured goods on the European and American continents is not in the least more conducive to the welfare of the human race than the system of protection, which aims at developing *the manufacturing power of the whole temperate zone,* for the benefit of *the agriculture of the whole torrid zone.*

The advance which England has made in manufactures, navigation, and commerce, need therefore not discourage any other nation which is fitted for manufacturing production, by the possession of suitable territory, of national power and intelligence, from entering into the lists with England's manufacturing supremacy. A future is approaching for manufactures, commerce, and navigation which will surpass the present as much as the present surpasses the past. Let us only have the courage to believe in a great national future, and in that belief to march onward. But above all things we must have enough national spirit at once to plant and protect the tree, which will yield its first richest fruits only to future generations. We must first gain possession of the home market of our own nation, at least as respects articles of general necessity, and try to procure the products of tropical countries direct from those countries which allow us to pay for them with our own manufactured goods. This is especially the task which the German commercial union has to solve, if the German nation is not to remain far behind the French and North Americans, nay, far behind even the Russians.

CHAPTER XVI.

POPULAR AND STATE FINANCIAL ADMINISTRATION, POLITICAL AND NATIONAL ECONOMY.

THAT which has reference to the raising, the expending, and the administration of the material means of government of a community (*the financial economy of the State*), must necessarily be distinguished everywhere from those institutions, regulations, laws, and conditions on which the economy of the individual subjects of a State is dependent, and by which it is regulated; i.e. from *the economy of the people*. The necessity for this distinction is apparent in reference to all political communities, whether these comprise a whole nation or merely fractions of a nation, and whether they are small or large.

In a confederated State, the financial economy of the State is again divided into the financial economy of the separate states and the financial economy of the entire union.

The economy of the people becomes identical with *national economy* where the State or the confederated State embraces a *whole nation* fitted for independence by the number of its population, the extent of its territory, by its political institutions, civilisation, wealth, and power, and thus fitted for stability and political influence. The economy of the people and national economy are, under these circumstances, one and the same. They constitute with the financial economy of the State the political economy of the nation.

But, on the other hand, in States whose population and territory merely consist of *the fraction of a nation* or of a national territory, which neither by complete and direct union, nor by means of a federal union with other fractions, constitutes a whole, we can only take into consideration an ' economy of the people ' which is directly opposed to ' private economy ' or to ' financial economy of the State.'

In such an imperfect political condition, the objects and requirements of a great nationality cannot be taken into consideration ; especially is it impossible to regulate the economy of the people with reference to the development of a nation complete in itself, and with a view to its independence, permanence, and power. Here politics must necessarily remain excluded from economy, here can one only take account of the natural laws of social economy, as these would develop and shape themselves if no large united nationality or national economy existed anywhere.

It is from this standpoint that that science has been cultivated in Germany which was formerly called ' State administration,' then ' national economy,' then ' political economy,' then ' popular administration,' without anyone having clearly apprehended the fundamental error of these systems.

The true conception and real character of national economy could not be recognised because no economically united nation was in existence, and because for the distinct and definite term ' *nation* ' men had everywhere substituted the general and vague term ' *society*,' an idea which is as applicable to entire humanity, or to a small country, or to a single town, as to the nation.

CHAPTER XVII.

IN a country devoted to mere raw agriculture, dullness of mind, awkwardness of body, obstinate adherence to old notions, customs, methods, and processes, want of culture, of prosperity, and of liberty, prevail. The spirit of striving for a steady increase in mental and bodily acquirements, of emulation, and of liberty, characterise, on the contrary, a State devoted to manufactures and commerce.

The cause of this difference lies partly in the different kind of social habits and of education which respectively characterise these two classes of people, partly in the different character of their occupation and in the things which are requisite for it. The agricultural population lives dispersed over the whole surface of the country; and also, in respect to mental and material intercourse, agriculturists are widely separated from one another. One agriculturist does almost precisely what the other does; the one produces, as a rule, what the other produces. The surplus produce and the requirements of all are almost alike; everybody is himself the best consumer of his own products; here, therefore, little inducement exists for mental intercourse or material exchange. The agriculturist has to deal less with his fellow-men than with inanimate nature. Accustomed to reap only after a long lapse of time where he has sown, and to leave the success of his exertions to the will of a higher power, contentment with little, patience, resignation, but also negligence and mental laziness, become to him a second nature. As his occupation keeps him apart from intercourse with his fellow-men, so also does the conduct of his ordinary business require but little mental exertion and bodily skill on his part. He learns it by imitation in the narrow circle of the family in which he was born, and the idea that it might be conducted differently and better seldom occurs to him. From the cradle to the grave he moves always in the same limited circle of men and of circumstances. Examples of special prosperity in consequence of extraordinary mental and bodily exertions are seldom brought before his eyes. The possession of means or a state of poverty are transmitted by inheritance in the occupation of mere agriculture from generation to generation, and almost all that power which originates in emulation lies dead.

The nature of manufactures is fundamentally different from that of agriculture. Drawn towards one another by their business, manufacturers live only in society, and consequently only in commercial intercourse and by means of that intercourse. The manufacturer procures from the market all that he requires of the necessaries of life and raw materials, and only the smallest part of his own products is destined for his own consumption. If the agriculturist expects a blessing on his exertions chiefly from nature, the prosperity and existence of the manufacturer mainly depend on his commercial intercourse. While the agriculturist does not know the purchasers of his produce, or at any rate need have little anxiety as to disposing of it, the very existence of the manufacturer depends on his customers. The prices of raw materials, of the necessaries of life and wages, of goods and of money, vary incessantly; the manufacturer is never certain how his profits will turn out. The favour of nature and mere ordinary industry do not guarantee to him existence and prosperity as they do to the agriculturist; both these depend entirely upon his own intelligence and activity. He must strive to gain more than enough in order to be certain of having enough of what is absolutely necessary; he must endeavour to become rich in order not to be reduced to poverty. If he goes on somewhat faster than others, he thrives; if he goes slower, he is certain of ruin.

He must always buy and sell, exchange and make bargains. Everywhere he has to deal with men, with changing circumstances, with laws and regulations; he has a hundred times more opportunity for developing his mind than the agriculturist. In order to qualify himself for conducting his business, he must become acquainted with foreign men and foreign countries; in order to establish that business, he must make unusual efforts. While the agriculturist simply has to do with his own neighbourhood, the trade of the manufacturer extends itself over all countries and parts of the world. The desire to gain the respect of his fellow-citizens or to retain it, and the continual competition of his rivals, which perpetually threaten his existence and prosperity, are to him a sharp stimulus to uninterrupted activity, to ceaseless progress. Thousands of examples prove to him, that by extraordinary performances and exertions it is possible for a man to raise himself from the lowest degree of well-being and position to the highest social rank, but that, on the other hand, by mental inactivity and negligence, he can sink from the most respectable to the meanest position. These circumstances produce in the manufacturer an energy which is not observable in the mere agriculturist.

If we regard manufacturing occupations as a whole, it must be evident at the first glance that they develop and bring into action an incomparably greater variety and higher type of mental qualities and abilities than agriculture does. Adam Smith certainly expressed one of those paradoxical opinions which (according to Dugald Stewart, his biographer) he was very fond of, when he maintained that agriculture requires more skill than manufactures and commerce. Without entering into the investigation whether the construction of a clock requires more skill than the management of a farm, we have merely to observe that all agricultural occupations are of the same kind, while in manufactures a thousand-fold variety exists. It must also not be forgotten, that for the purpose of the present comparison, agriculture must be regarded as it exists in the primitive state, and not as it has been improved by the

influence of manufactures. If the condition of English agriculturists appeared to Adam Smith much nobler than the
condition of English manufacturers, he had forgotten that
the condition of the former has been thus ennobled through
the influence of manufactures and commerce.

It is evident that by agriculture merely personal qualities of the same kind are put into requisition, and merely
those which combine bodily power and perseverance in
executing raw and manual labour with the simple idea of
order ; while manufactures require a thousand-fold variety
of mental ability, skill, and experience. The demand for
such a variety of talents makes it easy for every individual
in a manufacturing State to find an occupation and vocation corresponding with his individual abilities and taste,
while in an agricultural State but little choice exists. In
the former mental gifts are infinitely more prized than in
the latter, where as a rule the usefulness of a man is determined according to his bodily strength. The labour of the
weak and the cripple in the former is not unfrequently
valued at a much higher rate than that of the strongest
man is in the latter. Every power, even the smallest, that
of children and women, of cripples and old men, finds in
manufactures employment and remuneration.

Manufactures are at once the offspring, and at the
same time the supporters and the nurses, of science and the
arts. We may observe how little the condition of raw
agriculture puts sciences and arts into requisition, how
little of either is necessary to prepare the rude implements
which it employs. It is true that agriculture at first had,
by yielding rents of land, made it possible for men to
devote themselves to science and art ; but without manufactures they have always remained private treasures, and
have only extended their beneficial effects in a very slight
degree to the masses. In the manufacturing State the
industry of the masses is enlightened by science, and the
sciences and arts are supported by the industry of the
masses. There scarcely exists a manufacturing business
which has not relations to physics, mechanics, chemistry,
mathematics, or to the art of design &c. No progress,

no new discoveries and inventions, can be made in these sciences by which a hundred industries and processes could not be improved or altered. In the manufacturing State, therefore, sciences and arts must necessarily become popular. The necessity for education and instruction, through writings and lectures by a number of persons who have to bring into practice the results of scientific investigations, induces men of special talents to devote themselves to instruction and authorship. The competition of such talents, owing to the large demand for their efforts, creates both a division and co-operation of scientific activity, which has a most beneficial influence not merely on the further progress of science itself, but also on the further perfection of the arts and of industries. The effects of these improvements are soon afterwards extended even to agriculture. Nowhere can more perfect agricultural machines and implements be found, nowhere is agriculture carried on with so much intelligence, as in countries where industry flourishes. Under the influence of manufactures, agriculture itself is raised to a skilled industry, an art, a science.

The sciences and industry in combination have produced that great material power which in the new state of society has replaced with tenfold benefits the slave labour of ancient times, and which is destined to exercise on the condition of the masses, on the civilisation of barbarous countries, on the peopling of uninhabited lands, and on the power of the nations of primitive culture, such an immeasurable influence—namely, *the power of machinery.*

A manufacturing nation has a hundred times more opportunities of applying the power of machinery than an agricultural nation. A cripple can accomplish by directing a steam engine a hundred times more than the strongest man can with his mere hand.

The power of machinery, combined with the perfection of transport facilities in modern times, affords to the manufacturing State an immense superiority over the mere agricultural State. It is evident that canals, railways, and steam navigation are called into existence only by means of *the manufacturing power,* and can only by means of it be extended over the whole surface of the country. In the mere agricultural State, where everybody produces for himself the greater part of what he requires, and consumes himself the greater part of what he produces, where the individuals among themselves can only carry on a small amount of goods and passenger traffic, it is impossible that a sufficiently large traffic in either goods or passengers can take place to defray the costs of the erection and maintenance of the machinery of transport.

New inventions and improvements in the mere agricultural State are of but little value. Those who occupy themselves with such things in such a State fall themselves, as a rule, a sacrifice to their investigations and endeavours, while in the manufacturing State there is no path which leads more rapidly to wealth and position than that of invention and discovery. Thus, in the manufacturing State genius is valued and rewarded more highly than skill, and skill more highly than mere physical force. In the agricultural State, however, excepting in the public service, the reverse is almost the rule.

As, however, manufactures operate beneficially on the development of the mental powers of the nation, so also do they act on the development of the physical power of labour, by affording to the labourers means of enjoyment, inducements to exert their powers, and opportunities for making use of them. It is an undisputed observation, that in flourishing manufacturing States the workman, irrespective of the aid which he obtains from better machinery and tools, accomplishes a far larger day's work than in mere agricultural countries.

Moreover, the circumstance that in manufacturing States the value of time is recognised much more than in agricultural States, affords proof of the higher standing in the former of the power of labour. The degree of civilisation of a nation and the value of its labour power cannot be estimated more accurately than according to the degree of the value which it attributes to time. The savage lies for days idle in his hut. How can the shepherd learn to estimate the value of time, to whom time is simply a burden which

his pastoral pipe or sleep alone makes tolerable to him ?
How can a slave, a serf, a peasant, subject to tributes of
forced labour, learn to value time, he to whom labour is
penalty, and idleness gain ? Nations only arrive at the
recognition of the value of time through industry. At present time gained brings gain of profit; loss of time, loss of
profit. The zeal of the manufacturer to utilise his time in
the highest possible degree imparts itself to the agriculturist.
Through the increased demand for agricultural products
caused by manufactures, the rent and therefore the value of
land is raised, larger capital is employed in cultivating it,
profits are increased, a larger produce must be obtained
from the soil in order to be able to provide for the increased
rent and interest of capital, and for the increased consumption. One is in a position to offer higher wages, but one
also requires more work to be done. The workman begins
to feel that he possesses in his bodily powers, and in the
skill with which he uses them, the means of improving his
condition. He begins to comprehend why the Englishman
says, ' Time is money.'

Owing to the isolation in which the agriculturist lives,
and to his limited education, he is but little capable of
adding anything to general civilisation or learning to estimate the value of political institutions, and much less still
to take an active part in the administration of public affairs
and of justice, or to defend his liberty and rights. Hence
he is mostly in a state of dependence on the landed proprietor. Everywhere merely agricultural nations have
lived in slavery, or oppressed by despotism, feudalism, or
priestcraft. The mere exclusive possession of the soil gave
the despot, the oligarchy, or the priestly caste a power over
the mass of the agricultural population, of which the latter
could not rid themselves of their own accord.

Under the powerful influence of habit, everywhere among
merely agricultural nations has the yoke which brute force
or superstition and priestcraft imposed upon them so grown
into their very flesh, that they come to regard it as a necessary constituent of their own body, as a condition of their
very existence.

On the other hand, the separation and variety of the operations of business, and the confederation of the productive powers, press with irresistible force the various manufacturers towards one another. Friction produces sparks of the mind, as well as those of natural fire. Mental friction, however, only exists where people live together closely, where frequent contact in commercial, scientific, social, civil, and political matters exists, where there is large interchange both of goods and ideas. The more men live together in one and the same place, the more every one of these men depends in his business on the co-operation of all others, the more the business of every one of these individuals requires knowledge, circumspection, education, and the less that obstinacy, lawlessness, oppression, and arrogant opposition to justice interfere with the exertions of all these individuals and with the objects at which they aim, so much the more perfect will the civil institutions be found, so much larger will be the degree of liberty enjoyed, so much more opportunity will be given for self-improvement and for co-operation in the improvement of others. Therefore liberty and civilisation have everywhere and at all times emanated from towns; in ancient times in Greece and Italy; in the Middle Ages in Italy, Germany, Belgium, and Holland; later on in England, and still more recently in North America and France.

But there are two kinds of towns, one of which we may term the productive, the other the consuming kind. There are towns which work up raw materials, and pay the country districts for these, as well as for the means of subsistence which they require, by means of manufactured goods. These are the manufacturing towns, the productive ones. The more that these prosper, the more the agriculture of the country prospers, and the more powers that agriculture unfolds, so much the greater do those manufacturing towns become. But there are also towns where those live who simply consume the rents of the land. In all countries which are civilised to some extent, a large portion of the national income is consumed as rent in the towns. It would be false, however, were we to maintain as a general principle that this consumption is injurious to production, or does not tend to promote it. For the possibility of securing to oneself an independent life by the acquisition of rents, is a powerful stimulus to economy and to the utilisation of savings in agriculture and in agricultural improvements. Moreover, the man who lives on rents, stimulated by the inclination to distinguish himself before his fellow-citizens, supported by his education and his independent position, will promote civilisation, the efficiency of public institutions, of State administration, science and art. But the degree in which rent influences in this manner the industry, prosperity, and civilisation of the nation will always depend on the degree of liberty which that nation has already obtained. That inclination to become useful to the commonwealth by voluntary activity, and to distinguish oneself before one's fellow-citizens, will only develop itself in countries where this activity leads to public recognition, to public esteem, and to offices of honour, but not in countries where every attempt to gain public esteem and every manifestation of independence is regarded by the ruling power with a jealous eye. In such countries the man of independent income will give himself up to debauchery and idleness, and because in this manner he brings useful industry into contempt, and injures the morality as well as the industrious impulse of the nation, he will radically imperil the nation's productive power. Even if under such conditions the manufactures of towns are to some extent promoted by the consumption of the rentier, such manufactures are nevertheless to be regarded as barren and unsound fruits, and especially they will aid very little in promoting the civilisation, prosperity, and liberty of the nation. Inasmuch as a sound manufacturing industry especially tends to produce liberty and civilisation, it may also be said that through it rent itself is redeemed from forming a fund for idleness, debauchery, and immorality, and is converted into a fund for promoting mental culture, and consequently that through it the merely consuming towns are changed into productive towns. Another element by which the consuming towns are supported is, the consumption of the public servants and of the State administration. These also may occasion some apparent prosperity in a town; but whether such consumption especially promotes or is injurious to the productive power, prosperity, and institutions of the nation, depends altogether on the question how far the functions of the consumers tend to promote or to injure those powers.

From this the reason is evident why in mere agricultural States large towns can exist, which, although they contain a large number of wealthy inhabitants and manifold trades, exercise only a very inconsiderable influence on the civilisation, liberty, and productive power of the nation. The persons engaged in those trades necessarily participate in the views of their customers; they are to be regarded in a great measure as mere domestic servants of the rentiers and public employés. In contrast to great luxury in those towns, poverty, misery, narrow-mindedness, and a slavish disposition are found among the inhabitants of the surrounding country districts. A prosperous effect of manufactures on the civilisation, the improvement of public institutions, and the liberty of the nation, is only perceptible if in a country a manufacturing power is established which, quite independently of the rentiers and public servants, works for the large mass of the agricultural population or for export trade, and consumes the products of that population in large quantities for working up in manufacture and for subsistence. The more such a sound and healthy manufacturing power increases in strength, the more will it draw to its side the manufacturing power which originated in the consumption above named, and also the rentiers and public servants, and the more also will the public institutions be regulated with a view to the interest of the commonwealth.

Let us consider the condition of a large town in which the manufacturers are numerous, independent, lovers of liberty, educated, and wealthy, where the merchants participate in their interests and position, where the rentiers feel themselves compelled to gain the respect of the public, where the public servants are subject to the control of public opinion, where the men of science and art work for the public at large, and draw from it their means of subsistence; let us consider the mass of mental and material means which are combined together in such a narrow space, and further how closely this mass of power is united through the law of the division of the operations of business and the confederation of powers; we may note again how quickly every improvement, every progress in public institutions, and in social and economical conditions, on the one hand, and how, on the other hand, every retrogression, every injury of the public interests, must be felt by this mass; then, again; how easily this mass, living in one and the same place, can come to an agreement as to their common objects and regulations, and what enormous means it can concentrate on the spot for these purposes; and finally, in what a close union a community so powerful, enlightened, and liberty-loving, stands in relation to other similar communities in the same nation—if we duly consider all these things, we shall easily be convinced that the influence on the maintenance and improvement of the public welfare exercised by an agricultural population living dispersed over the whole surface of the country (however large its aggregate number may be) will be but slight in comparison with that of towns, whose whole power (as we have shown) depends upon the prosperity of their manufactures, and of those trades which are allied to and dependent on them.

The predominating influence of the towns on the political and municipal conditions of the nation, far from being disadvantageous to the rural population, is of inestimable advantage to it. The advantages which the towns enjoy make them feel it a duty to raise the agriculturists to the enjoyment of similar liberty, cultivation, and prosperity; for the larger the sum of these mental and social advantages is among the rural population, the larger will be the amount of the provisions and raw materials which they send into the towns, the greater also will be the quantity of the manufactured goods which they purchase from the towns, and consequently the prosperity of the towns.

The country derives energy, civilisation, liberty, and good institutions from the towns, but the towns insure to themselves the possession of liberty and good institutions by raising the country people to be partakers of these acquisitions. Agriculture, which hitherto merely supported landowners and their servants, now furnishes the commonwealth with the most independent and sturdy defenders of its liberty. In the culture of the soil, also, every class is now able to improve its position. The labourer can raise himself to become a farmer, the farmer to become a landed proprietor. The capital and the means of transport which industry creates and establishes now give prosperity to agriculture everywhere. Serfdom, feudal burdens, laws and regulations which injure industry and liberty, disappear. The landed proprietor will now derive a hundred times more income from his forest possessions than from his hunting. Those who formerly from the miserable produce of serf labour scarcely obtained the means of leading a rude country life, whose sole pleasure consisted in the keeping of horses and dogs and chasing game, who therefore resented every infringement of these pleasures as a crime against their dignity as lords of the soil, are now enabled by the augmentation of their rents (the produce of free labour) to spend a portion of the year in the towns. There, through the drama and music, through art and reading, their manners are softened ; they learn by intercourse with artists and learned men to esteem mind and talents. From mere Nimrods they become cultivated men. The aspect of an industrious community, in which everybody is striving to improve his condition, awakens in them also the spirit of improvement. They pursue instruction and new ideas instead of stags and hares. Returning to the country, they offer to the middle and small farmer examples worthy of imitation, and they gain his respect instead of his curse.

The more industry and agriculture flourish, the less can the human mind be held in chains, and the more are we compelled to give way to the spirit of toleration, and to put real morality and religious influence in the place of compulsion of conscience. Everywhere has industry given birth to tolerance; everywhere has it converted the priests into teachers of the people and into learned men. Everywhere have the cultivation of national language and literature, have the civilising arts, and the perfection of municipal institutions kept equal pace with the development of manufactures and commerce. It is from manufactures that the nation's capability originates of carrying on foreign trade with less civilised nations, of increasing its mercantile marine, of establishing a naval power, and by founding colonies, of utilising its surplus population for the further augmentation of the national prosperity and the national power.

Comparative statistics show that by the complete and relatively equal cultivation of manufactures and agriculture in a nation endowed with a sufficiently large and fertile territory, a population twice or three times as large can be maintained, and maintained, moreover, in a far higher degree of well-being than in a country devoted exclusively to agriculture. From this it follows that all the mental powers of a nation, its State revenues, its material and mental means of defence, and its security for national independence, are increased in equal proportion by establishing in it a manufacturing power.

At a time where technical and mechanical science exercise such immense influence on the methods of warfare, where all warlike operations depend so much on the condition of the national revenue, where successful defence greatly depends on the questions, whether the mass of the nation is rich or poor, intelligent or stupid, energetic or sunk in apathy; whether its sympathies are given exclusively to the fatherland or partly to foreign countries; whether it can muster many or but few defenders of the country—at such a time, more than ever before, must the value of manufactures be estimated from a political point of view.

CHAPTER XVIII.

THE MANUFACTURING POWER AND THE NATURAL PRODUCTIVE POWERS OF THE NATION.

THE more that man and the community perfect themselves, the more are they enabled to make use of the natural powers which are within their reach for the accomplishment of their objects, and the more does the sphere of what is within their reach extend itself.

The hunter does not employ the thousandth part, the shepherd not the hundredth part, of those natural advantages which surround him. The sea, foreign climates and countries, yield him either none, or at least only an inconsiderable amount of enjoyment, assistance, or stimulants to exertion.

In the case of a people in a primitive agricultural condition, a large portion of the existing natural resources lies yet unutilised, and man still continues limited to his nearest surroundings. The greater part of the water power and wind power which exists, or can be obtained, is unemployed; the various mineral products which the manufacturers so well understand how to utilise profitably, lie dead; various sorts of fuel are wasted or regarded (as, for instance, peat turf) as a mere hindrance to cultivation; stone, sand, and lime are used but little as building materials; the rivers, instead of being means of freight and transport for man, or of fertilising the neighbouring fields, are allowed to devastate the country by floods; warmer climates and the sea yield to the agricultural country but few of their products.

In fact, in the agricultural State, that power of nature on which production especially depends, the natural fertility of the soil, can only be utilised to a smaller extent so long as agriculture is not supported by manufacturing industry.

Every district in the agricultural State must itself produce as much of the things necessary to it as it requires to use, for it can neither effect considerable sales of that which it has in excess to other districts, nor procure that which it requires from other districts. A district may be ever so fertile and adapted for the culture of plants yielding oil, dyeing materials, and fodder, yet it must plant forests for fuel, because to procure fuel from distant mountain districts, over wretched country roads, would be too expensive. Land which if utilised for the cultivation of the vine and for garden produce could be made to yield three to four times more returns must be used for cultivating corn and fodder. He who could most profitably devote himself solely to the breeding of cattle must also fatten them: on the other hand, he who could most profitably devote himself merely to fattening stock, must also carry on cattle breeding. How advantageous it would be to make use of mineral manures (gypsum, lime, marl), or to burn peat, coal, &c. instead of wood, and to bring the forest lands under cultivation; but in such a State there exists no means of transport by means of which these articles can be conveyed with advantage for more than very short distances. What rich returns would the meadows in the valleys yield, if irrigation works on a large scale were established—the rivers now merely serve to wash down and carry away the fertile soil.

Through the establishment of manufacturing power in an agricultural State, roads are made, railways constructed, canals excavated, rivers rendered navigable, and lines of steamers established. By these not merely is the surplus produce of the agricultural land converted into machinery for yielding income, not merely are the powers of labour of those who are employed by it brought into activity, not only is the agricultural population enabled to obtain from the natural resources which it possesses an infinitely greater return than before, but all minerals, all metals, which heretofore were lying idle in the earth are now rendered useful and valuable. Articles which could formerly only bear a freight of a few miles, such as salt, coals, stone, marble, slate, gypsum, lime, timber, bark, &c., can now be distributed over the surface of an entire kingdom.   Hence such articles, formerly quite valueless, can now assume a degree of importance in the statistical returns of the national produce, which far surpasses the total of the entire agricultural production in previous times.   Not a cubic foot of water-fall will then exist which is not made to perform some service ; even in the most distant districts of a manufacturing country, timber and fuel will now become valuable, of which previously no one knew how to make any use.

Through the introduction of manufactures, a demand for a quantity of articles of food and raw materials is created, to the production of which certain districts can be far more profitably devoted than to the growth of corn (the usual staple article of rude agricultural countries).   The demand which now springs up for milk, butter, and meat adds a higher value to the existing pasture land, and leads to the breaking up of fallows and the erection of works of irrigation.   The demand for fruit and garden produce converts the former bare agricultural land into vegetable gardens and orchards.

The loss which the mere agricultural State sustains by not making use of these natural powers, is so much the greater the more it is fitted by nature for carrying on manufactures, and the more its territory is adapted for the production of raw materials and natural powers which manufacturers specially require ; that loss will therefore be the greatest in mountainous and hilly countries less suitable for agriculture on the whole, but which offer to manufactures plenty of water power, of minerals, timber, and stone, and to the farmer the opportunity of cultivating the products which are specially required by the manufacturer.

Countries with a temperate climate are (almost without exception) adapted for factories and manufacturing industry. The moderate temperature of the air promotes the development and exertion of power far more than a hot temperature.   But the severe season of the year, which appears to the superficial observer as an unfavourable effect of nature, is the most powerful promoter of habits of energetic activity, of forethought, order, and economy. A man who has the prospect before him of six months in which' he is not merely unable to obtain any fruits from the earth, but also requires special provisions and clothing materials for the sustenance of himself and his cattle, and for protection against the effects of cold, must necessarily become far more industrious and economical than the one who merely requires protection from the rain, and into whose mouth the fruits are ready to drop during the whole year. Diligence, economy, order, and forethought are at first produced by necessity, afterwards by habit, and by the steady cultivation of those virtues. Morality goes hand in hand with the exertion of one's powers and economy, and immorality with idleness and extravagance : each are reciprocally fertile sources, the one of power, the other of weakness.

An agricultural nation, which inhabits a country of temperate climate, leaves therefore the richest part of its natural resources unutilised.

The school, inasmuch as, in judging the influences of climate on the production of wealth, it has not distinguished between agriculture and manufacturing industry, has fallen into the gravest errors in respect to the advantages and disadvantages of protective regulations, which we cannot here omit thoroughly to expose, although we have already made mention of them in general terms elsewhere.

In order to prove that it is foolish to seek to produce everything in one and the same country, the school asks the question : whether it would be reasonable if we sought to produce wine by growing grapes in Scottish and English greenhouses ? It is of course possible to produce wine in this manner, only it would be of much worse quality and more expensive than that which England and Scotland could procure in exchange for their manufactured goods. To anyone who either is unwilling or unable to penetrate more deeply into the nature of things, this argument is a striking one, and the school is indebted to it for a large portion of its popularity ; at any rate among the French vine growers and silk manufacturers, and among the North

American cotton planters and cotton merchants. Regarded in the light of day, however, it is fundamentally false, since restrictions on commercial intercourse operate quite differently on the productive power of agriculture than they do on the productive power of manufacturing industry.

Let us first see how they operate on agriculture.

If France rejects from her frontiers German fat cattle, or corn, what will she effect thereby? In the first place, Germany will thereby be unable to buy French wines. France will therefore have to use those portions of her soil which are fitted for the cultivation of the vine less profitably in proportion as this destruction of commercial interchange lessens her exportation of wines. So many fewer persons will be exclusively occupied with the cultivation of the vine, and therefore so much less native agricultural products will be required, which these persons would have consumed, who would have otherwise devoted themselves exclusively to vine culture. This will be the case in the production of oil as well as in that of wine. France will therefore always lose in her agricultural power on other points much more than she gains on one single point, because by her exclusion of the German cattle she protects a trade in the rearing and fattening of cattle which had not been spontaneously developed, and for which, therefore, probably the agriculture of those districts where this branch of industry has had to be artificially developed is not adapted. Thus will it be if we consider France merely as an agricultural State opposed to Germany as a merely agricultural State, and if we also assume that Germany will not retaliate on that policy by a similar one. This policy, however, appears still more injurious if we assume that Germany, as she will be compelled to out of regard to her own interests, adopts similarly restrictive measures, and if we consider that France is not merely an agricultural, but also a manufacturing State. Germany will, namely, not merely impose higher duties on French wines, but on all those French products which Germany either produces herself, or can more or less do without, or procure elsewhere ; she will further restrict the importation

of those manufactured goods which she cannot at present
produce with special benefit, but which she can procure
from other places than from France. The disadvantage
which France has brought upon herself by those restrictions,
thus appears twice or three times greater than the advantage. It is evident that in France only so many persons
can be employed in the cultivation of the vine, in the
cultivation of olives, and in manufacturing industry, as the
means of subsistence, and raw materials which France
either produces herself or procures from abroad, are able
to support and employ. But we have seen that the restriction of importation has not increased the agricultural
production, but has merely transferred it from one district
to another. If free course had been permitted to the
interchange of products, the importation of products and
raw materials, and consequently the sale of wine, oil, and
manufactured goods, would have continually increased, and
consequently the number of persons employed in the cultivation of the vine and olives, and in manufactures; while
with the increasing traffic, on the one hand, the means of
subsistence and raw materials, and, on the other hand, the
demand for her manufactured products, would have augmented. The augmentation of this population would have
produced a larger demand for those provisions and raw
materials which cannot easily be imported from abroad,
and for which the native agriculture possesses a natural
monopoly; the native agriculture therefore would thus have
obtained a far greater profit. The demand for those
agricultural products for which the character of the French
soil is specially adapted, would be much more considerable
under this free interchange than that produced artificially
by restriction. One agriculturist would not have lost what
another gained; the whole agriculture of the country would
have gained, but still more the manufacturing industry.
Through restriction, the agricultural power of the country
therefore is not increased, but limited; and besides this,
that manufacturing power is annihilated which would have
grown up from the augmentation of the internal agriculture,
as well as from the foreign importation of provisions and

raw materials. All that has been attained through the restriction is an increase of prices in favour of the agriculturists of one district at the expense of the agriculturists of another district, but above all, at the expense of the total productive force of the country.

The disadvantages of such restrictions on the interchange of products are still more clearly brought to light in the case of England than in that of France. Through the corn laws, no doubt, a quantity of unfertile land is brought under cultivation; but it is a question whether these lands would not have been brought under cultivation without them. The more wool, timber, cattle, and corn that England would have imported, the more manufactured goods would she have sold, the greater number of workmen would have been enabled to live in England, the higher would the prosperity of the working classes have risen. England would probably have doubled the number of her workmen. Every single workman would have lived better, would have been better able to cultivate a garden for his pleasure and for the production of useful vegetables, and would have supported himself and his family much better. It is evident that such a large augmentation of the working population, as well as of its prosperity and of the amount of what it consumed, would have produced an enormous demand for those products for which the island possesses a natural monopoly, and it is more than probable that thereby double and three times as much land could have been brought into cultivation than by unnatural restrictions. The proof of this may be seen in the vicinity of every large town. However large the mass of products may be which is brought into this town from distant districts for miles around it, one cannot discover a single tract of land uncultivated, however much that land may have been neglected by nature. If you forbid the importation into such a town of corn from distant districts, you thereby merely effect a diminution of its population, of its manufacturing industry, and its prosperity, and compel the farmer who lives near the town to devote himself to less profitable culture

It will be perceived that thus far we are quite in accord with the prevailing theory. With regard to the interchange of raw products, the school is perfectly correct in supposing that the most extensive liberty of commerce is, under all circumstances, most advantageous to the individual as well as to the entire State.[1] One can, indeed, augment this production by restrictions ; but the advantage obtained thereby is merely apparent. We only thereby divert, as the school says, capital and labour into another and less useful channel. But the manufacturing productive power, on the contrary, is governed by other laws, which have, unfortunately, entirely escaped the observation of the school.

If restriction on the importation of raw products hinder (as we have seen) the utilisation of the natural resources and powers of a State, restrictions on the importation of manufactured goods, on the contrary, call into life and activity (in the case of a populous country already far advanced in agriculture and civilisation) a mass of natural powers ; indeed, without doubt, the greater half of all natural powers, which in the merely agricultural State lie idle and dead for ever. If, on the one hand, restrictions on the importation of raw products are a hindrance to the development not only of the manufacturing, but also of the agricultural productive, powers of a State, on the other hand, an internal manufacturing productive power produced by restrictions on the importation of foreign manufactures, stimulates the whole agricultural productive powers of a State to a degree which the most flourishing foreign trade is never able to do. If the importation of raw products makes the foreign country dependent on us and takes from it the means of manufacturing for itself, so in like manner, by the importation of foreign manufactures, are we rendered dependent on the foreign country, and the means are taken from us of manufacturing for ourselves. If the importation of products and raw materials withdraws from the foreign country the material for the employment and support of its population and diverts it to our nation, so does the importation of manufactured fabrics take from

[1] See Appendix C.

us the opportunity of increasing our own population and of providing it with employment. If the importation of natural products and raw materials increases the influence of our nation on the affairs of the world and gives us the means of carrying on commerce with all other nations and countries, so by the importation of manufactured fabrics are we chained to the most advanced manufacturing nation, which can rule over us almost as it pleases, as England rules over Portugal. In short, history and statistics alike prove the correctness of the dictum expressed by the ministers of George I. : that nations are richer and more powerful the more they export manufactured goods, and import the means of subsistence and raw materials. In fact, it may be proved that entire nations have been ruined merely because they have exported only means of subsistence and raw materials, and have imported only manufactured goods. Montesquieu,[1] who understood better than anyone either before or after him how to learn from History the lessons which she imparts to the legislator and politician, has well perceived this, although it was impossible for him in his times, when political economy was as yet but little studied, clearly to unfold the causes of it. In contradiction to the groundless system of the physiocratic school, he maintained that Poland would be more prosperous if she gave up altogether foreign commerce, i.e. if she established a manufacturing power of her own, and worked up and consumed her own raw materials and means of subsistence. Only by the development of an internal manufacturing power, by free, populous, and industrious cities, could Poland obtain a strong internal organisation, national industry, liberty, and wealth ; only thus could she maintain her independence and political superiority over less cultivated neighbours. Instead of foreign manufactured goods she should have introduced (as England did at one time, when she was on the same footing as regards culture with Poland) foreign manufacturers and foreign manufacturing capital. Her aristocracy, however, preferred to export the paltry fruits of serf labour to foreign markets, and to obtain in return

---

[1] *Esprit des Lois*, Livre XX. chap. xxiii.

the cheap and fine goods made by foreign countries. Their successors now may answer the question: whether it is advisable for a nation to buy the fabrics of a foreign country so long as its own native manufactures are not yet sufficiently strengthened to be able to compete in prices and quality with the foreigner. The aristocracy of other countries may bear her fate in mind whenever they are instigated by feudal inclinations; they may then cast a glance at the English aristocracy in order to inform themselves as to what is the value to the great landed proprietors of a strengthened manufacturing power, of free municipal institutions, and of wealthy towns.

Without here entering on an inquiry whether it would have been possible for the elective kings of Poland, under the circumstances under which they were placed, to introduce such a commercial system as the hereditary kings of England have gradually developed and established, let us imagine that it had been done by them: can we not perceive what rich fruits such a system would have yielded to the Polish nation? By the aid of large and industrious towns, the crown would have been rendered hereditary, the nobility would have been obliged to make it convenient to take part in legislation in a' House of Peers, and to emancipate their serfs; agriculture would have developed itself, as it has developed itself in England; the Polish nobility would now be rich and respected; the Polish nation would, even if not so respected and influential in the affairs of the world as the English nation is, would have long ago become so civilised and powerful as to extend its influence over the less cultivated East. Without a manufacturing power she has become ruined and partitioned, and were she not so already she must have become so. Of its own accord and spontaneously no manufacturing power was developed in her; it could not be so, because its efforts would have been always frustrated by further advanced nations. Without a system of protection, and under a system of free trade with further advanced nations, even if Poland had retained her independence up to the present time, she could never have carried on anything more than a crippled agriculture; she could never have become rich, powerful, and outwardly influential.

By the circumstance that so many natural resources and natural powers are converted by the manufacturing power into productive capital is the fact chiefly to be accounted for, that protective regulations act so powerfully on the augmentation of national wealth. This prosperity is not a false appearance, like the effects of restrictions on the trade in mere natural products, it is a reality. They are natural powers which were otherwise quite dead— natural resources which were otherwise quite valueless, which an agricultural nation calls to life and renders valuable by establishing a manufacturing power of its own.

It is an old observation, that the human race, like the various breeds of animals, is improved mentally and bodily by crossings; that man, if a few families always intermarry amongst one another, just as the plant if the seed is always sown in the same soil, gradually degenerates. We seem obliged to attribute to this law of nature the circumstance that among many wild or half-wild tribes in Africa and Asia, whose numbers are limited, the men choose their wives from foreign tribes. The fact which experience shows, that the oligarchies of small municipal republics, who continually intermarry among themselves, gradually die out or visibly degenerate, appears similarly attributable to such a natural law. It is undeniable that the mixing of two quite different races results, almost without exception, in a powerful and fine future progeny; and this observation extends to the mixing of the white race with the black in the third and the fourth generation. This observation seems to confirm more than any other thing the fact, that those nations which have emanated from a crossing of race frequently repeated and comprising the whole nation, have surpassed all other nations in power and energy of the mind and character, in intelligence, bodily strength, and personal beauty.[1]

[1] According to Chardin, the Guebres, an unmixed tribe of the old Persians, are an ugly, deformed, and clumsy race, like all nations of Morgol

We think we may conclude from this that men need not necessarily be such dull, clumsy, and unintellectual beings as we perceive them to be when occupied in crippled agriculture in small villages, where a few families have for thousands of years intermarried only with one another; where for centuries it has occurred to no one to make use of an implement of a new form, or to adopt a new method of culture, to alter the style of a single article of clothing, or to adopt a new idea; where the greatest art consisted, not in exerting one's bodily and mental powers in order to obtain as much enjoyment as possible, but to dispense with as much of it as possible.

This condition of things is entirely changed (and for the best purposes of the improvement of race of a whole nation) by establishing a manufacturing power. While a large portion of the increase of the agricultural population goes over into the manufacturing community, while the agricultural population of various districts becomes mixed by marriages between one another and with the manufacturing population, the mental, moral, and physical stagnation of the population is broken up. The intercourse which manufactures and the commerce between

descent, while the Persian nobility, which for centuries has intermarried with Georgian and Circassian women, is distinguished for beauty and strength. Dr. Pritchard remarks that the unmixed Celts of the Scottish Highlands are far behind the Scottish Lowlanders (descendants of Saxons and Celts) in height, bodily power, and fine figure. Pallas makes similar observations respecting the descendants of the Russians and Tartars in comparison with the unmixed tribes to which they are related. Azara affirms that the descendants of the Spaniards and the natives of Paraguay are a much more handsome and powerful race of men than their ancestors on both sides. The advantages of the crossing of race are not only apparent in the mixing of different nations, but also in the mixing of different family stocks in one and the same nation. Thus the Creole negroes far surpass those negroes who have sprung from unmixed tribes, and who have come direct from Africa to America, in mental gifts as well as in bodily power. The Caribbeans, the only Indian race which chooses regularly its women from neighbouring tribes, are in every respect superior to all other American tribes. If this is a law of nature, the rise and progress which the cities of the Middle Ages displayed shortly after their foundation, as well as the energy and fine bodily appearance of the American people, are hence partly explained.

various nations and districts which is based upon them bring about, brings new blood into the whole nation as well as into separate communities and families.

The development of the manufacturing power has no less important an influence on the improvement of the breeds of cattle. Everywhere, where woollen manufactures have been established, the race of sheep has quickly been improved. Owing to a greater demand for good meat, which a numerous manufacturing population creates, the agriculturist will endeavour to introduce better breeds of cattle. The greater demand for 'horses of luxury' is followed by the improvement of the breeds of horses. We shall then no longer see those wretched primitive breeds of cattle, horses, and sheep, which having resulted from the crippled state of agriculture and everywhere from neglect of crossing of breeds, exhibit a side spectacle worthy of their clumsy owners.

How much do the productive powers of the nations already owe to the importation of foreign breeds of animals and to the improvement of the native breeds; and how much has yet to be done in this respect! All the silkworms of Europe are derived from a few eggs, which (under Constantine) were brought to Constantinople in hollow sticks, by Greek monks from China, where their exportation was strictly prohibited. France is indebted to the importation of the Thibet goat for a beautiful product of her industry. It is very much to be regretted, that hitherto the breeding and improving of animals has been chiefly carried on in order to satisfy the requirements of luxury, and not in order to promote the welfare of the large masses. The descriptions of travellers show that in some countries of Asia a race of cattle has been seen which combines considerable draught power with great swiftness of pace, so that they can be used with almost the same advantage as horses for riding and driving. What immense advantages would such a breed of cattle confer on the smaller agriculturists of Europe! What an increase in means of subsistence, productive power, and convenience, would the working classes thereby obtain! But even far more than by improved breeds, and importation from one country into another of various animals, has the productive power of the human race been increased by the improvement and importation of trees and plants. This is at once evident, if we compare the original plants as they have sprung from the bosom of nature, with their improved species. How little do the primitive plants of the various species of corn and of fruit trees, of edible vegetables and of the olive, resemble in form and utility their improved offspring! What masses of means of nourishment, of enjoyment, and comfort, and what opportunities for the useful application of human powers, have been derived from them! The potato, the beet-root, the cultivation of root crops for cattle, together with the improved systems of manuring and improved agricultural machines, have increased ten-fold the returns of agriculture, as it is at present carried on by the Asiatic tribes.

Science has already done much with regard to the discovery of new plants and the improvement of them; but governments have not yet devoted to this important object so much attention as they ought to have done, in the interests of economy. Quite recently, species of grass are said to have been discovered in the savannas of North America, which from the poorest soil yield a higher produce than any fodder plants, which are as yet known to us, do from the richest soil. It is very probable that in the wild regions of America, Asia, Africa, and Australia, a quantity of plants still vegetate uselessly, the transplantation and improvement of which might infinitely augment the prosperity of the inhabitants of temperate climates.

It is clear that most of the improvements and transportations of animals and vegetables, most of the new discoveries which are made with respect to them, as well as all other progress, inventions, and discoveries, are chiefly calculated to benefit the countries of the temperate zone, and of those most of all, the manufacturing countries.

CHAPTER XIX.

THE MANUFACTURING POWER AND THE INSTRUMENTAL
POWERS (MATERIAL CAPITAL) OF THE NATION.

THE nation derives its productive power from the mental
and physical powers of the individuals; from their social,
municipal, and political conditions and institutions; from
the natural resources placed at its disposal, or from the instruments it possesses as the material products of former
mental and bodily exertions (material, agricultural, manufacturing, and commercial capital). In the last two chapters
we have dealt with the influence of manufactures on the
three first-named sources of the national productive powers;
the present and the following chapter are devoted to the
demonstration of its influence on the one last named.

That which we understand by the term '*instrumental
powers*' is called '*capital*' by the school. It matters but
little by what word an object is signified, but it matters
very much (especially with regard to scientific investigations)
that the word selected should always indicate one and the
same object, and never more or less. As often, therefore,
as different branches of a matter are discussed, the necessity
for a distinction arises. The school now understands by
the term '*capital*' not merely the material, but also all
mental and social means of and aids to production. It
clearly ought, therefore, to specify wherever it speaks of
capital, whether the material capital, the material instruments of production, or the mental capital, the moral and
physical powers which are inherent in individuals, or which
individuals derive from social, municipal, and political conditions, are meant. The omission of this distinction, where
it ought to be drawn, must necessarily lead to false reason-

ing, or else serve to conceal false reasoning. Meanwhile, however, as it is not so much our business to found a new nomenclature as to expose the errors committed under the cover of an inexact and inadequate nomenclature, we will adopt the term ' *capital*,' but distinguish between mental and material capital, between material, agricultural, manu- facturing, and commercial capital, between private and national capital.

Adam Smith (by means of the common expression, *capital*) urges the following argument against the protective commercial policy which is adopted to the present day by all his followers : ' A country can indeed by means of such (protective) regulations produce a special description of manufactures sooner than without them ; and this spe- cial kind of manufactures will be able to yield after some time as cheap or still cheaper productions than the foreign country. But although in this manner we can succeed in directing national industry sooner into those channels into which it would later have flowed of its own accord, it does not in the least follow that the total amount of industry or of the incomes of the community can be increased by means of such measures. *The industry of the community can only be augmented in proportion as its capital increases, and the capital of the community can only increase in accordance with the savings which it gradually makes from its income.* Now, the immediate effect of these measures is to decrease the income of the community. But it is certain that that which decreases that income cannot increase the *capital* more quickly than it would have been increased by itself, if it, as well as industry, had been left free.' [1]

As a proof of this argument, the founder of the school adduces the well-known example, refuted by us in the previous chapter, how foolish it would be to plant the vine in Scotland.

In the same chapter he states, the *annual income* of the community is nothing else but the *value in exchange* of those objects which the national industry produces annually.

In the above-named argument lies the chief proof of the

[1] *Wealth of Nations*, Book IV. chap. ii.

school against the protective commercial policy. It admits
that by measures of protection manufactories can be established and enabled to produce manufactured goods as
cheap or even cheaper than they can be obtained from
abroad; but it maintains that the immediate effect of these
measures is to decrease the income of the community (the
value in exchange of those things which the national industry
produces annually). It thereby weakens its power of acquiring capital, for capital is formed by the savings which
the nation makes out of its annual income; the total of
the capital, however, determines the total of the national
industry, and the latter can only increase in proportion
to the former. It therefore weakens its industry by means
of those measures—by producing an industry which, in the
nature of things, if they had been left to their own free
course would have originated of its own accord.

It is firstly to be remarked in opposition to this reasoning, that Adam Smith has merely taken the word *capital* in
that sense in which it is necessarily taken by rentiers or
merchants in their book-keeping and their balance-sheets,
namely as the grand total of their values of exchange in
contradistinction to the income accruing therefrom.

He has forgotten that he himself includes (in his definition of capital) the mental and bodily abilities of the producers under this term.

He wrongly maintains that the revenues of the nation
are dependent only on the sum of its material capital. His
own work, on the contrary, contains a thousand proofs that
these revenues are chiefly conditional on the sum of its
mental and bodily powers, and on the degree to which they
are perfected, in social and political respects (especially by
means of more perfect division of labour and confederation
of the national productive powers), and that although
measures of protection require sacrifices of material goods
for a time, these sacrifices are made good a hundred-fold
in powers, in the ability to acquire values of exchange, and
are consequently merely reproductive outlay by the nation.

He has forgotten that the ability of the whole nation to

increase the sum of its material capital consists mainly in the possibility of converting unused natural powers into material capital, into valuable and income-producing instruments, and that in the case of the merely agricultural nation a mass of natural powers lies idle or dead which can be quickened into activity only by manufactures. He has not considered the influence of manufactures on the internal and external commerce, on the civilisation and power of the nation, and on the maintenance of its independence, as well as on the capability arising from these of gaining material wealth.

He has e.g. not taken into consideration what a mass of capital the English have obtained by means of colonisation (Martin estimates the amount of this at more than two and a half milliards of pounds sterling).

He, who nevertheless elsewhere proves so clearly that the capital employed in intermediate commerce is not to be regarded as belonging to any given nation, so long as it is not equally embodied in that nation's land, has here not duly considered that the nationalisation of such capital is most effectually realised by favouring the nation's inland manufactures.

He has not taken into account, that by the policy of favouring native manufacture a mass of foreign capital, mental as well as material, is attracted into the country.

He falsely maintains that these manufactures have originated in the natural course of things and of their own accord ; notwithstanding that in every nation the political power interferes to give to this so-called natural course an artificial direction for the nation's own special advantage.

He has illustrated his argument, founded on an ambiguous expression and consequently fundamentally wrong, by a fundamentally wrong example, in seeking to prove that because it would be foolish to produce wine in Scotland by artificial methods, therefore it would be foolish to establish manufactures by artificial methods.

He reduces the process of the formation of capital in the nation to the operation of a private rentier, whose income is determined by the value of his material capital, and who can only increase his income by savings which he again turns into capital.

He does not consider that this theory of savings, which in the merchant's office is quite correct, if followed by a whole nation must lead to poverty, barbarism, powerlessness, and decay of national progress. Where everyone saves and economises as much as he possibly can, no motive can exist for production. Where everyone merely takes thought for the accumulation of values of exchange, the mental power required for production vanishes. A nation consisting of such insane misers would give up the defence of the nation from fear of the expenses of war, and would only learn the truth after all its property had been sacrificed to foreign extortion, that the wealth of nations is to be attained in a manner different to that of the private rentier.

The private rentier himself, as the father of a family, must follow a totally different theory to the shopkeeper theory of the material values of exchange which is here set up. He must at least expend on the education of his heirs as much value of exchange as will enable them to administer the property which is some day to fall to their lot.

The building up of the material national capital takes place in quite another manner than by mere saving as in the case of the rentier, namely in the same manner as the building up of the productive powers, chiefly by means of the reciprocal action between the mental and material national capital, and between the agricultural, manufacturing, and commercial capital.

The augmentation of the national material capital is dependent on the augmentation of the national mental capital, and *vice versâ*.

The formation of the material agricultural capital is dependent on the formation of the material manufacturing capital, and *vice versá*.

The material commercial capital acts everywhere as an intermediary, helping and compensating between both.

In the uncivilised state, in the state of the hunter and the fisher, the powers of nature yield almost everything, capital is almost *nil*. Foreign commerce increases the latter, but also in so doing (through fire-arms, powder, lead) totally destroys the productiveness of the former. The theory of savings cannot profit the hunter ; he must be ruined or become a shepherd.

In the pastoral state the material capital increases quickly, but only so far as the powers of nature afford spontaneously nourishment to the cattle. The increase of population, however, follows closely upon the increase of flocks and herds and of the means of subsistence. On the one hand, the flocks and herds as well as pastures become divided into smaller shares ; on the other hand, foreign commerce offers inducements to consumption. It would be in vain to preach to the pastoral nation the theory of savings ; it must sink into poverty or pass over into the agricultural State.

To the agricultural nation is open an immense, but at the same time limited, field for enriching itself by utilising the dormant powers of nature.

The agriculturist for himself alone can save provisions, improve his fields, increase his cattle ; but the increase of the means of subsistence always follows the increase of population. The material capital (namely, cultivated land and cattle), in proportion as the former becomes more fertile and the latter increase, becomes divided among a larger number of persons. Inasmuch, however, as the surface of the land cannot be increased by industry, and the land cannot be utilised up to the measure of its natural capacity, for want of means of transport, which (as we showed in the preceding chapter) must remain imperfect in such a state of things owing to lack of intercourse ; and as moreover the merely agricultural nation is mostly in want of those instruments, intelligence, motives to exertion, and also of that energy and social development which are imparted to the nation through manufactures and the commerce which originates from them, the mere agricultural population soon reaches a point in which the increase of material agricultural capital can no longer keep pace with the increase of population, and where consequently individual poverty increases more and more, notwithstanding that the total capital of the nation is continually increasing.

In such a condition the most important product of the nation consists of *men*, who, as they cannot find sufficient support in their own country, emigrate to other countries. It can be but little consolation to such a country, that the school regards man as an accumulated capital; for the exportation of men does not occasion return freights, but, on the contrary, causes the unproductive export of considerable amounts of material values (in the shape of implements, utensils, money &c.)

It is clear that in such a state of things, where the national division of labour is not properly developed, neither industry nor economy can bring about the augmentation of the material capital (material enrichment of individuals).

The agricultural country is, of course, rarely quite without any foreign commerce, and foreign commerce, as far as it extends, also supplies the place of internal manufactures with regard to the augmentation of capital, inasmuch as it places the manufacturer of the foreign country in commercial relation with the agriculturist of the home country. This, however, takes place only partially and very imperfectly : firstly, because this commerce extends merely to special staple products, and chiefly only to those districts which are situated on the sea-coast and on navigable rivers ; and secondly, because it is in any case but a very irregular one, and is liable to be frequently interrupted by wars, fluctuations in trade and changes in commercial legislation, by specially rich harvests, and by foreign importations.

The augmentation of the material agricultural capital can only take place on a large scale, with regularity and continuously, if a completely developed manufacturing power is established in the midst of the agriculturists.

By far the greatest portion of the material capital of a nation is bound to its land and soil. In every nation the value of landed property, of dwelling houses in rural districts and in towns, of workshops, manufactories, waterworks, mines, &c. amounts to from *two-thirds to nine-tenths of the entire property of the nation*. It must therefore be accepted as a rule, that all that increases or decreases the value of the fixed property, increases or decreases the total of the material capital of the nation. Now, it is evident that the capital value of land of equal natural fertility is incomparably larger in the proximity of a small town than in remote districts; that this value is incomparably larger still in the neighbourhood of a large town than in that of a small one; and that in manufacturing nations these values are beyond all comparison greater than in mere agricultural nations. We may observe (inversely) that the value of the dwelling houses and manufacturing buildings in towns, and that of building land, rises or falls (as a rule) in the same ratio in which the commercial intercourse of the town with the agriculturists is extended or restricted, or in which the prosperity of these agriculturists progresses or recedes. From this it is evident that the augmentation of the agricultural capital is dependent on the augmentation of the manufacturing capital; and (inversely) the latter on the former.[1]

----

[1] Compare the following paragraph, which appeared in the *Times* during 1883:

'MANUFACTURES AND AGRICULTURE.—The statistician of the Agricultural Department of the United States has shown in a recent report that the value of farm lands decreases in exact proportion as the ratio of agriculture to other industries increases. That is, where all the labour is devoted to agriculture, the land is worth less than where only half of the people are farm labourers, and where only a quarter of them are so engaged the farms and their products are still more valuable. It is, in fact, proved by statistics that diversified industries are of the greatest value to a State, and that the presence of a manufactory near a farm increases the value of the farm and its crops. It is further established that, dividing the United States into four sections or classes, with reference to the ratio of agricultural workers to the whole population, and putting those States having less than 30 per cent. of agricultural labourers in the first class, all having over 30 and less than 50 in the second, those between 50 and 70 in the third, and those having 70 or more in the fourth, the value of farms is in inverse ratio to the agricultural population; and that, whereas in the purely agricultural section, the fourth class, the value of the farms per acre is only $5 28c., in the next class it is $13 03c., in the third $22 21c., and in the manufacturing districts $40 91c. This shows an enormous advantage for a mixed district. Yet not only is the land more valuable—the production per acre is greater, and the wages paid to farm hands larger. Manufactures and varied industries thus not only benefit the manufacturers, but are of equal benefit and

This reciprocal action is, however, in the case of the change from the agricultural state into the manufacturing state much stronger on the part of manufacture than on the part of agriculture. For as the increase of capital which results from the change from the condition of the mere hunter to the pastoral condition is chiefly effected by the rapid increase of flocks and herds, as the increase of capital resulting from the change from the pastoral condition into the agricultural condition is chiefly effected by the rapid increase in cultivated land and in surplus produce, so, in the event of a change from the agricultural condition into the manufacturing condition, is the augmentation of the material capital of the nation chiefly effected by those values and powers which are devoted to the establishment of manufactures, because thereby a mass of formerly unutilised natural and mental powers are converted into mental and material capital. Far from hindering the saving of material capital, the establishment of manufactures is the first thing which affords to the nation the means of employing its agricultural savings in an economical manner, and it is the first means by which the nation can be incited to agricultural economy.

In the legislative bodies of North America it has often been mentioned that corn there rots in the ear from want of sale, because its value will not pay the expense of harvesting it. In Hungary it is asserted that the agriculturist is almost choked with excess of produce, while manufactured goods are three to four times dearer there than in England. Germany even can remember such times. In agricultural States, therefore, all surplus agricultural produce is not material capital. By means of manufactures it first becomes commercial capital by being warehoused, and then by being sold to the manufacturers it is turned into manufacturing capital. What may be unutilised stock in the band of the agriculturist, becomes productive capital in the hand of the manufacturer, and *vice versâ*.

advantage to the farmers as well. The latter would, therefore, do well to abandon their prejudice against factories, which really increase the value of their property instead of depreciating it.'—Tʀ.

Production renders consumption possible, and the desire to consume incites to production. The mere agricultural nation is in its consumption dependent on foreign conditions, and if these are not favourable to it, that production dies out which would have arisen in consequence of the desire to consume. But in that nation which combines manufactures with agriculture in its territory, the reciprocal inducement continually exists, and therefore, also, there will be continuous increase of production and with it augmentation of capital on both sides.

As the agricultural-manufacturing nation is (for the reasons which we have already given) always incomparably richer in material capital than the mere agricultural nation (which is evident at a glance), so in the former the rate of interest is always much lower, and larger capital and more favourable conditions are at the disposal of men of enterprise, than in the purely agricultural nation. It follows that the former can always victoriously compete with the newly formed manufactories in the agricultural nation ; that the agricultural nation remains continually in debt to the manufacturing nation, and that in the markets of the former continual fluctuations in the prices of produce and manufactured goods and in the value of money take place, whereby the accumulation of material wealth in the purely agricultural nation is no less endangered than its morality and its habits of economy.

The school distinguishes fixed capital from circulating capital, and classes under the former in a most remarkable manner a multitude of things which are in circulation without making any practical application whatever of this distinction. The only case in which such a distinction can be of value, it passes by without notice. The material as well as the mental capital is (namely) bound in a great measure to agriculture, to manufactures, to commerce, or to special branches of either—nay often, indeed, to special localities. Fruit trees, when cut down, are clearly not of the same value to the manufacturer (if he uses them for wood-work) as they are to the agriculturist (if he uses them for the production of fruit). Sheep, if, as has already frequently happened in Germany and North America, they have to be slaughtered in masses, have evidently not the value which they would possess when used for the production of wool. Vineyards have (as such) a value which, if used as arable fields, they would lose. Ships, if used for timber or for firewood, have a much lower value than when they serve as' means of transport. What use can be made of manufacturing buildings, water-power, and machinery if the spinning industry is ruined? In like manner individuals lose, as a rule, the greatest part of their productive power, consisting in experience, habits, and skill, when they are displaced. The school gives to all these objects and properties the general name of capital, and would transplant them (by virtue of this terminology) at its pleasure from one field of employment to another. J. B. Say thus advises the English to divert their manufacturing capital to agriculture. How this wonder is to be accomplished he has not informed us, and it has probably remained a secret to English statesmen to the present day. Say has in this place evidently confounded private capital with national capital. A manufacturer or merchant can withdraw his capital from manufactures or from commerce by selling his works or his ships and buying landed property with the proceeds. A whole nation, however, could not effect this operation except by sacrificing a large portion of its material and mental capital. The reason why the school so deliberately obscures things which are so clear is apparent enough. If things are called by their proper names, it is easily comprehended that the transfer of the productive powers of a nation from one field of employment to another is subject to difficulties and hazards which do not always speak in favour of 'free trade,' but very often in favour of national protection.

CHAPTER XX.

THE MANUFACTURING POWER AND THE AGRICULTURAL
INTEREST.

IF protective duties in favour of home manufactures proved
disadvantageous to the consumers of manufactured goods
and served only to enrich the manufacturer, this disadvantage would especially be felt by the landed proprietor
and the agriculturist, the most numerous and important
class of those consumers. But it can be proved that even
this class derives far greater advantages from the establishment of manufactures, than the manufacturers themselves
do ; for by means of these manufactures a demand for
greater variety and for larger quantities of agricultural
products is created, the value in exchange of these products
is raised, the agriculturist is placed in a position to utilise
his land and his powers of labour more profitably. Hence
emanates an increase of rent, of profits, and wages ; and the
augmentation of rents and capital is followed by an increase
in the selling value of land and in the wages of labour.

The selling value of landed property is nothing else than
capitalised rent ; it is dependent, on the one hand, on the
amount and the value of the rent, but, on the other hand,
and chiefly, on the quantities of mental and material
capital existing in the nation.

Every individual and social improvement, especially
every augmentation of productive power in the nation, but,
most of all, of the manufacturing power, raises the amount
of rents, while at the same time it lessens the proportion
which rent bears to the gross produce. In an agricultural
nation little developed and scantily peopled, e.g. in Poland,
the proportion of rent amounts to one-half or one-third the

gross produce; in a well-developed, populous, and wealthy nation, e.g. England, it only amounts to one-fourth or one-fifth part of that produce. Nevertheless, the actual worth of this smaller proportion is disproportionately greater than the worth of that larger proportion—in money value especially, and still more in manufactured goods. For the *fifth* part of twenty-five bushels (the average produce of wheat in England) equals five bushels; the *third* part, however, of nine bushels (the average produce of wheat in Poland) amounts only to three bushels; further, these five bushels in England are worth on an average 25s. to 30s.; while these three bushels in the interior of Poland are at the most worth 8s. to 9s.; and finally, manufactured goods in England are at least twice as cheap as in Poland: consequently the English landed proprietor is able to buy for his 30s. of money-rent ten yards of cloth, but the Polish landowner for his 9s. of rent can obtain scarcely two yards, from which it is evident that the English landed proprietor by the fifth part of the gross produce is as rentier three times, and as consumer of manufactured goods five times, better off than the Polish landowner is by the third part of his gross produce. But that farmers and agricultural labourers also must in England (especially as consumers of manufactured goods) be disproportionately better off than in Poland, is shown by the fact that out of the produce of twenty-five bushels in England twenty bushels go for sowing, for cultivation of the field, wages, and profits: half of which (or ten bushels) devoted to the last two items have an average value of 60s. or twenty yards of cloth (at 3s. per yard), while from the produce of nine bushels in Poland only six bushels go for sowing, cultivation of the field, profit, and wages, half of which, or three bushels, devoted to the last two items, have merely a value of 10s. to 12s. or three and a half yards of cloth.

Rent is a chief means of usefully employing material capital. Its price, therefore, depends also on the quantity of the capital existing in the nation and the proportion of the supply of it to the demand. By the surplus of the capital which accumulates in a manufacturing nation as the result of its home and foreign commerce, by the low rate of interest which there exists, and the circumstance that in a manufacturing and commercial nation a number of individuals who have become wealthy are always seeking to invest their surplus capital in land, the selling price of a given amount of rent of land is always disproportionately higher in such a nation than in the mere agricultural nation. In Poland the rent of land is sold at ten or twenty years' purchase; in England at thirty or forty years' purchase.

In the proportion in which the selling value of the rent of land is higher in the manufacturing and commercial nation than in the agricultural nation, so also is the selling value of the land itself higher in the former than in the latter. For land of equal natural fertility in each country, the value is in England ten to twenty times higher than in Poland.

That manufactures have an influence on the amount of rent, and therefore on the value in exchange of the land, is a fact which Adam Smith certainly notices at the conclusion of the ninth chapter of his first book, but only incidentally and without bringing the vast importance of manufactures in this respect properly to light. He there distinguishes those causes which influence *directly* the augmentation of rent (such as the improvement of the land itself, the increase in the number and the value of the cattle maintained upon it) from those causes which have only an *indirect* influence on that augmentation, among which latter he classes manufactures. In this manner he places *the main cause of the augmentation of the rent* and of the value of land (namely, the *manufactures*) in the background so that it is scarcely perceptible ; while he places the improvement of the land itself and the increase of cattle, which are themselves for the most part the result of manufactures and of the commerce proceeding from them, as the chief cause, or at least as an equal cause, of that augmentation.

Adam Smith and his followers have not recognised by any means to its full extent the value of manufactures in this respect.

We have remarked that in consequence of manufactures and of the commerce connected with them, the value of land of equal natural fertility in England is ten to twenty times greater than in Poland. If we now compare the total produce of the English manufacturing production and of the English manufacturing capital with the total produce of the English agricultural production and of the English agricultural capital, we shall find that the greatest part of the wealth of the nation shows itself in the thus increased value of landed property.

MacQueen [1] has prepared the following estimate of the national wealth and national income of England :

I. National Capital.

1. In agriculture, lands, mines, and fisheries . . . . 2,604 mill.
   Working capital in cattle, implements, stocks, and money . 655 „
   Household furniture and utensils of the agriculturists . . 52 „

   $\overline{\hspace{1cm}}$ 3,311 „

2. Invested in manufactures and commerce :
   Manufactures, and home trade in manufactured
   goods . . . . 178½ mill.
   Trade in colonial goods . . . . . 11 „
   Foreign trade in manufactured goods . . 16½ „

   $\overline{\hspace{1cm}}$ 206 „

   To this add increase since 1835 (in which year
   this estimate was made) . . . . 12 „

   218 mill.

   Then in town buildings of all kinds, and in
   manufacturing buildings . . . . 605 mill.
   In ships . . . . 33¼ „
   In bridges, canals, and railways . . ; 118 „
   In horses which are not used in agriculture . 20 „

   776¼ mill.

   Amount of the whole national capital (exclusive of the
   capital invested in the colonies, in foreign loans, and in
   the English public funds) . . . . . . 4,305½ mill.

II. Gross National Production.

1. Of agriculture, mines, and fisheries . . . . 539 mill.
2. Manufacturing production . . . . 259¼ „

   $\overline{\hspace{1cm}}$ 798¼ „

From this estimate it may be seen :

1. That the value of the land devoted to agriculture

[1] *General Statistics of the British Empire.* London, 1836.

amounts to $\frac{26}{43}$ of the whole English national property, and is about twelve times more than the value of the whole capital invested in manufactures and in commerce.

2. That the whole capital invested in agriculture amounts to over three-fourths of the English national capital.

3. That the value of the whole fixed property in England, namely:

Of the land, &c.	2,604 mill.
Of houses in towns, and manufacturing buildings .	605 „
Of canals and railways	118 „
	3,327 „

is therefore equal to more than three-fourths of the whole English national capital.

4. That the manufacturing and commercial capital, inclusive of ships, does not altogether amount to more than $241\frac{1}{2}$ millions, and therefore to only about $\frac{1}{18}$ of the English national wealth.

5. That the whole English agricultural capital, with 3,311 millions, yields a gross income of 539 millions, consequently about 16 per cent.; while manufacturing and commercial capital, amounting to 218 millions, gives a gross annual production of $259\frac{1}{2}$ millions or of 120 per cent.

It must here, above all things, be noted that the 218 millions manufacturing capital, with an annual production of $259\frac{1}{2}$ millions, constitute the chief reason why the English agricultural capital could have attained to the enormous amount of 3,311 millions, and its annual produce to the sum of 539 millions. By far the greatest part of the agricultural capital consists in the value of land and cattle. Manufactures, by doubling and trebling the population of the country, by furnishing the means for an immense foreign commerce, for the acquisition and exploration of a number of colonies, and for a large mercantile marine, have increased in the same proportion the demand for means of subsistence and raw materials, have afforded to the agriculturist at once the means and the motive for satisfying this increased demand, have increased the exchangeable value of these products, and thus caused the proportionate increase in the amount and the selling value of the rent of land, consequently of the land itself. Were these 218 millions of manufacturing and commercial capital destroyed, we should see not merely the 259½ millions manufacturing production, but also the greatest part of the 3,311 millions agricultural capital, and consequently of the 539 millions agricultural production, disappear. The English national production would not merely lose 259½ millions (the value of its manufacturing production), but the value of land would decline to the value which it has in Poland, i.e. to the tenth or twentieth part of its present value.

From this it follows that all capital which is devoted by the agricultural nation in a profitable manner to manufactures, increases in the course of time the value of the land tenfold. Experience and statistics everywhere confirm this statement. Everywhere it has been seen that in consequence of the establishment of manufactures the value of land and also that of the stock of cattle rapidly increases. Let anyone compare these values in France (in 1789 and in 1840), in North America (in 1820 and in 1830), or in Germany (in 1830 and in 1840), how they have corresponded with a less developed or a more fully developed condition of manufactures, and he will find our observation everywhere confirmed.

The reason for this appearance lies in the increased power of production in the nation, which emanates from the regular division of labour and from the strengthened confederation of the national powers, also from a better use of the mental and natural powers placed at the disposal of the nation, and from foreign commerce.

These are the very same causes and effects which we may perceive in respect to improved means of transport; which not merely yield in themselves a revenue, and through it a return for the capital spent upon them, but also powerfully promote the development of manufactures and agriculture, whereby they increase in the course of time the value of the landed property within their districts to tenfold the value of the actual material capital which has been employed in creating them. The agriculturist, in comparison with the undertaker of such works (improved means of transport), has the great advantage of being quite sure of his tenfold gain on his invested capital and of obtaining this profit without making any sacrifices, while the contractor for the works must stake his whole capital. The position of the agriculturist is equally favourable as compared with that of the erector of new manufactories.

If, however, this effect of manufactures on agricultural production, on rent, and therefore on the value of landed property, is so considerable and advantageous for all who are interested in agriculture ; how, then, can it be maintained that protective measures would favour manufactures merely at the cost of the agriculturists ?

The material prosperity of agriculturists, as well as of all other private persons, principally depends on the point that the value of what they produce shall exceed the value of what they consume. It, therefore, is not so important to them that manufactured goods should be cheap, as especially that a large demand for various agricultural products should exist, and that these should bear a high value in exchange. Now, if measures of protection operate so that the agriculturist gains more by the improvement of the market for his own produce than he loses by the increase of the prices of such manufactured goods as he requires to buy, he cannot rightly be described as making a sacrifice in favour of the manufacturer. This effect is, however, always observable in the case of all nations who are capable of establishing a manufacturing power of their own, and in their case is most apparent during the first period of the rise of the native manufacturing industry ; since just at that time most of the capital transferred to manufacturing industry is spent on the erection of dwelling houses and manufactories, the application of water power &c., an expenditure which chiefly benefits the agriculturist. However much in the beginning the advantages of the greater sale of agricultural produce and of its increased value outweighs the disadvantage of the increased price of manufactured goods, so must this favourable condition always increase further to the advantage of the agriculturists, because the flourishing of the manufactories always tends in the course of time continually more and more to increase the prices obtainable for agricultural produce and to lessen the prices of manufactured goods.

Further, the prosperity of the agriculturist and landed proprietor is especially dependent on the circumstance that the value of the instrument from which his income is derived, namely his landed property, at least maintains its former-position. This is not merely the chief condition of his prosperity, but frequently of his entire economical existence. For instance, it frequently happens that the annual production of the agriculturist exceeds his consumption, and nevertheless he finds himself ruined. This occurs if while his landed property is encumbered with money debts, the general credit becomes fluctuating; if on one side the demand for money capital exceeds the supply of it, and on the other hand the supply of land exceeds the demand. In such cases a general withdrawal of money loans and a general offer of land for sale arises, and consequently land becomes almost valueless, and a large number of the most enterprising, active, and economical land cultivators are ruined, not because their consumption has exceeded their production, but because the instrument of their production, their landed property, has lost in their hands a considerable portion of its value, in consequence of causes over which they had no control ; further, because their credit has thereby become destroyed ; and finally, because the amount of the money debts with which their landed property is encumbered is no longer in proportion to the money value of their possessions, which has become depressed by the general worthlessness of landed property. Such crises have occurred in Germany and North America during the last fifty years more than once, and in this manner a large proportion of the German nobility find themselves no longer in possession of property or landed estate, without having clearly perceived that they really owe this fate to the policy adopted by their brothers in

England, the Tories whom they regard as so well disposed. The condition of the agriculturist and landed proprietor is, however, totally different in countries where manufactures flourish vigorously.   There, while the productive capabilities of the land and the prices of produce are increased, he not merely gains the amount by which the value of his production exceeds the value of his consumption ; he gains, as landed proprietor, not only an increase of annual rent, but the amount of capital represented by the increase of rent. His property doubles and trebles itself in value, not because he works more, improves his fields more, or saves more, but because the value of his property has been increased in consequence of the establishment of manufactures.   This effect affords to him means and inducement for greater mental and bodily exertions, for improvement of his land, for the increase of his live stock, and for greater economy, notwithstanding increased consumption.   With the increase in the value of his land his credit is raised, and with it the capability of procuring the material capital required for his improvements.

Adam Smith passes over these conditions of the exchangeable value of land in silence.   J. B. Say, on the contrary, believes that the exchangeable value of land is of little importance, inasmuch as, whether its value be high or low, it always serves equally well for production.   It is sad to read from an author whom his German translators regard as a universal national authority, such fundamentally wrong views about a matter which affects so deeply the prosperity of nations.   We, on the contrary, believe it essential to maintain that there is no surer test of national prosperity than the rising and falling of the value of the land, and that fluctuations and crises in that are to be classed among the most ruinous of all plagues that can befall a country.

Into this erroneous view the school has also been led by its predilection for the theory of free trade (as it desires the latter term to be understood).   For nowhere are fluctuations and crises in the value and price of land greater than in those purely agricultural nations which are in unrestricted commercial intercourse with rich and powerful manufacturing and commercial nations.

Foreign commerce also, it is true, acts on the increase of rent and the value of land, but it does so incomparably less decidedly, uniformly, and permanently, than the establishment of home manufactures, the continuous regular increase of manufacturing production, and the exchange of home manufacturing products for home agricultural products.

So long as the agricultural nation still possesses a large quantity of uncultivated or badly cultivated land, so long as it produces staple articles which are readily taken by the richer manufacturing nation in exchange for manufactured goods, so long as these articles are easy of transport, so long also as the demand for them is lasting and capable of annual increase at a rate corresponding with the growth of the productive powers of the agricultural nation, and so long as it is not interrupted by wars or foreign tariff regulations, under such circumstances foreign commerce has a powerful effect on the increase of rents and on the exchangeable value of land. But as soon as any one of these conditions fails or ceases to operate, foreign commerce may become the cause of national stagnation, nay frequently of considerable and long-continued retrogression.

The fickleness of foreign demand has the most baneful effect of all in this respect, if in consequence of wars, failure of crops, diminution of importation from other parts, or owing to any other circumstances and occurrences, the manufacturing nation requires larger quantities especially of the necessaries of life or raw materials, or of the special staple articles referred to, and then if this demand again to a great extent ceases, in consequence of the restoration of peace, of rich harvests, of larger importation from other countries, or in consequence of political measures. If the demand lasts merely for a short time, some benefit may result from it to the agricultural nation; but if it last for years or a series of years then all the circumstances of the agricultural nation, the scale of expenditure of all private establishments, will have become regulated by it. The

producer becomes accustomed to a certain scale of consumption; and certain enjoyments, which under other
circumstances he would have regarded as luxuries, become
necessaries to him.   Relying on the increased yield and
value of his landed property, he undertakes improvements
in cultivation, in buildings, and makes purchases which
otherwise he would never have done.   Purchases and
sales, contracts of letting land, loans, are concluded according to the scale of increased rents and values.   The
State itself does not hesitate to increase its expenses in
accordance with the increased prosperity of private persons.   But if this demand afterwards suddenly ceases, disproportion between production and consumption follows;
disproportion between the decreased values of land and
the money encumbrances upon it which continue undiminished in amount; disproportion between the money
rent payable under the leases, and the money produce of
the land which has been taken on lease; disproportion
between national income and national expenditure; and in
consequence of these disproportions, bankruptcy, embarrass-
ment, discouragement, retrogression in the economical as
well as in the mental and political development of the
nation.   Agricultural prosperity would under these circumstances act like the stimulant of opium or strong
drink, stimulating merely for a moment, but weakening for
a whole lifetime.   It would be like Franklin's flash of
lightning, which for a moment displayed the objects in a
shining light, but only to throw them back into deeper
darkness.

A period of temporary and passing prosperity in agriculture is a far greater misfortune than uniform and
lasting poverty.   If prosperity is to bring real benefit to
individuals and nations, it must be continuous.   It, however,
becomes continuous only in case it increases gradually, and
in case the nation possesses guarantees for this increase
and for its duration.   A lower value of land is incomparably better than fluctuations in its value; it is only a
gradual but steady increase in that value that affords to the
nation lasting prosperity.   And only by the possession of

a manufacturing power of their own, can well-developed nations possess any guarantee for the steady and permanent increase of that value.

To how very small an extent clear ideas prevail as to the effect of a home manufacturing power on the rent and value of land in comparison with the effect which foreign trade has on them, is shown most plainly by the circumstance that the proprietors of vineyards in France still always believe that they are injuriously affected by the French system of protection, and demand the greatest possible freedom of commerce with England in hopes of thereby increasing their rents.

Dr. Bowring, in his report of the commercial relations existing between England and France, the fundamental tendency of which is to show the benefit to France which a larger importation of English fabrics and a consequently increasing exportation of French wines would occasion, has adduced facts from which the most striking proof against his own argument can be brought.

Dr. Bowring quotes the importation of French wines into the Netherlands (2,515,193 gallons, 1829) against the annual importation into England (431,509 gallons) to prove how greatly the sale of French wines in England could be increased by freer commercial interchange between the two countries.

Now supposing (although it is more than improbable that the sale of French wines in England would not find obstacles in the predilection existing there for spirituous liquors, for strong beer, and for the strong and cheap wines of Portugal, Spain, Sicily, Teneriffe, Madeira, and the Cape)—supposing that England really was to extend her consumption of French wines to the same proportion as that of the Netherlands, she would certainly (calculating according to her population) be able to increase her consumption to five or six million gallons (i.e. to from ten to fifteen fold her present amount); and from a superficial point of view this certainly appears to promise great advantage to France, and to the French vineyard proprietors.

If, however, we investigate this matter to the bottom,

we obtain another result.   By as much freedom of trade as
is possible—we will not say complete freedom of trade,
although the latter would have to be accepted according to
the principle enunciated, and to Bowring's arguments—it
can scarcely be doubted that the English would draw to
themselves a large part of the French market for manufactured goods (especially as regards the manufactures of
woollens, cotton, linen, iron, and pottery).   On the most
moderate estimate we must assume, that in consequence of
this decreased French manufacturing production one million
fewer inhabitants would live in the French towns, and that
one million fewer persons would be employed in agriculture
for the purpose of supplying the citizens of those towns
with raw material and necessaries of life.   Now, Dr. Bowring
himself estimates the consumption of the country population
in France at 16½ gallons per head, and that of the town
population at double that quantity, or 33 gallons per head.
Thus in consequence of the diminution of the home manufacturing power effected by free trade, the internal consumption of wines would decrease by 50 million gallons,
while the exportation of wine could only increase by 5 or 6
million gallons.   Such a result could scarcely be to the
special advantage of the French proprietors of vineyards,
since the internal demand for wines would necessarily suffer
ten times more than the external demand could possibly
gain.

In one word : it is evident as respects the production of
wine, as also in that of meat, of corn, and of raw materials
and provisions generally, that in the case of a great nation
well fitted to establish a manufacturing power of its own,
the internal manufacturing production occasions ten to
twenty times more demand for the agricultural products of
temperate climates, consequently acts ten to twenty times
more effectually on the increase of the rent and exchangeable
value of real estate, than the most flourishing exportation
of such products can do.   The most convincing proof of
this may also be seen in the amount of rents and the
exchangeable value of land near large towns, as compared
with their amount and value in distant provinces, even

though these latter are connected with the capital by good roads and conveniences for commercial intercourse.

The doctrine of rent can either be considered from the point of view of values or from the point of view of *productive powers* ; it can further be considered with respect merely to private relations, namely the relations between landed proprietor, farmer, and labourer, or with especial regard to the social and national relations and conditions. The school has taken up this doctrine chiefly from the sole point of view of private economy. So far as we know, for instance, nothing has been adduced by it to show how the consumption of the rents of the nation is the more advantageous the more it takes place in the proximity of the place whence it is derived, but how nevertheless in the various States that consumption takes place principally at the seat of the sovereign (e.g. in absolute monarchies mostly in the national metropolis), far away from the provinces where it is produced, and therefore in a manner the least advantageous to agriculture, to the most useful industries, and to the development of the mental powers of the nation. Where the landowning aristocracy possess no rights and no political influence unless they live at the Court, or occupy offices of State, and where all public power and influence is centralised in the national metropolis, landowners are attracted to that central point, where almost exclusively they can find the means of satisfying their ambition, and opportunities for spending the income of their landed property in a pleasant manner ; and the more that most landowners get accustomed to live in the capital, and the less that a residence in the provinces offers to each individual opportunities for social intercourse and for mental and material enjoyments of a more refined character, the more will provincial life repel him and the metropolis attract him. The province thereby loses and the metropolis gains almost all those means of mental improvement which result from the spending of rents, especially those manufactures and mental producers which would have been maintained by the rent. The metropolis under those circumstances, indeed, appears extremely attractive because it unites in itself all the talents of the intellectual workers and the greatest part of the material trades which produce articles of luxury.   But the provinces are thereby deprived of those mental powers, of those material means, and especially of those industries, which chiefly enable the agriculturist to undertake agricultural improvements, and stimulate him to effect them.

In these circumstances lies to a great extent the reason why in France, especially under absolute monarchy, alongside of a metropolis surpassing in intellect and splendour all towns of the European continent, agriculture made but slight progress, and the provinces were deficient in mental culture and in useful industries.   But the more that the landed aristocracy gains in independence of the Court, and in influence in legislation and administration, the more that the representative system and the system of administration grants to the towns and provinces the right of administering their own local affairs and of taking part in the legislation and government of the State, and consequently the more that respect and influence can be attained in the provinces and by living there, so much the more will the landed aristocracy, and the educated and well-to-do citizens, be drawn to those localities from which they derived their rents, the greater also will be the influence of the expenditure of those rents on the development of the mental powers and social institutions, on the promotion of agriculture, and on the development of those industries which are useful to the great masses of the people in the province.

The economical conditions of England afford proof of this observation.   The fact that the English landed proprietor lives for the greatest portion of the year on his estates, promotes in manifold ways the improvement of English agriculture : directly, because the resident landowner devotes a portion of his rent to undertaking on his own account improvements in agriculture, or to supporting such improvements when undertaken by his tenants ; indirectly, because his own consumption tends to support the manufactures and agencies of mental improvement and civilisation existing in the neighbourhood. From these circumstances it can further partly be explained why in Germany and in Switzerland, in spite of the want of large towns, of important means of transport, and of national institutions, agriculture and civilisation in general are in a much higher condition than in France.

But the great error into which in this matter Adam Smith and his school have fallen is that which we have already before indicated, but which can be here more clearly shown, viz. that he did not clearly recognise the influence of manufactures on the increase of rents, on the market value of landed property itself, and on the agricultural capital, and did not state this by any means to its full extent, but, on the contrary, has drawn a comparison between agriculture and manufactures in such a manner that he would make it appear that agriculture is far more valuable and important to a nation than manufactures, and that the prosperity resulting from it is far more lasting than the prosperity resulting from the latter. Adam Smith in so doing merely sanctioned the erroneous view of the physiocratic school, although in a somewhat modified manner. He was evidently misled by the circumstance that—as we have already demonstrated by the statistical conditions of England – the material agricultural capital is (even in the richest manufacturing country) ten to twenty times more important than the material manufacturing capital; in fact, even the annual *agricultural production* far exceeds in value the total *manufacturing capital*. The same circumstance may also have induced the physiocratic school to over-estimate the value of agriculture in comparison with manufactures. Superficially considered, it certainly appears as if agriculture enriches a country ten times more, and consequently deserves ten times more consideration, and is ten times more important to the State than manufactures. This, however, is merely apparent. If we investigate the causes of this agricultural prosperity to their basis, we find them principally in the existence of manufactures. It is those 218 millions of manufacturing capital which have principally called into existence those

8,311 millions of agricultural capital. The same consideration holds good as respects means of transport; it is the money expended in constructing them which has made those lands which are within the reach of the canals more valuable. If the means of transport along a canal be destroyed, we may use the water which has been hitherto employed for transport, for irrigating meadows—apparently, therefore, for increasing agricultural capital and agricultural rents, &c.; but even supposing that by such a process the value of these meadows rose to millions, this alteration, apparently profitable to agriculture, will nevertheless lower the total value of the landed property which is within reach of the canal ten times more.

Considered from this point of view, from the circumstance that the total manufacturing capital of a country is so small in comparison with its total agricultural capital, conclusions must be drawn of a totally different character from those which the present and preceding school have drawn from it. The maintenance and augmentation of the manufacturing power seem now, even to the agriculturist, the more valuable, the less capital as compared with agriculture it requires to absorb in itself and to put into circulation. Yes, it must now become evident to the agriculturist, and especially to the rent-owners and the landed proprietors of a country, that it would be to their interest to maintain and develop an internal manufacturing power, even had they to procure the requisite capital without hope of direct recompense; just as it is to their interest to construct canals, railways, and roads even if these undertakings yield no real nett profit. Let us apply the foregoing considerations to those industries which lie nearest and are most necessary to agriculture, e.g. flour mills; and there will be no room for doubt as to the correctness of our views. Compare, on the one hand, the value of landed property and rent in a district where a mill is not within reach of the agriculturist, with their value in those districts where this industry is carried on in their very midst, and we shall find that already this single industry has a considerable effect on the value of land and on rent; that there, under similar conditions of natural fertility, the total value of the land has not merely increased to double, but to ten or twenty times more than the cost of erecting the mill amounted to ; and that the landed proprietors would have obtained considerable advantage by the erection of the mill, even if they had built it at their common expense and presented it to the miller. The latter circumstance, in fact, takes place every day in the backwoods of North America, where, in cases when an individual has not adequate capital to erect such works entirely at his own expense, the landowner gladly helps him by contributing labour, by team work, free gifts of timber, &c. In fact, the same thing also occurred, although in another form, in countries of earlier civilisation ; here must undoubtedly be sought the origin of many ancient feudal ' common mill ' rights.

As it is in the case of the corn mill, so is it in those of saw, oil, and plaster mills, so is it in that of iron works ; everywhere it can be proved that the rent and the value of landed property rise in proportion as the property lies nearer to these industries, and especially according as they are in closer or less close commercial relations with agriculture.

And why should this not be the case with woollen, flax, hemp, paper, and cotton mills ? Why not with all manufacturing industries ? We see, at least, everywhere that rent and value of landed property rise in exactly the same proportion with the proximity of that property to the town, and with the degree in which the town is populous and industrious. If in such comparatively small districts we calculate the value of the landed property and the capital expended thereon, and, on the other hand, the value of the capital employed in various industries, and compare their total amount, we shall find everywhere that the former is at least ten times larger than the latter. But it would be folly to conclude from this that a nation obtains greater advantages by investing its material capital in agriculture than in manufactures, and that the former is in itself more favourable to the augmentation of capital than the latter.

The increase of the material agricultural capital depends for the most part on the increase of the material manufacturing capital; and nations which do not recognise this truth, however much they may be favoured by nature in agriculture, will not only not progress, but will retrograde in wealth, population, culture, and power.

We see, nevertheless, how the proprietors of rent and of landed property not unfrequently regard those fiscal and political regulations which aim at the establishment of a native manufacturing power as privileges which serve merely to enrich the manufacturers, the burden of which they (the landed interest) have exclusively to bear. They, who at the beginning of their agricultural operations so clearly perceived what great advantages they might obtain if a corn mill, a saw mill, or an iron work were established in their neighbourhood, that they themselves submitted to the greatest sacrifices in order to contribute towards the erection of such works, can no longer, when their interests as agriculturists have somewhat improved, comprehend what immense advantages the total agricultural interest of the country would derive from a perfectly developed national industry of its own, and how its own advantage demands that it should submit to those sacrifices without which this object cannot be attained. It therefore happens, that, only in a few and only in very well educated nations, the mind of each separate landed proprietor, though it is generally keenly enough alive to those interests which lie close at hand, is sagacious enough to appreciate those greater ones which are manifest to a more extended view.

It must not, moreover, be forgotten that the popular theory has materially contributed to confuse the opinions of landed proprietors. Smith and Say endeavoured everywhere to represent the exertions of manufacturers to obtain measures of protection as inspirations of mere self-interest, and to praise, on the contrary, the generosity and disinterestedness of the landed proprietors, who are far from claiming any such measures for themselves. It appears, however, that the landed proprietors have merely become mindful of and been stimulated to the virtue of disinterestedness, which is so highly attributed to them, in order to rid themselves of it. For in the greatest number of, and in the most important, manufacturing states, these landowners have also recently demanded and obtained measures of protection, although (as we have shown in another place) it is to their own greatest injury. If the landed proprietors formerly made sacrifices to establish a national manufacturing power of their own, they did what the agriculturist in a country place does when he makes sacrifices in order that a corn mill or an iron forge may be established in his vicinity. If the landed proprietors now require protection also for their agriculture, they do what those former landed proprietors would have done if, after the mill has been erected by their aid, they required the miller to help in cultivating their fields. Without doubt that would be a foolish demand. Agriculture can only progress, the rent and value of land can only increase, in the ratio in which manufactures and commerce flourish; and manufactures cannot flourish if the importation of raw materials and provisions is restricted. This the manufacturers everywhere felt. For the fact, however, that the landed proprietors notwithstanding obtained measures of protection in most large states, there is a double reason. Firstly, in states having representative government, the landowner's influence is paramount in legislation, and the manufacturers did not venture to oppose themselves perseveringly to the foolish demand of the landowners, fearing lest they might thereby incline the latter to favour the principles of free trade; they preferred to agree with the landed proprietors.

It was then insinuated by the school to the landed proprietors that it is just as foolish to establish manufactures by artificial means as it would be to produce wine in cold climates in greenhouses; that manufactures would originate in the natural course of things of their own accord; that agriculture affords incomparably more opportunity for the increase of capital than manufactures; that the capital of the nation is not to be augmented by artificial measures; that laws and State regulations can only induce a condition of things less favourable to the augmentation of wealth. Finally, where the admission could not be avoided that manufactures had an influence over agriculture, it was sought at least to represent that influence to be as little and as uncertain as possible. In any case (it was said) if manufactures had an influence over agriculture, at least everything is injurious to agriculture that is injurious to manufactures, and accordingly manufactures also had an influence on the increase of the rent of land, but merely an *indirect* one. But, on the other hand, the increase of population and of cattle, the improvements in agriculture, the perfection of the means of transport, &c. had a direct influence on the increase of rent. The case is the same here in reference to this distinction between *direct* and *indirect* influence as on many other points where the school draws this distinction (e.g. in respect of the results of mental culture), and here also is the example already mentioned by us applicable; it is like the fruit of the tree, which clearly (in the sense of the school) is an indirect result, inasmuch as it grows on the twig, which again is a fruit of the branch, this again is a fruit of the trunk, and the latter a fruit of the root, which alone is a direct product of the soil. Or would it not be just as sophistical to speak of the population, the stock of cattle, the means of transport, &c. as direct causes ; but of manufactures, on the contrary, as an indirect cause of the augmentation of rents, while, nevertheless, one's very eyesight teaches one in every large manufacturing country that manufactures themselves are a chief cause of the augmentation of population, of the stock of cattle, and of means of transport, &c. ? And would it be logical and just to co-ordinate these effects of manufactures with their cause—in fact, to put these results of manufactures at the head as main causes, and to put the manufactures themselves as an indirect (consequently, almost as a secondary) cause behind the former ? And what else can have induced so deeply investigating a genius as Adam Smith to make use of an argument so perverted and so little in accordance with the actual nature of things, than a desire to put especially into the shade manufactures, and their influence on the prosperity and the power of the nation, and on the augmentation of the rent and the value of the land ? And from what other motive can this have taken place than a wish to avoid explanations whose results would speak too loudly in favour of the system of prc-tection ? The school has been especially unfortunate since the time of Adam Smith in its investigations as to the nature of rent. Ricardo, and after him Mill, M'Culloch, and others, are of opinion that rent is paid on account of the natural productive fertility inherent in the land itself. Ricardo has based a whole system on this notion. If he had made an excursion to Canada, he would have been able to make observations there in every valley, on every hill, which would have convinced him that his theory is based on sand. As he, however, only took into account the circumstances of England, he fell into the erroneous idea that these English fields and meadows for whose pretended natural productive capability such handsome rents are now paid, have at all times been the same fields and meadows. The original natural productive capability of land is evi-dently so unimportant, and affords to the person using it so small an excess of products, that the rent derivable from it alone is not worth mentioning. All Canada in its original state (inhabited merely by hunters) would yield in meat and skins scarcely enough income to pay the salary of a single Oxonian professor of political economy. The natural productive capability of the soil in Malta consists of rocks, which would scarcely have yielded a rent at any time. If we follow up with the mind's eye the course of the civilisa-tion of whole nations, and of their conversion from the condition of hunters to the pastoral condition, and from this to that of agriculturists &c., we may easily convince ourselves that the rent everywhere was originally *nil*, and that it rose everywhere with the progress of civilisation, of population, and with the increase of mental and material capital. By comparing the mere agricultural nation with the agricultural, manufacturing, and commercial nation, it will be seen that in the latter twenty times more people live on rents than in the former. According to Marshal's statistics of Great Britain, for example, in England and Scotland 16,537,398 human beings were living in 1831, among whom were 1,116,398 rentiers.   We could scarcely find in Poland on an equal space of land the twentieth part of this number.   If we descend from generals to particulars and investigate the origin and cause of the rental of separate estates, we find everywhere that it is the result of a productive capability which has been bestowed on it not spontaneously by nature, but chiefly (directly or indirectly) through the mental and material labour and capital employed thereon and through the development of society. We see, indeed, how pieces of land yield rents which the hand of men has never stirred by cultivation, as, for instance, quarries, sand pits, pasture grounds ; but this rent is merely the effect of the increase of culture, capital, and population in the vicinity.   We see, on the other hand, that those pieces of land bring most rent whose natural productive capability has been totally destroyed, and which serve for no other use than for men to eat and drink, sit, sleep, or walk, work, or enjoy themselves, teach or be taught upon, viz. building sites.

The basis of rent is the exclusive benefit or advantage which the ground yields to that individual at whose exclusive disposal it is placed, and the greatness of this benefit is determined especially according to the amount of available mental and material capital in the community in which he is placed, and also according to the opportunity which the special situation and peculiar character of the property and the utilisation of capital previously invested therein affords to the person exclusively possessing the property for obtaining material values, or for satisfying mental and bodily requirements and enjoyments.

Rent is the interest of a capital which is fixed to a natural fund, or which is a capitalised natural fund. The territory, however, of that nation which has merely capitalised the natural funds devoted to agriculture, and which does so in that imperfect manner which is the case in mere agriculture, yields incomparably less rent than the territory of that nation which combines agricultural and manufacturing industry on its territory. The rentiers of such a country live mostly in the same nation which supplies the manufactured goods. But when the nation which is far advanced in agriculture and population establishes a manufacturing industry of its own, it capitalises (as we have already proved in a former chapter) not merely those powers of nature which are specially serviceable for manufactures and were hitherto unemployed, but also the greatest part of the manufacturing powers serving for agriculture. The increase of rent in such a nation, therefore, infinitely exceeds the interest of the material capital required to develop the manufacturing power.

CHAPTER XXI.

THE MANUFACTURING POWER AND COMMERCE.

WE have hitherto merely spoken of the relations between agriculture and manufactures, because they form the fundamental ingredients of the national production, and because, before obtaining a clear view of their mutual re-lations, it is impossible to comprehend correctly the actual function and position of commerce. Commerce is also certainly productive (as the school maintains); but it is so in quite a different manner from agriculture and manu-factures. These latter actually produce goods, commerce only brings about the exchange of the goods between agri-culturists and manufacturers, between producers and con-sumers. From this it follows that commerce must be regulated according to the interests and wants of agri-culture and manufactures, not *vice versâ*.

But the school has exactly reversed this last dictum by adopting as a favourite expression the saying of old Gourney, ' Laissez faire, laissez passer,' an expression which sounds no less agreeably to robbers, cheats, and thieves than to the merchant, and is on that account rather doubt-ful as a maxim. This perversity of surrendering the interests of manufactures and agriculture to the demands of commerce, without reservation, is a natural consequence of that theory which everywhere merely takes into con-sideration present values, but nowhere the powers that produce them, and regards the whole world as but one *in-divisible republic of merchants.* The school does not discern that the merchant may be accomplishing his purpose (viz. gain of values by exchange) at the expense of the agri-culturists and manufacturers, at the expense of the nation's productive powers, and indeed of its independence. It is all

the same to him ; and according to the character of his
business and occupation, he need not trouble himself much
respecting the manner in which the goods imported or
exported by him act on the morality, the prosperity, or the
power of the nation.   He imports poisons as readily as
medicines.   He enervates whole nations through opium
and spirituous liquors.   Whether he by his importations
and smugglings brings occupation and sustenance to hundreds of thousands, or whether they are thereby reduced
to beggary, does not signify to him as a man of business,
if only his own balance is increased thereby.   Then if
those who have been reduced to want bread seek to escape
the misery in their fatherland by emigrating, he can still
obtain profit by the business of arranging their emigration.
In the time of war he provides the enemy with arms and
ammunition.   He would, if it were possible, sell fields and
meadows to foreign countries, and when he had sold the
last bit of land would place himself on board his ship and
export himself.

It is therefore evident that the interest of individual
merchants and the interest of the commerce of a whole
nation are widely different things.   In this sense Montesquieu has well said, ' If the State imposes restrictions on
the individual merchant, it does so in the interest of commerce, and his trade is nowhere more restricted than in
free and rich nations, and nowhere less so than in nations
governed by despots.'[1]   Commerce emanates from manufactures and agriculture, and no nation which has not
brought within its own borders both these main branches
of production to a high state of development can attain
(in our days) to any considerable amount of internal and
external commerce.   In former times there certainly existed
separate cities or leagues of cities which were enabled by
means of foreign manufacturers and foreign agriculturists
to carry on a large exchange trade ; but since the great
agricultural manufacturing commercial states have sprung
up, we can no longer think of originating a mere exchange
trade such as the Hanse Towns possessed.   In any case

[1] *Esprit des Lois*, Book XX. chap. xii.

such a trade is of so precarious a character, that it hardly deserves consideration in comparison with that which is based on the nation's own production.

The most important objects of internal commerce are articles of food, salt, fuel, and building material, clothing materials, then agricultural and manufacturing utensils and implements, and the raw materials of agricultural and mining production which are necessary for manufactures. The extent of this internal interchange is beyond all comparison greater in a nation in which manufacturing industry has attained a high stage of development than in a merely agricultural nation. At times in the latter the agriculturist lives chiefly on his own productions. From want of much demand for various products and lack of means of transport, he is obliged to produce for himself all his requirements without regard to what his land is more specially fitted to produce; from want of means of exchange he must manufacture himself the greater part of the manufactured articles which he requires. Fuel, building materials, provisions, and mineral products can find only a very limited market because of the absence of improved means of transport, and hence cannot serve as articles for a distant trade.

Owing to the limited market and the limited demand for such products, no inducement for storing them or for the accumulation of capital exists. Hence the capital devoted by mere agricultural nations to internal commerce is almost *nil*; hence all articles of production, which depend especially on good or bad weather, are subject to extraordinary fluctuation in prices; hence the danger of scarcity and famine is therefore greater the more any nation restricts itself to agriculture.

The internal commerce of a nation mainly arises in consequence of and in proportion to the activity of its internal manufactures, of the improved means of transport called forth by them, and of the increase of population, and attains an importance which is ten to twenty fold greater than the internal trade of a merely agricultural nation, and five to ten fold that of the most flourishing foreign trade.

If anyone will compare the internal commerce of England with that of Poland or Spain, he will find this observation confirmed.

The foreign commerce of agricultural nations of the temperate zone, so long as it is limited to provisions and raw materials, cannot attain to importance.

Firstly, because the exports of the agricultural nation are directed to a few manufacturing nations, which themselves carry on agriculture, and which indeed, because of their manufactures and their extended commerce, carry it on on a much more perfect system than the mere agricultural nation; that export trade is therefore neither certain nor uniform. The trade in mere products is always a matter of extraordinary speculation, whose benefits fall mostly to the speculating merchants, but not to the agriculturists or to the productive power of the agricultural nation.

Secondly, because the exchange of agricultural products for foreign manufactured goods is liable to be greatly interrupted by the commercial restrictions of foreign states and by wars.

Thirdly, because the export of mere products chiefly benefits countries which are situated near sea coasts and the banks of navigable rivers, and does not benefit the inland territory, which constitutes the greater part of the territory of the agricultural nation.

Fourthly and finally, because the foreign manufacturing nation may find it to its interest to procure its means of subsistence and raw materials from other countries and newly formed colonies.

Thus the export of German wool to England is diminished by importations into England from Australia; the exports of French and German wines to England by importations from Spain, Portugal, Sicily, the Spanish and Portuguese islands, and from the Cape; the exports of Prussian timber by importations from Canada. In fact, preparations have already been made to supply England with cotton chiefly from the East Indies. If the English succeed in restoring the old commercial route, if the new

State of Texas becomes strong, if civilisation in Syria and Egypt, in Mexico and the South American states progresses, the cotton planters of the United States will also begin to perceive that their own internal market will afford them the safest, most uniform, and constant demand.

In temperate climates, by far the largest part of a nation's foreign commerce originates in its internal manufactures, and can only be maintained and augmented by means of its own manufacturing power.

Those nations only which produce all kinds of manufactured goods at the cheapest prices, can have commercial connections with the people of all climates and of every degree of civilisation; can supply all requirements, or if they cease, create new ones; can take in exchange every kind of raw materials and means of subsistence. Such nations only can freight ships with a variety of objects, such as are required by a distant market which has no internal manufactured goods of its own. Only when the export freights themselves suffice to indemnify the voyage, can ships be loaded with less valuable return freights.

The most important articles of importation of the nations of the temperate zone consist in the products of tropical climates, in sugar, coffee, cotton, tobacco, tea, dye stuffs, cacao, spices, and generally in those articles which are known under the name of colonial produce. By far the greatest part of these products is paid for with manufactured goods. In this interchange chiefly consists the cause of the progress of industry in manufacturing countries of the temperate zone, and of the progress of civilisation and production in the countries of the torrid zone. This constitutes the division of labour, and combination of the powers of production to their greatest extent, as these never existed in ancient times, and as they first originated from the Dutch and English.

Before the discovery of the route round the Cape, the East still far surpassed Europe in manufactures. Besides the precious metals and small quantities of cloth, linen, arms, iron goods, and some fabrics of luxury, European articles were but little used there. The transport by land rendered both inward and outward conveyance expensive. The export of ordinary agricultural products and common manufactured goods, even if they had been produced in excess, in exchange for the silks and cotton stuffs, sugar, and spices, of the East, could not be hoped for. Whatever we may, therefore, read of the importance of Oriental commerce in those times, must always be understood relatively; it was important only for that time, but unimportant compared with what it is now.

The trade in the products of the torrid zone became more important to Europe through the acquisition of larger quantities of the precious metals in the interior and from America, and through the direct intercourse with the East by the route round the Cape. It could not, however, attain to universal importance as long as the East produced more manufactured goods than she required.

This commerce attained its present importance through the colonisation of Europeans in the East and West Indies, and in North and South America through the transplantation of the sugar cane, of the coffee tree, of cotton, rice, indigo, &c., through the transportation of negroes as slaves to America and the West Indies, then through the successful competition of the European with the East Indian manufacturers, and especially through the extension of the Dutch and English sovereignty in foreign parts of the world, while these nations, in contrast to the Spaniards and Portuguese, sought and found their advantage more in the exchange of manufactured goods for colonial goods, than in extortion.

This commerce at present employs the most important part of the large shipping trade and of the commercial and manufacturing capital of Europe which is employed in foreign commerce; and all the hundreds of millions in value of such products which are transported annually from the countries of the torrid zone to those of the temperate zone are, with but little exception, *paid for in manufactured goods.*

The exchange of colonial products for manufactured goods is of manifold use to the productive powers of the countries of the temperate zone. These articles serve either, as e.g. sugar, coffee, tea, tobacco, partly as stimulants to agricultural and manufacturing production, partly as actual means of nourishment; the production of the manufactured goods which are required to pay for the colonial products, occupies a larger number of manufacturers; manufactories and manufacturing business can be conducted on a much larger scale, and consequently more profitably; this commerce, again, employs a larger number of ships, of seamen, and merchants; and through the manifold increase of the population thus occasioned, the demand for native agricultural products is again very greatly increased.

In consequence of the reciprocal operation which goes on between manufacturing production and the productions of the torrid zone, the English consume on an average two to three times more colonial produce than the French, three to four times more than the Germans, five to ten times more than the Poles.

Moreover, the further extension of which colonial production is still capable, may be recognised from a superficial calculation of the area which is required for the production of those colonial goods which are at present brought into commerce.

If we take the present consumption of cotton at ten million centners, and the average produce of an acre (40,000 square feet) only at eight centners, this production requires not more than $1\frac{1}{4}$ million acres of land. If we estimate the quantity of sugar brought into commerce at 14 million centners, and the produce of an acre at 10 centners, this total production requires merely $1\frac{1}{2}$ million acres.

If we assume for the remaining articles (coffee, rice, indigo, spices, &c.) as much as for these two main articles, all the colonial goods at present brought into commerce require no more than seven to eight million acres, an area which is probably not the fiftieth part of the surface of the earth which is suitable for the culture of such articles.

The English in the East Indies, the French in the Antilles, the Dutch in Java and Sumatra, have recently afforded actual proof of the possibility of increasing these productions in an extraordinary manner.

England, especially, has increased her imports of cotton from the East Indies fourfold, and the English papers confidently maintain that Great Britain (especially if she succeeds in getting possession of the old commercial route to the East Indies) could procure all her requirements of colonial products in the course of a few years from India. This anticipation will not appear exaggerated if we take into consideration the immense extent of the English East Indian territory, its fertility, and the cheap wages paid in those countries.

While England in this manner gains advantage from the East Indies, the progress in cultivation of the Dutch in the islands will increase ; in consequence of the dissolution of the Turkish Empire a great portion of Africa and the west and middle of Asia will become productive ; the Texans will extend North American cultivation over the whole of Mexico ; orderly governments will settle down in South America and promote the yield of the immense productive capacity of these tropical countries.

If thus the countries of the torrid zone produce enormously greater quantities of colonial goods than heretofore, they will supply themselves with the means of taking from the countries of the temperate zone much larger quantities of manufactured goods ; and from the larger sale of manufactured goods the manufacturers will be enabled to consume larger quantities of colonial goods. In consequence of this increased production, and increase of the means of exchange, the commercial intercourse between the agriculturists of the torrid zone and the manufacturers of the temperate zone, i.e. the great commerce of the world, will increase in future in a far larger proportion than it has done in the course of the last century.

This present increase, and that yet to be anticipated, of the now great commerce of the world, has its origin partly in the great progress of the manufacturing powers of production, partly in the perfection of the means of transport by water and by land, partly in political events and developments.

Through machinery and new inventions the imperfect manufacturing industry of the East has been destroyed for the benefit of the European manufacturing power, and the latter enabled to supply the countries of the torrid zone with large quantities of fabrics at the cheapest prices; and thus to give them motives for augmenting their own powers of labour and production.

In consequence of the great improvements in means of transport, the countries of the torrid zone have been brought infinitely nearer to the countries of the temperate zone; their mutual commercial intercourse has infinitely increased through diminution of risk, of time employed and of freights, and through greater regularity; and it will increase infinitely more as soon as steam navigation has become general, and the systems of railways extend themselves to the interior of Asia, Africa, and South America.

Through the secession of South America from Spain and Portugal, and through the dissolution of the Turkish Empire, a mass of the most fertile territories of the earth have been liberated, which now await with longing desire for the civilised nations of the earth to lead them in peaceful concord along the path of the security of law and order, of civilisation and prosperity; and which require nothing more than that manufactured goods should be brought to them, and their own productions taken in exchange.

One may see that there is sufficient room here for all countries of Europe and North America which are fitted to develop a manufacturing power of their own, to bring their manufacturing production into full activity, to augment their own consumption of the products of tropical countries, and to extend in the same proportion their direct commercial intercourse with the latter.

CHAPTER XXII.

THE MANUFACTURING POWER AND NAVIGATION, NAVAL POWER
AND COLONISATION.

MANUFACTURES as the basis of a large home and foreign
commerce are also the fundamental conditions of the existence of any considerable mercantile marine. Since the
most important function of inland transport consists in supplying manufacturers with fuel and building materials, raw
materials and means of subsistence, the coast and river
navigation cannot well prosper in a merely agricultural
State. The coast navigation, however, is the school and
the depôt of sailors, ships' captains, and of shipbuilding,
and hence in merely agricultural countries the main foundation for any large maritime navigation is lacking.

International commerce consists principally (as we have
shown in the previous chapter) in the interchange of
manufactured goods for raw materials and natural products, and especially for the products of tropical countries.
But the agricultural countries of the temperate zone
have merely to offer to the countries of the torrid zone
what they themselves produce, or what they cannot make
use of, namely raw materials and articles of food ; hence
direct commercial intercourse between them and the countries of the torrid zone, and the ocean transport which
arises from it, is not to be expected. Their consumption
of colonial produce must be limited to those quantities for
which they can pay by the sale of agricultural products and
raw materials to the manufacturing and commercial nations ;
they must consequently procure these articles second-hand.
In the commercial intercourse between an agricultural
nation and a manufacturing commercial nation, however,
the greatest part of the sea transport must fall to the

latter, even if it is not in its power by means of navigation laws to secure the lion's share to itself.

Besides internal and international commerce, sea fisheries occupy a considerable number of ships ; but again from this branch of industry, as a rule, nothing or very little falls to the agricultural nation ; as there cannot exist in it much demand for the produce of the sea, and the manufacturing commercial nations are, out of regard to the maintenance of their naval power, accustomed to protect their home market exclusively for their own sea fisheries.

The fleet recruits its sailors and pilots from the private mercantile marine, and experience has as yet always taught that able sailors cannot be quickly drilled like land troops, but must be trained up by serving in the coasting and international navigation and in sea fisheries. The naval power of nations will therefore always be on the same footing with these branches of maritime industry, it will consequently in the case of the mere agricultural nation be almost *nil*.

The highest means of development of the manufacturing power, of the internal and external commerce proceeding from it, of any considerable coast and sea navigation, of extensive sea fisheries, and consequently of a respectable naval power, are *colonies*.

The mother nation supplies the colonies with manufactured goods, and obtains in return their surplus produce of agricultural products and raw materials; this interchange gives activity to its manufactures, augments thereby its population and the demand for its internal agricultural products, and enlarges its mercantile marine and naval power. The superior power of the mother country in population, capital, and enterprising spirit, obtains through colonisation an advantageous outlet, which is again made good with interest by the fact that a considerable portion of those who have enriched themselves in the colony bring back the capital which they have acquired there, and pour it into the lap of the mother nation, or expend their income in it.

Agricultural nations, which already need the means of forming colonies, also do not possess the power of utilising and maintaining them.   What the colonies require, cannot be offered by them, and what they can offer the colony itself possesses.

The exchange of manufactured goods for natural products is the fundamental condition on which the position of the present colonies continues.   On that account the United States of North America seceded from England as soon as they felt the necessity and the power of manufacturing for themselves, of carrying on for themselves navigation and commerce with the countries of the torrid zone ; on that account Canada will also secede after she has reached the same point, on that account independent agricultural manufacturing commercial States will also arise in the countries of temperate climate in Australia in the course of time.

But this exchange between the countries of the temperate zone and the countries of the torrid zone is based upon natural causes, and will be so for all time.   Hence India has given up her manufacturing power with her independence to England ; hence all Asiatic countries of the torrid zone will pass gradually under the dominion of the manufacturing commercial nations of the temperate zone ; hence the islands of the torrid zone which are at present dependent colonies can hardly ever liberate themselves from that condition; and the States of South America will always remain dependent to a certain degree on the manufacturing commercial nations.

England owes her immense colonial possessions solely to her surpassing manufacturing power.   If the other European nations wish also to partake of the profitable business of cultivating waste territories and civilising barbarous nations, or nations once civilised but which are again sunk in barbarism, they must commence with the development of their own internal manufacturing powers, of their mercantile marine, and of their naval power.   And should they be hindered in these endeavours by England's manufacturing, commercial, and naval supremacy, in the union of their powers lies the only means of reducing such unreasonable pretensions to reasonable ones.

CHAPTER XXIII.

IF the experience of the last twenty-five years has confirmed, as being partly correct, the principles which have been set up by the prevailing theory in contradiction to the ideas of the so-called 'mercantile' system on the circulation of the precious metals and on the balance of trade, it has, on the other hand, brought to light important weak points in that theory respecting those subjects.

Experience has proved repeatedly (and especially in Russia and North America) that in agricultural nations, whose manufacturing market is exposed to the free competition of a nation which has attained manufacturing supremacy, the value of the importation of manufactured goods exceeds frequently to an enormous extent the value of the agricultural products which are exported, and that thereby at times suddenly an extraordinary exportation of precious metals is occasioned, whereby the economy of the agricultural nation, especially if its internal interchange is chiefly based on paper circulation, falls into confusion, and national calamities are the result.

The popular theory maintains that if we provide ourselves with the precious metals in the same manner as every other article, it is in the main indifferent whether large or small quantities of precious metals are in circulation, as it merely depends on the relation of the price of any article in exchange whether that article shall be cheap or dear ; a derangement in the rate of exchange acts simply like a premium on a larger exportation of goods from that country, in favour of which it oscillates from time to time : consequently the stock of metallic money and the balance between the imports and exports, as well as all the other economical circumstances of the nation, would regulate themselves in the safest and best manner by the operation of the natural course of things.

This argument is perfectly correct as respects the *internal* interchange of a nation; it is demonstrated in the commercial intercourse between town and town, between town and country districts, between province and province, as in the union between State and State. Any political economist would be deserving of pity who believed that the balance of the mutual imports and exports between the various states of the American Union or the German Zollverein, or between England, Scotland, and Ireland, can be regulated better through State regulations and laws than through free interchange. On the hypothesis that a similar union existed between the various states and nations of the earth, the argument of the theory of trusting to the natural course of things would be quite consistent. Nothing, however, is more contrary to experience than to suppose under the existing conditions of the world that in international exchange things act with similar effect.

The imports and exports of independent nations are regulated and controlled at present not by what the popular theory calls the natural course of things, but mostly by the commercial policy and the power of the nation, by the influence of these on the conditions of the world and on foreign countries and peoples, by colonial possessions and internal credit establishments, or by war and peace. Here, accordingly, all conditions shape themselves in an entirely different manner than between societies which are united by political, legal, and administrative bonds in a state of unbroken peace and of perfect unity of interests.

Let us take into consideration as an example the conditions between England and North America. If England from time to time throws large masses of manufactured goods on to the North American market; if the Bank of England stimulates or restricts, in an extraordinary degree, the exports to North America and the credit granted to her

by its raising or lowering its discount rates ; if, in addition
to and as a consequence of this extraordinary glut of the
American market for manufactured goods, it happens that
the English manufactured goods can be obtained cheaper
in North America than in England, nay, sometimes much
below the cost price of production ; if thus North America
gets into a state of perpetual indebtedness and of an unfavourable condition of exchange towards England, yet
would this disorganised state of things readily rectify itself
under a state of perfectly unrestricted exchange between the
two countries.   North America produces tobacco, timber,
corn, and all sorts of means of subsistence very much cheaper
than England does.   The more English manufactured goods
go to North America, the greater are the means and inducements to the American planter to produce commodities of
value sufficient to exchange for them ; the more credit is
given to him the greater is the impulse to procure for him
self the means of discharging his liabilities ; the more the
rate of exchange on England is to the disadvantage of
North America, the greater is the inducement to export
American agricultural products, and hence the more successful will be the competition of the American agriculturist in the English produce market.

In consequence of these exportations the adverse rate
of exchange would speedily rectify itself ; indeed, it could
not even reach any very unfavourable point, because the
certain anticipation in North America that the indebtedness
which had been contracted through the large importation
of manufactured goods in the course of the present year,
would equalise itself through the surplus production and
increased exports of the coming year, would be followed
by easier accommodation in the money market and in
credit.

Such would be the state of things if the interchange
between the English manufacturer and the American
agriculturist were as little restricted as the interchange
between the English manufacturer and the Irish agriculturist is.   But they are and must be different : if England
imposes a duty on American tobacco of from five hundred

to one thousand per cent.; if she renders the importation of American timber impossible by her tariffs, and admits the American means of subsistence only in the event of famine, for at present the American agricultural production cannot balance itself with the American consumption of English manufactured goods, nor can the debt incurred for those goods be liquidated by agricultural products; at present the American exports to England are limited by narrow bounds, while the English exports to North America are practically unlimited; the rate of exchange between both countries under such circumstances cannot equalise itself, and the indebtedness of America towards England must be discharged by exports of bullion to the latter country.

These exports of bullion, however, as they undermine the American system of paper circulation, necessarily lead to the ruin of the credit of the American banks, and therewith to general revolutions in the prices of landed property and of the goods in circulation, and especially to those general confusions of prices and credit which derange and overturn the economy of the nation, and with which, we may observe, that the North American free States are visited whenever they have found themselves unable to restore a balance between their imports and their exports by State tariff regulations.

It cannot afford any great consolation to the North American that in consequence of bankruptcies and diminished consumption, the imports and exports between both countries are at a later period restored to a tolerable proportion to one another. For the destruction and convulsions of commerce and in credit, as well as the reduction in consumption, are attended with disadvantages to the welfare and happiness of individuals and to public order, from which one cannot very quickly recover and the frequent repetition of which must necessarily leave permanently ruinous consequences.

Still less can it afford any consolation to the North Americans, if the popular theory maintains that it is an indifferent matter whether large or small quantities of precious, metals are in circulation; that we exchange products merely for products; whether this exchange is made by means of large or small quantities of metallic circulation is of no importance to individuals. To the producer or proprietor it certainly may be of no consequence whether the object of his production or of his possession is worth 100 centimes or 100 francs, provided always that he can procure with the 100 centimes as large a quantity of objects of necessity and of enjoyment as he can with the 100 francs. But low or high prices are thus a matter of indifference only in case they remain on the same footing uninterruptedly for a long period of time.

If, however, they fluctuate frequently and violently, disarrangements arise which throw the economy of every individual, as well as that of society, into confusion. Whoever has purchased raw materials at high prices, cannot under low prices, by the sale of his manufactured article, realise again that sum in precious metals which his raw materials have cost him. Whoever has bought at high prices landed property and has left a portion of the purchase money as a mortgage debt upon it, loses his ability of payment and his property; because, under diminished prices, probably the value of the entire property will scarcely equal the amount of the mortgage. Whoever has taken leases of property under a state of high prices, finds himself ruined by the decrease in prices, or at least unable to fulfil the covenants of his leases. The greater the rising and falling of prices, and the more frequently that fluctuations occur, the more ruinous is their effect on the economical conditions of the nation and especially on credit. But nowhere are these disadvantageous effects of the unusual influx or efflux of precious metals seen in a more glaring light than in those countries which are entirely dependent on foreign nations in respect of their manufacturing requirements and the sale of their own products, and whose commercial transactions are chiefly based on paper circulation.

It is acknowledged that the quantity of bank notes which a country is able to put into and to maintain in circulation, is dependent on the largeness of the amount of metallic money which it possesses. Every bank will endeavour to extend or limit its paper circulation and its business in proportion to the amount of precious metals lying in its vaults. If the increase in its own money capital or in deposits is large, it will give more credit; and through this credit, increase the credit given by its debtors, and by so doing raise the amount of consumption and prices; especially those of landed property. If, on the contrary, an efflux of precious metals is perceptible, such a bank will limit its credit, and thereby occasion restriction of credit and consumption by its debtors, and by the debtors of its debtors, and so on to those who by credit are engaged in bringing into consumption the imported manufactured goods. In such countries, therefore, the whole system of credit, the market for goods and products, and especially the money value of all landed property, is thrown into confusion by any unusual drain of metallic money.

The cause of the latest as well as of former American commercial crises, has been alleged to exist in the American banking and paper system. The truth is that the banks have helped to bring about these crises in the manner above named, but the main cause of their occurrence is that since the introduction of the 'compromise' bill the value of the English manufactured goods has far surpassed the value of the exported American products, and that thereby the United States have become indebted to the English to the amount of several hundreds of millions for which they could not pay in products. The proof that these crises are occasioned by disproportionate importation is, that they have always taken place whenever (in consequence of peace having set in or of a reduction being made in the American customs duties) importation of manufactured goods into the United States has been unusually large, and that they have never occurred as long as the imports of goods have been prevented by customs duties on imports from exceeding the value of the exports of produce.

The blame for these crises has further been laid on the large capital which has been expended in the United States in the construction of canals and railways, and which has mostly been procured from England by means of loans. The truth is that these loans have merely assisted in delaying the crisis for several years, and in increasing it when it arose ; but these very loans themselves have evidently been incurred through the inequality which had arisen between the imports and exports, and but for that inequality would not have been made and could not have been made.

While North America became indebted to the English for large sums through the large importation of manufactured goods which could not be paid for in produce, but only in the precious metals, the English were enabled, and in consequence of the unequal rates of exchange and interest found it to their advantage, to have this balance paid for in American railway, canal, and bank stocks, or in American State paper.

The more the import of manufactured goods into America surpassed her exports in produce, and the greater that the demand for such paper in England became, the more were the North Americans incited to embark in public. enterprises ; and the more that capital was invested in such enterprises in North America, the greater was the demand for English manufactured goods, and at the same time the disproportion between the American imports and exports.

If on the one hand the importation of English manufactured goods into North America was promoted by the credit given by the American banks, the Bank of England on the other side through the credit facilities which it gave and by its low rates of discount operated in the same direction. It has been proved by an official account of the English Committee on Trade and Manufactures, that the Bank of England lessened (in consequence of these discounts) the cash in its possession from eight million pounds to two millions. It thereby on the one hand weakened the effect of the American protective system to the advantage of the English competition with the American manufactories ; on the other hand it thus offered facilities for, and stimulated, the placing of American stocks and State paper in England.

For as long as money could be got in England at three per cent. the American contractors and loan procurers who offered six per cent. interest had no lack of buyers of their paper in England.

These conditions of exchange afforded the appearance of much prosperity, although under them the American manufactories were being gradually crushed. For the American agriculturists sold a great part of that surplus produce which under free trade they would have sold to England, or which under a moderate system of protection of their own manufactories they would have sold to the working men employed therein, to those workmen who were employed in public works and who were paid with English capital. Such an unnatural state of things could not, however, last long in the face of opposing and divided national interests, and the break up of it was the more disadvantageous to North America the longer it was repressed. As a creditor can keep the debtor on his legs for a long time by renewals of credit, but the bankruptcy of the debtor must become so much the greater the longer he is enabled to prolong a course of ruinous trading by means of continually augmented credit from the creditor, so was it also in this case.

The cause of the bankruptcy in America was the unusual export of bullion which took place from England to foreign countries in consequence of insufficient crops and in consequence of the Continental protective systems. We say in consequence of the Continental protective systems, because the English—if the European Continental markets had remained open to them—would have covered their extraordinary importations of corn from the Continent chiefly by means of extraordinary export of English manufactured goods to the Continent, and because the English bullion—even had it flown over for a time to the continent—would again have found its way back to England in a short time in consequence of the augmented export of manufactured goods. In such a case the Continental manufactories would undoubtedly have fallen a sacrifice to the English-American commercial operations.

As matters stood, however, the Bank of England could

only help itself by limiting its credit and increasing its rate
of discount. In consequence of this measure not only the
demand for more American stocks and State paper fell off
in England, but also such paper as was already in circulation now forced itself more on the market. The United
States were thereby not merely deprived of the means of
covering their current deficit by the further sale of paper,
but payment of the whole debt they had contracted in the
course of many years with England by means of their sales
of stocks and State paper became liable to be demanded in
money. It now appeared that the cash circulation in
America really belonged to the English. It appeared yet
further that the English could dispose of that ready money
on whose possession the whole bank and paper system of
the United States was based, according to their own inclination. If, however, they disposed of it, the American bank
and paper system would tumble down like a house built of
cards, and with it the foundation would fall whereon rested
the prices of landed property, consequently the economical
means of existence of a great number of private persons.

The American banks tried to avoid their fall by sus-
pending specie payments, and indeed this was the only
means of at least modifying it; on the one hand they tried
by this means to gain time so as to decrease the debt of the
United States through the yield of the new cotton crops
and to pay it off by degrees in this manner; on the other
hand they hoped by means of the reduction of credit occasioned by the suspension to lessen the imports of English
manufactured goods and to equalise them in future with
their own country's exports.

How far the exportation of cotton can afford the means
of balancing the importation of manufactured goods is,
however, very doubtful. For more than twenty years the
production of this article has constantly outstripped the
consumption, so that with the increased production the
prices have fallen more and more. Hence it happens that,
on the one hand, the cotton manufacturers are exposed to
severe competition with linen manufactures, perfected as
these are by greatly improved machinery; while the cotton

planters, on the other hand, are exposed to it from the planters of Texas, Egypt, Brazil, and the East Indies.

It must, in any case, be borne in mind that the exports of cotton of North America benefit those States to the least extent which consume most of the English manufactured goods.

In these States, namely those which derive from the cultivation of corn and from cattle-breeding the chief means of procuring manufactured goods, a crisis of another kind now manifests itself. In consequence of the large importation of English manufactured goods the American manufactures were depressed. All increase in population and capital was thereby forced to the new settlements in the west. Every new settlement increases at the commencement the demand for agricultural products, but yields after the lapse of a few years considerable surplus of them. This has already taken place in those settlements. The Western States will therefore pour, in the course of the next few years, into the Eastern States considerable surplus produce, by the newly constructed canals and railways; while in the Eastern States, in consequence of their manufactories being depressed by foreign competition, the number of consumers has decreased and must continually decrease. From this, depreciation in the value of produce and of land must necessarily result, and if the Union does not soon prepare to stop up the sources from which the above described money crises emanate, a general bankruptcy of the agriculturists in the corn-producing States is unavoidable.

The commercial conditions between England and North America which we have above explained, therefore teach:

(1) That a nation which is far behind the English in capital and manufacturing power cannot permit the English to obtain a predominating competition on its manufacturing market without becoming permanently indebted to them; without being rendered dependent on their money institutions, and drawn into the whirlpool of their agricultural industrial, and commercial crises.

(2) That the English national bank is able by it

operations to depress the prices of English manufactured goods in the American markets which are placed under its influence—to the advantage of the English and to the disadvantage of the American manufactories.

(3) That the English national bank could effect by its operations the consumption by the North Americans, for a series of years, of a much larger value of imported goods than they would be able to repay by their exportation of products, and that the Americans had to cover their deficit during several years by the exportation of stocks and State paper.

(4) That under such circumstances the Americans carried on their internal interchange and their bank and paper-money system with ready money, which the English bank was able to draw to itself for the most part by its own operations whenever it felt inclined so to do.

(5) That the fluctuations in the money market under all circumstances act on the economy of the nations in a highly disadvantageous manner, especially in countries where an extensive bank and paper-money system is based on the possession of certain quantities of the precious metals.

(6) That the fluctuations in the money market and the crises which result therefrom can only be prevented, and that a solid banking system can only be founded and maintained, if the imports of the country are placed on a footing of equality to the exports.

(7) *That this equality can less easily be maintained in proportion as foreign manufactured goods can successfully compete in the home manufacturing markets, and in proportion as the exportation of native agricultural products is limited by foreign commercial restrictions ; finally, that this equality can less easily be disturbed in proportion as the nation is independent of foreign nations for its supply of manufactured goods, and for the disposal of its own produce.*

These doctrines are also confirmed by the experience of Russia. We may remember to what convulsions public credit in the Russian Empire was subjected as long as the market there was open to the overwhelming consignments of English manufactured goods, and that since the introduction of the tariff of 1821 no similar convulsion has occurred in Russia.

The popular theory has evidently fallen into the opposite extreme to the errors of the so-called mercantile system. It would be of course false if we maintained that the wealth of nations consisted merely in precious metals ; that a nation can only become wealthy if it exports more goods than it imports, and if hence the balance is discharged by the importation of precious metals. But it is also erroneous if the popular theory maintains, under the existing conditions of the world, that it does not signify how much or how little precious metals circulate in a nation ; that the fear of possessing too little of the precious metals is a frivolous one, that we ought rather to further their exportation than favour their importation, &c. &c. This manner of reasoning would only be correct in case we could consider all nations and countries as united under one and the same system of law; if no commercial restrictions of any kind against the exportation of our products existed in those nations for whose manufactured goods we can only repay with the productions of our agriculture ; if the changes wrought by war and peace caused no fluctuations in production and consumption, in prices, and on the money market; if the great credit institutions do not seek to extend their influence over other nations for the special interest of the nation to which they belong. But as long as separate national interests exist, a wise State policy will advise every great nation to guard itself by its commercial system against extraordinary money fluctuations and revolutions in prices which overturn its whole internal economy, and it will attain this purpose only by placing its internal manufacturing production in a position of proper equality with its internal agricultural production and its imports with its exports.

The prevailing theory has evidently not sufficiently discriminated between the mere *possession* of the precious metals and the power of *disposition* of the precious metals in international interchange. Even in private exchange, the necessity of this distinction is clearly evident. No one wishes to keep money by him, everyone tries to remove it from the house as soon as possible; but everybody at the same time seeks to be able to dispose at any time of the sums which he requires. The indifference in regard to the actual possession of ready money is manifested everywhere in proportion to wealth. The richer the individual is, the less he cares about the actual possession of ready money if only he is able at any hour to dispose of the ready cash lying in the safes of other individuals; the poorer, however, the individual is, and the smaller his power of disposing of the ready money lying in other people's hands, the more anxiously must he take care to have in readiness what is required. The same is the case with nations which are rich in industry or poor in industry. If England cares but little as a rule about how great or how small a quantity of gold or silver bars are exported out of the country, she is perfectly well aware that an extraordinary export of precious metals occasions on the one hand a rise in the value of money and in discount rates, on the other hand a fall in the prices of fabrics, and that she can regain through larger exportation of fabrics or through realisation of foreign stocks and State paper speedy possession of the ready money required for her trade. England resembles the rich banker who, without having a thaler in his pocket, can draw for any sum he pleases on neighbouring or more distant business connections. If, however, in the case of merely agricultural nations extraordinary exports of coin take place, they are not in the same favourable position, because their means of procuring the ready money they require are very limited, not merely on account of the small *value in exchange* of their products and agricultural values, but also on account of the hindrances which foreign laws put in the way of their exportation. They resemble the poor man who can draw no bills on his business friends, but who is drawn upon if the rich man gets into any difficulty; who can, therefore, not even call what is actually in his hands, his own.

A nation obtains *the power of disposition* of the amount

of ready money which is always required for its internal
trade, mainly through the possession or the production of
those goods and values whose facility of exchange approaches most nearly to that of the precious metals.

The diversity of this property of the facility of exchange
in respect to the various articles of commerce and of
property, has been as little taken into consideration by the
popular school of economists in judging of international
commerce, as the power of disposition of the precious
metals. If we consider in this respect the various articles
of value existing in private interchange, we perceive that
many of them are fixed in such a way that their value is
exchangeable only on the spot where they are, and that
even there their exchange is attended with great costs and
difficulties. To that class belong more than three-fourths
of all national property—namely, immovable properties
and fixed plant and instruments. However large the
landed property of an individual may be, he cannot send
his fields and meadows to town in order to obtain money or
goods for them. He can, indeed, raise mortgages on such
property, but he must first find a lender on them; and the
further from his estate that such an individual resides, the
smaller will be the probability of the borrower's requirements being satisfied.

Next after property thus fixed to the locality, the greatest
part of agricultural products (excepting colonial produce
and a few less valuable articles) have in regard to international intercourse the least facility for exchange. The
greatest part of these values, as e.g. building materials and
wood for fuel, bread stuffs, &c., fruit, and cattle, can only be
sold within a reasonable distance of the place where they
are produced, and if a great surplus of them exists they
have to be warehoused in order to become realisable. So
far as such products can be exported to foreign countries
their sale again is limited to certain manufacturing and
commercial nations, and in these also their sale is generally
limited by duties on importation and is affected by the
larger or smaller produce of the purchasing nation's own
harvests. The inland territories of North America might

be completely overstocked with cattle and products, but it would not be possible for them to procure through exportation of this excess considerable amounts of the precious metals from South America, from England, or from the European continent. The valuable manufactured goods of common use, on the other hand, possess incomparably greater facilities for exchange. They find at ordinary times a sale in all open markets of the world; and at extraordinary crises they also find a sale (at lower prices) in those markets whose protective tariffs are calculated to operate adversely merely in ordinary times. The power of exchange of these articles clearly approaches most nearly to that of the precious metals, and the experience of England shows that if in consequence of deficient harvests money crises occur, the increased exportation of fabrics, and of foreign stocks and State paper, quickly rectifies the balance. The latter, the foreign stocks and State paper, which are evidently the results of former favourable balances of exchange caused by exportations of fabrics, constitute in the hands of the nation which is rich in manufacturing industry so many bills which can be drawn on the agricultural nation, which at the time of an extraordinary demand for the precious metals are indeed drawn with loss to the individual owner of them (like the manufactured goods at the time of money crises), but, nevertheless, with immense advantage to the maintenance of the economical conditions of that nation which is rich in manufacturing industry.

However much the doctrine of the balance of trade may have been scorned by the popular school, observations like those above described encourage us nevertheless to express the opinion that between large and independent nations something of the nature of a balance of trade must exist; that it is dangerous for great nations to remain for a long period at very considerable disadvantage in respect of this balance, and that a considerable and lasting efflux of the precious metals must always be followed as a consequence by important revolutions in the system of credit and in the condition of prices in the interior of the nation. We are far from wishing in these remarks to revive the doctrine of

the balance of trade as it existed under the so-called 'mercantile system,' and to maintain that the nation ought to
impose obstacles in the way of the exportation of precious
metals, or that we must keep a specially exact account
with each individual nation, or that in the commerce between
great nations a few millions difference between the imports
and exports is of great moment. What we deny is merely
this : that a great and independent nation, as Adam Smith
maintains at the conclusion of his chapter devoted to this
subject,[1] 'may continually import every year considerably
larger values in products and fabrics than it exports; that
the quantities of precious metals existing in such a nation
may decrease considerably from year to year and be replaced by paper circulation in the interior ; moreover, that
such a nation may allow its indebtedness towards another
nation continually to increase and expand, and at the same
time nevertheless make progress from year to year in
prosperity.'[2]

This opinion, expressed by Adam Smith and maintained
since that time by his school, is alone that which we here
characterise as one that has been contradicted a hundred
times by experience, as one that is contrary in the very
nature of things to common sense, in one word (to retort
upon Adam Smith his own energetic expression) as 'an
absurdity.'

It must be well understood that we are not speaking
here of countries which carry on the production of the precious metals themselves at a profit, from which therefore
the export of these articles has quite the character of an
export of manufactured goods. We are also not speaking
of that difference in the balance of trade which must necessarily arise if the nation rates its exports and imports at
those prices which they have in their own seaport towns.
That in such a case the amount of imports of every nation
must exceed its exports by the total amount of the nation's
own commercial profits (a circumstance which speaks to
its advantage rather than to its disadvantage), is clear and

---

[1] *Wealth of Nations*, Book IV. chapter iii.
[2] See Appendix D.

indisputable. Still less do we mean to deny the extraordinary cases where the greater exportation rather denotes
loss of value than gain, as e.g. if property is lost by shipwreck. The popular school has made clever use of all those
delusions arising from a shopkeeper-like calculation and
comparison of the value of the exchanges arising from the
exports and imports, in order to make us disbelieve in the
disadvantages which result from a real and enormous disproportion between the exports and imports of any great
and independent nation, even though such disproportion be
not permanent, which shows itself in such immense sums
as for instance in the case of France in 1786 and 1789, in
that of Russia in 1820 and 1821, and in that of the United
States of North America after the ' Compromise Bill.'

Finally, we desire to speak (and this must be specially
noted) not of colonies, not of dependent countries, not of
small states or of single independent towns, but of entire,
great, independent nations, which possess a commercial
system of their own, a national system of agriculture and
industry, a national system of money and credit.

It evidently consists with the character of *colonies* that
their exports can surpass their imports considerably and
continuously, without thereby involving any conclusion as
to the decrease or increase of their prosperity. The colony
always prospers in the proportion in which the *total amount*
of its exports and imports increases year by year. If its
export of colonial produce exceeds its imports of manufactured goods considerably and lastingly, the main cause
of this may be that the landed proprietors of the colony
live in the mother country, and that they receive their income
in the shape of colonial goods, in produce, or in the money
which has been obtained for them. If, however, the exports
of fabrics to the colony exceed the imports of colonial goods
considerably, this may be chiefly due to the fact that by
emigrations or loans from year to year large masses of
capital go to the colony. This latter circumstance is, of
course, of the utmost advantage to the prosperity of the
colony. It can continue for centuries and yet commercial
crises under such circumstances may be infrequent or im-

possible, because the colony is endangered neither by wars nor by hostile commercial measures, nor by operations of the national bank of the mother country, because it possesses no independent system of commerce, credit, and industry peculiar to itself, but is, on the contrary, supported and constantly upheld by the institutions of credit and political measures of the mother country.

Such a condition existed for more than a century with advantage between North America and England, exists still between England and Canada, and will probably exist for centuries between England and Australia.

This condition becomes fundamentally changed, however, from the moment in which the colony appears as an independent nation with every claim to the attributes of a great and independent nationality—in order that it may develop a power and policy of its own and its own special system of commerce and credit. The former colony then enacts laws for the special benefit of its own navigation and naval power—it establishes in favour of its own internal industry a customs tariff of its own ; it establishes a national bank of its own, &c., provided namely that the new nation thus passing from the position of a colony to independence feels itself capable, by reason of the mental, physical, and economical endowments which it possesses, of becoming an industrial and commercial nation. The mother country, in consequence, places restrictions, on its side, on the navigation, commerce, and agricultural production of the former colony, and acts, by its institutions of credit, exclusively for the maintenance of its own national economical conditions.

But it is precisely the instance of the North American colonies as they existed before the American War of Independence by which Adam Smith seeks to prove the above-mentioned highly paradoxical opinion : that a country can continually increase its exportation of gold and silver, decrease its circulation of the precious metals, extend its paper circulation, and increase its debts contracted with other nations while enjoying simultaneously steadily increasing prosperity ; Adam Smith has been very careful not to cite the example of two nations which have been in-

dependent of one another for some time, and whose interests
of navigation, commerce, industry, and agriculture are in
competition with those of other rival nations, in proof of
his opinion—he merely shows us the relation of a colony to
its mother country. If he had lived to the present time
and only written his book now, he would have been very
careful not to cite the example of North America, as this
example proves in our days just the opposite of what he
attempts by it to demonstrate.

Under such circumstances, however, it may be urged
against us that it would be incomparably more to the
advantage of the United States if they returned again to
the position of an English colony. To this we answer, yes,
provided always that the United States do not know how
to utilise their national independence so as to cultivate and
develop a national industry of their own, and a self-support-
ing system of commerce and credit which is independent
of the world outside. But (it may be urged) is it not
evident that if the United States had continued to exist as
a British colony, no English corn law would ever have been
passed ; that England would never have imposed such high
duties on American tobacco ; that continual quantities of
timber would have been exported from the United States
to England ; that England, far from ever entertaining the
idea of promoting the production of cotton in other countries,
would have endeavoured to give the citizens of the United
States a monopoly in this article, and to maintain it; that
consequently commercial crises such as have occurred
within the last decades in North America, would have been
impossible ? Yes ; if the United States do not manufacture,
if they do not found a durable system of credit of their
own ; if they do not desire or are not able to develop a
naval power. But then, in that case, the citizens of Boston
have thrown the tea into the sea in vain ; then all their
declamation as to independence and future national greatness is in vain : then indeed would they do better if they
re-enter as soon as possible into dependence on England
as her colony. In that event England will favour them
instead of imposing restrictions on them ; she will rather

impose restrictions on those who compete with the North Americans in cotton culture and corn production &c. than raise up with all possible energy competitors against them. The Bank of England will then establish branch banks in the United States, the English Government will promote emigration and the export of capital to America, and through the entire destruction of the American manufactories, as well as by favouring the export of American raw materials and agricultural produce to England, take maternal care to prevent commercial crises in North America, and to keep the imports and exports of the colony always at a proper balance with one another. In one word, the American slaveholders and cotton planters will then realise the fulfilment of their finest dreams. In fact, such a position has already for some time past appeared to the patriotism, the interests, and requirements of these planters more desirable than the national independence and greatness of the United States. Only in the first emotions of liberty and independence did they dream of industrial independence. They soon, however, grew cooler, and for the last quarter of a century the industrial prosperity of the middle and eastern states is to them an abomination ; they try to persuade the Congress that the prosperity of America depends on the industrial sovereignty of England over North America. What else can be meant by the assertion that the United States would be richer and more prosperous if they again went over to England as a colony ?

In general it appears to us that the defenders of free trade would argue more consistently in regard to money crises and the balance of trade, as well as to manufacturing industry, if they openly advised all nations to prefer to subject themselves to the English as dependencies of England, and to demand in exchange the benefits of becoming English colonies, which condition of dependence would be, in economical respects, clearly more favourable to them than the condition of half independence in which those nations live who, without maintaining an independent system of industry, commerce, and credit of their own, nevertheless always want to assume towards England the attitude of independence. Do not we see what Portugal would have gained if she had been governed since the Methuen Treaty by an English viceroy—if England had transplanted her laws and her national spirit to Portugal, and taken that country (like the East Indian Empire) altogether under her wings ? Do not we perceive how advantageous such a condition would be to Germany—to the whole European continent ?

India, it is true, has lost her manufacturing power to England, but has she not gained considerably in her internal agricultural production and in the exportation of her agricultural products ? Have not the former wars under her Nabobs ceased ? Are not the native Indian princes and kings extremely well off ? Have they not preserved their large private revenues ? Do not they find themselves thereby completely relieved of the weighty cares of government ?

Moreover, it is worthy of notice (though it is so after the manner of those who, like Adam Smith, make their strong points in maintaining paradoxical opinions) that this renowned author, in spite of all his arguments against the existence of a balance of trade, maintains, nevertheless, the existence of a thing which he calls the balance between the consumption and production of a nation, which, however, when brought to light, means nothing else but our actual balance of trade. A nation whose exports and imports tolerably well balance each other, may rest assured that, in respect to its national interchange, it does not consume much more in value than it produces, while a nation which for a series of years (as the United States of America have done in recent years) imports larger quantities in value of foreign manufactured goods than it exports in value of products of its own, may rest assured that, in respect to international interchange, it consumes considerably larger quantities in value of foreign goods than it produces at home. For what else did the crises of France (1786–1789), of Russia (1820–1821), and of the United States since 1833, prove ?

In concluding this chapter we must be permitted to put a few questions to those who consider the whole doctrine of the balance of trade as a mere exploded fallacy.

How is it that a decidedly and continuously disadvantageous balance of trade has always and without exception been accompanied in those countries to whose detriment it existed (with the exception of colonies) by internal commercial crises, revolutions in prices, financial difficulties, and general bankruptcies, both in the public institutions of credit, and among the individual merchants, manufacturers, and agriculturists ?

How is it that in those nations which possessed a balance of trade decidedly in their favour, the opposite appearances have always been observed, and that commercial crises in the countries with which such nations were connected commercially, have only affected such nations detrimentally for periods which passed away very quickly ?

How is it that since Russia has produced for herself the greatest part of the manufactured goods which she requires, the balance of trade has been decidedly and lastingly in her favour, that since that time nothing has been heard of economical convulsions in Russia, and that since that time the internal prosperity of that empire has increased year by year ?

How is it that in the United States of North America the same effects have always resulted from similar causes ?

How is it that in the United States of North America, under the large importation of manufactured goods which followed the 'Compromise Bill,' the balance of trade was for a series of years so decidedly adverse to them, and that this appearance was accompanied by such great and continuous convulsions in the internal economy of that nation ?

How is it that we, at the present moment, see the United States so glutted with primitive products of all kinds (cotton, tobacco, cattle, corn, &c.) that the prices of them have fallen everywhere one-half, and that at the same time these states are unable to balance their exports with their imports, to satisfy their debt contracted with England, and to put their credit again on sound footing ?

How is it, if no balance of trade exists, or if it does not signify whether it is in our favour or not, if it is a matter of indifference whether much or little of the precious metals flows to foreign countries, that England in the case of failures of harvests (the only case where the balance is adverse to her) strives, with fear and trembling, to equalise her exports with her imports, that she then carefully estimates every ounce of gold or silver which is imported or exported, that her national bank endeavours most anxiously to stop the exportation of precious metals and to promote their importation—how is it, we ask, if the balance of trade is an ' exploded fallacy,' that at such a time no English newspaper can be read wherein this ' exploded fallacy ' is not treated as a matter of the most important concern to the nation ?

How is it that, in the United States of North America, the same people who before the Compromise Bill spoke of the balance of trade as an exploded fallacy, since the Compromise Bill cannot cease speaking of this exploded fallacy as a matter of the utmost importance to their country ?

How is it, if the nature of things itself always suffices to provide every country with exactly the quantity of precious metals which it requires, that the Bank of England tries to turn this so-called nature of things in her own favour by limiting her credits and increasing her rates of discount, and that the American banks are obliged from time to time to suspend their cash payments till the imports of the United States are reduced to a tolerably even balance with the exports ?

CHAPTER XXIV.

THE MANUFACTURING POWER AND THE PRINCIPLE OF STABILITY AND CONTINUITY OF WORK.

IF we investigate the origin and progress of individual branches of industry, we shall find that they have only gradually become possessed of improved methods of operation, machinery, buildings, advantages in production, experiences, and skill, and of all those knowledges and connections which insure to them the profitable purchase of their raw materials and the profitable sale of their products. We may rest assured that it is (as a rule) incomparably easier to perfect and extend a business already established than to found a new one. We see everywhere old business establishments that have lasted for a series of generations worked with greater profits than new ones. We observe that it is the more difficult to set a new business going in proportion as fewer branches of industry of a similar character already exist in a nation; because, in that case, masters, foremen, and workmen must first be either trained up at home or procured from abroad, and because the profitableness of the business has not been sufficiently tested to give capitalists confidence in its success. If we compare the conditions of distinct classes of industry in any nation at various periods, we everywhere find, that when special causes had not operated to injure them, they have made remarkable progress, not only in regard to cheapness of prices, but also with respect to quantity and quality, from generation to generation. On the other hand, we observe that in consequence of external injurious causes, such as wars and devastation of territory, &c., or oppressive tyrannical or fanatical measures of government and finance (as e.g. the revocation of the Edict of Nantes), whole nations have been thrown back for centuries, either in their entire industry or in certain branches of it, and have in this manner been far outstripped by nations in comparison with which they had previously been far advanced.

One can see at a glance that, as in all human institutions so also in industry, a law of nature lies at the root of important achievements which has much in common with the natural law of the division of labour and of the confederation of the productive forces, whose principle, namely, consists in the circumstance that several generations following one another have equally united their forces towards the attainment of one and the same object, and have participated in like manner in the exertions needed to attain it.

It is the same principle which in the cases of hereditary kingdoms has been incomparably more favourable to the maintenance and increase of the power of the nation than the constant changes of the ruling families in the case of electoral kingdoms.

It is partly this natural law which secures to nations who have lived for a long time past under a rightly ordered constitutional form of government, such great successes in industry, commerce, and navigation.

Only through this natural law can the effect of the invention of printing on human progress be partially explained. Printing first rendered it possible to hand down the acquisitions of human knowledge and experience from the present to future generations more perfectly and completely than could be done by oral tradition.

To the recognition of this natural law is undoubtedly partly attributable the division of the people into castes, which existed among the nations of antiquity, and also the law of the old Egyptians—that the son must continue to follow the trade or profession of his father. Before the invention and general dissemination of printing took place, these regulations may have appeared to be indispensable for the maintenance and for the development of arts and trades.

Guilds and trade societies also have partly originated from this consideration. For the maintenance and bringing to perfection of the arts and sciences, and their transfer from one generation to another, we are in great measure indebted to the priestly castes of ancient nations, to the monasteries and universities.

What power and what influence have the orders of priesthood and orders of knights, as well as the papal chair, attained to, by the fact that for centuries they have aspired to one and the same aim, and that each successive generation has always continued to work where the other had left off.

The importance of this principle becomes still more evident in respect to material achievements.

Individual cities, monasteries, and corporations have erected works the total cost of which perhaps surpassed the value of their whole property at the time. They could only obtain the means for this by successive generations devoting their savings to one and the same great purpose.

Let us consider the canal and dyke system of Holland; it comprises the labours and savings of many generations. Only to a series of generations is it possible to complete systems of national transport or a complete system of fortifications and defensive works.

The system of State credit is one of the finest creations of more recent statesmanship, and a blessing for nations, inasmuch as it serves as the means of dividing among several generations the costs of those achievements and exertions of the present generation which are calculated to benefit the nationality for all future times, and which guarantee to it continued existence, growth, greatness, power, and increase of the powers of production; it becomes a curse only if it serves for useless national expenditure, and thus not merely does not further the progress of future generations, but deprives them beforehand of the means of undertaking great national works, or also if the burden of the payment of interest of the national debt is thrown on the consumptions of the working classes instead of on capital,

State debts are bills which the present generation draws on future ones. This can take place either to the special advantage of the present generation or the special advantage of the future one, or to the common advantage of both. In the first case only is this system an objectionable one. But all cases in which the object in view is the maintenance and promotion of the greatness and welfare of the nationality, so far as the means required for the purpose surpass the powers of the present generation, belong to the last category.

No expenditure of the present generation is so decidedly and specially profitable to future generations as that for the improvement of the means of transport, especially because such undertakings as a rule, besides increasing the powers of production of future generations, do also in a constantly increasing ratio not merely pay interest on the cost in the course of time, but also yield dividends. The present generation is, therefore, not merely entitled to throw on to future generations the capital outlay of these works and fair interest on it (as long as they do not yield sufficient income), but further acts unjustly towards itself and to the true fundamental principles of national economy, if it takes the burden or even any considerable part of it on its own shoulders.

If in our consideration of the subject of the continuity of national industry we revert to the main branches which constitute it, we may perceive, that while this continuity has an important influence on agriculture, yet that interruptions to it, in the case of that industry, are much less decided and much less injurious when they occur, also that their evil consequences can be much more easily and quickly made good than in the case of manufactures.

However great may be any damage or interruption to agriculture, the actual personal requirements and consumption of the agriculturist, the general diffusion of the skill and knowledge required for agriculture, and the simplicity of its operations and of the implements which it requires, suffice to prevent it from coming entirely to an end.

Even after devastations by war it quickly raises itself

up again. Neither the enemy nor the foreign competitor can take away the main instrument of agriculture, the land; and it needs the oppressions of a series of generations to convert arable fields into uncultivated waste, or to deprive the inhabitants of a country of the capability of carrying on agriculture.

On manufactures, however, the least and briefest interruption has a crippling effect; a longer one is fatal. The more art and talent that any branch of manufacture requires, the larger the amounts of capital which are needful to carry it on, the more completely this capital is sunk in the special branch of industry in which it has been invested, so much the more detrimental will be the interruption. By it machinery and tools are reduced to the value of old iron and fire-wood, the buildings become ruins, the workmen and skilled artificers emigrate to other lands or seek subsistence in agricultural employment. Thus in a short time a complex combination of productive powers and of property becomes lost, which had been created only by the exertions and endeavours of several generations.

Just as by the establishment and continuance of industry one branch of trade originates, draws after it, supports and causes to flourish many others, so is the ruin of one branch of industry always the forerunner of the ruin of several others, and finally of the chief foundations of the manufacturing power of the nation.

The conviction of the great effects produced by the steady continuation of industry and of the irretrievable injuries caused by its interruption, and not the clamour and egotistical demands of manufacturers and traders for special privileges, has led to the idea of protective duties for native industry.

In cases where the protective duty cannot help, where the manufactories, for instance, suffer from want of export trade, where the Government is unable to provide any remedy for its interruption, we often see manufacturers continuing to produce at an actual loss. They want to avert, in expectation of better times, the irrecoverable injury which they would suffer from a stoppage of their works.

By free competition it is often hoped to oblige the competitor to discontinue work which has compelled the manufacturer or merchant to sell his products under their legitimate price and often at an actual loss. The object is not merely to prevent the interruption of our own industry, but also to force others to discontinue theirs in the hope later on of being able by better prices to recoup the losses which have been suffered.

In any case striving after monopoly forms part of the very nature of manufacturing industry. This circumstance tends to justify and not to discredit a protective policy ; for this striving, when restricted in its operation to the home market, tends to promote cheaper prices and improvements in the art of production, and thus increases the national prosperity ; while the same thing, in case it presses from without with overwhelming force on the internal industry, will occasion the interruption of work and downfall of the internal national industry.

The circumstance that there are no limits to manufacturing production (especially since it has been so extraordinarily aided and promoted by machinery) except the limits of the capital which it possesses and its means of effecting sales, enables that particular nation whose manufacturing industry has continued for a century, which has accumulated immense capitals, extended its commerce all over the world, dominated the money market by means of large institutions of credit (whose operations are able to depress the prices of fabrics and to induce merchants to export), to declare a war of extermination against the manufacturers of all other countries. Under such circumstances it is quite impossible that in other nations, ' in the natural course of things ' (as Adam Smith expresses himself), merely in consequence of their progress in agriculture, immense manufactures and works should be established, or that those manufactures which have originated in consequence of the commercial interruptions caused by war should be able, ' in the natural course of things,' to continue to maintain themselves. The reason for this is the same as that why a child or a boy in wrestling with a strong man can scarcely be victorious or even offer steady resistance. The manufactories which constitute the commercial and industrial supremacy (of England) have a thousand advantages over the newly born or half-grown manufactories of other nations. The former, for instance, can obtain skilled and experienced workmen in the greatest number and at the cheapest wages, the best technical men and foremen, the most perfect and the cheapest machinery, the greatest benefit in buying and selling advantageously ; further, the cheapest means of transport, as respects raw materials and also in respect of transporting goods when sold, more extended credit for the manufacturers with banks and money institutions at the lowest rates of interest, greater commercial experience, better tools, buildings, arrangements, connections, such as can only be acquired and established in the course of generations ; an enormous home market, and, what is equally good, a colonial market equally enormous. Hence under all circumstances the English manufacturers can feel certainty as to the sale of large quantities of manufactured products by vigorous efforts, and consequently possess a guarantee for the continuance of their business and abundant means to sell on credit for years to come in the future, if it is required to acquire the control of a foreign market. If we enumerate and consider these advantages one after another, we may easily be convinced that in competition with such a power it is simply foolish to rest our hopes on the operation of ' the natural course of things ' under free competition, where, as in our case, workmen and technical men have in the first place yet to be trained, where the manufacture of machinery and proper means of transport are merely in course of erection, where even the home market is not secured to the manufacturer—not to mention any important export market, where the credit that the manufacturer can obtain is under the most fortunate circumstances limited to the lowest point, where no man can be certain even for a day that, in consequence of English commercial crises and bank operations, masses of foreign goods may not be thrown on the home market at prices which scarcely recoup the value of the raw materials of which they are made, and which bring to a stand for years the progress of our own manufacturing industries.

It would be in vain for such nations to resign themselves to a state of perpetual subordination to the English manufacturing supremacy, and content themselves with the modest determination to supply it with what it may not be able to produce for itself or to procure elsewhere. Even by this subordination they would find no permanent benefit. What benefit is it to the people of the United States, for instance, that they sacrifice the welfare of their finest and most cultivated states, the states of free labour, and perhaps their entire future national greatness, for the advantage of supplying England with raw cotton? Do they thereby restrict the endeavours of England to procure this material from other districts of the world? In vain would the Germans be content to obtain their requirements of manufactured goods from England in exchange for their fine sheep's wool; they would by such a policy hardly prevent Australia from flooding all Europe with fine wool in the course of the next twenty years.

Such a condition of dependence appears still more deplorable when we consider that such nations lose in times of war their means of selling their agricultural products, and thereby the means of purchasing the manufacturing products of the foreigner. At such times all economical considerations and systems are thrust into the background. It is the principle of self-maintenance, of self-defence, which counsels the nations to work up their agricultural products themselves, and to dispense with the manufactured goods of the enemy. Whatever losses may be involved in adopting such a war-prohibitive system, cannot be taken into account during such a state of things. However great the exertions and the sacrifices may have been by which the agricultural nation during the time of war has called into existence manufactures and works, the competition of the manufacturing supremacy which sets in on the recurrence of peace will again destroy all these creations of the times of necessity. In short, it is an eternal alternation of erecting and destroying, of prosperity and calamity, which those nations have to undergo who do not strive to insure, through realisation of their national division of labour and through the confederation of their own powers of production, the benefits of the continuation of their own industries from generation to generation.

CHAPTER XXV.

THE MANUFACTURING POWER AND THE INDUCEMENT TO PRODUCTION AND CONSUMPTION.

In society man is not merely productive owing to the circumstance that he directly brings forth products or creates powers of production, but he also becomes productive by creating inducements to production and to consumption, or to the formation of productive powers.

The artist by his works acts in the first place on the ennobling and refinement of the human spirit and on the productive power of society ; but inasmuch as the enjoyment of art presupposes the possession of those material means whereby it must be purchased, the artist also offers inducements to material production and to thrift.

Books and newspapers act on the mental and material production by giving information ; but their acquisition costs money, and so far the enjoyment which they afford is also an inducement to material production.

The education of youth ennobles society ; but what great exertions do parents make to obtain the means of giving their children a good education !

What immense performances in both mental and material production arise out of the endeavour to move in better society !

We can live as well in a house made of boards as in a villa, we can protect ourselves for a few florins against rain and cold as well as by means of the finest and most elegant clothing. Ornaments and utensils of gold and silver add no more to comfort than those of iron and tin ; but the distinction connected with the possession of the former acts as an inducement to exertions of the body and the mind, and to order and thrift ; and to such inducements society owes a large part of its productiveness. Even the man living on his private property who merely occupies himself with preserving, increasing, and consuming his income, acts in manifold ways on mental and material production : firstly by supporting through his consumption art and science, and artistic trades ; next by discharging, as it were, the function of a preserver and augmenter of the material capital of society ; finally, by inciting through his display all other classes of society to emulation. As a whole school is encouraged to exertions by the offer of prizes, although only a few become winners of the principal prizes, so does the possession of large property, and the appearance and display connected with it, act on civil society. This action of course ceases when the great property is the fruit of usurpation, of extortion, or fraud, or where the possession of it and the enjoyment of its fruits cannot be openly displayed.

Manufacturing production yields either productive instruments or the means of satisfying the necessities of life and the means of display: The last two advantages are frequently combined. The various ranks of society are everywhere distinguished by the manner in which and where they live, and how they are furnished and clothed, by the costliness of their equipages and the quality, number, and external appearance of their servants. Where the commercial production is on a low scale, this distinction is but slight, i.e. almost all people live badly and are poorly clothed, emulation is nowhere observable. It originates and increases according to the ratio in which industries flourish. In flourishing manufacturing countries almost everyone lives and dresses well, although in the quality of manufactured goods which are consumed the most manifold degrees of difference take place. No one who feels that he has any power in him to work is willing to appear outwardly needy. Manufacturing industry, therefore, furthers production by the community by means of inducements which agriculture, with its mean domestic manufacture, its productions of raw materials and provisions, cannot offer.

There is of course an important difference between various modes of living, and everyone feels some inducement to eat and drink well; but we do not dine in public; and a German proverb says strikingly, 'Man sieht mir auf den Kragen, nicht auf den Magen' (One looks at my shirt collar, not at my stomach). If we are accustomed from youth to rough and simple fare, we seldom wish for better. The consumption of provisions also is restricted to very narrow limits where it is confined to articles produced in the immediate neighbourhood. These limits are extended in countries of temperate climate, in the first instance, by procuring the products of tropical climates. But as respects the quantity and the quality of these products, in the enjoyment of which the whole population of a country can participate, they can only be procured (as we have shown in a former chapter) by means of foreign commerce in manufactured goods.

Colonial products, so far as they do not consist of raw materials for manufacturing purposes, evidently act more as stimulants than necessary means of subsistence. No one will deny that barley coffee without sugar is as nutritious as mocha coffee with sugar; and admitting also that these products contain some nutritious matter, their value in this respect is nevertheless so unimportant that they can scarcely be considered as substitutes for native provisions. With regard to spices and tobacco, they are certainly mere stimulants, i.e. they chiefly produce a useful effect on society only so far as they augment the enjoyments of the masses, and incite them to mental and bodily labour.

In many countries very erroneous notions prevail among those who live by salaries or rents, respecting what they are accustomed to call the luxurious habits of the lower classes; such persons are shocked to observe that labourers drink coffee with sugar, and regret the times when they were satisfied with gruel; they deplore that the peasant has exchanged his poor clothing of coarse home-spun for woollen cloth; they express fears that the maid-servant will soon not be distinguishable from the lady of the house; they praise the legal restrictions on dress of previous centuries. But if we compare the result of the labour of the workman in countries where he is clad and nourished like

the well-to-do man with the result of his labour where he
has to be satisfied with the coarsest food and clothing, we
shall find that the increase of his comfort in the former case
has been attained not at the expense of the general welfare, but to the advantage of the productive powers of the
community.   The day's work of the workman is double or
three times greater in the former case than in the latter.
Attempts to regulate dress and restrictions on luxury have
destroyed wholesome emulation in the large masses of
society, and have merely tended to the increase of mental
and bodily idleness.

In any case products must be created before they can
be consumed, and thus production must necessarily generally precede consumption.   In popular and national practice, however, consumption frequently precedes production.
Manufacturing nations, supported by large capital and less
restricted in their production than mere agricultural nations,
make, as a rule, advances to the latter on the yield of
future crops; the latter thus consume before they produce—
they produce later on because they have previously consumed.   The same thing manifests itself in a much greater
degree in the relation between town and country : the closer
the manufacturer is to the agriculturist, the more will the
former offer to the latter both an inducement to consume
and means for consumption, the more also will the latter
feel himself stimulated to greater production.

Among the most potent stimulants are those afforded
by the civil and political institutions of the country.   Where
it is not possible to raise oneself by honest exertions and
by prosperity from one class of society to another, from the
lowest to the highest; where the possessor necessarily hesi-
tates to show his property publicly or to enjoy the fruits of
it because it would expose his property to risk, or lest
he should be accused of arrogance or impropriety; where
persons engaged in trade are excluded from public honour,
from taking part in administration, legislation, and juries;
where distinguished achievements in agriculture, industry,
and commerce do not lead also to public esteem and to
social and civil distinction, there the most important

motives for consumption as well as for production are wanting.

Every law, every public regulation, has a strengthening or weakening effect on production or on consumption or on the productive forces.

The granting of patent privileges offers a prize to inventive minds. The hope of obtaining the prize arouses the mental powers, and gives them a direction towards industrial improvements. It brings honour to the inventive mind in society, and roots out the prejudice for old customs and modes of operation so injurious among uneducated nations. It provides the man who merely possesses mental faculties for new inventions with the material means which he requires, inasmuch as capitalists are thus incited to support the inventor, by being assured of participation in the anticipated profits.

Protective duties act as stimulants on all those branches of internal industry the produce of which foreign countries can provide better than the home country, but of the production of which the home country is capable. They guarantee a reward to the man of enterprise and to the workman for acquiring new knowledge and skill, and offer to the inland and foreign capitalist means for investing his capital for a definite and certain time in a specially remunerative manner.

CHAPTER XXVI.

CUSTOMS DUTIES AS A CHIEF MEANS OF ESTABLISHING AND PROTECTING THE INTERNAL MANUFACTURING POWER.

It is not part of our plan to treat of those means of promoting internal industry whose efficacy and applicability are nowhere called in question. To these belong e.g. educational establishments (especially technical schools), industrial exhibitions, offers of prizes, transport improvements, patent laws &c.; in short, all those laws and institutions by means of which industry is furthered, and internal and external commerce facilitated and regulated. We have here merely to speak of the institution of customs duties as a means for the development of industry.

According to our system, prohibitions of, or duties on, exports can only be thought of as exceptional things; the imports of natural products must everywhere be subject to revenue duties only, and never to duties intended to protect native agricultural production. In manufacturing states, articles of luxury from warm climates are chiefly subject to duties for revenue, but not the common necessaries of life, as e.g. corn or fat cattle; but the countries of warmer climate or countries of smaller population or limited territory, or countries not yet sufficiently populous, or such as are still far behind in civilisation and in their social and political institutions, are those which should only impose mere revenue duties on manufactured goods.

Revenue duties of every kind, however, should everywhere be so moderate as not essentially to restrict importation and consumption; because, otherwise, not only would the internal productive power be weakened, but the object of raising revenue be defeated.

Measures of protection are justifiable only for the purpose of furthering and protecting the internal manufacturing power, and only in the case of nations which through an extensive and compact territory, large population, possession of natural resources, far advanced agriculture, a high degree of civilisation and political development, are qualified to maintain an equal rank with the principal agricultural manufacturing commercial nations, with the greatest naval and military powers.

Protection can be afforded, either by the prohibition of certain manufactured articles, or by rates of duty which amount wholly, or at least partly, to prohibition, or by moderate import duties.   None of these kinds of protection are invariably beneficial or invariably objectionable ; and it depends on the special circumstances of the nation and on the condition of its industry which of these is the right one to be applied to it.

War exercises a great influence on the selection of the precise system of protection, inasmuch as it effects a compulsory prohibitive system.   In time of war, exchange between the belligerent parties ceases, and every nation must endeavour, without regard to its economical conditions, to be sufficient to itself.   Hence, on the one hand, in the less advanced manufacturing nations commercial industry, on the other hand, in the most advanced manufacturing nation agricultural production, becomes stimulated in an extraordinary manner, indeed to such a degree that it appears advisable to the less advanced manufacturing nation (especially if war has continued for several years) to allow the exclusion which war has occasioned of those manufactured articles in which it cannot yet freely compete with the most advanced manufacturing nation, to continue for some time during peace.

France and Germany were in this condition after the general peace.   If in 1815 France had allowed English competition, as Germany, Russia, and North America did, she would also have experienced the same fate ; the greatest part of her manufactories which had sprung up during the war would have come to grief; the progress which has since been made in all branches of manufacture, in improving the internal means of transport, in foreign commerce, in steam river and sea navigation, in the increase in the value of land (which, by the way, has doubled in value during this time in France), in the augmentation of population and of the State's revenues, could not have been hoped for. The manufactories of France at that time were still in their childhood; the country possessed but few canals; the mines had been but little worked; political convulsions and wars had not yet permitted considerable capital to accumulate, sufficient technical cultivation to exist, a sufficient number of really qualified workmen or an industrial and enterprising spirit to have been called into existence; the mind of the nation was still turned more towards war than towards the arts of peace; the small capital which a state of war permitted to accumulate, still flowed principally into agriculture, which had declined very much indeed. Then, for the first time, could France perceive what progress England had made during the war; then, for the first time, was it possible for France to import from England machinery, artificers, workmen, capital, and the spirit of enterprise; then, to secure the home market exclusively for the benefit of home industry, demanded the exertion of her best powers, and the utilisation of all her natural resources. The effects of this protective policy are very evident; nothing but blind cosmopolitanism can ignore them, or maintain that France would have, under a policy of free competition with other nations, made greater progress. Does not the experience of Germany, the United States of America, and Russia, conclusively prove the contrary?

If we maintain that the prohibitive system has been useful to France since 1815, we do not by that contention wish to defend either her mistakes or her excess of protection, nor the utility or necessity of her continued maintenance of that excessive protective policy. It was an error for France to restrict the importation of raw materials and agricultural products (pig-iron, coal, wool, corn, cattle) by import duties; it would be a further error if France, after her manufacturing power has become sufficiently strong and established, were not willing to revert gradually to a moderate system of protection, and by permitting a limited amount of competition incite her manufacturers to emulation.

In regard to protective duties it is especially important to discriminate between the case of a nation which contemplates passing from a policy of free competition to one of protection, and that of a nation which proposes to exchange a policy of prohibition for one of moderate protection; in the former case the duties imposed at first must be low, and be gradually increased, in the latter they must be high at first and be gradually diminished.

A nation which has been formerly insufficiently protected by customs duties, but which feels itself called upon to make greater progress in manufactures, must first of all endeavour to develop those manufactures which produce articles of general consumption. In the first place the total value of such industrial products is incomparably greater than the total value of the much more expensive fabrics of luxury. The former class of manufactures, therefore, brings into motion large masses of natural, mental, and personal productive powers, and gives—by the fact that it requires large capital—inducements for considerable saving of capital, and for bringing over to its aid foreign capital and powers of all kinds. The development of these branches of manufacture thus tends powerfully to promote the increase of population, the prosperity of home agriculture, and also especially the increase of the trade with foreign countries, inasmuch as less cultivated countries chiefly require manufactured goods of common use, and the countries of temperate climates are principally enabled by the production of these articles to carry on direct interchange with the countries of tropical climates. A country e.g. which has to import cotton yarns and cotton goods cannot carry on direct trade with Egypt, Louisiana, or Brazil, because it cannot supply those countries with the cotton goods which they require, and cannot take from them their raw cotton. Furthermore, these articles, on account of the magnitude of their total value, serve especially to equalise the exports of the nation tolerably well with its imports, and always to retain in the nation the amount of circulating medium which it requires, or to provide it with the same. Thus it is by the prosperity and preservation of these important branches of industry that the industrial independence of the nation is gained and maintained, for the disturbance of trade resulting from wars is of little importance if it merely hinders the purchase of expensive articles of luxury, but, on the other hand, it always occasions great calamities if it is attended by scarcity and rise in price of common manufactured goods, and by the interruption of a previously considerable sale of agricultural products. Finally, the evasion of customs duties by smuggling and false declarations of value is much less to be feared in the case of these articles, and can be much more easily prevented than in the case of costly fabrics of luxury.

Manufactures and manufactories are always plants of slow growth, and every protective duty which suddenly breaks off formerly existing commercial connections must be detrimental to the nation for whose benefit it is professedly introduced. Such duties ought only to be increased in the ratio in which capital, technical abilities, and the spirit of enterprise are increasing in the nation or are being attracted to it from abroad, in the ratio in which the nation is in a condition to utilise for itself its surplus of raw materials and natural products which it had previously exported. It is, however, of special importance that the scale by which the import duties are increased should be determined beforehand, so that an assured remuneration can be offered to the capitalists, artificers, and workmen, who are found in the nation or who can be attracted to it from abroad. It is indispensable to maintain these scales of duty inviolably, and not to diminish them before the appointed time, because the very fear of any such breach of promise would already destroy for the most part the effect of that assurance of remuneration.

To what extent import duties should be increased in the case of a change from free competition to the protective system, and how much they ought to be diminished in the case of a change from a system of prohibition to a moderate system of protection, cannot be determined theoretically : that depends on the special conditions as well as on the relative conditions in which the less advanced nation is placed in relation to the more advanced ones.   The United States of North America e.g. have to take into special consideration their exports of raw cotton to England, and of agricultural and maritime products to the English colonies, also the high rate of wages existing in the United States ; whereby they again profit by the fact that they can depend more than any other nation on attracting to themselves English capital, artificers, men of enterprise, and workmen.

It may in general be assumed that where any technical industry cannot be established by means of an original protection of forty to sixty per cent. and cannot continue to maintain itself under a continued protection of twenty to thirty per cent. the fundamental conditions of manufacturing power are lacking.

The causes of such incapacity can be removed more or less readily : to the class more readily removable belong want of internal means of transport, want of technical knowledge, of experienced workmen, and of the spirit of industrial enterprise ; to the class which it is more difficult to remove belong the lack of industrious disposition, civilisation, education, morality, and love of justice on the part of the people ; want of a sound and vigorous system of agriculture, and hence of material capital ; but especially defective political institutions, and want of civil liberty and of security of justice ; and finally want of compactness of territory, whereby it is rendered impossible to put down contraband trade.

Those industries which merely produce expensive articles of luxury require the least consideration and the least amount of protection ; firstly, because their production requires and assumes the existence of a high degree of technical attainment and skill ; secondly, because their total value is inconsiderable in proportion to that of the whole national production, and the imports of them can be readily paid for by means of agricultural products and raw materials, or with manufactured products of common use ; further, because the interruption of their importation occasions no important inconvenience in time of war ; lastly, because high protective duties on these articles can be most readily evaded by smuggling.

Nations which have not yet made considerable advances in technical art and in the manufacture of machinery should allow all complicated machinery to be imported free of duty, or at least only levy a small duty upon them, until they themselves are in a position to produce them as readily as the most advanced nation. Machine manufactories are in a certain sense the manufacturers of manufactories, and every tax on the importation of foreign machinery is a restriction on the internal manufacturing power. Since it is, however, of the greatest importance, because of its great influence on the whole manufacturing power, that the nation should not be dependent on the chances and changes of war in respect of its machinery, this particular branch of manufacture has very special claims for the direct support of the State in case it should not be able under moderate import duties to meet competition. The State should at least encourage and directly support its home manufactories of machinery, so far as their maintenance and development may be necessary to provide at the commencement of a time of war the most necessary requirements, and under a longer interruption by war to serve as patterns for the erection of new machine factories.

Drawbacks can according to our system only be entertained in cases where half-manufactured goods which are still imported from abroad, as for instance cotton yarn, must be subjected to a considerable protective duty in order to enable the country gradually to produce them itself.

Bounties are objectionable as permanent measures to render the exports and the competition of the native manufactories possible with the manufactories of further advanced nations in neutral markets ; but they are still more objectionable as the means of getting possession of the inland markets for manufactured goods of nations which have themselves already made progress in manufactures. Yet there are cases where they are to be justified as temporary means of encouragement, namely where the slumbering spirit of enterprise of a nation merely requires stimulus and assistance in the first period of its revival, in order to evoke in it a powerful and lasting production and an export trade to countries which themselves do not possess flourishing manufactures. But even in these cases it ought to be considered whether the State would not do better by making advances free of interest and granting special privileges to individual men of enterprise, or whether it would not be still more to the purpose to promote the formation of companies to carry into effect such primary experimental adventures, to advance to such companies a portion of their requisite share capital out of the State treasury, and to allow to the private persons taking shares in them a preferential interest on their invested capital. As instances of the cases referred to, we may mention experimental undertakings in trade and navigation to distant countries, to which the commerce of private persons has not yet been extended; the establishment of lines of steamers to distant countries; the founding of new colonies, &c.

CHAPTER XXVII.

THE CUSTOMS SYSTEM AND THE POPULAR SCHOOL.

THE popular school does not discriminate (in respect of the operation of protective duties) between natural or primitive products and manufactured products. It perverts the fact that such duties always operate injuriously on the production of primitive or natural products, into the false conclusion that they exercise an equally detrimental influence on the production of manufactured goods.

The school recognises no distinction in reference to the establishment of manufacturing industry in a State between those nations which are not adapted for such industry and those which, owing to the nature of their territory, to perfectly developed agriculture, to their civilisation, and to their just claims for guarantees for their future prosperity, for their permanence, and for their power, are clearly qualified to establish such an industry for themselves.

The school fails to perceive that under a system of perfectly free competition with more advanced manufacturing nations, a nation which is less advanced than those, although well fitted for manufacturing, can never attain to a perfectly developed manufacturing power of its own, nor to perfect national independence, without protective duties.

It does not take into account the influence of war on the necessity for a protective system; especially it does not perceive that war effects a compulsory prohibitive system, and that the prohibitive system of the custom-house is but a necessary continuation of that prohibitive system which war has brought about.

It seeks to adduce the benefits which result from free

internal trade as a proof that nations can only attain to the highest degree of prosperity and power by absolute freedom in international trade; whereas history everywhere proves the contrary.

It maintains that protective measures afford a monopoly to inland manufacturers, and thus tend to induce indolence; while, nevertheless, all the time internal competition amply suffices as a stimulus to emulation among manufacturers and traders.

It would have us believe that protective duties on manufactured goods benefit manufacturers at the expense of agriculturists; whereas it can be proved that enormous benefits accrue to home agriculture from the existence of a home manufacturing power, compared to which the sacrifices which the former has to make to the protective system are inconsiderable.

As a main point against protective duties, the popular school adduces the expenses of the custom-house system and the evils caused by contraband trade. These evils cannot be denied; but can they be taken seriously into account in comparison of measures which exercise such enormous influence on the existence, the power, and the prosperity of the nation? Can the evils of standing armies and wars constitute an adequate motive for the nation to neglect means of defence? If it is maintained that protective duties which far exceed the limit which offers an assured remuneration to smuggling, serve merely to favour contraband trade, but not to benefit home manufactures, that can apply only to ill-regulated customs establishments, to countries of small extent and irregular frontiers, to the consumption which takes place on the frontiers, and only to high duties on articles of luxury of no great aggregate bulk.

But experience everywhere teaches us that with well-ordered customs establishments, and with wisely devised tariffs, the objects of protective duties in large and compact states cannot be materially impeded by contraband trade.

So far as regards the mere expenses of the customs system, a large portion of these would, if it were abolished,

have to be incurred in the collection of revenue duties; and
that revenue duties can be dispensed with by great nations,
even the school itself does not maintain.

Moreover, the school itself does not condemn all protective duties.

Adam Smith allows in three cases the special protection
of internal industry: firstly, as a measure of *retaliation* in
case a foreign nation imposes restrictions on our imports,
and there is hope of inducing it by means of reprisals to
repeal those restrictions; secondly, for the *defence of the
nation*, in case those manufacturing requirements which
are necessary for defensive purposes could not under open
competition be produced at home; thirdly, as a *means of
equalisation* in case the products of foreigners are taxed
lower than those of our home producers. J. B. Say objects
to protection in all these cases, but admits it in a fourth
case—namely, when some branch of industry is expected
to become after the lapse of a few years so remunerative
that it will then no longer need protection.

Thus it is Adam Smith who wants to introduce the
principle of retaliation into commercial policy—a principle
which would lead to the most absurd and most ruinous
measures, especially if the retaliatory duties, as Smith
demands, are to be repealed as soon as the foreign nation
agrees to abolish its restrictions. Supposing Germany
made reprisals against England, because of the duties imposed by the latter on German corn and timber, by excluding from Germany English manufactured goods, and by
this exclusion called artificially into existence a manufacturing power of her own; must Germany then allow this
manufacturing industry, created at immense sacrifice, to
come to grief in case England should be induced to reopen
her ports to German corn and timber? What folly! It
would have been ten times better than that if Germany
had submitted quietly to all measures of restriction on the
part of England, and had discouraged the growth of any
manufacturing power of her own which might grow up
notwithstanding the English import prohibitions, instead
of stimulating its growth.

The principle of retaliation is reasonable and applicable only if it coincides with the principle of the *industrial development of the nation*, if it serves as it were as an assistance to this object.

Yes, it is reasonable and beneficial that other nations should retaliate against the English import restrictions on their agricultural products, by imposing restrictions on the importation of manufactured goods, but only *when those nations are qualified to establish a manufacturing power of their own and to maintain it for all times.*

By the second exception, Adam Smith really justifies not merely the necessity of protecting such manufactures as supply the immediate requirements of war, such as, for instance, manufactories of arms and powder, but the whole system of protection as we understand it; for by the establishment in the nation of a manufacturing power of its own, protection to native industry tends to the augmentation of the nation's population, of its material wealth, of its machine power, of its independence, and of all mental powers, and, therefore, of its means of national defence, in an infinitely higher degree than it could do by merely manufacturing arms and powder.

The same must be said of Adam Smith's third exception. If the burden of taxation to which our productions are subjected, affords a just ground for imposing protective duties on the less taxed products of foreign countries, why should not also the other disadvantages to which our manufacturing industry is subjected in comparison with that of the foreigner afford just grounds for protecting our native industry against the overwhelming competition of foreign industry?

J. B. Say has clearly perceived the contradictory character of this exception, but the exception substituted by him is no better; for in a nation qualified by nature and by its degree of culture to establish a manufacturing power of its own, almost every branch of industry must become remunerative under continued and powerful protection; and it is ridiculous to allow a nation merely a *few years* for the task of bringing to perfection one great branch of national industry or the whole industry of the nation; just as a shoemaker's apprentice is allowed only a few years to learn shoemaking.

In its eternal declamations on the immense advantages of absolute freedom of trade, and the disadvantages of protection, the popular school is accustomed to rely on the examples of a few nations ; that of *Switzerland* is quoted to prove that industry can prosper without protective duties, and that absolute liberty of international commerce forms the safest basis of national prosperity. The fate of *Spain* is quoted to exhibit to all nations which seek aid and preservation in the protective system, a frightful example of its ruinous effects. The case of England, which, as we have shown in a former chapter, affords such an excellent example for imitation to all nations which are capable of developing a manufacturing power, is adduced by these theorists merely to support their allegation that capability for manufacturing production is a natural gift exclusively peculiar to certain countries, like the capability to produce Burgundy wines; and that nature has bestowed on England, above all other countries of the earth, the destiny and the ability to devote herself to manufacturing industry and to an extensive commerce.

Let us now take these examples more closely into consideration.

As for *Switzerland*, it must be remarked in the first place that she does not constitute a nation, at least not one of normal magnitude which can be ranked as a great nation, but is merely a conglomeration of municipalities. Possessing no sea-coast, hemmed in between three great nations, she lacks all inducement to strive to obtain a native commercial marine, or direct trade with tropical countries ; she need pay no regard to the establishment of a naval power, or to founding or acquiring colonies. Switzerland laid the foundation of her present very moderate degree of prosperity at the time when she still belonged to the German Empire. Since that time, she has been almost entirely free from internal wars, her capital has been permitted to increase from generation to generation, as scarcely any of it was required by her municipal governments for discharging their expenses. Amid the devastations occasioned by the despotism, fanaticism, wars, and revolutions, with which Europe was perturbed during the last centuries, Switzerland offered an asylum to all who desired to transfer their capital and talents to another country than their own, and thus acquired considerable wealth from abroad. Germany has never adopted strong commercial restrictions against Switzerland, and a large part of the manufactured products of the latter has obtained a market in Germany. Moreover, the industry of Switzerland was never a national one, one comprising the production of articles of common use, but chiefly an industry in articles of luxury, the products of which could be easily smuggled into the neighbouring countries or transported to distant parts of the world. Furthermore, her territory is most favourably situated for intermediate trade, and in this respect is in some measure privileged. Again, their excellent opportunity of becoming acquainted with the languages, laws, institutions, and circumstances of the three nations which adjoin her must have given the Swiss important advantages in intermediate commerce and in every other respect. Civil and religious liberty and universal education have evoked in the Swiss, activity and a spirit of enterprise which, in view of the narrow limits of their country's internal agriculture, and of her internal resources for supporting her population, drove the Swiss to foreign countries, where they amassed wealth, by means of military service, by commerce, by industries of every kind, in order to bring it home to their Fatherland. If under such special circumstances they managed to acquire mental and material resources, in order to develop a few branches of industry for producing articles of luxury, if these industries could maintain themselves without protective duties by sales to foreign countries, it cannot thence be concluded that great nations could follow a similar policy under wholly different circumstances. In her small national expenditure Switzerland possesses an advantage which great nations could only attain if they, like Switzerland, resolved themselves into mere municipalities and thus exposed their nationality to foreign attacks.

That *Spain* acted foolishly in preventing the exportation of the precious metals, especially since she herself produced such a large excess of these articles, must be admitted by every reasonable person. It is a mistake, however, to attribute the decline of the industry and national well-being of Spain to her restrictions against the importation of manufactured goods. If Spain had not expelled the Moors and Jews, and had never had an Inquisition; if Charles V. had permitted religious liberty in Spain; if the priests and monks had been changed into teachers of the people, and their immense property secularised, or at least reduced to what was actually necessary for their maintenance; if, in consequence of these measures, civil liberty had gained a firm footing, the feudal nobility had been reformed and the monarchy limited; if, in a word, Spain had politically developed herself in consequence of a Reformation, as England did, and if the same spirit had extended to her colonies, a prohibitive and protective policy would have had similar effects in Spain as it had in England, and this all the more because at the time of Charles V. the Spaniards were more advanced than the English and French in every respect, and the Netherlands only (of all countries) occupied a more advanced position than Spain, whose industrial and commercial spirit might have been transferred to Spain by means of the protective policy, provided that the institutions and conditions of Spain were such as would have invited foreign talents and capital to her shores, instead of driving her own native talents and capital into foreign countries.

To what causes England owes her manufacturing and commercial supremacy, we have shown in our fifth chapter.

It is especially owing to her civil, mental, and religious liberty, to the nature and excellence of her political institutions, that the commercial policy of England has been enabled to make the most of the natural riches of the country, and fully to develop the productive powers of the nation. But who would deny that other nations are capable of raising themselves to the same degree of liberty? Who would venture to maintain that nature has denied to other nations the means which are requisite for manufacturing industry ?

In the latter respect the great natural wealth in coal and iron which England possesses has often been adduced as a reason why the English are specially destined to be a manufacturing nation. It is true that in this respect England is greatly favoured by nature; but against this it may be stated that even in respect of these natural products, nature has not treated other countries merely like a stepmother; for the most part the want of good transport facilities is the chief obstacle to the full utilisation of these products by other nations; that other countries possess enormous unemployed water power, which is cheaper than steam power; that where it is necessary they are able to counterbalance the want of coal by the use of other fuels; that many other countries possess inexhaustible means for the production of iron, and that they are also able to procure these raw materials from abroad by commercial exchange.

In conclusion, we must not omit here to make mention of *commercial treaties* based on mutual concessions of duties. The school objects to these conventions as unnecessary and detrimental, whereas they appear to us as the most effective means of gradually diminishing the respective restrictions on trade, and of leading the nations of the world gradually to freedom of international intercourse. Of course, the specimens of such treaties which the world has hitherto seen, are not very encouraging for imitation. We have shown in former chapters what injurious effects the *Methuen* Treaty has produced in Portugal, and the *Eden* Treaty has produced in France. It is on these injurious effects of reciprocal alleviation of duties, that the objections of the school to commercial treaties appear principally to be founded. Its principle of absolute commercial liberty has evidently experienced a practical contradiction in these cases, inasmuch as, according to that principle, those treaties ought to have operated beneficially to both contracting nations, but not to the ruin of the one, and to the immense advantage of the other. If, however, we inves-

tigate the cause of this disproportionate effect, we find that
Portugal and France, in consequence of those conventions,
abandoned in favour of England the progress they had
already made in manufacturing industry, as well as that
which they could expect to make in it in the future, with
the expectation of increasing by that means their exportation of natural products to England; that, accordingly,
both those nations have declined, in consequence of the
treaties thus concluded, from a higher to a lower standpoint of industrial development. From this, however, it
merely follows that a nation acts foolishly if it sacrifices its
manufacturing power to foreign competition by commercial
treaties, and thereby binds itself to remain for all future
time dependent on the low standpoint of merely agricultural
industry; but it does not in the least follow from this, that
those treaties are also detrimental and objectionable whereby
the reciprocal exchange of agricultural products and raw
materials, or the reciprocal exchange of manufactured products, is promoted.

We have previously explained that free trade in agricultural products and raw materials is useful to all nations at
all stages of their industrial development; from this it
follows that every commercial treaty which mitigates or
removes prohibitions and restrictions on freedom of trade in
such articles must have a beneficial effect on both contracting
nations, as e.g. a convention between France and England
whereby the mutual exchange of wines and brandies for
pig-iron and coal, or a treaty between France and Germany
whereby the mutual exchange of wine, oil, and dried fruit,
for corn, wool, and cattle, were promoted.

According to our former deductions, protection is only
beneficial to the prosperity of the nation so far as it corresponds with the degree of the nation's industrial development. Every exaggeration of protection is detrimental;
nations can only obtain a perfect manufacturing power by
degrees. On that account also, two nations which stand at
different stages of industrial cultivation, can with mutual
benefit make reciprocal concessions by treaty in respect
to the exchange of their various manufacturing products.

The less advanced nation can, while it is not yet able to produce for itself with profit finer manufactured goods, such as fine cotton and silk fabrics, nevertheless supply the further advanced nation with a portion of its requirements of coarser manufactured goods.

Such treaties might be still more allowable and beneficial between nations which stand at about the same degree of industrial development, between which, therefore, competition is not overwhelming, destructive, or repressive, nor tending to give a monopoly of everything to one side, but merely acts, as competition in the inland trade does, as an incentive to mutual emulation, perfection, and cheapening of production. This is the case with most of the Continental nations. France, Austria, and the German Zollverein might, for instance, anticipate only very prosperous effects from moderately low reciprocal protective duties. Also, between these countries and Russia mutual concessions could be made to the advantage of all sides. What they all have to fear at this time is solely the preponderating competition of England.

Thus it appears also from this point of view, that the supremacy of that island in manufactures, in trade, in navigation, and in her colonial empire, constitutes the greatest existing impediment to all nations drawing nearer to one another ; although it must be at the same time admitted that England, in striving for this supremacy, has immeasurably increased, and is still daily increasing, the productive power of the entire human race.

THE SYSTEMS

CHAPTER XXVIII.

ITALY has been the forerunner of all modern nations, in the theory as well as in the practice of Political Economy. Count Pechio has given us a laboriously written sketch of that branch of Italian literature ; only his book is open to the observation, that he has clung too slavishly to the popular theory, and has not duly set forth the fundamental causes of the decline of Italy's national industry— the absence of national unity, surrounded as she was by great nationalities united under hereditary monarchies ; further, priestly rule and the downfall of municipal freedom in the Italian republics and cities. If he had more deeply investigated these causes, he could not have failed to apprehend the special tendency of the ' Prince ' of Macchiavelli, and he would not have passed that author by with merely an incidental reference to him.[1]

Through a remark of Pechio, that Macchiavelli in a letter to his friend Guicciardini (in 1525) had proposed a union of all the Powers of Italy against the foreigner, and that as that letter was communicated to Pope Clement VII. he had thus exercised considerable influence in the formation of the ' Holy League ' (in 1526), we were led to imagine that the same tendency must underlie the ' Prince.' As soon as we referred to that work, we found our anticipation confirmed at first sight. The object of the ' Prince ' (written in 1513) was clearly to impress the Medici with the idea,

---

[1] During a journey in Germany which the author undertook while this work was in the press, he learned for the first time that Doctors Von Ranke and Gervinus have criticised Macchiavelli's *Prince* from the same point of view as himself

that they were called upon to unite the whole of Italy under one sovereignty ; and to indicate to them the means whereby that end might be attained. The title and form of that book, as though its general intention was to treat of the nature of absolute government, were undoubtedly selected from motives of prudence. It only alludes incidentally to the various hereditary Princes and their governments. Everywhere the author has in view only one Italian usurper. Principalities must be overthrown, dynasties destroyed, the feudal aristocracy brought under subjection, liberty in the republics rooted out. The virtues of heaven and the artifices of hell, wisdom and audacity, valour and treachery, good fortune and chance, must all be called forth, made use of, and tried by the usurper, in order to found an Italian empire. And to this end a secret is confided to him, the power of which has been thoroughly made manifest three hundred years later—a national army must be created, to whom victory must be assured by new discipline and by newly invented arms and manœuvres.[1]

If the general character of his arguments leaves room for doubt as to the special bias of this author, such doubt will be removed by his last chapter. There he plainly declares that foreign invasions and internal divisions are the fundamental causes of all the evils prevailing in Italy ; that the House of the Medici, under whose dominion were (fortunately) Tuscany and the States of the Church, were called by Providence itself to accomplish that great work ; that the present was the best time and opportunity for introducing a new *régime*, that now a new Moses must arise to deliver his people from the bondage of Egypt, that nothing conferred on a Prince more distinction and fame than great enterprises.[2]

---

[1] Everything that Macchiavelli has written, whether before or after the publication of the *Prince*, indicates that he was revolving in his mind plans of this kind. How otherwise can it be explained, why he, a civilian, a man of letters, an ambassador and State official, who had never borne arms, should have occupied himself so much in studying the art of war, and that he should have been able to write a work upon it which excited the wonder of the most distinguished soldiers of his time ?

[2] Frederick the Great in his *Anti-Macchiavel* treats of the *Prince* as

That anyone may read between the lines the tendency of that book in the other chapters also, may be best seen by the manner in which the author in his ninth chapter speaks of the States of the Church.   It is merely an irony when he says, ' The priests possessed lands but did not govern them, they held lordships but did not defend them ; these happiest of all territories were directly protected by God's Providence, it would be presumption to utter a criticism upon them.'   He clearly by this language meant it to be understood without saying so in plain words : This country presents no special impediment to a bold conqueror, especially to a Medici whose relative occupies the Papal chair.

But how can we explain the advice which Macchiavelli gives to his proposed usurper respecting the republics, considering his own republican sentiments ?   And must it be solely attributed to a design on his part to ingratiate himself with the Prince to whom his book is dedicated, and thus to gain private advantages, when he, the zealous republican, the great thinker and literary genius, the patriotic martyr, advised the future usurper utterly to destroy the freedom of the Italian republics ?   It cannot be denied that Macchiavelli, at the time when he wrote the ' Prince,' was languishing in poverty, that he regarded the future with anxiety, that he earnestly longed and hoped for employment and support from the Medici.   A letter which he wrote on October 10, 1513, from his poor dwelling in the country to his friend Bettori, at Florence, places that beyond doubt.[1]

Nevertheless, there are strong reasons for believing that he by this book did not merely design to flatter the

simply a scientific treatis on the rights and duties of princes generally. Here it is remarkable that he, while contradicting Macchiavelli chapter by chapter, never mentions the last or twenty-sixth chapter, which bears the heading, ' A Summons to free Italy from the Foreigners,' and instead of it inserts a chapter which is not contained in Macchiavelli's work with the heading, ' On the different kinds of Negotiations, and on the just Reasons for a Declaration of .War.'

[1] First published in the work, *Pensieri intorno allo scopo di Nicolo Macchiavelli nel libro ' Il Principe.'*   Milano, 1810.

Medici, and to gain private advantage, but to promote the realisation of a plan of usurpation ; a plan which was not opposed to his republican-patriotic ideas, though according to the moral ideas of our day it must be condemned as reprehensible and wicked. His writings and his deeds in the service of the State prove that Macchiavelli was thoroughly acquainted with the history of all periods, and with the political condition of all States. But an eye which could see so far backwards, and so clearly what was around it, must also have been able to see far into the future. A spirit which even at the beginning of the sixteenth century recognised the advantage of the national arming of Italy, must also have seen that the time for small republics was past, that the period for great monarchies had arrived, that nationality could, under the circumstances then existing, be won only by means of usurpation, and maintained only by despotism, that the oligarchies as they then existed in the Italian republics constituted the greatest obstacle to national unity, that consequently they must be destroyed, and that national freedom would one day grow out of national unity. Macchiavelli evidently desired to cast away the worn-out liberty of a few cities as a prey to despotism, hoping by its aid to acquire national union, and thus to insure to future generations freedom on a greater and a nobler scale.

The earliest work written specially on Political Economy in Italy, is that of Antonio Serra of 'Naples (in 1613), on the means of providing ' the Kingdoms ' with an abundance of gold and silver.

J. B. Say and M'Culloch appear to have seen and read only the title of this book : they each pass it over with the remark that it merely treats of money ; and its title certainly shows that the author laboured under the error of considering the precious metals as the sole constituents of wealth. If they had read farther into it, and duly considered its contents, they might perhaps have derived from it some wholesome lessons. Antonio Serra, although he fell into the error of considering an abundance of gold and silver as the tokens of wealth, nevertheless expresses himself tolerably clearly on the causes of it.

He certainly puts mining in the first place as the direct source of the precious metals; but he treats very justly of the indirect means of acquiring them. Agriculture, manufactures, commerce, and navigation, are, according to him, the chief sources of national wealth. The fertility of the soil is a sure source of prosperity; manufactures are a still more fruitful source, for several reasons, but chiefly because they constitute the foundation of an extensive commerce. The productiveness of these sources depends on the characteristic qualifications of the people (viz. whether they are industrious, active, enterprising, thrifty, and so forth), also on the nature and circumstances of the locality (whether, for instance, a city is well situated for maritime trade). But above all these causes, Serra ranks the form of government, public order, municipal liberty, political guarantees, the stability of the laws. 'No country can prosper,' says he, 'where each successive ruler enacts new laws, hence the States of the Holy Father cannot be so prosperous as those countries whose government and legislation are more stable. In contrast with the former, one may observe in Venice the effect which a system of order and legislation, which has continued for centuries, has on the public welfare.' This is the quintessence of a system of Political Economy which in the main, notwithstanding that its object appears to be only the acquisition of the precious metals, is remarkable for its sound and natural doctrine. The work of J. B. Say, although it comprises ideas and matter on Political Economy of which Antonio Serra had in his day no foreknowledge, is far inferior to Serra's on the main points, and especially as respects a due estimate of the effect of political circumstances on the wealth of nations. Had Say studied Serra instead of laying his work aside, he could hardly have maintained (in the first page of his system of Political Economy) that ' the constitution of countries cannot be taken into account in respect to Political Economy; that the people have become rich, and become poor, under every form of government; that the only important point is, that its administration should be good.'

We are far from desiring to maintain the *absolute* pre-

ferableness of any one form of government compared with
others. One need only cast a glance at the Southern States
of America, to be convinced that democratic forms of
government among people who are not ripe for them can
become the cause of decided retrogression in public prosperity. One need only look at Russia, to perceive that
people who are yet in a low degree of civilisation are capable
of making most remarkable progress in their national well-
being under an absolute monarchy. But that in no way
proves that people have become rich, i.e. have attained the
highest degree of economical well-being, under all forms of
government. History rather teaches us that such a degree
of public well-being, namely a flourishing state of manufactures and commerce, has been attained in those countries
only whose political constitution (whether it bear the name
of democratic or aristocratic republic, or limited monarchy)
has secured to their inhabitants a high degree of personal
liberty and of security of property, whose administration
has guaranteed to them a high degree of activity and power
successfully to strive for the attainment of their common
objects, and of steady continuity in those endeavours. For
in a state of highly advanced civilisation, it is not so important that the administration should be good for a *certain
period*, but that it should be *continuously* and *conformably*
good; that the next administration should not destroy the
good work of the former one; that a thirty years' administration of Colbert should not be followed by a Revocation of
the Edict of Nantes, that for successive centuries one should
follow one and the same system, and strive after one and
the same object. Only under those political constitutions
in which the national interests are represented (and not
under an absolute Government, under which the State administration is necessarily always modified according to the
individual will of the ruler) can such a steadiness and con-
sistency of administration be secured, as Antonio Serra
rightly observes. On the other hand, there are undoubtedly
certain grades of civilisation in which the administration by
absolute power may prove far more favourable to the economical and mental progress of the nation (and generally is

so) than that of a limited monarchy. We refer to periods of slavery and serfdom, of barbarism and superstition, of national disunity, and of caste privileges. For, under such circumstances, the constitution tends to secure not only the interests of the nation, but also the continuance of the prevailing evils, whereas it is the interest and the nature of absolute government to destroy the latter, and it is also possible that an absolute ruler may arise of distinguished power and sagacity, who may cause the nation to make advances for centuries, and secure to its nationality existence and progress for all future time.

It is consequently only a conditional commonplace truth on the faith of which J. B. Say would exclude politics from his doctrine. In every case it is the chief desideratum that the administration should be good; but the efficiency of the administration depends on the form of government, and that form of government is clearly the best which most promotes the moral and material welfare and the future progress of any given nation. Nations have made some progress under all forms of government. But a high degree of economical development has only been attained in those nations whose form of government has been such as to secure to them a high degree of freedom and power, of steadiness of laws and of policy, and efficient institutions.

Antonio Serra sees the nature of things as it actually exists, and not through the spectacles of previous systems, or of some one principle which he is determined to advocate and carry out. He draws a comparison between the condition of the various States of Italy, and perceives that the greatest degree of wealth is to be found where there is extensive commerce; that extensive commerce exists where there is a well-developed manufacturing power, but that the latter is to be found where there is municipal freedom.

The opinions of Beccaria are pervaded by the false doctrines of the physiocratic school. That author indeed either discovered, or derived from Aristotle, the principle of the division of labour, either before, or contemporaneously with, Adam Smith; he, however, carries it farther than Adam

Smith, inasmuch as he not only applies it to the division of the work in a single manufactory, but shows that the public welfare is promoted by the division of occupation among the members of the community. At the same time he does not hesitate, with the physiocrats, to assert that manufactures are non-productive.

The views of the great philosophical jurist, Filangieri, are about the narrowest of all. Imbued with false cosmopolitanism, he considers that England, by her protective policy, has merely given a premium to contraband trade, and weakened her own commerce.

Verri, as a practical statesman, could not err so widely as that. He admits the necessity of protection to native industry against foreign competition; but did not or could not see that such a policy is conditional on the greatness and unity of the nationality.

CHAPTER XXIX.

THE INDUSTRIAL SYSTEM (FALSELY TERMED BY THE SCHOOL
'THE MERCANTILE SYSTEM ').

AT the period when great nationalities arose, owing to the
union of entire peoples brought about by hereditary monarchy
and by the centralisation of public power, commerce and
navigation, and hence wealth and naval power, existed· for
the most part (as we have before shown) in republics of cities,
or in leagues of such republics. The more, however, that
the institutions of these great nationalities became developed, the more evident became the necessity of establishing
on their own territories these main sources of power and of
wealth.

Under the conviction that they could only take root and
flourish under municipal liberty, the royal power favoured
municipal freedom and the establishment of guilds, both
which it regarded as counterpoises against the feudal aristocracy, who were continually striving for independence,
and always hostile to national unity. But this expedient
appeared insufficient, for one reason, because the total of
the advantages which individuals enjoyed in the *free* cities
and republics was much greater than the total of those
advantages which the monarchical governments were able
to offer, or chose to offer, in their own municipal cities ; in
the second place, because it is very difficult, indeed impossible, for a country which has always been principally
engaged in agriculture, successfully to displace in free competition those countries which for centuries have acquired
supremacy in manufactures, commerce, and navigation ;
lastly, because in the great monarchies the feudal institutions acted as hindrances to the development of their

internal agriculture, and consequently to the growth of their internal manufactures. Hence, the nature of things led the great monarchies to adopt such political measures as tended to restrict the importation of foreign manufactured goods, and foreign commerce and navigation, and to favour the progress of their own manufactures, and their own commerce and navigation.

Instead of raising revenue as they had previously done by duties on the raw materials which they exported, they were henceforth principally levied on the imported manufactured goods. The benefits offered by the latter policy stimulated the merchants, seamen, and manufacturers of more highly civilised cities and countries to immigrate with their capital into the great monarchies, and stimulated the spirit of enterprise of the subjects of the latter. The growth of the national industry was followed by the growth of the national freedom. The feudal aristocracy found it necessary in their own interest to make concessions to the industrial and commercial population, as well as to those engaged in agriculture; hence resulted progress in agriculture as well as in native industry and native commerce, which had a reciprocally favourable influence on those two other factors of national wealth. We have shown how England, in consequence of this system, and favoured by the Reformation, made forward progress from century to century in the development of her productive power, freedom, and might. We have stated how in France this system was followed for some time with success, but how it came to grief there, because the institutions of feudalism, of the priesthood, and of the absolute monarchy, had not yet been reformed. We have also shown how the Polish nationality succumbed, because the elective system of monarchy did not possess influence and steadiness enough to bring into existence powerful municipal institutions, and to reform the feudal aristocracy. As a result of this policy, there was created in the place of the commercial and manufacturing city, and of the agricultural province which chiefly existed outside the political influence of that city, the agricultural-manufacturing-commercial State; a nation complete in itself, an harmonious and compact whole, in which, on the one hand, the formerly prevailing differences between monarchy, feudal aristocracy, and citizenhood gave place to one harmonious accord, and, on the other hand, the closest union and reciprocally beneficial action took place between agriculture, manufactures, and commerce. This was an immeasurably more perfect commonwealth than the previously existing one, because the manufacturing power, which in the municipal republic had been confined to a narrow range, now could extend itself over a wider sphere; because now all existing resources were placed at its disposition; because the division of labour and the confederation of the productive powers in the different branches of manufactures, as well as in agriculture, were made effectual in an infinitely greater degree; because the numerous classes of agriculturists became politically and commercially united with the manufacturers and merchants, and hence perpetual concord was maintained between them; the reciprocal action between manufacturing and commercial power was perpetuated and secured for ever; and finally, the agriculturists were made partakers of all the advantages of civilisation arising from manufactures and commerce. The agricultural-manufacturing-commercial State is like a city which spreads over a whole kingdom, or a country district raised up to be a city. In the same proportion in which material production was promoted by this union, the mental powers must necessarily have been developed, the political institutions perfected, the State revenues, the national military power, and the population, increased. Hence we see at this day, that nation which first of all perfectly developed the agricultural, manufacturing, and commercial State, standing in these respects at the head of all other nations.

The Industrial System was not defined in writing, nor was it a theory devised by authors, it was simply acted upon in practice, until the time of Stewart, who deduced it for the most part from the actual English practice, just as Antonio Serra deduced his system from a consideration of the circumstances of Venice. Stewart's treatise, however, cannot be considered a scientific work. The greater part of it is devoted to money, banking, the paper circulation—commercial crises—the balance of trade, and the doctrine of population;—discussions from which even in our day much may be learned, but which are carried on in a very illogical and unintelligible way, and in which one and the same idea is ten times repeated. The other branches of political economy are either superficially treated, or passed over altogether. Neither the productive powers, nor the elements of price, are thoroughly discussed. Everywhere the author appears to have in view only the experiences and circumstances of England. In a word, his book possesses all the merits and demerits of the practice of England, and of that of Colbert. The merits of the Industrial System as compared with later ones, are :

1. That it clearly recognises the value of native manufactures and their influence on native agriculture, commerce, and navigation, and on the civilisation and power of the nation ; and expresses itself unreservedly to that effect.

2. That it indicates what is in general the right means whereby a nation which is qualified for establishing a manufacturing power, may attain a national industry.[1]

3. That it is based on the idea of 'the nation,' and regarding the nations as individual entities, everywhere takes into account the national interests and national conditions.

On the other hand, this system is chargeable with the following chief faults :

1. That it does not generally recognise the fundamental principle of the industrial development of the nation and the conditions under which it can be brought into operation.

2. That it consequently would mislead peoples who live

---

[1] Stewart says (Book I. chapter xxix.) : ' In order to promote industry, a nation must act as well as permit, and protect. Could ever the woollen manufacture have been introduced into France from the consideration of the great advantage which England had drawn from it, if the king had not undertaken the support of it by granting many privileges to the undertakers, and by laying strict prohibitions on all foreign cloths ? Is there any other way of establishing a new manufacture anywhere ? '

in a climate unsuited for manufacturing, and small and uncivilised states and peoples, into the adoption of the protective system.

3. That it always seeks to apply protection to agriculture, and especially to the production of raw materials— to the injury of agriculture—whereas agricultural industry is sufficiently protected against foreign competition by the nature of things.[1]

4. That it seeks to favour manufactures unjustly by imposing restrictions on the export of raw materials, to the detriment of agriculture.

5. That it does not teach the nation which has already attained manufacturing and commercial supremacy to preserve her own manufacturers and merchants from indolence, by permitting free competition in her own markets.

6. That in the exclusive pursuit of the political object, it ignores the cosmopolitical relations of all nations, the objects of the whole human race ; and hence would mislead governments into a prohibitory system, where a protective one would amply suffice, or imposing duties which are practically prohibitory, when moderate protective duties would better answer the purpose. Finally :

7. That chiefly owing to its utterly ignoring the principle of cosmopolitanism, it does not recognise the future union of all nations, the establishment of perpetual peace, and of universal freedom of trade, as the goal towards which all nations have to strive, and more and more to approach.

The subsequent schools have, however, falsely reproached this system for considering the precious metals as the sole constituents of wealth, whereas they are merely merchandise like all other articles of value; and that hence it would follow that we ought to sell as much as possible to other nations and to buy from them as little as possible.

As respects the former objection, it cannot be truly alleged of either Colbert's administration or of that of the English since George I. that they have attached an unreasonable degree of importance to the importation of the precious metals.

[1] See Appendix C.

To raise their own native manufactures, their own navigation, their foreign trade, was the aim of their commercial policy ; which indeed was chargeable with many mistakes, but which on the whole produced important results. We have observed that since the Methuen Treaty (1703) the English have annually exported great quantities of the precious metals to the East Indies, without considering these exports as prejudicial.

The Ministers of George I. when they prohibited (in 1721) the importation of the cotton and silk fabrics of India did not assign as a reason for that measure that a nation ought to sell as much as possible to the foreigner, and buy as little as possible from him ; that absurd idea was grafted on to the industrial system by a subsequent school ; what they asserted was, that it is evident that a nation can only attain to wealth and power by the export of its own manufactured goods, and by the import from abroad of raw materials and the necessaries of life. England has followed this maxim of State policy to the present day, and by following it has become rich and mighty ; this maxim is the only true one for a nation which has been long civilised, and which has already brought its own agriculture to a high degree of development.

CHAPTER XXX.

THE PHYSIOCRATIC OR AGRICULTURAL SYSTEM.

HAD the great enterprise of Colbert been permitted to succeed—had not the Revocation of the Edict of Nantes, the love of splendour and false ambition of Louis XIV., and the debauchery and extravagance of his successors, nipped in the bud the seeds which Colbert had sown—if consequently a wealthy manufacturing and commercial interest had arisen in France, if by good fortune the enormous properties of the French clergy had been given over to the public, if these events had resulted in the formation of a powerful lower house of Parliament, by whose influence the feudal aristocracy had been reformed— the physiocratic system would hardly have ever come to light. That system was evidently deduced from the then existing circumstances of France, and was only applicable to those circumstances.

At the period of its introduction the greater part of the landed property in France was in the hands of the clergy and the nobility. It was cultivated by a peasantry languishing under a state of serfdom and personal oppression, who were sunk in superstition, ignorance, indolence, and poverty. The owners of the land, who constituted its productive instruments, were devoted to frivolous pursuits, and had neither mind for, nor interest in, agriculture. The actual cultivators had neither the mental nor material means for agricultural improvements. The oppression of feudalism on agricultural production was increased by the insatiable demands made by the monarchy on the producers, which were made more intolerable by the freedom from taxation enjoyed by the clergy and nobility. Under such circumstances it was impossible that the most important branches

of trade could succeed, those namely which depend on the
productiveness of native agriculture, and the consumption
of the great masses of the people ; those only could manage
to thrive which produced articles of luxury for the use of
the privileged classes.   The foreign trade was restricted
by the inability of the material producers to consume any
considerable quantity of the produce of tropical countries,
and to pay for them by their own surplus produce; the
inland trade was oppressed by provincial customs duties.

Under .such circumstances, nothing could be more
natural than that thoughtful men, in their investigations
into the causes of the prevailing poverty and misery, should
have arrived at the conviction, that national welfare could
not be attained so long as agriculture was not freed from
its fetters, so long as the owners of land and capital took
no interest in agriculture, so long as the peasantry remained
sunk in personal subjection, in superstition, idleness, and
ignorance, so long as taxation remained undiminished and
was not equally borne by all classes, so long as internal
tariff restrictions existed, and foreign trade did not flourish.

But these thoughtful men (we must remember) were
either physicians to the King and his Court, Court favourites,
or confidants and friends of the aristocracy and the clergy,
they could not and would not declare open war against
either absolute power or against clergy and nobility.
There remained to them but one method of disseminating
their views, that of concealing their. plan of reform under
the obscurity of a profound system, just as, in earlier as
well as later times, ideas of political and religious reform
have been embedded in the substance of philosophical
systems.   Following the philosophers of their own age and
country, who, in view of the total disorganisation of the
national condition of France, sought consolation in the
wider field of philanthropy and cosmopolitanism (much as
the father of a family, in despair at the break-up of his
household, goes to seek comfort in the tavern), so the
physiocrats caught at the cosmopolitan idea of universal
free trade, as a panacea by which all prevailing evils might
be cured.   When they had got hold of this point of truth

by exalting their thoughts above, they then directed them
beneath, and discovered in the 'nett revenue' of the soil
a basis for their preconceived ideas.   Thence resulted the
fundamental maxim of their system, 'the soil alone yields
nett revenue, therefore agriculture is the sole source of
wealth.   That is a doctrine from which wonderful consequences might be inferred—first feudalism must fall, and
if requisite, landowning itself; then all taxation ought to
be levied on the land, as being the source of all wealth;
then the exemption from taxation enjoyed by the nobility
and clergy must cease; finally the manufacturers must be
deemed an unproductive class, who ought to pay no taxes,
but also ought to have no State-protection, hence custom-
houses must be abolished.

In short, people contrived by means of the most absurd
arguments and contentions to prove those great truths
which they had determined beforehand to prove.

Of the nation, and its special circumstances and condition in relation to other nations, no further account was to
be taken, for that is clear from the 'Encyclopédie Méthodique,' which says, 'The welfare of the individual is
conditional on the welfare of the entire human race.'
Here, therefore, no account was taken of any nation, of
any war, of any foreign commercial measures: history and
experience must be either ignored or misrepresented.

The great merit of this system was, that it bore the
appearance of an attack made on the policy of Colbert and
on the privileges of the manufacturers, for the benefit of the
landowners; while in reality its blows told with most effect
on the special privileges of the latter.   Poor Colbert had to
bear all the blame of the sufferings of the French agriculturists, while nevertheless everyone knew that France
possessed a great industry for the first time since Colbert's
administration; and that even the dullest intellect was
aware that manufactures constitute the chief means for
promoting agriculture and commerce.   The Revocation of
the Edict of Nantes—the wanton wars of Louis XIV.—the
profligate expenditure of Louis XV.—were utterly ignored
by these philosophers.

Quesnay in his writings has adduced, and replied to, point by point, the objections which were urged against his system. One is astonished at the mass of sound sense which he puts into the mouth of his opponents, and at the mass of mystical absurdity which he opposes to those objections by way of argument. Notwithstanding, all that absurdity was accepted as wisdom by the contemporaries of this reformer, because the tendency of his system accorded with the circumstances of France at that time, and with the philanthropic and cosmopolitan ideas prevalent in that century.

CHAPTER XXXI.

THE SYSTEM OF VALUES OF EXCHANGE (FALSELY TERMED BY
THE SCHOOL, THE 'INDUSTRIAL' SYSTEM)—ADAM SMITH.

ADAM SMITH's doctrine is, in respect to national and
international conditions, merely a continuation of the
physiocratic system. Like the latter, it ignores the very
nature of nationalities, seeks almost entirely to exclude
politics and the power of the State, presupposes the existence of a state of perpetual peace and of universal union,
underrates the value of a national manufacturing power,
and the means of obtaining it, and demands absolute
freedom of trade.

Adam Smith fell into these fundamental errors in
exactly the same way as the physiocrats had done before
him, namely by regarding absolute freedom in international
trade as an axiom assent to which is demanded by common
sense, and by not investigating to the bottom how far
history supports this idea.

Dugald Stewart (Adam Smith's able biographer) informs
us that Smith, at a date twenty-one years before his work
was published in 1776 (viz. in 1755), claimed priority in
conceiving the idea of universal freedom of trade, at a
literary party at which he was present, in the following
words :

'Man is usually made use of by statesmen and makers
of projects, as the material for a sort of political handiwork.
The project makers, in their operations on human affairs,
disturb Nature, whereas people ought simply to leave her
to herself to act freely, in order that she may accomplish
her objects. In order to raise a State from the lowest
depth of barbarism to the highest degree of wealth, all that

is requisite is peace, moderate taxation, and good administration of justice; everything else will follow of its own
accord in the natural course of things. All governments
which act in a contrary spirit to this natural course, which
seek to divert capital into other channels, or to restrict the
progress of the community in its spontaneous course, act
contrary to nature, and, in order to maintain their position,
become oppressive and tyrannical.'

Adam Smith set out from this fundamental idea, and
to prove it and to illustrate it was the sole object of all his
later works. He was confirmed in this idea by Quesnay,
Turgot, and the other coryphæi of the physiocratic school,
whose acquaintance he had made in a visit to France in
the year 1765.

Smith evidently considered the idea of freedom of trade
as an intellectual discovery which would constitute the
foundation of his literary fame. How natural, therefore,
it was that he should endeavour in his work to put aside
and to refute everything that stood in the way of that idea;
that he should consider himself as the professed advocate
of absolute freedom of trade, and that he thought and
wrote in that spirit.

How could it be expected, that with such preconceived
opinions, Smith should judge of men and of things, of
history and statistics, of political measures and of their
authors, in any other light than as they confirmed or contradicted his fundamental principle?

In the passage above quoted from Dugald Stewart,
Adam Smith's whole system is comprised as in a nutshell.
The power of the State can and ought to do nothing, except to allow justice to be administered, to impose as little
taxation as possible. Statesmen who attempt to found a
manufacturing power, to promote navigation, to extend
foreign trade, to protect it by naval power, and to found or
to acquire colonies, are in his opinion project makers who
only hinder the progress of the community. For him no
nation exists, but merely a community, i.e. a number of
individuals dwelling together. These individuals know best
for themselves what branches of occupation are most to

their advantage, and they can best select for themselves the means which promote their prosperity.

This entire nullification of nationality and of State power, this exaltation of individualism to the position of author of all effective power, could be made plausible only by making the main object of investigation to be not the power which effects, but the thing effected, namely material wealth, or rather the value in exchange which the thing effected possesses. Materialism must come to the aid of individualism, in order to conceal what an enormous amount of power accrues to individuals from nationality, from national unity, and from the national confederation of the productive powers. A bare theory of values must be made to pass current as national economy, because individuals alone produce values, and the State, incapable of creating values, must limit its operations to calling into activity, protecting, and promoting the productive powers of individuals. In this combination, the quintessence of political economy may be stated as follows, viz. : Wealth consists in the possession of objects of exchangeable value ; objects of exchangeable value are produced by the labour of individuals in combination with the powers of nature and with capital. By the division of labour, the productiveness of the labour is increased ; capital is accumulated by savings, by production exceeding consumption. The greater the total amount of capital, so much the greater is the division of labour, and hence the capacity to produce. Private interest is the most effectual stimulus to labour and to economy. Therefore the highest wisdom of statecraft consists in placing no obstacle in the way of private industry, and in caring only for the good administration of justice. And hence also it is folly to induce the subjects of a State, by means of State legislative measures, to produce for themselves anything which they can buy cheaper from abroad. A system so consistent as this is, which sets forth the elements of wealth, which so clearly explains the process of its production, and apparently so completely exposes the errors of the previous schools, could not fail, in default of any other, to meet with acceptance. The mistake has been simply, that this system at bottom is nothing else than a system of the *private economy of all the individual persons in a country, or of the individuals of the whole human race, as that economy would develop and shape itself, under a state of things in which there were no distinct nations, nationalities, or national interests—no distinctive political constitutions or degrees of civilisation—no wars or national animosities*; that it is nothing more than a theory of values; a mere shopkeeper's or individual merchant's theory—not a scientific doctrine, showing how the productive powers of an entire nation can be called into existence, increased, maintained, and preserved—for the special benefit of its civilisation, welfare, might, continuance, and independence.

This system regards everything from the shopkeeper's point of view. The value of anything is wealth, according to it, so its sole object is to gain values. The establishment of powers of production, it leaves to chance, to nature, or to the providence of God (whichever you please), only the State must have nothing at all to do with it, nor must politics venture to meddle with the business of accumulating exchangeable values. It is resolved to buy wherever it can find the cheapest articles—that the home manufactories are ruined by their importation, matters not to it. If foreign nations give a bounty on the export of their manufactured goods, so much the better; it can buy them so much the cheaper. In its view no class is productive save those who actually produce things valuable in exchange. It well recognises how the division of labour promotes the success of a business in detail, but it has no perception of the effect of the division of labour as affecting a whole nation. It knows that only by individual economy can it increase its capital, and that only in proportion to the increase in its capital can it extend its individual trades; but it sets no value on the increase of the productive power, which results from the establishment of native manufactories, or on the foreign trade and national power which arise out of that increase. What may become of the entire nation in the future, is to it a matter of perfect in-

difference, so long as private individuals can gain wealth.
It takes notice merely of the rent yielded by land, but pays
no regard to the value of landed property; it does not perceive that the greatest part of the wealth of a nation consists in the value of its land and its fixed property.   For
the influence of foreign trade on the value and price of
landed property, and for the fluctuations and calamities
thence arising, it cares not a straw.   In short, this system
is the strictest and most consistent 'mercantile system,'
and it is incomprehensible how that term could have been
applied to the system of Colbert, the main tendency of
which is towards an 'industrial system'—i.e. a system
which has solely in view the founding of a national industry
—a national commerce—without regarding the temporary
gains or losses of values in exchange.

Notwithstanding, we would by no means deny the great
merits of Adam Smith.   He was the first who successfully
applied the analytical method to political economy.   By·
means of that method and an unusual degree of sagacity,
he threw light on the most important branches of the
science, which were previously almost wholly obscure.
Before Adam Smith only a practice existed; his works
rendered it possible to constitute a science of political
economy, and he has contributed a greater amount of
materials for that object than all his predecessors or
successors.

But that very peculiarity of his mind by which, in
analysing the various constituent parts of political economy,
he rendered such important service, was the cause why he
did not take a comprehensive view of the community in its
entirety; that he was unable to combine individual interests
in one harmonious whole; that he would not consider the
nation in preference to mere individuals; that out of mere
anxiety for the freedom of action of the individual producers,
he lost sight of the interests of the entire nation.   He who
so clearly perceived the benefits of the division of labour
in a single manufactory, did not perceive that the same
principle is applicable with equal force to entire provinces
and nations.

With this opinion, that which Dugald Stewart says of him exactly agrees. Smith could judge individual traits of character with extraordinary acuteness; but if an opinion was needed as to the entire character of a man or of a book, one could not be sufficiently astonished at the narrowness and obliquity of his views. Nay, he was incapable of forming a correct estimate of the character of those with whom he had lived for many years in the most intimate friendship. 'The portrait,' says his biographer, 'was ever full of life and expression, and had a strong resemblance to the original if one compared it with the original from a certain point of view; but it never gave a true and perfect representation according to all its dimensions and circumstances.'

CHAPTER XXXII.

THE SYSTEM OF VALUES OF EXCHANGE (CONTINUED) — JEAN BAPTISTE SAY AND HIS SCHOOL.

THIS author on the whole has merely endeavoured to systematise, to elucidate, and to popularise, the materials which Adam Smith had gathered together after an irregular fashion. In that he has perfectly succeeded, inasmuch as he possessed in a high degree the gift of systematisation and elucidation. Nothing new or original is to be found in his writings, save only that he asserted the productiveness of mental labours, which Adam Smith denied. Only, this view, which is quite correct according to the theory of the productive powers, stands opposed to the theory of exchangeable values, and hence Smith is clearly more consistent than Say. Mental labourers produce directly no exchangeable values; nay, more, they diminish by their consumption the total amount of material productions and savings, and hence the total of material wealth. Moreover, the ground on which Say from his point of view includes mental labourers among the productive class, viz. because they are paid with exchangeable values, is an utterly baseless one, inasmuch as those values have been already produced before they reach the hands of the mental labourers; their possessor alone is changed, but by that change their amount is not increased. We can only term mental labourers productive if we regard the productive powers of the nation, and not the mere possession of exchangeable values, as national wealth. Say found himself opposed to Smith in this respect, exactly as Smith had found himself opposed to the physiocrats.

In order to include manufacturers among the productive class, Smith had been obliged to enlarge the idea of what constitutes wealth; and Say on his part had no other alternative than either to adopt the absurd view that mental labourers are not productive, as it was handed down to him by Adam Smith, or else to enlarge the idea of wealth as Adam Smith had done in opposition to the physiocrats, namely to make it comprise productive power; and to argue, national wealth does not consist in the possession of exchangeable values, but in the possession of power to produce, just as the wealth of a fisherman does not consist in the possession of fish, but in the ability and the means of continually catching fish to satisfy his wants.

It is noteworthy, and, so far as we are aware, not generally known, that Jean Baptiste Say had a brother whose plain clear common sense led him clearly to perceive the fundamental error of the theory of values, and that J. B. Say himself expressed to his doubting brother doubts as to the soundness of his own doctrine.

Louis Say wrote from Nantes, that a technical language had become prevalent in political economy which had led to much false reasoning, and that his brother Jean himself was not free from it.[1] According to Louis Say, the wealth of nations does not consist in material goods and their value in exchange, but in the ability continuously to produce such goods. The exchange theory of Smith and J. B. Say regards wealth from the narrow point of view of an individual merchant, and this system, which would reform the (so-called) mercantile system, is itself nothing else than a restricted mercantile system.[2] To these doubts and

---

[1] Louis Say, *Etudes sur la Richesse des Nations*, Preface, p. iv.

[2] The following are the actual words of Louis Say (p. 10) : ' La richesse ne consiste pas dans les choses qui satisfont nos besoins ou nos goûts, mais dans le pouvoir d'en jouir annuellement.' And further (pp. 14 to 15) : ' Le faux système mercantil, fondé sur la richesse en métaux précieux, a été remplacé par un autre fondé sur la richesse en valeurs vénales ou échangeables, qui consiste à n'évaluer ce qui compose la richesse d'une nation que comme le fait un marchand.' And (note, p. 14) : ' L'école moderne qui refute le système mercantil a elle-même créé un système qui lui-même doit être appelé le système mercantil.'

objections J. B. Say replied to his brother that 'his (J. B. Say's) method (method?) (viz. the theory of exchangeable values) was certainly not the best, but that the difficulty was, to find a better.' [1]

What! difficult to find a better? Had not brother Louis, then, found one? No, the real difficulty was that people had not the requisite acuteness to grasp and to follow out the idea which the brother had (certainly only in general terms) expressed; or rather, perhaps, because it was very distasteful to have to overturn the already established school, and to have to teach the precise opposite of the doctrine by which one had acquired celebrity. The only original thing in J. B. Say's writings is the form of his system, viz. that he defined political economy as the science which shows how *material wealth is produced, distributed, and consumed.* It was by this classification and by his exposition of it that J. B. Say made his success and also his school, and no wonder: for here everything lay ready to his hand; he knew how to explain so clearly and intelligibly the special process of production, and the individual powers engaged in it; he could set forth so lucidly (within the limits of his own narrow circle) the principle of the division of labour, and so clearly expound the trade of individuals. Every working potter, every huckster could understand him, and do so the more readily, the less J. B. Say told him that was new or unknown. For that in the work of the potter, hands and skill (labour) must be combined with clay (natural material) in order by means of the potter's wheel, the oven, and fuel (capital), to produce pots (valuable products or values in exchange), had been well known long before in every respectable potter's workshop, only they had not known how to describe these things in scientific language, and by means of it to generalise upon them. Also there were probably very few hucksters who did not know before J. B. Say's time, that by exchange both parties could gain values in exchange, and that if anyone exported 1,000 thalers' worth

---

[1] *Etudes sur la Richesse des Nations*, p. 36 (quoting J. B. Say's words): 'Que cette méthode était loin d'être bonne, mais que la difficulté était d'en trouver une meilleure.'

of goods, and got for them 1,500 thalers' worth of other goods from abroad, he would gain 500 thalers.

It was also well known before, that work leads to wealth, and idleness to beggary; that private self-interest is the most powerful stimulus to active industry; and that he who desires to obtain young chickens, must not first eat the eggs. Certainly people had not known before that all this was political economy; but they were delighted to be initiated with so little trouble into the deepest mysteries of the science, and thus to get rid of the hateful duties which make our favourite luxuries so dear, and to get perpetual peace, universal brotherhood, and the millennium into the bargain. It is also no cause for surprise that so many learned men and State officials ranked themselves among the admirers of Smith and Say; for the principle of ' laissez faire et laissez aller ' demands no sagacity from any save those who first introduced and expounded it; authors who succeeded them had nothing to do but to reiterate, embellish, and elucidate their argument; and who might not feel the wish and have the ability to be a great statesman, if all one had to do was to fold one's hands in one's bosom ? It is a strange peculiarity of these systems, that one need only adopt their first propositions, and let oneself be led credulously and confidingly by the hand by the author, through a few chapters, and one is lost. We must say to M. Jean Baptiste Say at the outset that *political* economy is not, in our opinion, that science which teaches only how values in exchange are produced by individuals, distributed among them, and consumed by them ; we say to him that a statesman will know and must know, over and above that, how the productive powers of a whole *nation* can be awakened, increased, and protected, and how on the other hand they are weakened, laid to sleep, or utterly destroyed; and how by means of those national productive powers the national resources can be utilised in the wisest and best manner so as to produce national existence, national independence, national prosperity, national strength, national culture, and a national future.

This system (of Say) has rushed from one extreme view —that the State can and ought to regulate everything—

into the opposite extreme—that the State can and ought to do nothing: that the individual is everything, and the State nothing at all. The opinion of M. Say as to the omnipotence of individuals and the impotence of the State verges on the ridiculous. Where he cannot forbear from expressing a word of praise on the efficacy of Colbert's measures for the industrial education of France, he exclaims, ' One could hardly have given *private persons* credit for such a high degree of wisdom.'

If we turn our attention from the system to its author, we see in him a man who, without a comprehensive knowledge of history, without deep insight into State policy or State administration, without political or philosophical views, with merely one idea adopted from others in his head, rummages through history, politics, statistics, commercial and industrial relations, in order to discover isolated proofs and facts which may serve to support his idea. If anyone will read his remarks on the Navigation Laws, the Methuen Treaty, the system of Colbert, the Eden Treaty, &c. he will find this judgment confirmed. It did not suit him to follow out connectedly the commercial and industrial history of nations. That nations have become rich and mighty under protective tariffs he admits, only in his opinion they became so in spite of that system and not in consequence of it; and he requires that we should believe that conclusion on his word alone. He maintains that the Dutch were induced to trade directly with the East Indies, because Philip II. forbade them to enter the harbour of Portugal; as though the protective system would justify that prohibition, as though the Dutch would not have found their way to the East Indies without it. With statistics and politics M. Say is as dissatisfied as with history; with the former because no doubt they produce the inconvenient facts which he says ' have so often proved contradictory of his system '—with the latter because he understood nothing at all of it. He cannot desist from his warnings against the pitfalls into which statistical facts may mislead us, or from reminding us that politics have nothing to do with political economy,

which sounds about as wise as if anyone were to maintain
that pewter must not be taken into account in the consideration of a pewter platter.

First a merchant, then a manufacturer, then an unsuccessful politician, Say laid hold of political economy
just as a man grasps at some new undertaking when the
old one cannot go on any longer. We have his own con-
fession on record, that he stood in doubt at first whether
he should advocate the (so-called) mercantile system, or
the system of free trade. Hatred of the Continental system
(of Napoleon) which had ruined his manufactory, and
against the author of it who had turned him out of the
magistracy, determined him to espouse the cause of absolute freedom of trade.

The term ‘ freedom ’ in whatever connection it is used
has for fifty years past exercised a magical influence in
France. Hence it happened that Say, under the Empire
as well as under the Restoration, belonged to the Opposition, and that he incessantly advocated economy. Thus
his writings became popular for quite other reasons than
what they contained. Otherwise would it not be incomprehensible that their popularity should have continued
after the fall of Napoleon, at a period when the adoption of
Say’s system would inevitably have ruined the French
manufacturers ? His firm adherence to the cosmopolitical
principle under such circumstances proves how little political
insight the man had. How little he knew the world, is
shown by his firm belief in the cosmopolitical tendencies of
Canning and Huskisson. One thing only was lacking to
his fame, that neither Louis XVIII. nor Charles X. made
him minister of commerce and of finance. In that case
history would have coupled his name with that of Colbert,
the one as the creator of the national industry, the other as
its destroyer.

Never has any author with such small materials exercised such a wide scientific terrorism as J. B. Say; the
slightest doubt as to the infallibility of his doctrine was
branded as obscurantism; and even men like Chaptal
feared the anathemas of this politico-economical Pope.

Chaptal's work on the industry of France, from the beginning to the end, is nothing else than an exposition of the effects of the French protective system ; he states that expressly ; he says distinctly that under the existing circumstances of the world, prosperity for France can only be hoped for under the system of protection. At the same time Chaptal endeavours by an article in praise of free trade, directly in opposition to the whole tendency of his book, to solicit pardon for his heresy from the school of Say. Say imitated the Papacy even so far as to its ' Index.' He certainly did not prohibit heretical writings individually by name, but he was stricter still ; he prohibits all, the non-heretical as well as the heretical ; he warns the young students of political economy not to read too many books, as they might thus too easily be misled into errors ; they ought to read only a few, but those good books, which means in other words, ' You ought only to read me and Adam Smith, no others.' But that none too great sympathy should accrue to the immortal father of the school from the adoration of his disciples, his successor and interpreter on earth took good care, for, according to Say, Adam Smith's books are full of confusion, imperfection, and contradictions ; and he clearly gives us to understand that one can only learn from himself ' how one ought to read Adam Smith.'

Notwithstanding, when Say was at the zenith of his fame, certain young heretics arose who attacked the basis of his system so effectually and so boldly, that he preferred privately to reply to them, and meekly to avoid any public discussion. Among these, Tanneguy du Châtel (more than once a minister of State) was the most vigorous and the most ingenious.

' Selon vous, mon cher critique,' said Say to Du Châtel in a private letter, ' il ne reste plus dans mon économie politique que des actions sans motifs, des faits sans explication, une chaîne de rapports dont les extrémités manquent et dont les anneaux les plus importants sont brisés. Je partage donc l'infortune d'Adam Smith, dont un de nos critiques a dit qu'il avait fait rétrograder l'économie poli-

tique.' [1] In a postscript to this letter he remarks very
naïvely, ' Dans le second article que vous annoncez, il est
bien inutile de revenir sur cette polémique, *par laquelle
nous pouvions bien ennuyer le public.'*

At the present day the school of Smith and Say has
been exploded in France, and the rigid and spiritless
influence of the Theory of Exchangeable Values has been
succeeded by a revolution and an anarchy, which neither
M. Rossi nor M. Blanqui are able to exorcise. The Saint-
Simonians and the Fourrierists, with remarkable talent at
their head, instead of reforming the old doctrines, have cast
them entirely aside, and have framed for themselves a
Utopian system. Quite recently the most ingenious persons
among them have been seeking to discover the connection
of their doctrines with those of the previous schools, and to
make their ideas compatible with existing circumstances.
Important results may be expected from their labours,
especially from those of the talented Michel Chevalier. The
amount of truth, and of what is practically applicable in
our day, which their doctrines contain, consists chiefly in
their expounding the *principle of the confederation and the
harmony of the productive powers.* Their annihilation of
individual freedom and independence is their weak side ;
with them the individual is entirely absorbed in the community, in direct contradiction to the Theory of Exchangeable Values, according to which the individual ought to be
everything and the State nothing.

It may be that the spirit of the world is tending to the
realisation of the state of things which these sects dream
of or prognosticate ; in any case, however, I believe that
many centuries must elapse before that can be possible. It
is given to no mortal to estimate the progress of future
centuries in discoveries and in the condition of society.
Even the mind of a Plato could not have foretold that after
the lapse of thousands of years the instruments which do
the work of society would be constructed of iron, steel, and
brass, nor could that of a Cicero have foreseen that the
printing press would render it possible to extend the

[1] Say, *Cours complet d'Economie politique pratique*, vii. p. 378.

representative system over whole kingdoms, perhaps over whole quarters of the globe, and over the entire human race. If meanwhile it is given to only a few great minds to foresee a few instances of the progress of future thousands of years, yet to every age is assigned its own special task. But the task of the age in which we live appears not to be to break up mankind into Fourrierist 'phalanstères,' in order to give each individual as nearly as possible an equal share of mental and bodily enjoyments, but to perfect the productive powers, the mental culture, the political condition, and the power of whole nationalities, and by equalising them in these respects as far as is possible, to prepare them beforehand for universal union. For even if we admit that under the existing circumstances of the world the immediate object which its apostles had in view could be attained by each 'phalanstère,' what would be its effect on the power and independence of the nation? And would not the nation which was broken up into 'phalanstères,' run the risk of being conquered by some less advanced nation which continued to live in the old way, and of thus having its premature institutions destroyed together with its entire nationality? At present the Theory of Exchangeable Values has so completely lost its influence, that it is almost exclusively occupied with inquiries into the nature of Rent, and that Ricardo in his 'Principles of Political Economy' could write, 'The chief object of political economy is to determine the laws by which the produce of the soil ought to be shared between the landowner, the farmer, and the labourer.'

While some persons are firmly convinced that this science is complete, and that nothing essential can further be added to it, those, on the other hand, who read these writings with philosophical or practical insight, maintain, that as yet there is no political economy at all, that that science has yet to be constructed; that until it is so, what goes by its name is merely an astrology, but that it is both possible and desirable out of it to produce an astronomy.

Finally, we must remark, in order not to be misunderstood, that our criticism of the writings alike of J. B. Say and of his predecessors and successors refers only to their national and international bearing; and that we recognise their value as expositions of subordinate doctrines. It is evident that an author may form very valuable views and inductions on individual branches of a science, while all the while the basis of his system may be entirely erroneous.

FOURTH BOOK

THE POLITICS

CHAPTER XXXIII.

THE INSULAR SUPREMACY AND THE CONTINENTAL POWERS— NORTH AMERICA AND FRANCE.

In all ages there have been cities or countries which have been pre-eminent above all others in industry, commerce, and navigation; but a supremacy such as that which exists in our days, the world has never before witnessed. In all ages, nations and powers have striven to attain to the dominion of the world, but hitherto not one of them has erected its power on so broad a foundation. How vain do the efforts of those appear to us who have striven to found their universal dominion on military power, compared with the attempt of England to raise her entire territory into one immense manufacturing, commercial, and maritime city, and to become among the countries and kingdoms of the earth, that which a great city is in relation to its surrounding territory: to comprise within herself all industries, arts, and sciences; all great commerce and wealth; all navigation and naval power—a world's metropolis which supplies all nations with manufactured goods, and supplies herself in exchange from every nation with those raw materials and agricultural products of a useful or acceptable kind, which each other nation is fitted by nature to yield to her—a treasure house of all great capital—a banking establishment for all nations, which controls the circulating medium of the whole world, and by loans and the receipt of interest on them makes all the peoples of the earth her tributaries. Let us, however, do justice to this Power and to her efforts. The world has not been hindered in its progress, but immensely aided in it, by England. She has become an example and a pattern to all nations—in internal and in foreign policy, as well as in great inventions

and enterprises of every kind; in perfecting industrial processes and means of transport, as well as in the discovery
and bringing into cultivation uncultivated lands, especially
in the acquisition of the natural riches of tropical countries,
and in the civilisation of barbarous races or of such as
have retrograded into barbarism. Who can tell how far
behind the world might yet remain if no England had ever
existed? And if she now ceased to exist, who can estimate
how far the human race might retrograde? Let us then
congratulate ourselves on the immense progress of that nation, and wish her prosperity for all future time. But ought
we on that account also to wish that she may erect a universal dominion on the ruins of the other nationalities?
Nothing but unfathomable cosmopolitanism or shopkeepers'
narrow-mindedness can give an assenting answer to that
question. In our previous chapters we have pointed out
the results of such denationalisation, and shown that the
culture and civilisation of the human race can only be
brought about by placing many nations in similar positions
of civilisation, wealth, and power; that just as England
herself has raised herself from a condition of barbarism to
her present high position, so the same path lies open for
other nations to follow: and that at this time more than
one nation is qualified to strive to attain the highest degree
of civilisation, wealth, and power. Let us now state sum-
marily the maxims of State policy by means of which England has attained her present greatness. They may be
briefly stated thus:

Always to favour the importation of productive power,[1]
in preference to the importation of goods.

[1] Even a part of the production of wool in England is due to the obser-
vance of this maxim. Edward IV. imported under special privileges 3,000
head of sheep from Spain (where the export of sheep was prohibited), and
distributed them among various parishes, with a command that for seven
years none were to be slaughtered or castrated. (*Essai sur le Commerce
d'Angleterre*, tome i. p. 379.) As soon as the object of these measures had
been attained, England rewarded the Spanish Government for the special
privileges granted by the latter, by prohibiting the import of Spanish wool.
The efficacy of this prohibition (however unjust it may be deemed) can
as little be denied as that of the prohibitions of the import of wool by
Charles II. (1672 and 1674).

Carefully to cherish and to protect the development of the productive power

To import only raw materials and agricultural products, and to export nothing but manufactured goods.

To direct any surplus of productive power to colonisation, and to the subjection of barbarous nations.

To reserve exclusively to the mother country the supply of the colonies and subject countries with manufactured goods, but in return to receive on preferential terms their raw materials and especially their colonial produce.

To devote especial care to the coast navigation ; to the trade between the mother country and the colonies ; to encourage sea-fisheries by means of bounties; and to take as active a part as possible in international navigation.

By these means to found a naval supremacy, and by means of it to extend foreign commerce, and continually to increase her colonial possessions.

To grant freedom in trade with the colonies and in navigation only so far as she can gain more by it than she loses.

To grant reciprocal navigation privileges only if the advantage is on the side of England, or if foreign nations can by that means be restrained from introducing restrictions on navigation in their own favour.

To grant concessions to foreign independent nations in respect of the import of agricultural products, only in case concessions in respect of her own manufactured products can be gained thereby.

In cases where such concessions cannot be obtained by treaty, to attain the object of them by means of contraband trade.

To make wars and to contract alliances with exclusive regard to her manufacturing, commercial, maritime, and colonial interests.   To gain by these alike from friends and foes : from the latter by interrupting their commerce at sea ; from the former by ruining their manufactures through subsidies which are paid in the shape of English manufactured goods.[1]

These maxims were in former times plainly professed by

---

[1] See Appendix A.

all English ministers and parliamentary speakers. The ministers of George I. in 1721 openly declared, on the occasion of the prohibition of the importation of the manufactures of India, that it was clear that a nation could only become wealthy and powerful if she imported raw materials and exported manufactured goods. Even in the times of Lords Chatham and North, they did not hesitate to declare in open Parliament that it ought not to be permitted that even a single horse-shoe nail should be manufactured in North America. In Adam Smith's time, a new maxim was for the first time added to those which we have above stated, namely, to conceal the true policy of England under the cosmopolitical expressions and arguments which Adam Smith had discovered, in order to induce foreign nations not to imitate that policy.

It is a very common clever device that when anyone has attained the summit of greatness, he kicks away the ladder by which he has climbed up, in order to deprive others of the means of climbing up after him. In this lies the secret of the cosmopolitical doctrine of Adam Smith, and of the cosmopolitical tendencies of his great contemporary William Pitt, and of all his successors in the British Government administrations.

Any nation which by means of protective duties and restrictions on navigation has raised her manufacturing power and her navigation to such a degree of development that no other nation can sustain free competition with her, can do nothing wiser than to throw away these ladders of her greatness, to preach to other nations the benefits of free trade, and to declare in penitent tones that she has hitherto wandered in the paths of error, and has now for the first time succeeded in discovering the truth.

William Pitt was the first English statesman who clearly perceived in what way the cosmopolitical theory of Adam Smith could be properly made use of, and not in vain did he himself carry about a copy of the work on the Wealth of Nations. His speech in 1786, which was addressed neither to Parliament nor to the nation, but clearly to the ears of the statesmen of France, who were destitute of all experience and political insight, and solely intended to influence the latter in favour of the Eden Treaty, is an excellent specimen of Smith's style of reasoning. By nature he said France was adapted for agriculture and the production of wine, as England was thus adapted to manufacturing production. These nations ought to act towards one another just as two great merchants would do who carry on different branches of trade and who reciprocally enrich one another by the exchange of goods.[1] Not a word here of the old maxim of England, that a nation can only attain to the highest degree of wealth and power in her foreign trade by the exchange of manufactured products against agricultural products and raw materials. This maxim was then, and has remained since, an English State secret; it was never again openly professed, but was all the more persistently followed. If, however, England since William Pitt's time had really cast away the protective system as a useless crutch, she would now occupy a much higher position than she does, and she

---

[1] France, said Pitt, has advantages above England in respect of climate and other natural gifts, and therefore excels England in its raw produce ; on the other hand, England has the advantage over France in its artificial products. The wines, brandies, oils, and vinegars of France, especially the first two, are articles of such importance and of such value, that the value of our natural products cannot be in the least compared with them. But, on the other hand, it is equally certain that England is the exclusive producer of some kinds of manufactured goods, and that in respect of other kinds she possesses such advantages that she can defy without doubt all the competition of France. This is a reciprocal condition and a basis on which an advantageous commercial treaty between both nations should be founded. As each of them has its peculiar staple commodities, and each possesses that which is lacking to the other, so both should deal with one another like two great merchants who are engaged in different branches of trade, and by a reciprocal exchange of their goods can at once become useful to one another. Let us further only call to mind on this point the wealth of the country with which we stand in the· position of neighbours, its great population, its vicinity to us, and the consequent quick and regular exchange. Who could then hesitate a moment to give his approval to the system of freedom, and who would not earnestly and impatiently wish for the utmost possible expedition in establishing it ? The possession of such an extensive and certain market must give quite an extraordinary impulse to our trade, and the customs revenue which would then be diverted from the hands of the smuggler into the State revenue would benefit our finances, and thus two main springs of British wealth and of British power would be made more productive.

would have got much nearer to her object, which is to monopolise the manufacturing power of the whole world. · The favourable moment for attaining this object was clearly just after the restoration of the general peace. Hatred of Napoleon's Continental system had secured a reception among all nations of the Continent of the doctrines of the cosmopolitical theory. Russia, the entire North of Europe, Germany, the Spanish peninsula, and the United States of North America would have considered themselves fortunate in exchanging their agricultural produce and raw materials for English manufactured goods. France herself would perhaps have found it possible, in consideration of some decided concessions in respect of her wine and silk manufactures, to depart from her prohibitive system.

Then also the time had arrived when, as Priestley said of the English navigation laws, *it would be just as wise to repeal the English protective system as it had formerly been to introduce it.*

The result of such a policy would have been that all the surplus raw materials and agricultural produce from the two hemispheres would have flowed over to England, and all the world would have clothed themselves with English fabrics. All would have tended to increase the wealth and the power of England. Under such circumstances the Americans or the Russians would hardly have taken it into their heads in the course of the present century to introduce a protective system, or the Germans to establish a customs union. People would have come to the determination with difficulty to sacrifice the advantages of the present moment to the hopes of a distant future.

But Providence has taken care that trees should not grow quite up to the sky. Lord Castlereagh gave over the commercial policy of Englan1 into the hands of the landed aristocracy, and these killed the hen which had laid the golden eggs. Had they permitted the English manufactures to monopolise the markets of all nations, Great Britain would have occupied the position in respect to the world which a manufacturing town does in respect to the open country; the whole territory of the island of England would have been covered with houses and manufactories, or devoted to pleasure gardens, vegetable gardens, and orchards; to the production of milk and of meat, or of the cultivation of market produce, and generally to such cultivation as only can be carried on in the neighbourhood of great cities. The production of these things would have become much more lucrative for English agriculture than the production of corn, and consequently after a time the English landed aristocracy would have obtained much higher rents than by the exclusion of foreign grain from the home market. Only, the landed aristocracy having only their present interests in view, preferred by means of the corn laws to maintain their rents at the high rate to which they had been raised by the involuntary exclusion of foreign raw materials and grain from the English market which had been occasioned by the war; and thus they compelled the nations of the Continent to seek to promote their own welfare by another method than by the free exchange of agricultural produce for English manufactures, viz. by the method of establishing a manufacturing power of their own. The English restrictive laws thus operated quite in the same way as Napoleon's Continental system had done, only their operation was somewhat slower.

When Canning and Huskisson came into office, the landed aristocracy had already tasted too much of the forbidden fruit for it to be possible to induce them by reasons of common sense to renounce what they had enjoyed. These statesmen found themselves in the difficult position of solving an impossible problem—a position in which the English Ministry still finds itself. They had at one and the same time to convince the Continental nations of the advantages of free trade, and also maintain the restrictions on the import of foreign agricultural produce for the benefit of the English landed aristocracy. Hence it was impossible that their system could be developed in such a manner that justice could be done to the hopes of the advocates of free trade on both continents. With all their liberality with philanthropical and cosmopolitical phrases which they uttered in general discussions respecting the commercial systems of England and other countries, they nevertheless did not think it inconsistent, whenever the question arose of the alteration of any particular English duties, to base their arguments on the principle of protection.

Huskisson certainly reduced the duties on several articles, but he never omitted to take care that at that lower scale of duty the home manufactories were still sufficiently protected. He thus followed pretty much the rules of the Dutch water administration. Wherever the water on the outside rises high, these wise authorities erect high dykes ; wherever it rises less, they only build lower dykes. After such a fashion the reform of the English commercial policy which was announced with so much pomp reduced itself to a piece of mere politico-economical jugglery. Some persons have adduced the lowering of the English duty on silk goods as a piece of English liberality, without duly considering that England by that means only sought to discourage contraband trade in these articles to the benefit of her finances and without injury to her own silk manufactories, which object it has also by that means perfectly attained. But if a protective duty of 50 to 70 per cent. (which at this day foreign silk manufacturers have to pay in England, including the extra duty [1]) is to be accepted as a proof of liberality,

---

[1] Since List wrote these lines, the duties which foreign silk manufacturers had to pay on the import of their goods into England have been totally abolished. The results of their abolition may be learned from Mr. Wardle's report on the English silk trade, as follows : London, in 1825, contained 24,000 looms and 60,000 operatives engaged in silk manufacture. At the present time these have dwindled to 1,200 looms and less than 4,000 operatives. In Coventry, in 1861, the ribbon trade is stated to have given subsistence to 40,600 persons ; while at the present time probably not more than 10,000 persons are supported by it, and the power-looms at work in Coventry have decreased from 1,800 to 600. In Derby the number of operatives employed in silk manufacture has decreased from 6,650 (in 1350) to 2,400 at present. In the Congleton district they have decreased from 5,186 (in 1860) to 1,530 (in 1884) ; while of the forty silk-throwsters' works which that district contained (in 1859) only twelve now remain, with ' about three-fourths of their machinery employed.' In Manchester this trade has practically died out, while at Middleton the industry is ' simply ruined.' These results (stated by Mr. Wardle) may account for the decrease in England's imports of raw silk, from 8,000,000 pounds (in 1871) to less than 3,000,000 pounds.

On the other hand, since List wrote, the United States of America have

most nations may claim that they have rather preceded the English in that respect than followed them.

As the demonstrations of Canning and Huskisson were specially intended to produce an effect in France and North America, it will not be uninteresting to call to mind in what way it was that they suffered shipwreck in both countries. Just as formerly in the year 1786, so also on this occasion, the English received great support from the theorists, and the liberal party in France, carried away by the grand idea of universal freedom of trade and by Say's superficial arguments, and from feelings of opposition towards a detested Government and supported by the maritime towns, the wine growers, and the silk manufacturers, the liberal party clamorously demanded, as they had done in the year 1786, extension of the trade with England as the one true method of promoting the national welfare.

For whatever faults people may lay to the charge of the Restoration, it rendered an undeniable service to France, a service which posterity will not dispute; it did not allow itself to be misled into a false step as respects commercial policy either by the stratagems of the English or by the outcry of the liberals. Mr. Canning laid this business so much to heart that he himself made a journey to Paris in order to convince Monsieur Villèle of the excellence of his

increased and steadily maintained a considerable protective duty on the importation of foreign silk manufactures. The results of that policy were publicly stated by Mr. Robert P. Porter (member of the United States' Tariff Commission), in a speech in 1883, to have been as follows:

Five thousand persons were employed in silk manufacture in the United States before the Morill tariff (1861). In 1880 their number had increased to 30,000. The value of silk manufactures produced in the States increased from 1,200,000*l.* in 1860 to more than 8,000,000*l.* in 1880. ' Yet the cost of the manufactured goods to the consumer, estimated on a gold basis, has steadily declined at a much greater rate than the cost of the raw material.' After reference to the earthenware and plate-glass manufactures, Mr. Porter adds: ' The testimony before the Tariff Commission showed unquestionably that the competition *in* the United States had resulted in a reduction in the cost to the American consumer. In this way, gentlemen, I contend, and am prepared to prove statistically, that protection, so far as the United States are concerned, ha*s* *in every case* ultimately *benefited the consumer*; and on this ground I defend it and believe in it.'—TRANSLATOR.

measures, and to induce him to imitate them. M. Villèle was, however, much too practical not to see completely through this stratagem ; he is said to have replied to Mr. Canning, ' If England in the far advanced position of her industry permits greater foreign competition than formerly, that policy corresponds to England's own well-understood interests. But at this time it is to the well-understood interests of France that she should secure to her manufactories which have not as yet attained perfect development, that protection which is at present indispensable to them for that object. But whenever the moment shall have arrived when French manufacturing industry can be better promoted by permitting foreign competition than by restricting it, then he (M. Villèle) would not delay to derive advantage from following the example of Mr. Canning.'

Annoyed by this conclusive answer, Canning boasted in open Parliament after his return, how he had hung a millstone on the neck of the French Government by means of the Spanish intervention, from which it follows that the cosmopolitan sentiments and the European liberalism of Mr. Canning were not spoken quite so much in earnest as the good liberals on the Continent might have chosen to believe. For how could Mr. Canning, if the cause of liberalism on the Continent had interested him in the least, have sacrificed the liberal constitution of Spain to the French intervention owing to the mere desire to hang a millstone round the neck of the French Government ? The truth is, that Mr. Canning was every inch an Englishman, and he only permitted himself to entertain philanthropical or cosmopolitical sentiments, when they could prove serviceable to him in strengthening and still further extending the industry and commercial supremacy of England, or in throwing dust into the eyes of England's rivals in industry and commerce.

In fact, no great sagacity was needed on the part of M. Villèle to perceive the snare which had been laid for him by Mr. Canning. In the experience of neighbouring Germany, who after the abolition of the Continental system had continually retrograded farther and farther in respect of her industry, M. Villèle possessed a striking proof of the true value of the principle of commercial freedom as it was understood in England. Also France was prospering too well under the system which she had adopted since 1815, for her to be willing to attempt, like the dog in the fable, to let go the substance and snap at the shadow. Men of the deepest insight into the condition of industry, such as Chaptal and Charles Dupin, had expressed themselves on the results of this system in the most unequivocal manner.

Chaptal's work on French industry is nothing less than a defence of the French commercial policy, and an exposition of its results as a whole and in every particular. The tendency of this work is expressed in the following quotation from it. 'Instead of losing ourselves in the labyrinth of metaphysical abstractions, we maintain above all that which exists, and seek above all to make it perfect. Good customs legislation is the bulwark of manufacturing industry. It increases or lessens import duties according to circumstances; it compensates the disadvantages of higher wages of labour and of higher prices of fuel; it protects arts and industries in their cradle until they at length become strong enough to bear foreign competition; it creates the industrial independence of France and enriches the nation through labour, which, as I have already often remarked, is the chief source of wealth.'[1]

Charles Dupin had, in his work 'On the Productive Powers of France, and on the Progress of French Industry from 1814 to 1847,' thrown such a clear light on the results of the commercial policy which France had followed since the Restoration, that it was impossible that a French minister could think of sacrificing this work of half a century, which had cost such sacrifices, which was so rich in fruits, and so full of promise for the future, merely for the attractions of a Methuen Treaty.

The American tariff for the year 1828 was a natural and necessary result of the English commercial system, which shut out from the English frontiers the North American timber, grain, meal, and other agricultural products, and only permitted raw cotton to be received by

---

[1] Chaptal, *De l'Industrie Française*, vol. ii. 147.

England in exchange for her manufactured goods. On this system the trade with England only tended to promote the agricultural labour of the American slaves, while on the other hand, the freest, most enlightened, and most powerful States of the Union found themselves entirely arrested in their economical progress, and thus reduced to dispose of their annual surplus of population and capital by emigration to the waste lands of the West. Mr. Huskisson understood this position of affairs very well. It was notorious that the English ambassador in Washington had more than once correctly informed him of the inevitable consequence of the English policy. If Mr. Huskisson had really been the man that people in other countries supposed him to be, he would have made use of the publication of the American tariff as a valuable opportunity for making the English aristocracy comprehend the folly of their corn laws, and the necessity of abolishing them. But what did Mr. Huskisson do? He fell into a passion with the Americans (or at least affected to do so), and in his excitement he made allegations—the incorrectness of which was well known to every American planter—and permitted himself to use threats which made him ridiculous. Mr. Huskisson said the exports of England to the United States amounted to only about the sixth part of all the exports of England, while the exports of the United States to England constituted more than half of all their exports. From this he sought to prove that the Americans were more in the power of the English than the latter were in that of the former; and that the English had much less reason to fear interruptions of trade through war, cessation of intercourse, and so forth, than the Americans had. If one looks merely at the totals of the value of the imports and exports, Huskisson's argument appears sufficiently plausible; but if one considers the nature of the reciprocal imports and exports, it will then appear incomprehensible how Mr. Huskisson could make use of an argument which proves the exact opposite of that which he desired to prove. All or by far the greater part of the exports of the United States to England consisted of raw materials, whose value is increased tenfold by the English, and which they cannot dispense with, and also could not at once obtain from other countries, at any rate not in sufficient quantity, while on the other hand all the imports of the North Americans from England consisted of articles which they could either manufacture for themselves or procure just as easily from other nations. If we now consider what would be the operation of an interruption of commerce between the two nations according to the theory of values, it will appear as if it must operate to the disadvantage of the Americans; whereas if we judge of it according to the theory of the productive powers, it must occasion incalculable injury to the English. For by it two-thirds of all the English cotton manufactories would come to a standstill and fall into ruin. England would lose as by magic a productive source of wealth, the annual value of which far exceeds the value of her entire exports, and the results of such a loss on the peace, wealth, credit, commerce, and power of England would be incalculable. What, however, would be the consequences of such a state of things for the North Americans? Compelled to manufacture for themselves those goods which they had hitherto obtained from England, they would in the course of a few years gain what the English had lost. No doubt such a measure must occasion a conflict for life and death, as formerly the navigation laws did between England and Holland. But probably it would also end in the same way as formerly did the conflict in the English Channel. It is unnecessary here to follow out the consequences of a rivalry which, as it appears to us, must sooner or later, from the very nature of things, come to a rupture. What we have said suffices to show clearly the futility and danger of Huskisson's argument, and to demonstrate how unwisely England acted in compelling the North Americans (by means of her corn laws) to manufacture for themselves, and how wise it would have been of Mr. Huskisson had he, instead of trifling with the question by such futile and hazardous arguments, laboured to remove out of the way the causes which led to the adoption of the American tariff of 1828.

In order to prove to the North Americans how advantageous to them the trade of England was, Mr. Huskisson pointed out the extraordinary increase in the English importations of cotton, but the Americans also knew how to estimate this argument at its true value. For the production of cotton in America had for more than ten years previously so greatly exceeded the consumption of, and the demand for, this article from year to year, that its prices had fallen in almost the same ratio in which the export had increased; as may be seen from the fact that in the year 1816 the Americans had obtained for 80,000,000 pounds of cotton 24,000,000 dollars, while in the year 1826 for 204,000,000 pounds of cotton they only obtained 25,000,000 dollars.

Finally, Mr. Huskisson threatened the North Americans with the organisation of a wholesale contraband trade by way of Canada. It is true that under existing circumstances an American protective system can be endangered by nothing so seriously as by the means indicated by Mr. Huskisson. But what follows from that? Is it that the Americans are to lay their system at the feet of the English Parliament, and await in humility whatever the latter may be pleased to determine from year to year respecting their national industry? How absurd! The only consequence would be that the Americans would annex Canada and include it in their Union, or else assist it to attain independence as soon as ever the Canadian smuggling trade became unendurable. Must we not, however, deem the degree of folly absolutely excessive if a nation which has already attained industrial and commercial supremacy, first of all compels an agricultural nation connected with her by the closest ties of race, of language, and of interest, to become herself a manufacturing nation, and then, in order to hinder her from following the impulse thus forcibly given to her, compels her to assist that nation's own colonies to attain independence?

After Huskisson's death Mr. Poulett Thompson undertook the direction of the commercial affairs of England; this statesman followed his celebrated predecessor in his policy as well as in his office. In the meantime, so far as concerned North America, there remained little for him to do, for in that country, without special efforts on the part of the English, by means of the influence of the cotton planters and the importers, and by the aid of the Democratic party, especially by means of the so-called Compromise Bill in 1832, a modification of the former tariff had taken place, which, although it certainly amended the excesses and faults of the former tariff, and also still secured to the American manufactories a tolerable degree of protection in respect of the coarser fabrics of cotton and woollen, nevertheless gave the English all the concessions which they could have desired without England having been compelled to make any counter concessions.

Since the passing of that Bill, the exports of the English to America have enormously increased. And subsequently to this time they greatly exceed the English imports from North America, so that at any time it is in the power of England to draw to herself as much as she pleases of the precious metals circulating in America, and thereby to occasion commercial crises in the United States as often as she herself is in want of money. But the most astonishing thing in this matter is that that Bill had for its author Henry Clay, the most eminent and clearsighted defender of the American manufacturing interest. For it must be remembered that the prosperity of the American manufacturers which resulted from the tariff of 1828 excited so greatly the jealousy of the cotton planters, that the Southern States threatened to bring about a dissolution of the Union in case the tariff of 1828 was not modified. The Federal Government, which was dominated by the Democratic party, had sided with the Southern planters from purely party and electioneering motives, and also managed to get the agriculturists of the Middle and Western States, who belonged to that party, to adopt the same views.

These last had lost their former sympathy with the manufacturing interest in consequence of the high prices of produce which had prevailed, which, however, were the result for the most part of the prosperity of the home manufactories and of the numerous canals and railways which were undertaken. They may also have actually feared that the Southern States would press their opposition so far as to bring about a real dissolution of the Union and even civil war. Hence it became the party interests of the Democrats of the Central and Eastern States not to alienate the sympathies of the Democrats of the Southern States. In consequence of these political circumstances, public opinion veered round so much in favour of free trade with England, that there was reason to fear that all the manufacturing interests of the country might be entirely sacrificed in favour of English free competition. Under such circumstances the Compromise Bill of Henry Clay appeared to be the only means of at least partially preserving the protective system. By this Bill part of the American manufactures, viz. those of finer and more expensive articles, was sacrificed to foreign competition, in order to preserve another class of them, viz. the manufacture of articles of a coarser and a less expensive character. In the meantime all appearances seem to indicate that the protective system in North America in the course of the next few years will again raise its head and again make new progress. However much the English may desire to lessen and mitigate the commercial crises in North America, however large also may be the amount of capital which may pass over from England to North America in the form of purchases of stock or of loans or by means of emigration, the existing and still increasing disproportion between the value of the exports and that of imports cannot possibly in the long run be equalised by those means. Alarming commercial crises, which continually increase in their magnitude, must occur, and the Americans must at length be led to recognise the sources of the evil and to determine to put a stop to them.

It thus lies in the very nature of things, that the number of the advocates of the protective system must again increase, and those of free trade again diminish. Hitherto, the prices of agricultural produce have been maintained at an unusually high level, owing to the previous prosperity of the manufactories, through the carrying out of great public undertakings, through the demand for necessaries of life arising from the great increase of the production of cotton, also partially through bad harvests. One may, however, foresee with certainty, that these prices in the course of the next few years will fall as much below the average as they have hitherto ranged above it. The greater part of the increase of American capital has since the passing of the Compromise Bill been devoted to agriculture, and is only now beginning to become productive. While thus agricultural production has unusually increased, on the other hand the demand for it must unusually diminish. Firstly, because public works are no more being undertaken to the same extent ; secondly, because the manufacturing population in consequence of foreign competition can no more increase to an important extent ; and thirdly, because the production of cotton so greatly exceeds the consumption that the cotton planters will be compelled, owing to the low prices of cotton, to produce for themselves those necessaries of life which they have hitherto procured from the Middle and Western States. If in addition rich harvests occur, then the Middle and Western States will again suffer from an excess of produce, as they did before the tariff of 1828. But the same causes must again produce the same results ; viz. the agriculturists of the Middle and Western States must again arrive at the conviction, that the demand for agricultural produce can only be increased by the increase of the manufacturing population of the country, and that that increase can only be brought about by an extension of the protective system. While in this manner the partisans of protection will dai'y increase in number and influence, the opposite party will diminish in like proportion until the cotton planters under such altered circumstances must necessarily come to the conviction that the increase of the manufacturing population of the country and the increase of the demand for agricultural produce and raw materials both consist with their own interests if rightly understood.

Because, as we have shown, the cotton planters and the Democrats in North America were striving most earnestly of their own accord to play into the hands of the commercial interests of England, no opportunity was offered at the moment on this side for Mr. Poulett Thompson to display his skill in commercial diplomacy.

Matters were quite in another position in France. There people still steadily clung to the prohibitive system. There were indeed many State officials who were disciples of theory, and also deputies who were in favour of an extension of commercial relations between England and France, and the existing alliance with England had also rendered this view to a certain extent popular. But how to attain that object, opinions were less agreed, and in no respect were they quite clear. It seemed evident and also indisputable that the high duties on the foreign necessaries of life and raw materials, and the exclusion of English coal and pig-iron, operated very disadvantageously to French industry, and that an increase in the exports of wines, brandy, and silk fabrics would be extremely advantageous to France.

In general, people confined themselves to universal declamation against the disadvantages of the prohibitive system. But to attack this in special cases did not appear at the time to be at all advisable For the Government of July had their strongest supporters among the rich bourgeoisie, who for the most part were interested in the great manufacturing undertakings.

Under these circumstances Mr. Poulett Thompson formed a plan of operations which does all honour to his breadth of thought and diplomatic adroitness. He sent to France a man thoroughly versed in commerce and industry, and in the commercial policy of France, well known for his liberal sentiments, a learned man and a very accomplished writer, Dr. Bowring, who travelled through the whole of France, and subsequently through Switzerland also, to gather on the spot materials for arguments against the prohibitive system and in favour of free trade. Dr. Bowring accomplished this task with his accustomed ability and adroitness. Especially he clearly indicated the before-mentioned advantages of a freer commercial intercourse between the two countries in respect of coal, pig-iron, wines, and brandies. In the report which he published, he chiefly confined his arguments to these articles ; in reference to the other branches of industry he only gave statistics, without committing himself to proofs or propositions how these could be promoted by means of free trade with England.

Dr. Bowring acted in precise accordance with the instructions given to him by Mr. Poulett Thompson, which were framed with uncommon art and subtlety, and which appear at the head of his report. In these Mr. Thompson makes use of the most liberal expressions. He expresses himself, with much consideration for the French manufacturing interests, on the improbability that any important result was to be expected from the contemplated negotiations with France. This instruction was perfectly adapted for calming the apprehensions respecting the views of England entertained by the French woollen and cotton manufacturing interests which had become so powerful. According to Mr. Thompson, it would be folly to ask for important concessions respecting these.

On the other hand, he gives a hint how the object might more easily be attained in respect of ' *less important articles.*' These less important articles are certainly not enumerated in the instruction, but the subsequent experience of France has completely brought to light what Mr. Thompson meant by it, for at the time of the writing of this instruction the exports of linen yarn and linen fabrics of England to France were included in the term ' less important.'

The French Government, moved by the representations and explanations of the English Government and its agents, and with the intention of making to England a comparatively unimportant concession, which would ultimately prove advantageous to France herself, lowered the duty on linen yarn and linen fabrics to such an extent that they no longer gave any protection to French industry in face of the great improvements which the English had made in these branches of manufacture, so that even in the next few years the export of these articles from England to France increased enormously (1838, 32,000,000 francs) ; and that France stood in danger, owing to the start which England had thus obtained, of losing its entire linen industry, amounting to many hundred millions in value, which was of the greatest importance for her agriculture and for the welfare of her entire rural population, unless means could be found to put a check on the English competition by increasing the duties.

That France was duped by Mr. Poulett Thompson was clear enough. He had already clearly seen in the year 1834 what an impulse the linen manufacture of England would receive in the next few years in consequence of the new inventions which had been made there, and in this negotiation he had calculated on the ignorance of the French Government respecting these inventions and their necessary consequences. The advocates of this lowering of duties now indeed endeavoured to make the world believe that by it they only desired to make a concession to the Belgian linen manufactures. But did that make amends for their lack of acquaintance with the advances made by the English, and their lack of foresight as to the necessary consequences?

Be that as it may, this much is clearly demonstrated, that it was necessary for France to protect herself still more, under penalty of losing the greater part of her linen manufacturing for the benefit of England; and that the first and most recent experiment of the increase of freedom of trade between England and France remains as an indelible memorial of English craft and of French inexperience, as a new Methuen Treaty, as a second Eden Treaty. But what did Mr. Poulett Thompson do when he perceived the complaints of the French linen manufacturers and the inclination of the French Government to repair the mistake which had been made? He did what Mr. Huskisson had done before him, he indulged in threats, he threatened to exclude French wines and silk fabrics. This is English cosmopolitanism. France must give up a manufacturing industry of a thousand years' standing, bound up in the closest manner with the entire economy of her lower classes and especially with her agriculture, the products of which must be reckoned as chief necessaries of life for all classes, and of the entire amount of between three and four hundred millions, in order thereby to purchase the privilege of exporting to England some few millions more in value of wines and silk manufactures. Quite apart from this disproportion in value, it must be considered in what a position France would be placed if the commercial relations between both nations became interrupted in consequence of a war ; in case viz. that France could no more export to England her surplus products of silk manufactures and wines, but at the same time suffered from the want of such an important necessary of life as linen.

If anyone reflects on this he will see that the linen question is not simply a question of economical well-being, but, as everything is which concerns the national manufacturing power, is still more a question of the independence and power of the nation.

It seems indeed as if the spirit of invention had set itself the task, in this perfecting of the linen manufacture, to make the nations comprehend the nature of the manufacturing interest, its relations with agriculture, and its influence on the independence and power of the State, and to expose the erroneous arguments of the popular theory. The school maintains, as is well known, that every nation possesses special advantages in various branches of production, which she has either derived from nature, or which she has partly acquired in the course of her career, and which under free trade compensate one another. We have in a previous chapter adduced proof that this argument is only true in reference to agriculture, in which production depends for the most part on climate and on the fertility of the soil, but that it is not true in respect to manufacturing industry, for which all nations inhabiting temperate climates have equal capability provided that they possess the necessary material, mental, social, and political qualifications. England at the present day offers the most striking proof of this. If any nations whatever are specially adapted by their past experience and exertions, and through their natural qualifications, for the manufacture of linen, those are the Germans, the Belgians, the Dutch, and the inhabitants of the North of France for a thousand years past. The English, on the other hand, up to the middle of the last century, had notoriously made such small progress in that industry, that they imported a great proportion of the linen which they required, from abroad. It would never have been possible for them, without the duties by which they continuously protected this manufacturing industry, even to supply their own markets and colonies with linen of their own manufacture. And it is well known how Lords Castlereagh and Liverpool adduced proof in Parliament, that without protection it was impossible for the Irish linen manufactures to sustain competition with those of Germany. At present, however, we see how the English threaten to monopolise the linen manufacture of the whole of Europe, in consequence of their inventions, notwithstanding that they were for a hundred years the worst manufacturers of linen in all Europe, just as they have monopolised for the last fifty years the cotton markets of the East Indies, notwithstanding that one hundred years previously they could not even compete in their own market with the Indian cotton manufacturers. At this moment it is a matter of dispute in France how it happens that England has lately made such immense progress in the manufacture of linen, although Napoleon was the first who offered such a great reward for the invention of a machine for spinning cotton, and that the French machinists and manufacturers had been engaged in this trade before the English. The inquiry is made whether the English or the French possessed more mechanical talent. All kinds of explanations are offered except the true and the natural one. It is absurd to attribute specially to the English greater mechanical talent, or greater skill and perseverance in industry, than to the Germans or to the French. Before the time of Edward III. the English were the greatest bullies and good-for-nothing characters in Europe; certainly it never occurred to them to compare themselves with the Italians and Belgians or with the Germans in respect to mechanical talent or industrial skill; but since then their Government has taken their education in hand, and thus they have by degrees made such progress that they can dispute the palm of industrial skill with their instructors. If the English in the last twenty years have made more rapid progress in machinery for linen manufacture than other nations, and especially the French, have done, this has only occurred because, firstly, they had attained greater eminence in mechanical skill; secondly, that they were further advanced in machinery for spinning and weaving cotton, which is so similar to that for spinning and weaving linen; thirdly, that in consequence of their previous commercial policy, they had become possessed of more capital than the French; fourthly, that in consequence of that commercial policy their home market for linen goods was far more extensive than that of the French; and lastly, that their protective duties, combined with the circumstances above named, afforded to the mechanical talent of the nation greater stimulus and more means to devote itself to perfecting this branch of industry.

The English have thus given a striking confirmation of the opinions which we in another place have propounded and explained—that all individual branches of industry have the closest reciprocal effect on one another; that the perfecting of one branch prepares and promotes the perfecting of all others; that no one of them can be neglected without the effects of that neglect being felt by all; that, in short, the whole manufacturing power of a nation constitutes an inseparable whole. Of these opinions they have by their latest achievements in the linen industry offered a striking confirmation.

CHAPTER XXXIV.

THE INSULAR SUPREMACY AND THE GERMAN COMMERCIAL UNION.

WHAT a great nation is at the present day without a vigorous commercial policy, and what she may become by the adoption of a vigorous commercial policy, Germany has learnt for herself during the last twenty years. Germany was that which Franklin once said of the State of New Jersey, 'a cask which was tapped and drained by its neighbours on every side.' England, not contented with having ruined for the Germans the greater part of their own manufactories and supplied them with enormous quantities of cotton and woollen fabrics, excluded from her ports German grain and timber, nay from time to time also even German wool. There was a time when the export of manufactured goods from England to Germany was ten times greater than that to her highly extolled East Indian Empire. Nevertheless the all-monopolising islanders would not even grant to the poor Germans what they conceded to the conquered Hindoos, viz. to pay for the manufactured goods which they required by agricultural produce. In vain did the Germans humble themselves to the position of hewers of wood and drawers of water for the Britons. The latter treated them worse than a subject people. Nations, like individuals, if they at first only permit themselves to be ill-treated by one, soon become scorned by all, and finally become an object of derision to the very children. France, not contented with exporting to Germany enormous quantities of wine, oil, silk, and millinery, grudged the Germans their exports of cattle, grain, and flax; yes, even a small maritime province formerly possessed by Germany and inhabited by Germans, which having become wealthy and powerful by means of Germany, at all times was only able to maintain itself with and by means of Germany, barred for half a generation Germany's greatest river by means of contemptible verbal quibbles. To fill up the measure of this contempt, the doctrine was taught from a hundred professorial chairs, that nations could only attain to wealth and power by means of universal free trade. Thus it was; but how is it now? Germany has advanced in prosperity and industry, in national self-respect and in national power, in the course of ten years as much as in a century. And how has this result been achieved? It was certainly good and beneficial that the internal tariffs were abolished which separated Germans from Germans; but the nation would have derived small comfort from that if her home industry had thenceforth remained freely exposed to foreign competition. It was especially the protection which the tariff of the Zollverein secured to manufactured articles of common use, which has wrought this miracle. Let us freely confess it, for Dr. Bowring [1] has incontrovertibly shown it, that the Zollverein tariff has not, as was before asserted, imposed merely duties for revenue—that it has not confined itself to duties of ten to fifteen per cent. as Huskisson believed—let us freely admit that it has imposed protective duties of from twenty to sixty per cent. as respects the manufactured articles of common use.

But what has been the operation of these protective duties? Are the consumers paying for their German manufactured goods twenty to sixty per cent. more than they formerly paid for foreign ones (as must be the case if the popular theory is correct), or are these goods at all worse than the foreign ones? Nothing of the sort. Dr. Bowring himself adduces testimony that the manufactured goods produced under the high customs tariff are both better and cheaper than the foreign ones.[2] The internal competition and the security from destructive competition by the foreigner has wrought this miracle, of which the popular

---

[1] *Report on the German Zollverein to Lord Viscount Palmerston*, by John Bowring, 1840.
[2] See statement of R. B. Porter, note to p. 372.

school knows nothing and is determined to know nothing. Thus, that is not true, which the popular school maintains, that a protective duty increases the price of the goods of home production by the amount of the protective duty. For a short time the duty may increase the price, but in every nation which is qualified to carry on manufacturing industry the consequence of the protection will be, that the internal competition will soon reduce the prices lower than they had stood at when the importation was free.

But has agriculture at all suffered under these high duties? Not in the least; it has gained—gained tenfold during the last ten years. The demand for agricultural produce has increased. The prices of it everywhere are higher. It is notorious that solely in consequence of the growth of the home manufactories the value of land has everywhere risen from fifty to a hundred per cent., that everywhere higher wages are being paid, and that in all directions improvements in the means of transport are either being effected or projected.

Such brilliant results as these must necessarily encourage us to proceed farther on the system which we have commenced to follow. Other States of the Union have also proposed to take similar steps, but have not yet carried them into effect; while, as it would appear, some other States of the Union only expect to attain prosperity solely by the abolition of the English duties on grain and timber, and while (as it is alleged) there are still to be found influential men who believe in the cosmopolitical system and distrust their own experience. Dr. Bowring's report gives us most important explanations on these points as well as on the circumstances of the German Commercial Union and the tactics of the English Government. Let us endeavour to throw a little light on this report.

First of all, we have to consider the point of view from which it was written. Mr. Labouchere, President of the Board of Trade under the Melbourne Ministry, had sent Dr. Bowring to Germany for the same purpose as that for which Mr. Poulett Thompson had sent him to France in the year 1834. Just as it was intended to mislead the

French by concessions in respect of wines and brandies to open their home market to English manufactured goods, so it was intended to mislead the Germans to do the same by concessions in respect of grain and timber; only there was a great difference between the two missions in this respect, that the concession which was to be offered to the French had to fear no opposition in England, while that which had to be offered to the Germans had first to be fought for in England herself.

Hence the tendency of these two reports was of necessity of quite a different character. The report on the commercial relations between France and England was written exclusively for the French; to them it was necessary to represent that Colbert had accomplished nothing satisfactory through his protective regulations; it was necessary to make people believe that the Eden Treaty,was beneficial to France, and that Napoleon's Continental system, as well as the then existing French prohibitive system, had been extremely injurious to her. In short, in this case it was necessary to stick closely to the theory of Adam Smith; and the good results of the protective system must be completely and unequivocally denied. The task was not quite so simple with the other report, for in this, one had to address the English landowners and the German Governments at one and the same time. To the former it was necessary to say: See, there is a nation which has already in consequence of protective regulations made enormous advances in her industry, and which, in possession of all necessary means for doing so, is making rapid steps to monopolise her own home market and to compete with England in foreign markets. This, you Tories in the House of Lords —this, you country squires in the House of Commons, is your wicked doing. This has been brought about by your unwise corn laws; for by them the prices of provisions and raw materials and the wages of labour have been kept low in Germany. By them the German manufactories have been placed in an advantageous position compared to the English ones. Make haste, therefore, you fools, to abolish these corn laws. By that means you will doubly and trebly damage the German manufactories: firstly, because the prices of provisions and raw materials and the wages of labour will be raised in Germany and lowered in England; secondly, because by the export of German grain to England the export of English manufactured goods to Germany will be promoted; thirdly, because the German Commercial Union has declared that it is disposed to reduce their duties on common cotton and woollen goods in the same proportion in which England facilitates the import of German grain and timber. Thus we Britons cannot fail once more to crush the German manufactories. But the question cannot wait. Every year the manufacturing interests are gaining greater influence in the German Union; and if you delay, then your corn-law abolition will come too late. It will not be long before the balance will turn. Very soon the German manufactories will create such a great demand for agricultural produce that Germany will have no more surplus corn to sell to foreign countries. What concessions, then, are you willing to offer to the German Governments to induce them to lay hands on their own manufactures in order to hinder them from spinning cotton for themselves, and from encroaching upon your foreign markets in addition?

All this the writer of the report was compelled to make clear to the landowners in Parliament. The forms of the British State administration permit no secret Government reports. Dr. Bowring's report must be published, must therefore be seen by the Germans in translations and extracts. Hence one must use no expressions which might lead the Germans to a perception of their true interests. Therefore to every method which was adapted to influence Parliament, an antidote must be added for the use of the German Governments. It must be alleged, that in consequence of the protective system much German capital had been diverted into improper channels. The agricultural interests of Germany would be damaged by the protective system. That interest for its part ought only to turn its attention to foreign markets; agriculture was in Germany by far the most important productive industry, for three-fourths of the inhabitants of Germany were engaged in it.

It was mere nonsense to talk about protection for the producers; the manufacturing interest itself could only thrive
under foreign competition: public opinion in Germany desired freedom of trade. Intelligence in Germany was too
universal for a desire for high duties to be entertained.
The most enlightened men in the country were in favour
of a reduction of duties on common woollen and cotton
fabrics, *in case the English duties on corn and timber were
reduced*.

In short, in this report two entirely different voices
speak, which contradict one another like two opponents.
Which of the two must be deemed the true one—that
which speaks to the Parliament, or that which speaks to the
German Governments? There is no difficulty in deciding
this point, for everything which Dr. Bowring adduces in
order to induce Parliament to lower the import duties on
grain and timber is supported by statistical facts, calculations, and evidence; while everything that he adduces to
dissuade the German Governments from the protective
system is confined to mere superficial assertions.

Let us consider in detail the arguments by which Dr.
Bowring proves to the Parliament that in case a check is
not put to the progress of the German protective system in
the way which he pointed out, the German market for
manufactured goods must become irrecoverably lost to
England.

The German people is remarkable, says Dr. Bowring, for
temperance, thrift, industry, and intelligence, and enjoys a
system of universal education. Excellent polytechnic schools
diffuse technical instruction throughout the entire country.

The art of design is especially much more cultivated
there than in England. The great annual increase of its
population, of its head of cattle, and especially of sheep,
proves what progress agriculture there has achieved. (The
report makes no mention of the improvement in the value
of property, though that is an important feature, nor of the
increase in the value of produce.) The wages of labour have
risen thirty per cent. in the manufacturing districts. The
country possesses a great amount of water power, as yet

unused, which is the cheapest of all motive powers. Its mining industry is everywhere flourishing, more than at any previous time. From 1832 up to 1837 the imports of raw cotton have increased from 118,000 centners to 240,000 centners; the imports of cotton yarn from 172,000 centners to 322,000 centners; the exports of cotton fabrics from 26,000 centners to 75,000 centners; the number of cotton-weaving looms in Prussia from 22,000 in 1825 to 32,000 in 1834; the imports of raw wool from 99,000 centners to 195,000 centners; the exports of the same from 100,000 centners to 122,000 centners; the imports of woollen articles from 15,000 centners to 18,000 centners; the exports of the same from 49,000 centners to 69,000 centners.

The manufacture of linen cloths contends with difficulty against the high duties in England, France, and Italy, and has not increased. On the other hand, the imports of linen yarn have increased from 30,000 centners in 1832 to 86,000 centners in 1835, chiefly through the imports from England, which are still increasing. The consumption of indigo increased from 12,000 centners in 1831 to 24,000 centners in 1837; a striking proof of the progress of German industry. The exports of pottery have been more than doubled from 1832 to 1836. The imports of stoneware have diminished from 5,000 centners to 2,000 centners, and the exports of it increased from 4,000 centners to 18,000 centners. The imports of porcelain have diminished from 4,000 centners to 1,000 centners, and the exports of it have increased from 700 centners to 4,000 centners. The output of coal has increased from 6,000,000 Prussian tons in 1832 to 9,000,000 in 1836. In 1816 there were 8,000,000 sheep in Prussia; and in 1837, 15,000,000.

In Saxony in 1831 there were 14,000 stocking-weaving machines; in 1836, 20,000. From 1831 to 1837, the number of manufactories for spinning woollen yarn and of spindles had increased in Saxony to more than double their previous number. Everywhere machine manufactories had arisen, and many of these were in the most flourishing condition.

In short, in all branches of industry, in proportion as they have been protected, Germany has made enormous advances, especially in woollen and cotton goods for common use, the importation of which from England had entirely ceased. At the same time Dr. Bowring admits, in consequence of a trustworthy opinion which had been expressed to him, ' that the price of the Prussian stuffs was decidedly lower than that of the English ; that certainly in respect of some of the colours they were inferior to the best English tints, but that others were perfect and could not be surpassed ; that in spinning, weaving, and all preparatory processes, the German goods .were fully equal to the British, but only in the finish a distinct inferiority might be observed, but that the want of this would disappear after a little time.'

It is very easy to understand how by means of such representations as these the English Parliament may at length be induced to abandon its corn laws, which have hitherto operated as a protective system to Germany. But it appears to us utterly incomprehensible how the German Union, which has made such enormous advances in consequence of the protective system, should be induced by this report to depart from a system which has yielded them such excellent results.

It is very well for Dr. Bowring to assure us that the home industry of Germany is being protected at the expense of the agriculturists. But how can we attach any credence to his assurance, when we see, on the contrary, that the demand for agricultural produce, prices of produce, the wages of labour, the rents, the value of property, have everywhere considerably risen, without the agriculturist having to pay more than he did before for the manufactured goods which he requires ?

It is very well for Dr. Bowring to give us an estimate showing that in Germany three persons are engaged in agriculture to every one in manufactures, but that statement convinces us that the number of Germans engaged in manufacturing is not yet in proper proportion to the number of German agriculturists. And we cannot see by what other means this disproportion can be equalised, than by increasing the protection on those branches of manufacture which are still carried on in England for the supply of the German market by persons who consume English instead of German agricultural produce. It is all very well for Dr. Bowring to assert that German agriculture must only direct its attention to foreign countries if it desires to increase its sale of produce ; but that a great demand for agricultural produce can only be attained by a flourishing home manufacturing Power is taught us not alone by the experience of England, but Dr. Bowring himself implicitly admits this, by the apprehension which he expresses in his report, that if England delays for some time to abolish her corn laws, Germany will then have no surplus of either corn or timber to sell to foreign countries.

Dr. Bowring is certainly right when he asserts that the agricultural interest in Germany is still the predominant one, but just for the very reason that it is predominant it must (as we have shown in former chapters), by promoting the manufacturing interests, seek to place itself in a just proportion with them, because the prosperity of agriculture depends on its being in equal proportion with the manufacturing interest, but not on its own preponderance over it.

Further, the author of the report appears to be utterly steeped in error when he maintains that foreign competition in German markets is necessary for the German manufacturing interest itself, because the German manufacturers, as soon as they are in a position to supply the German markets, must compete with the manufacturers of other countries for the disposal of their surplus produce, which competition they can only sustain by means of cheap production. But cheap production will not consist with the existence of the protective system, inasmuch as the object of that system is to secure higher prices to the manufacturers.

This argument contains as many errors and falsehoods as words. Dr. Bowring cannot deny that the manufacturer can offer his products at cheaper prices, the more he is enabled to manufacture— that, therefore, a manufacturing Power which exclusively possesses its home market can work so much the cheaper for foreign trade. The proof of this he can find in the same tables which he has published on the advances made by German industry; for in the same proportion in which the German manufactories have acquired possession of their own home market, their export of manufactured goods has also increased. Thus the recent experience of Germany, like the ancient experience of England, shows us that high prices of manufactured goods are by no means a necessary consequence of protection.

Finally, German industry is still very far from entirely supplying her home market. In order to do that, she must first manufacture for herself the 13,000 centners of cotton fabrics, the 18,000 centners of woollen fabrics, the 500,000 centners of cotton yarn, thread, and linen yarn, which at present are imported from England. If, however, she accomplishes that, she will then import 500,000 centners more raw cotton than before, by which she will carry on so much the more direct exchange trade with tropical countries, and be able to pay for the greater part if not the whole of that requirement with her own manufactured goods.

We must correct the view of the author of the report, that public opinion in Germany is in favour of free trade, by stating that since the establishment of the Commercial Union people have acquired a clearer perception of what it is that England usually understands by the term 'free trade,' for, as he himself says, ' Since that period the sentiments of the German people have been diverted from the region of hope and of fantasy to that of their actual and material interests.' The author of the report is quite right when he says that intelligence is very greatly diffused amongst the German people, but for that very reason people in Germany have ceased to indulge in cosmopolitical dreams. People here now think for themselves—they trust their own conclusions, their own experience, their own sound common sense, more than one-sided systems which are opposed to all experience. They begin to comprehend why it was that Burke declared in confidence to Adam Smith ' that a nation must not be governed according to cosmo-

political systems, but according to knowledge of their special
national interests acquired by deep research.' People in
Germany distrust counsellors who blow both cold and hot
out of the same mouth. People know also how to estimate
at their proper value the interests and the advice of those
who are our industrial competitors. Finally, people in
Germany bear in mind as often as English offers are under
discussion the well-known proverb of the presents offered by
the Danaidæ.

For these very reasons we may doubt that influential
German statesmen have seriously given grounds for hope
to the author of the report, that Germany is willing to
abandon her protective policy for the benefit of England, in
exchange for the pitiful concession of permission to export
to England a little grain and timber. At any rate public
opinion in Germany would greatly hesitate to consider such
statesmen to be thoughtful ones. In order to merit that
title in Germany in the present day, it is not enough that
a man should have thoroughly learned superficial phrases
and arguments of the cosmopolitical school. People require that a statesman should be well acquainted with the
powers and the requirements of the nation, and, without
troubling himself with scholastic systems, should develop
the former and satisfy the latter. But that man would
betray an unfathomable ignorance of those powers and
wants, who did not know what enormous exertions are
requisite to raise a national industry to that stage to which
the German industry has already attained ; who cannot in
spirit foresee the greatness of its future ; who could so
grievously disappoint the confidence which the German
industrial classes have reposed in their Governments, and
so deeply wound the spirit of enterprise in the nation ; who
was incapable of distinguishing between the lofty position
which is occupied by a manufacturing nation of the first
rank, and the inferior position of a country which merely
exports corn and timber ; who is not intelligent enough to
estimate how precarious a foreign market for grain and
timber is even in ordinary times, how easily concessions of
this kind can be again revoked, and what convulsions are

involved in an interruption of such a trade, occasioned by wars or hostile commercial regulations; who, finally, has not learned from the example of other great states how greatly the existence, the independence, and the power of the nation depends on its possession of a manufacturing power of its own, developed in all its branches.

Truly one must greatly under-estimate the spirit of nationality and of unity which has arisen in Germany since 1830, if one believed, as the author of the report does (p. 26), that the policy of the Commercial Union will follow the separate interests of Prussia, because two-thirds of the population of the Union are Prussian. But Prussia's interests demand the export of grain and timber to England; the amount of her capital devoted to manufactures is unimportant; Prussia will therefore oppose every system which impedes the import of foreign manufactures, and all the heads of departments in Prussia are of that opinion. Nevertheless the author of the report says at the beginning of his report: ' The German Customs Union is an incarnation of the idea of national unity which widely pervades this country. If this Union is well led, it must bring about the fusion of all German interests in one common league. The experience of its benefits has made it popular. It is the first step towards the nationalisation of the German people. By means of the common interest in commercial questions, it has paved the way for political nationality, and in place of narrow-minded views, prejudices, and customs, it has laid down a broader and stronger element of German national existence.' Now, how does the opinion agree with these perfectly true prefatory observations, that Prussia will sacrifice the independence and the future greatness of the nation to a narrow regard to her own supposed (but in any case only momentary) private interest—that Prussia will not comprehend that Germany must either rise or fall with her national commercial policy, as Prussia herself must rise or fall with Germany? How does the assertion that the Prussian heads of departments are opposed to the protective system, agree with the fact that the high duties on ordinary woollen and cotton fabrics emanated from Prussia herself?

And must we not be compelled to conjecture from these contradictions, and from the fact that the author of the report paints in such glowing colours the condition and the progress of the industry of Saxony, that he himself is desirous of exciting the private jealousy of Prussia ?

Be that as it may, it is very strange that Dr. Bowring attaches such great importance to the private statements of heads of departments, he an English author who ought to be well aware of the power of public opinion—who ought to know that in our days the private views of heads of departments even in unconstitutional states count for very little if they are opposed to public opinion, and especially to the material interests of the whole nation, and if they favour retrograde steps which endanger the whole nationality. The author of the report also feels this well enough himself, when he states at page 98 that the Prussian Government has sufficiently experienced, as the English Government has done in connection with the abolition of the English corn laws, that the views of public officials cannot everywhere be carried into effect, that hence it might be necessary to consider whether German grain and timber should not be admitted to the English markets even without previous concessions on the part of the German Union, because by that very means the way might be paved for the admission of the English manufactured goods into the German market. This view is in any case a correct one. Dr. Bowring sees clearly that the German industry would never have been strengthened but for those laws ; that consequently the abolition of the corn laws would not only check the further advances of German industry, but must cause it again to retrograde greatly, provided always that in that case the German customs legislation remains unchanged. It is only a pity that the British did not perceive the soundness of this argument twenty years ago ; but now, after that the legislation of England has itself undertaken the divorce of German agriculture from English manufactures, after that Germany has pursued the path of perfecting her industry for twenty years, and has made enormous sacrifices for this object, it would betoken political blindness if Germany were now, owing to the abolition of the English corn laws, to abstain in any degree from pursuing her great national career. Indeed, we are firmly convinced that in such a case it would be necessary for Germany to increase her protective duties in the same proportion in which the English manufactories would derive advantage from the abolition of the corn laws as compared with those of Germany. Germany can for a long time follow no other policy in respect to England than that of a less advanced manufacturing nation which is striving with all her power to raise herself to an equal position with the most advanced manufacturing nation. Every other policy or measure than that, involves the im- perilling of the German nationality. If the English are in want of foreign corn or timber, then they may get it in Germany or where else they please. Germany will not on that account any the less protect the advances in industry which she has made up to this time, or strive any the less to make future advances. If the British will have nothing to do with German grain and timber, so much the better. In that case the industry, the navigation, the foreign trade of Germany will raise their heads so much the quicker, the German internal means of transport will be so much the sooner completed, the German nationality will so much the more certainly rest on its natural foundation. Perhaps Prussia may not in this way so soon be able to sell the corn and timber of her Baltic provinces at high prices as if the English markets were suddenly opened to her. But through the completion of the internal means of trans- port, and through the internal demand for agricultural pro- duce created by the manufactories, the sales of those pro- vinces to the interior of Germany will increase fast enough, and every benefit to these provinces which is founded on the home demand for agricultural produce will be gained by them for all future time. They will never more have to oscillate as heretofore between calamity and prosperity from one decade to another. But further, as a political power Prussia will gain a hundred-fold more in concentrated strength in the interior of Germany by this policy than the material values which she sacrifices for the moment in her maritime provinces, or rather invests for repayment in the future.

The object of the English ministry in this report is clearly to obtain the admission into Germany of ordinary English woollen and cotton fabrics, partly through the abolition or at least modification of charging duties by weight, partly through the lowering of the tariff, and partly by the admission of the German grain and timber into the English market. By these means the first breach can be made in the German protective system. These articles of ordinary use (as we have already shown in a former chapter) are by far the most important, they are the fundamental element of the national industry. Duties of ten per cent. *ad valorem*, which are clearly aimed at by England, would, with the assistance of the usual tricks of under declaration of value, sacrifice the greater part of the German industry to English competition, especially if in consequence of commercial crises the English manufacturers were sometimes induced to throw on the market their stocks of goods at any price. It is therefore no exaggeration if we maintain that the tendency of the English proposals aims at nothing less than the overthrow of the entire German protective system, in order to reduce Germany to the position of an English agricultural colony. With this object in view, it is impressed on the notice of Prussia how greatly her agriculture might gain by the reduction of the English corn and timber duties, and how unimportant her manufacturing interest is. With the same view, the prospect is offered to Prussia of a reduction of the duties on brandy. And in order that the other states may not go quite empty away, a five per cent. reduction of the duties on Nüremberg wares, children's toys, eau de Cologne, and other trifles, is promised. That gives satisfaction to the small German states, and also does not cost much.

The next attempt will be to convince the German governments, by means of this report, how advantageous to them it would be to let England spin cotton and linen yarns for them. It cannot be doubted that hitherto the policy adopted by the Union, first of all to encourage and protect the printing of cloths and then weaving, and to import the medium and finer yarns, has been the right one. But from that it in nowise follows that it would continue to be the right one for all time. The tariff legislation must advance as the national industry advances if it is rightly to fulfil its purpose. We have already shown that the spinning factories, quite apart from their importance in themselves, yet are the source of further incalculable benefits, inasmuch as they place us in direct commercial communication with the countries of warm climate, and hence that they exercise an incalculable influence on our navigation and on our export of manufactures, and that they benefit our manufactories of machinery more than any other branch of manufacture. Inasmuch as it cannot be doubted that Germany cannot be hindered either by want of water power and of capable workmen, or by lack of material capital or intelligence, from carrying on for herself this great and fruitful industry, so we cannot see why we should not gradually protect the spinning of yarns from one number to another, in such a way that in the course of five to ten years we may be able to spin for ourselves the greater part of what we require. However highly one may estimate the advantages of the export of grain and timber, they cannot nearly equal the benefits which must accrue to us from the spinning manufacture. Indeed, we have no hesitation in expressing the belief that it could be incontestably proved, by a calculation of the consumption of agricultural products and timber which would be created by the spinning industry, that from this branch of manufacture alone far greater benefits must accrue to the German landowners than the foreign market will ever or can ever offer them.

Dr. Bowring doubts that Hanover, Brunswick, the two Mecklenburgs, Oldenburg, and the Hanse Towns will join the Union, unless the latter is willing to make a radical reduction in its import duties. The latter proposal, however, cannot be seriously considered, because it would be immeasurably worse than the evil which by it, it is desired to remedy.

Our confidence in the prosperity of the future of Germany is, however, by no means so weak as that of the author of the report. Just as the Revolution of July has proved beneficial 'to the German Commercial Union, so must the next great general convulsion make an end of all the minor hesitations by which these small states have hitherto been withheld from yielding to the greater requirements of the German nationality. Of what value the commercial unity has been to the nationality, and of what value it is to German governments, quite apart from mere material interests, has been recently for the first time very strongly demonstrated, when the desire to acquire the Rhine frontier has been loudly expressed in France.

From day to day it is necessary that the governments and peoples of Germany should be more convinced that national unity is the rock on which the edifice of their welfare, their honour, their power, their present security and existence, and their future greatness, must be founded. Thus from day to day the apostasy of these small maritime states will appear more and more, not only to the states in the Union, but to these small states themselves, in the light of a national scandal which must be got rid of at any price. Also, if the matter is intelligently considered, the material advantages of joining the Union are much greater for those states themselves than the sacrifice which it requires. The more that manufacturing industry, that the internal means of transport, the navigation, and the foreign trade of Germany, develop themselves, in that degree in which under a wise commercial policy they can and must be developed in accordance with the resources of the nation, so much the more will the desire become more vigorous on the part of those small states directly to participate in these advantages, and so much the more will they leave off the bad habit of looking to foreign countries for blessings and prosperity.

In reference to the Hanse Towns especially, the spirit of imperial citizenship of the sovereign parish of Hamburg in no way deters us from our hopes. In those cities, according to the testimony of the author of the report himself, dwell a great number of men who comprehend that Hamburg, Bremen, and Lübeck are and must be to the German nation that which London and Liverpool are to the English, that which New York, Boston, and Philadelphia are to the Americans—men who clearly see that the Commercial Union can offer advantages to their commerce with the world which far exceed the disadvantages of subjection to the regulations of the Union, and that a prosperity without any guarantee for its continuance is fundamentally a delusion.

What sensible inhabitant of those seaports could heartily congratulate himself on the continual increase of their tonnage, on the continual extension of their commercial relations, if he reflected that two frigates, which coming from Heligoland could be stationed at the mouths of the Weser and the Elbe, would be in a position to destroy in twenty-four hours this work of a quarter of a century? But the Union will guarantee to these seaports their prosperity and their progress for all future time, partly by the creation of a fleet of its own and partly by alliances. It will foster their fisheries, secure special advantages to their shipping, protect and promote their foreign commercial relations, by effective consular establishments and by treaties. Partly by their means it will found new colonies, and by their means carry on its own colonial trade. For a union of States comprising thirty-five millions of inhabitants (for the Union will comprise that number at least when it is fully completed), which owing to an annual increase of population of one and a half per cent. can easily spare annually two or three hundred thousand persons, whose provinces abound with well-informed and cultivated inhabitants who have a peculiar propensity to seek their fortune in distant countries, people who can take root anywhere and make themselves at home wherever unoccupied land is to be cultivated, are called upon by Nature herself to place themselves in the first rank of nations who colonise and diffuse civilisation.

The feeling of the necessity for such a perfect completion

of the Commercial Union is so universally entertained in Germany, that hence the author of the report could not help remarking, ' More coasts, more harbours, more navigation, a Union flag,' the possession of a navy and of a mercantile marine, are wishes very generally entertained by the supporters of the Commercial Union, but there is little prospect at present of the Union making head against the increasing fleet of Russia and the commercial marine of Holland and the Hanse Towns.' Against them certainly not, but so much the more with them and by means of them. It lies in the very nature of every power to seek to divide in order to rule. After the author of the report has shown why it would be foolish on the part of the maritime states to join the Union, he desires also to separate the great seaports from the German national body for all time, inasmuch as he speaks to us of the warehouses of Altona which must become dangerous to the warehouses of Hamburg, as though such a great commercial empire could not find the means of making the warehouses of Altona serviceable to its objects. We will not follow the author through his acute inferences from this point; we will only say, that if they were applied to England, they would prove that London and Liverpool would increase their commercial prosperity in an extraordinary degree if they were, separated from the body of the English nation. The spirit which underlies these arguments is unmistakably expressed in the report of the English consul at Rotterdam. ' For the commercial interests of Great Britain,' says Mr. Alexander Ferrier at the end of his report, ' it appears of the greatest possible importance that no means should be left untried to prevent the aforesaid states, and also Belgium, from entering the Zollverein, for reasons which are too clear to need any exposition.' Who could possibly blame Mr. Ferrier for speaking thus, or Dr. Bowring for speaking thus, or the English ministers for acting as the others speak? The national instinct of England speaks and acts through them. But to expect prosperity and blessing to Germany from proposals which proceed from such a source as that, would appear to exceed even a decent degree of national good nature. 'Whatever may happen,' adds Mr. Ferrier to the words above quoted, ' Holland must at all times be considered as the main channel for the commercial relations of South Germany with other countries.'   Clearly Mr. Ferrier understands by the term ' other countries,' merely England ; clearly he means to say that if the English manufacturing supremacy should lose its means of access to Germany on the North Sea and the Baltic, Holland would still remain to it as the great means of access by which it could predominate over the markets for manufactured goods and colonial produce of the south of Germany.

But we from a national point of view say and maintain that Holland is in reference to its geographical position, as well as in respect to its commercial and industrial circumstances, and to the origin and language of its inhabitants, a German province, which has been separated from Germany at a period of German national disunion, without whose reincorporation in the German Union Germany may be compared to a house the door of which belongs to a stranger.: Holland belongs as much to Germany as Brittany and Normandy belong to France, and so long as Holland is determined to constitute an independent kingdom of her own, Germany can as little attain independence and power as France would have been enabled to attain these if those provinces had remained in the hands of the English.   That the commercial power of Holland has declined, is owing to the unimportance of the country.   Holland will and must also, notwithstanding the prosperity of her colonies, continue to decline, because the nation is too weak to support the enormous expense of a considerable military and naval power.   Through her exertions to maintain her nationality Holland must become more and more deeply involved in debt.   Notwithstanding her great colonial prosperity, she is and remains all the same a country dependent on England, and by her seeming independence she only strengthens the English supremacy.   This is also the secret reason why England at the congress of Vienna took under her protection the restoration of the Dutch seeming independence. The case is exactly the same as with the Hanse Towns.   On the side of England, Holland is a satellite for the English fleet—unite it with Germany, she is the leader of the German naval power.   In her present position Holland cannot nearly so well derive profit from her colonial possessions as if they became a constituent part of the German Union, especially because she is too weak in the elements which are necessary for colonisation—in population and in mental powers.   Further than this, the profitable development of her colonies, so far as that has hitherto been effected, depends for the most part on German good nature, or rather on the non-acquaintance of the Germans with their own national commercial interests ; for while all other nations reserve their market for colonial produce for their own colonies and for the countries subject to them, the German market is the only one which remains open to the Dutch for the disposal of their surplus colonial produce. As soon as the Germans clearly comprehend that those from whom they purchase colonial produce must be made to understand that they on their part must purchase manufactured goods from Germany under differentially favourable treatment, then the Germans will also clearly see that they have it in their power to compel Holland to join the Zollverein.   That union would be of the greatest advantage to both countries.   Germany would give Holland the means not only of deriving profit from her colonies far better than at present, but also to found and to acquire new colonies.   Germany would grant special preferential privileges to the Dutch and Hanseatic shipping, and grant special preferential privileges to Dutch colonial produce in the German markets.   Holland and the Hanse Towns, in return, would preferentially export German manufactures, and preferentially employ their surplus capital in the manufactories and the agriculture of the interior of Germany.

Holland, as she has sunk from her eminence as a commercial power because she, the mere fraction of a nation, wanted to make herself pass as an entire nation ; because she sought her advantage in the oppression and the weakening of the productive powers of Germany, instead of basing her greatness on the prosperity of the countries which lie behind her, with which every maritime state must stand or fall; because she sought to become great by her separation from the German nation instead of by her union with it; Holland can only again attain to her ancient state of prosperity by means of the German Union and in the closest connection with it. Only by this union is it possible to constitute an agricultural manufacturing commercial nationality of the first magnitude.

Dr. Bowring groups in his tables the imports and exports of the German Customs Union with the Hanse Towns and Holland and Belgium all together, and from this grouping it clearly appears how greatly all these countries are dependent on the English manufacturing industry, and how immeasurably they might gain in their entire productive power by union. He estimates the imports of these countries from England at 19,842,121*l*. sterling of official value, or 8,550,347*l*. of declared value, but the exports of those countries to England (on the other hand) at only 4,804,491*l*. sterling; in which, by the way, are included the great quantities of Java coffee, cheese, butter, &c. which England imports from Holland. These totals speak volumes. We thank the Doctor for his statistical grouping together— would that it might betoken a speedy political grouping.

CHAPTER XXXV.

CONTINENTAL POLITICS.

THE highest ultimate aim of rational politics is (as we have shown in our Second Book) the uniting of all nations under a common law of right, an object which is only to be attained through the greatest possible equalisation of the most important nations of the earth in civilisation, prosperity, industry, and power, by the conversion of the antipathies and conflicts which now exist between them into sympathy and harmony. But the solution of this problem is a work of immensely long duration. At the present time the nations are divided and repelled from one another by manifold causes ; chief among these are conflicts about territory. As yet, the apportionment of territory to the European nations does not correspond to the nature of things. Indeed, even in theory, people are not yet agreed upon the fundamental conditions of a just and natural apportionment of territory. Some desire that their national territory should be determined according to the requirements of their metropolis without regard to language, commerce, race, and so forth, in such a way that the metropolis should be situated in the centre and be protected as much as possible against foreign attacks. They desire to have great rivers for their frontiers. Others maintain, and apparently with greater reason, that sea-coasts, mountains, language, and race, constitute better frontiers than great rivers. There still are nations who are not in possession of those mouths of rivers and sea-coasts which are indispensable to them for the development of their commerce with the world and for their naval power.

If every nation was already in possession of the territory

which is necessary for its internal development, and for the maintenance of its political, industrial, and commercial independence, then every conquest of territory would be contrary to sound policy, because by the unnatural increase of territory the jealousy of the nation which is thus encroached upon would be excited and kept alive, and consequently the sacrifices which the conquering nation would have to make for retaining such provinces would be immeasurably greater than the advantages accruing from their possession. A just and wise apportionment of territory is, however, at this day not to be thought of, because this question is complicated by manifold interests of another nature. At the same time it must not be ignored that rectification of territory must be reckoned among the most important requirements of the nations, that striving to attain it is legitimate, that indeed in many cases it is a justifiable reason for war.

Further causes of antipathy between the nations are, at the present time, the diversity of their interests in respect to manufactures, commerce, navigation, naval power, and colonial possessions, also the difference in their degrees of civilisation, of religion, and of political condition. All these interests are complicated in manifold ways through the interests of dynasties and powers.

The causes of antipathy are, on the other hand, causes of sympathy. The less powerful nations sympathise against the most powerful, those whose independence is endangered sympathise against the aggressors, territorial powers against naval supremacy, those whose industry and commerce are defective sympathise against those who are striving for an industrial and commercial monopoly, the half-civilised against the civilised, those who are subjects of a monarchy against those whose government is entirely or partially democratic.

Nations at this time pursue their own interests and sympathies by means of alliances of those who are like-minded and have like interests against the interests and tendencies which conflict with theirs. As, however, these interests and tendencies conflict with one another in various ways, these alliances are liable to change. Those nations

who are friends to-day may be enemies to-morrow, and
vice versâ, as soon as ever some one of the great interests
or principles is at stake by which they feel themselves
repelled from or drawn towards one another.

Politicians have long felt that the equalisation of the
nations must be their ultimate aim. That which people
call the *maintenance of the European balance of power* has
always been nothing else than the endeavours of the less
powerful to impose a check on the encroachments of the
more powerful. Yet politics have not seldom confounded
their proximate object with their ultimate one, and *vice
versâ*.

The proximate task of politics always consists in clearly
perceiving in what respect the alliance and equalisation of
the different interests is at the moment most pressing, and
to strive that until this equalisation is attained all other
questions may be suspended and kept in the background.

When the dynastic, monarchic, and aristocratic interests
of Europe allied themselves against the revolutionary tendencies of 1789, disregarding all considerations regarding
power and commerce, their policy was a correct one.

It was just as correct when the French Empire introduced the tendency of conquest in place of that of
revolution.

Napoleon sought by his Continental system to establish
a Continental coalition against the predominant naval and
commercial power of England ; but in order to succeed, it
was necessary for him, first of all, to take away from the
Continental nations the apprehension of being conquered
by France. He failed, because on their part the fear of his
supremacy on land greatly outweighed the disadvantages
which they suffered from the naval supremacy.

With the fall of the French Empire, the object of the
great alliance ceased. From that time forth, the Continental
powers were menaced neither by the revolutionary tendencies nor by the lust of conquest of France. England's predominance in manufactures, navigation, commerce, colonial
possessions, and naval power, had, on the other hand,
enormously increased during the conflicts against the

Revolution and against the French conquest. From that time forth, it became the interest of the Continental powers to ally themselves with France against the commercial and naval predominance. Solely from fear of the skin of the dead lion, the Continental powers did not heed sufficiently the living leopard who had hitherto fought in their ranks. The Holy Alliance was a political error.

This error also brought about its own punishment through the revolution of Italy. The Holy Alliance had unnecessarily called into life a counter force which no longer existed, or which at least would not for a long time have revived again. Fortunately for the Continental powers, the dynasty of July contrived to appease the revolutionary tendency in France. France concluded the alliance with England in the interests of the dynasty of July and of strengthening the constitutional monarchy. England concluded it in the interest of the maintenance of her commercial supremacy.

The Franco-English alliance ceased as soon as ever the dynasty of July and the constitutional monarchy in France felt themselves to be sufficiently firmly established; but, on the other hand, the interests of France in respect of naval power, navigation, commerce, industry, and foreign possessions came again more to the front. It is clear that France has again an equal interest with the other Continental powers in these questions, and the establishing of a Continental alliance against the naval predominance of England appears to be becoming a question of the day, provided the dynasty of July can succeed in creating perfect unity of will between the different organs of State administration, also to thrust into the background those territorial questions which are excited by the revolutionary tendencies, and entirely to appease in the minds of the monarchical Continental powers the fear of the tendencies of France towards revolution and aggression.

Nothing, however, at this time so greatly impedes a closer union of the continent of Europe as the fact that the centre of it still never takes the position for which it is naturally fitted. Instead of being a mediator between the east and the west of that continent, on all questions of arrangement of territory, of the principle of their constitutions, of national independence and power, for which it is qualified by its geographical position, by its federal constitution which excludes all apprehension of aggression in the minds of neighbouring nations, by its religious toleration, and its cosmopolitical tendencies, and finally by its civilisation and the elements of power which it possesses, this central part of Europe constitutes at present the apple of discord for which the east and the west contend, while each party hopes to draw to its own side this middle power, which is weakened by want of national unity, and is always uncertainly wavering hither and thither.

If, on the other hand, Germany could constitute itself with the maritime territories which appertain to it, with Holland, Belgium, and Switzerland, as a powerful commercial and political whole—if this mighty national body could fuse representative institutions with the existing monarchical, dynastic, and aristocratic interests, so far as these are compatible with one another—then Germany could secure peace to the continent of Europe for a long time, and at the same time constitute herself the central point of a durable Continental alliance.

That the naval power of England greatly exceeds that of all other nations, if not in the number of ships, yet certainly in fighting power—that hence the nations which are less powerful at sea can only match England at sea by uniting their own naval power, is clear. From hence it follows, that every nation which is less powerful at sea has an interest in the maintenance and prosperity of the naval power of all other nations who are similarly weak at sea; and further, that fractions of other nations which, hitherto divided, have possessed either no naval power whatever or only an unimportant one, should constitute themselves into one united naval power. In regard to England, France and North America sustain loss if the naval power of Russia declines, and *vice versâ*.. They all gain, if Germany, Holland, and Belgium constitute together a common naval power; for while separated these last are mere satellites to the supremacy of England, but if united they strengthen the opposition to that supremacy of all nations at sea.

None of these less powerful nations possesses a mercantile marine which exceeds the requirements of its own international trade—none of these nations possesses a manufacturing power which would maintain important preponderance over that of the others. None of them, therefore, has any ground to fear the competition of the others. On the other hand, all have a common interest in protecting themselves against the destructive competition of England. Hence it must be to the interests of all that the predominating manufacturing power of England should lose those means of access (Holland, Belgium, and the Hanse Towns) by means of which England has hitherto dominated the markets of the Continent.

Inasmuch as the products of tropical climates are chiefly paid for by the manufactured products of temperate climates, and hence the consumption of the former depends on the sale of the latter, therefore every manufacturing nation should endeavour to establish direct intercourse with tropical countries. And thus, if all manufacturing nations of the second rank understand their own interests and act accordingly, no nation will be permitted to maintain a predominant amount of colonial possessions in tropical countries. If, for instance, England could succeed in the object for which she is at present striving, viz. to produce in India the colonial produce which she requires—in that case England could only carry on trade with the West Indies to the extent to which she was able to sell to other countries the colonial produce which she now obtains from the West Indies in exchange for her manufactured goods. If, however, she could not dispose of these to other countries, then her West Indian possessions would become useless to her. She would then have no other option than either to let them go free, or to surrender the trade with them to other manufacturing countries. Hence it follows that all manufacturing nations less powerful at sea have a common interest in following this policy and in reciprocally supporting one another in it, and it follows further that no one of these nations would lose by the accession of Holland to the German Commercial Union, and through the closer connection of Germany with the Dutch colonies.

Since the emancipation of the Spanish and Portuguese colonies in South America and the West Indies, it is no longer indispensably necessary that a manufacturing nation should possess colonies of its own in tropical climates in order to put itself in a position to carry on directly the exchange of manufactured goods against colonial produce. As the markets of these emancipated tropical countries are free, every manufacturing nation which is able to compete in these free markets can carry on direct trade with them. But these free tropical countries can only produce great quantities of colonial products, and only consume great quantities of manufactured goods, if prosperity and morality, peace and repose, lawful order and religious tolerance, prevail within them. All nations not powerful at sea, especially those who possess no colonies, or only unimportant ones, have hence a common interest in bringing about such a state of things by their united power. To England, with her commercial supremacy, the circumstances of these countries cannot matter so much because she is sufficiently supplied, or at least hopes to become sufficiently supplied, with colonial produce from her own exclusive and subject markets in the East and West Indies. From this point of view also we must partly judge respecting the extremely important question of slavery. We are very far from ignoring that much philanthropy and good motive lies at the root of the zeal with which the object of the emancipation of the negroes is pursued by England, and that this zeal does great honour to the character of the English nation. But at the same time, if we consider the immediate effects of the measures adopted by England in reference to this matter, we cannot get rid of the idea that also much political motive and commercial interest are mingled with it. These effects are : (1) That by the sudden emancipation of the blacks, through their rapid transition from a condition of disorder and carelessness little removed from that of wild animals to a high degree of individual independence, the yield of tropical produce of South America and the West Indies will be extremely diminished and ultimately reduced to nothing, as the example of St. Domingo incontestably shows, inasmuch as there since the expulsion of the French and Spaniards the production has greatly decreased from year to year, and continues to do so. (2) That the free negroes continually seek to obtain an increase in their wages, whilst they limit their labour to the supply of their most indispensable wants ; that hence their freedom merely leads to idleness. (3) That, on the other hand, England possesses in the East Indies ample means for supplying the whole world with colonial products. It is well known that the Hindoos, owing to great industry and great moderation in their food and other wants, especially in consequence of the precepts of their religion, which forbid the use of animal food, are excessively frugal. To these must be added the want of capital among the natives, the great fruitfulness of the soil in vegetable products, and the restriction of caste and the great competition of those in want of work.

The result of all this is, that wages in India are incomparably lower than in the West Indies and South America, whether the plantations there are cultivated by free blacks or by slaves ; that consequently the production of India, after trade has been set free in that country, and wiser principles of administration have prevailed, must increase at an enormous rate, and the time is no longer distant when England will not only be able to supply all her own requirements of colonial produce from India, but also export great quantities to other countries. Hence it follows that England cannot lose through the diminution of production in the West Indies and South America, to which countries other nations also export manufactured goods, but she will gain if the colonial production in India becomes preponderant, which market England exclusively supplies with manufactured goods. (4) Finally, it may be asserted, that by the emancipation of the slaves England desires to hang a sword over the head of the North American slave states, which is so much the more menacing to the Union the more this

emancipation extends and the wish is excited among the
negroes of North America to partake of similar liberty.
The question if rightly viewed must appear a philanthropical experiment of doubtful benefit towards those
on whose behalf it was undertaken from motives of general
philanthropy, but must in any case appear to those nations
who rely on the trade with South America and the West
Indies as not advantageous to them; and they may not
unreasonably inquire: Whether a sudden transition from
slavery to freedom may not prove more injurious to the
negroes themselves than the maintenance of the existing
state of things?—whether it may not be the task of several
generations to educate the negroes (who are accustomed to
an almost animal state of subjection) to habits of voluntary
labour and thrift?—whether it might not better attain the
object if the transition from slavery to freedom was made
by the introduction of a mild form of serfdom, whereby at
first some interest might be secured to the serf in the land
which he cultivates, and a fair share of the fruits of his
labour, allowing sufficient rights to the landlord in order to
bind the serf to habits of industry and order?—whether
such a condition would not be more desirable than that of
a miserable, drunken, lazy, vicious, mendicant horde called
free negroes, in comparison with which Irish misery in its
most degraded form may be deemed a state of prosperity
and civilisation? If, however, we are required to believe that
the zeal of the English to make everything which exists
upon earth partakers of the same degree of freedom which
they possess themselves, is so great and irrepressible' that
they must be excused if they have forgotten that nature
makes no advances by leaps and bounds, then we must
venture to put the questions: Whether the condition of the
lowest caste of the Hindoos is not much more wretched and
intolerable than that of the American negroes?—and how
it happens that the philanthropic spirit of England has
never been excited on behalf of these most miserable of
mankind?—how it happens that English legislation has
never intervened for their benefit?—how it happens that
England has been active enough in deriving means for her

own enrichment out of this miserable state of things, without thinking of any direct means of ameliorating it ?

The English-Indian policy leads us to the Eastern question. If we can dismiss from the politics of the day all that which at this moment has reference to territorial conflicts, to the dynastic, monarchic, aristocratic, and religious interests, and to the circumstances of the various powers, it cannot be ignored that the Continental powers have a great national economic interest in common in the Eastern question. However successful the present endeavours of the powers may be to keep this question in the background for a time, it will continually again come to the front with renewed force. It is a conclusion long arrived at by all thoughtful men, that a nation so thoroughly undermined in her religious, moral, social, and political foundations as Turkey is, is like a corpse, which may indeed be held up for a time by the support of the living, but must none the less pass into corruption. The case is quite the same with the Persians as with the Turks, with the Chinese and Hindoos and all other Asiatic people. Wherever the mouldering civilisation of Asia comes into contact with the fresh atmosphere of Europe, it falls to atoms ; and Europe will sooner or later find herself under the necessity of taking the whole of Asia under her care and tutelage, as already India has been so taken in charge by England. In this utter chaos of countries and peoples there exists no single nationality which is either worthy or capable of maintenance and regeneration. Hence the entire dissolution of the Asiatic nationalities appears to be inevitable, and a regeneration of Asia only possible by means of an infusion of European vital power, by the general introduction of the Christian religion and of European moral laws and order, by European immigration, and the introduction of European systems of government.

If we reflect on the course which such a regeneration might possibly pursue, the first consideration that strikes one is that the greater part of the East is richly provided by nature with resources for supplying the manufacturing nations of Europe with great quantities of raw materials and necessary articles of every kind, but especially for producing tropical products, and in exchange for these for opening unlimited markets to European manufacturers. From this circumstance, nature appears to have given an indication that this .egeneration, as generally is the case with the civilisation of barbarous peoples, must proceed by the path of free exchange of agricultural produce against manufactured goods. For that reason the principle must be firmly maintained above all by the European nations, that no exclusive commercial privileges must be reserved to any European nation in any part of Asia whatever, and that no nation must be favoured above others there in any degree. It would be especially advantageous to the extension of this trade, if the chief commercial emporiums of the East were constituted free cities, the European population of which should have the right of self-government in consideration of an annual payment of tax to the native rulers. But European agents should be appointed to reside with these rulers, after the example of English policy in India, whose advice the native rulers should be bound to follow in respect of the promotion of public security, order, and civilisation.

All the Continental powers have especially a common interest that neither of the two routes from the Mediterranean to the Red Sea and to the Persian Gulf should fall into the exclusive possession of England, nor remain impassable owing to Asiatic barbarism. To commit the duty of protecting these important points to Austria, would insure the best guarantees to all European nations.

Further, the Continental powers in general have a common interest with the United States in maintaining the principle that 'free ships cover free goods,' and that only an effectual blockade of individual ports, but not a mere proclamation of the blockade of entire coasts, ought to be respected by neutrals. Finally, the principle of the annexation of wild and uninhabited territories appears to require revision in the common interest of the Continental powers. People ridicule in our days the fact that the Holy Father formerly undertook to make presents of islands and parts of the globe, nay even to divide the world into two parts with a stroke of the pen, and to apportion this part to one man and that to another. Can it, however, be deemed much more sensible to acknowledge the title to an entire quarter of the globe to vest in the man who first erected somewhere on the earth a pole adorned with a piece of silk ? That in the case of islands of moderate size the right of the discoverer should be respected, may be admitted consistently with common sense ; but when the question arises as to islands which are as large as a great European kingdom (like New Zealand) or respecting a continent which is larger than the whole of Europe (like Australia), in such a case by nothing less than an actual occupation by colonisation, and then only for the actually colonised territory, can a claim to exclusive possession be admitted consistently with common sense. And it is not clear why the Germans and the French should not have the right to found colonies in those parts of the world at points which are distant from the English stations.

If we only consider the enormous interests which the nations of the Continent have in common, as opposed to the English maritime supremacy, we shall be led to the conviction that nothing is so necessary to these nations as union, and nothing is so ruinous to them as Continental wars. The history of the last century also teaches us that every war which the powers of the Continent have waged against one another has had for its invariable result to increase the industry, the wealth, the navigation, the colonial possessions, and the power of the insular supremacy.

Hence, it cannot be denied that a correct view of the wants and interests of the Continent underlaid the Continental system of Napoleon, although it must not be ignored that Napoleon desired to give effect to this idea (right in itself) in a manner which was contrary to the independence and to the interests of the other Continental powers. The Continental system of Napoleon suffered from three capital defects. In the first place, it sought to establish, in the place of the English maritime supremacy, a French Continental supremacy ; it sought the humiliation, or destruction and dissolution, of other nationalities on the Continent for the benefit of France, instead of basing itself on the elevation and equalisation of the other Continental nations. Furthermore, France followed herself an exclusive commercial policy against the other countries of the Continent, while she claimed for herself free competition in those countries. Finally, the system almost entirely destroyed the trade between the manufacturing countries of the Continent and tropical countries, and found itself compelled to find a remedy for the destruction of this international trade by the use of substituted articles.[1]

That the idea of this Continental system will ever recur, that the necessity of realising it will the more forcibly impress itself on the Continental nations in proportion as the preponderance of England in industry, wealth, and power further increases, is already very clear, and will continually become more evident. But it is not less certain that an alliance of the Continental nations can only have a good result if France is wise enough to avoid the errors of Napoleon. Hence, it is foolish of France if she raises (contrary to all justice, and to the actual nature of circumstances) claims for extension of frontiers at the expense of Germany, and thereby compels other nations of the Continent to ally themselves with England.

It is foolish of France if she speaks of the Mediterranean sea as of a French lake, and seeks to acquire exclusive influence in the Levant and in South America.

An effective Continental system can only originate from the free union of the Continental powers, and can succeed only in case it has for its object (and also effects) an equal participation in the advantages which result from it, for in that way only, and in no other, can the maritime powers of second rank command respect from the predominant power of England in such a way that the latter without any recourse to the force of arms will concede all the just requirements of the less powerful states. Only by such an alliance as that will the Continental manufacturing powers be able

[1] This fact is confirmed by Mad. Junot, in *Mémoires de la Duchesse d'Abrantis.*—[TRANSLATOR.]

to maintain their relations with tropical countries, and assert and secure their interests in the East and the West.

In any case the British, who are ever too anxious for supremacy, must feel it hard when they perceive in this manner how the Continental nations will reciprocally raise their manufacturing power by mutual commercial concessions and by treaties; how they will reciprocally strengthen their navigation and their naval power; how they will assert their claim to that share for which they are fitted by nature in civilising and colonising barbarous and uncultivated countries, and in trade with tropical regions. Nevertheless, a glance into the future ought sufficiently to console the Britons for these anticipated disadvantages.

For the same causes which have raised Great Britain to her present exalted position, will (probably in the course of the next century) raise the United States of America to a degree of industry, wealth, and power, which will surpass the position in which England stands, as far as at present England excels little Holland. In the natural course of things the United States will increase their population within that period to hundreds of millions of souls; they will diffuse their population, their institutions, their civilisation, and their spirit over the whole of Central and South America, just as they have recently diffused them over the neighbouring Mexican province. The Federal Union will comprise all these immense territories, a population of several hundred millions of people will develop the resources of a continent which infinitely exceeds the continent of Europe in extent and in natural wealth. The naval power of the western world will surpass that of Great Britain, as greatly as its coasts and rivers exceed those of Britain in extent and magnitude.

Thus in a not very distant future the natural necessity which now imposes on the French and Germans the necessity of establishing a Continental alliance against the British supremacy, will impose on the British the necessity of establishing a European coalition against the supremacy of America. Then will Great Britain be compelled to seek and to find in the leadership of the united powers of Europe protection, security, and compensation against the predominance of America, and an equivalent for her lost supremacy.

It is therefore good for England that she should practise resignation betimes, that she should by timely renunciations gain the friendship of European Continental powers, that she should accustom herself betimes to the idea of being only the first among equals.

CHAPTER XXXVI.

THE COMMERCIAL POLICY OF THE GERMAN ZOLLVEREIN.

IF any nation whatever is qualified for the establishment of a national manufacturing power, it is Germany; by the high rank which she maintains in science and art, in literature and education, in public administration and in institutions of public utility; by her morality and religious character, her industry and domestic economy; by her perseverance and steadfastness in business occupations; as also by her spirit of invention, by the number and vigour of her population; by the extent and nature of her territory, and especially by her highly advanced agriculture, and her physical, social, and mental resources.

If any nation whatever has a right to anticipate rich results from a protective system adapted to her circumstances, for the progress of her home manufactures, for the increase of her foreign trade and her navigation, for the perfecting of her internal means of transport, for the prosperity of her agriculture, as also for the maintenance of her independence and the increase of her power abroad, it is Germany.

Yes, we venture to assert, that on the development of the German protective system depend the existence, the independence, and the future of the German nationality. Only in the soil of general prosperity does the national spirit strike its roots, produce fine blossoms and rich fruits; only from the unity of material interests does mental power arise, and only from both of these national power. But of what value are all our endeavours, whether we are rulers or subjects, nobles or simple citizens, learned men, soldiers, or civilians, manufacturers, agriculturists, or merchants, without *nationality and without guarantees for the continuance of our nationality?*

Meanwhile, however, the German protective system only accomplishes its object in a very imperfect manner, so long as Germany does not spin for herself the cotton and linen yarn which she requires; so long as she does not directly import from tropical countries the colonial produce which she requires, and pay for it with goods of her own manufacture; so long as she does not carry on this trade with her own ships; so long as she has no means of protecting her own flag; so long as she possesses no perfect system of transport by river, canal, or railway; so long as the German Zollverein does not include all German maritime territories and also Holland and Belgium. We have treated these subjects circumstantially in various places in this book, and it is only necessary for us here to recapitulate what we have already thus treated.

If we import raw cotton from Egypt, Brazil, and North America, we in that case pay for it in our own manufactured goods; if, on the other hand, we import cotton yarn from England, we have to pay the value of it in raw materials and articles of food which we could more advantageously work up or consume ourselves, or else we must pay for it in specie which we have acquired elsewhere, and with which we could more advantageously purchase foreign raw materials to work up for ourselves, or colonial produce for our own consumption.

In the same way the introduction of spinning linen yarn by machinery offers us the means not only of increasing our home consumption of linen, and of perfecting our agriculture, but also of enormously increasing our trade with tropical countries.

For the two above-named branches of industry, as well as for the manufacture of woollens, we are as favourably circumstanced as any other nation, by an amount of water power hitherto not utilised, by cheap necessaries of life, and by low wages. What we lack is simply and solely a guarantee for our capitalists and artisans by which they may be protected against loss of capital and want of work.

A moderate protective duty of about twenty-five per cent. during the next five years, which could be maintained for a few years at that rate and then be lowered to fifteen to twenty per cent., ought completely to accomplish this object. Every argument which is adduced by the supporters of the theory of values against such a measure, has been refuted by us. On the other hand, we may add a further argument in favour of that measure, that these great branches of industry especially offer us the means for establishing extensive machine manufactories and for the development of a race of competent technical instructors and practical foremen.

In the trade in colonial produce Germany, as France and England have done, has to follow the principle—that in respect to the purchase of the colonial produce which we require, we should give a preference to those tropical countries which purchase manufactured goods from us; or, in short, *that we should buy from those who buy from us.* That is the case in reference to our trade with the West Indies and to North and South America.

But it is not yet the case in reference to our trade with Holland, which country supplies us with enormous quantities of her colonial produce, but only takes in return disproportionately small quantities of our manufactured goods.

At the same time Holland is naturally directed to the market of Germany for the disposal of the greater part of her colonial produce, inasmuch as England and France derive their supplies of such produce for the most part from their own colonies and from subject countries (where they exclusively possess the market for manufactured goods), and hence they only import small quantities of Dutch colonial produce.

Holland has no important manufacturing industry of her own, but, on the other hand, has a great productive industry in her colonies, which has recently greatly increased and may yet be immeasurably further increased. But Holland desires of Germany that which is unfair, and acts contrary to her own interests if rightly understood, inasmuch as she desires to dispose of the greater part of

her colonial produce to Germany, while she desires to
supply her requirements of manufactured goods from any
quarter she 'likes best. This is, for Holland, an only
apparently beneficial and a short-sighted policy ; for if
Holland would give preferential advantages to German
manufactured goods both in the mother country and in
her colonies, the demand in Germany for Dutch colonial
produce would increase in the same proportion in which
the sale of German manufactured goods to Holland and
her colonies increased, or, in other words, Germany would
be able to purchase so much the more colonial produce in
proportion as she sold more manufactured goods to Holland ; Holland would be able to dispose of so much more
colonial produce to Germany as she purchased from
Germany manufactured goods. This reciprocal exchange
operation is, at present, rendered impracticable by Holland
if she sells her colonial produce to Germany while she
purchases her requirements in manufactured goods from
England, because England (no matter how much of manufactured goods she sells to Holland) will always supply the
greater part of her own requirements of colonial produce
from her own colonies, or from the countries which are
subject to her.

Hence the interests of Germany require that she should
either demand from Holland a differential duty in favour
of Germany's manufacturing production, by which the
latter can secure to herself the exclusive market for manufactured goods in Holland and her colonies, or, in case of
refusal, that Germany should impose a differential duty on
the import of colonial produce in favour of the produce of
Central and South America and of the free markets of the
West Indies.

The above-named policy would constitute the most
effective means of inducing Holland to join the German
Zollverein.

As matters now stand, Germany has no reason for sacrificing her own manufactories of beetroot sugar to the trade
with Holland ; for only in case Germany can pay for her
requirements of this article by means of her own manufac-

tured goods, is it more to her advantage to supply that requirement by an exchange trade with tropical countries, than by producing it herself at home.

Hence the attention of Germany should be at once chiefly directed to the extension of her trade with Northern, Central, and South America, and with the free markets of the West Indies. In connection with that, the following measures, in addition to that above adverted to, appear desirable : the establishment of a regular service of steamships between the German seaports and the principal ports of those countries, the promotion of emigration thither, the confirmation and extension of friendly relations between them and the Zollverein, and especially the promotion of the civilisation of those countries.

Recent experience has abundantly taught us how enormously commerce on a large scale is promoted by a regular service of steamships. France and Belgium are already treading in the footsteps of England in this respect, as they well perceive that every nation which is behindhand in this more perfect means of transport must retrograde in her foreign trade. The German seaports also have already recognised this; already one public company has been completely formed in Bremen for building two or three steam vessels for the trade with the United States. This, however, is clearly an insufficient provision. The commercial interests of Germany require not only a regular service of steam vessels with North America, especially with New York, Boston, Charleston, and New Orleans, but also with Cuba, San Domingo, and Central and South America. Germany ought to be behind no other nation in respect to these latter lines of steam navigation. It must certainly not be ignored that the means which are required for these objects will be too great for the spirit of enterprise, and perhaps also for the power of the German seaports, and it seems to us they can only be carried into effect by means of liberal subsidies on the part of the states of the Zollverein. The prospect of such subsidies as well as of differential duties in favour of German shipping, ought at once to constitute a strong motive for these seaports to become included in the Commercial Union. When one considers how greatly the exports of manufactured goods and the imports of colonial produce, and consequently also the customs revenue, of the states of the Zollverein would be increased by such a measure, one cannot doubt that even a considerable expenditure for this object must appear as only a reproductive investment of capital from which rich returns are to be expected.

Through the increase of the means of intercourse of Germany with the above-named countries, the emigration of Germans to those countries and their settlement there as citizens would be no less promoted ; and by that means the foundation would be laid for future increase of commerce with them.   For this object the states of the Zollverein ought to establish everywhere consulates and diplomatic agencies, by means of which the settlement and undertakings of German citizens could be promoted, and especially to assist those states in every practicable way in giving stability to their governments and improving their degree of civilisation.

We do not share in the least the opinion of those who think that the tropical countries of America offer less advantages to German colonisation than those of temperate climate in North America.   However great, as we have openly confessed, is our attachment for the last-named country, and however little we are able or desire to deny that an individual German emigrant who possesses a little capital has greater hope of permanently making his fortune in Western North America, we must nevertheless here express our opinion that emigration to Central and South America, if it were well led and undertaken on a large scale, offers in a *national* point of view much greater advantages for Germany than emigration to North America.   What good is it if the emigrants to North America become ever so prosperous ?   In their personal relation they are lost for ever to the German nationality, and also from their material production Germany can expect only unimportant fruits. It is a pure delusion if people think that the German language can be maintained by the Germans who live in the interior of the United States, or that after a time it may be possible to establish entire German states there. We once ourselves entertained this illusion, but after ten years' observation in the country itself, on the spot, we have entirely given it up. It lies in the very spirit of every nationality, and above all in that of the United States, to assimilate itself in language, literature, administration, and legislation; and it is good that that is so. However many Germans may now be living in North America, yet certainly not one of them is living there whose great-grandchildren will not greatly prefer the English language to the German, and that for the very natural reason that the former is the language of the educated people, of the literature, the legislation, the administration, the courts of justice, and the trade and commerce of the country. The same thing can and will happen to the Germans in North America as happened to the Huguenots in Germany and the French in Louisiana. They naturally must and will be amalgamated with the predominant population : some a little sooner, others a little later, according as they dwell more or less together with fellow-countrymen.

Still less dependence can be placed on an active intercourse between Germany and the German emigrants to the west of North America. The first settler is always compelled by necessity to make for himself the greater part of his articles of clothing and utensils ; and these customs, which originated from mere necessity, continue for the most part to the second and third generation. Hence it is that North America itself is a country which makes powerful efforts in manufacturing industry, and will continually strive more and more to gain possession of her home market for manufactured goods, for her own industry.

On the other hand, we would on that account by no means maintain that the American market for manufactured goods is not a very important one, and well worthy of regard, especially for Germany. On the contrary, we are of opinion that for many articles of luxury and for manufactured articles which are easy of transport, and in which the wages of labour constitute a chief element of the price, that market is one of the most important, and must from year to year, as respects the articles above named, become more important for Germany. What we contend is only this, that those Germans who emigrate to the west of North America give no important assistance in increasing the demand for German manufactured goods, and that in reference to that object emigration to Central and South America requires and deserves very much more direct encouragement.

The above-mentioned countries, including Texas, are for the most part adapted for raising colonial produce. They can and will never make great progress in manufacturing industry. Here there is an entirely new and rich market for manufactured goods to acquire; whoever has here established firm commercial relations, may remain in possession of them for all future time. These countries, without sufficient moral power of their own to raise themselves to a higher grade of civilisation, to introduce well-ordered systems of government, and to endue them with stability, will more and more come to the conviction that they must be aided from outside, namely by immigration. In these quarters the English and French are hated on account of their arrogance, and owing to jealousy for national independence—the Germans for the opposite reasons are liked. Hence the states of the Zollverein ought to devote the closest attention to these countries.

A vigorous German consular and diplomatic system ought to be established in these quarters, the branches of which should enter into correspondence with one another. Young explorers should be encouraged to travel through these countries and make impartial reports upon them. Young merchants should be encouraged to inspect them—young medical men to go and practise there. Companies should be founded and supported by actual share subscription, and taken under special protection, which companies should be formed in the German seaports in order to buy large tracts of land in those countries and to settle them with German colonists—companies for commerce and navigation, whose object should be to open new markets in those countries for German manufactures and to establish lines of steamships—mining companies, whose object should be to devote German knowledge and industry to winning the great mineral wealth of those countries. In every possible way the Zollverein ought to endeavour to gain the good-will of the population and also of the governments of those countries, and especially to promote by that means public security, means of communication, and public order; indeed, one ought not to hesitate, in case one could by that means put the governments of those countries under obligation to us, also to assist them by sending an important auxiliary corps.

A similar policy ought to be followed in reference to the East—to European Turkey and the Lower Danubian territories. Germany has an immeasurable interest that security and order should be firmly established in those countries, and in no direction so much as in this is the emigration of Germans so easy for individuals to accomplish, or so advantageous for the nation. A man dwelling by the Upper Danube could transport himself to Moldavia and Wallachia, to Servia, or also to the south-western shores of the Black Sea, for one fifth part of the expenditure of money and time which are requisite for his emigration to the shores of Lake Erie. What attracts him to the latter more than to the former is, the greater degree of liberty, security, and order which prevails in the latter. But under the existing circumstances of Turkey it ought not to be impossible to the German states, in alliance with Austria, to exercise such an influence on the improvement of the public condition of those countries, that the German colonist should no longer feel himself repelled from them, especially if the governments themselves would found companies for colonisation, take part in them themselves, and grant them continually their special protection.

In the meantime it is clear that settlements of this kind could only have a specially beneficial effect on the industry of the states of the Zollverein, if no obstacles were placed in the way of the exchange of German manufactured goods for the agricultural produce of the colonists, and if that exchange was promoted by cheap and rapid means of communication. Hence it is to the interest of the states of the Zollverein, that Austria should facilitate as much as possible the through traffic on the Danube, and that steam navigation on the Danube should be roused to vigorous activity—consequently that it should at the outset be actually subsidised by the Governments.

Especially, nothing is so desirable as that the Zollverein and Austria at a later period, after the industry of the Zollverein states has been better developed and has been placed in a position of greater equality to that of Austria, should make, by means of a treaty, reciprocal concessions in respect to their manufactured products.

After the conclusion of such a treaty, Austria would have an equal interest with the states of the Zollverein in making the Turkish provinces available for the benefit of their manufacturing industry and of their foreign commerce.

In anticipation of the inclusion in the Zollverein of the German seaports and Holland, it would be desirable that Prussia should now make a commencement by the adoption of a German commercial flag, and by laying the foundation for a future German fleet, and that she should try whether and how German colonies can be founded in Australia, New Zealand, or in or on other islands of Australasia.

The means for such attempts and commencements, and for the undertakings and subventions which we have previously recommended as desirable, must be acquired in the same way in which England and France have acquired the means of supporting their foreign commerce and their colonisation and of maintaining their powerful fleets, namely, by imposing duties on the imports of colonial produce. United action, order, and energy could be infused into these measures of the Zollverein, if the Zollverein states would assign the direction of them in respect to the North and transmarine affairs to Prussia, and in respect to the Danube and Oriental affairs to Bavaria. An addition of ten per cent. to the present import duties on manufactures and colonial produce would at present place one million and a half per annum at the disposal of the Zollverein. And as it may be expected with certainty, as a result of the continual increase in the export of manufactured goods, that in the course of time consumption of colonial produce in the states of the Zollverein will increase to double and treble its present amount, and consequently their customs revenue will increase in like proportion, sufficient provision will be made for satisfying the requirements above mentioned, if the states of the Zollverein establish the principle that over and above the addition of ten per. cent. *a part also of all future increase in import duties* should be placed at the disposal of the Prussian Government to be expended for these objects.

As regards the establishment of a German transport system, and especially of a German system of railways, we beg to refer to a work of our own which specially treats of that subject. This great enterprise will pay for itself, and all that is required of the Governments can be expressed in one word, and that is— ENERGY.

APPENDICES.

—◦◦◦—

APPENDIX A.

LIST's allegation as to this effect of the pecuniary subsidies granted by England to her allies on the Continent would appear to have some foundation in fact : any capital transferred by one country to another (other than by a mere transfer of existing securities between wealthy States) must in the long run be effected chiefly in commodities. It is probable that the large loans made by English capitalists to foreign States (notably from 1850 to 1870) resulted in temporary extra demand for British products, which helped to cause the increase of our prosperity 'by leaps and bounds.' So far they may have operated as 'bounties' to British producers, in the manner in which List maintains that the subsidies did. But the subsidies being absolute gifts for services in war, and the subsequent loans to repudiating or bankrupt States being practically (although involuntary) gifts, produced no interest return in future years. The English nation has paid heavily (in the increase to the national debt) for any temporary benefit afforded to English manufacturers by the 'bounties' of which List complains. And English holders of foreign State bonds have paid no less heavily for the temporary 'leaps and bounds' by which British manufacturing industry may have advanced in more recent times, owing to the loans.—TRANSLATOR.

APPENDIX B.

THE following instances (among others) in which the State has, with general assent of the public, interfered with the liberty of individuals in respect to their separate action, are adduced by the late Mr. Justice Byles.

The State provides defences against external aggression.

It conducts treaties with foreign nations.

It preserves internal peace and order.

It is the corner-stone of family ties, family duties, family affection, family education, by regulating and enforcing the marriage contract.

It institutes and protects property.

It regulates the transmission of property.

It enforces the repair of highways by the several districts through which they pass, or by those who use them.

It obliges each county to make and repair its own bridges.

It maintains ports and harbours.

It surveys and lights the sea coasts of the realm.

It coins money, and prohibits interference with this monopoly.

It regulates the issue of promissory notes payable to bearer.

It provides a uniform system of weights and measures, and proscribes the use of any other.

It assumes the distribution of intelligence by post.

By the patent and copyright laws it gives bounties on the exertion of the inventive faculties, in the shape of a *monopoly* for a limited period.

By requiring a public specification, explanatory of every patented discovery or invention, it takes care that the secret shall not be hidden from the public nor die with the inventor.

It imposes a bridle on the acquisition of property by corporate bodies.

It protects the public health by the prohibition of nuisances of thousands of kinds, and by making provision for their removal.

By the quarantine laws it prevents the importation of contagious diseases.

It provides for the cleanliness of towns.

It regulates the fares of hackney carriages and controls the drivers.

It forbids inoculation for the small-pox, and artificially promotes vaccination.

It assumes the distribution of insolvents' estates.

It provides for the maintenance of the poor.

It forbids perpetuities by avoiding all attempts to tie up property beyond a life or lives in being and twenty-one years afterwards.

Though it tolerates all religions, it does not leave the virtue and happiness of the multitude without the support and direction of an established faith and worship.

In the above cases Government interferes on behalf of *the public*. But there are others in which it does so to protect the helplessness or inexperience of individuals. Thus:

It shields infants by avoiding their contracts and protecting their persons and property;

And married women;

And persons of unsound mind;

And in many ways the helpless labouring poor.

It forbids the truck system.

It regulates the employment of women and children in mines and factories.

It controls pawnbrokers—grinding the tooth of usury, and securing facilities for redemption.

It prohibits and punishes, as we have seen, the use of unjust weights and measures;

And the sale of unwholesome provisions;

And the adulteration of coffee, tobacco, snuff, beer, tea, cocoa, chocolate, and pepper.

To guard against fraud, it directs the form and manner in which wills shall be executed.

If a man gives a money bond with a penalty if the money is not repaid at a day prefixed, the State forbids the penalty to be enforced.

A purchaser of gold or silver articles cannot tell whether they are real gold and silver or not, or how much of the weight is precious metal, and how much is alloy. The State steps in to his assistance, and requires the assay mark of a public officer.

A man buys a pocket of hops. He cannot always open it to
see whether it is of the growth alleged or of uniform quality.
The State interferes and makes it penal to mark or pack falsely.

An attorney sends in his bill. The client cannot tell whether
the charges are usual and fair. The State intervenes and provides a public officer who is empowered, not only to correct, but
also to punish overcharges.

The State compels the professional education of medical men
and attorneys.

The above are but some instances of the mode in which
nearly all governments have found it for the advantage of the
community to interpose.

What is the interposition of Government ?

Simply the concentrated action of the wisdom and power of
the whole society on a given point ; a mutual agreement by all,
that certain things shall be done or not done for the general
benefit.—'Sophisms of Free Trade examined,' by a Barrister
(the late Mr. Justice Byles), 1870.

APPENDIX C.

THAT List should reject the idea of protective duties on corn and agricultural produce as being in any degree beneficial to a country like Germany, is easy to understand. Her agriculture at the time when he wrote (1841) not only amply provided for the wants of her population, but yielded then, and had yielded for a long previous period, a large and steady surplus for export to other countries. No other European nation could profitably export such produce to her, while the high rates of freight then prevalent and the non-existence of ocean steam transport rendered such export to her from more distant countries impossible.

Whether, as a mere question of policy, the free importation of agricultural produce be approved or not, his contention, thus laid down by him as a sort of universal axiom, but apparently based on the circumstances of his own country and time, can scarcely be deemed consistent with some other arguments on which his general theory of national economy is based. Nor can it be deemed (of itself) conclusive as a solution of the question which is presented to Great Britain at the present time, viz. whether, under circumstances in which the necessary result of a policy of unrestricted importation of agricultural produce is to throw a large portion of the land of the nation out of cultivation, to deprive those who cultivated it of their accustomed employment, and to render the nation dependent for the major part of its food on foreign supplies, the nation's best interests are most effectually promoted by such a policy, or by one of such moderate protection of native agriculture as may retain in cultivation the national land, and greatly lessen the nation's dependence for its food on foreign importation. His contention leads rather to the inference that what may be good for one nation may be undesirable for another which exists under very different conditions, and still more to show that what may be beneficial to a people at one stage of their national history may be injurious

at another time—an opinion which the present German Government appears to sanction by its recent reversion to a protectionist
policy as respects the import of agricultural produce.

A policy of moderate protection appears to be advocated by
those who approve it as a sort of mutual assurance to the
industrious producers of the nation against the competition in
its own markets of producers who do not belong to the nation.
It is further advocated as an impost levied on the foreign
producing competitor in the shape of a contribution by him to
the revenue of the nation which imposes it, and as the condition
on which he is permitted to compete in the markets of the
latter nation with the native producers, who are subjected to
much taxation to which the foreigner does not otherwise contribute. It is noteworthy that Adam Smith himself expresses
approval of protective duties for the latter purpose in case the
foreign imported products are believed to be subjected to less
taxation than similar home products. ('Wealth of Nations,'
Book IV. chapter ii.)

If those views can be deemed sound in their application to
manufacturing industry, our author does not appear to have
clearly stated the reasons why that industry which, as he
admits, is the most important of any, and which employs more
capital and population than any other, should not (if its successful prosecution requires it) receive moderate protection as well
as manufacturing industry.

Whether, however, the principle of protective duties (either
generally or limited in their application to manufacturing industry alone) be admitted or not, two inferences seem to be
fairly deducible from the teaching of Adam Smith and not to be
disproved by that of List : firstly, that if the home agriculturist
is required (in the interest of the nation) to be exposed to free
competition by the foreigner in the home market, he is entitled
to be relieved from all such taxation, whether local or imperial,
as at all specially or disproportionately oppresses him ; secondly,
that differential duties are justifiable on imports from those
nations who impose restrictions on our export to them as compared with imports from those nations who impose no such
restrictions.—TRANSLATOR.

APPENDIX D.

THE example of Great Britain during the last few years may be deemed by many to furnish a refutation of List's doctrine on this point. The excess of her recorded imports over her recorded exports has increased from 58,000,000 in 1869 to 121,000,000 in 1883.

The induction of accurate conclusions as to the beneficial or injurious effects of this state of things on the national welfare, and consequently on the general truth or error of List's allegation, is rendered difficult chiefly by two considerations—first, by the circumstance that Great Britain possessed up to a few years ago, and still possesses to a considerable extent, large amounts of capital invested abroad, the dividends or interest on which, if not reinvested there, necessarily tend to increase her total recorded imports. The second is, that we have no statistical returns of British home production or consumption of manufactured goods, and only imperfect ones of her agricultual production. Hence it is impossible accurately to determine to what extent Great Britain's present enormous excess of imports represents merely the annual interest on previously acquired capital, and to what extent, on the other hand, it represents the substitution of the products of foreign labour in her own markets for those of her home industry.

To the extent to which the former of these two elements can be proved to exist, the excess of imports so accounted for is (in the case of England) special and abnormal, and proves nothing adverse to the general truth of List's allegation.

But even if it be correct (and it is difficult to believe that it can be so) that the excess in value of our imports (less carrying profits) is wholly accounted for by earnings on capital invested abroad (which earnings reach us in imported commodities), it would appear that, if the direct effect of such earnings so imported is to supplant and diminish production at home, there is a countervailing national loss, which goes far to neutralise the alleged national benefit of such excess of imports.

Supposing, for instance, that the nation as a whole possesses 1,000,000,000*l*. sterling invested abroad in various ways realising an annual income of 50,000,000*l*. sterling, that profit, if not re-invested abroad, no doubt reaches us in imported commodities and permeates through the community ; but when such commodities mainly consist of goods or produce which supplant home productions, we are then to a great extent losers.

Were such profit to reach us only in goods which we cannot produce, or in raw materials required for manufactures, it might all be deemed national gain ; but when it reaches us in the shape of food or other articles which could be produced at home, and only transfers our custom from native to foreign producers, the gain is questionable even for the present, and (viewed prospectively) would appear to involve absolute danger to the community.—TRANSLATOR.

INDEX.

———